The Prime Minister
of Taste

A Portrait of Horace Walpole

The Prime Minister of Taste

A Portrait of Horace Walpole

MORRIS R. BROWNELL

Yale University Press ~ New Haven and London

For Ann

sine qua non

Designed by Beatrix McIntyre
Printed in China

Published with assistance from the Annie Burr Lewis Fund.

Front endpaper: Michel Vincent, called Charles Brandoin: *The Exhibition of the Royal Academy of Painting in 1771*. Watercolour drawing, $9\frac{5}{16} \times 13\frac{3}{4}$ in. Courtesy of the Huntington Library, Art Collections, and Botanical Gardens, San Marino, California.
Back endpaper: Edward Francis Burney: *The Royal Academy Exhibition at Somerset House*, 1784. Pen, ink and watercolour drawing, $13\frac{1}{2} \times 19\frac{1}{4}$ in. British Museum, Department of Prints and Drawings. © The British Museum.

Frontispiece: Sir Joshua Reynolds: *Portrait of Horace Walpole*, 1756. Oil on canvas, 50 × 40 ins. By courtesy of the National Portrait Gallery, London. Photo: NPG Picture Library.

Library of Congress Cataloging-in-Publication Data
Brownell, Morris R.
     The prime minister of taste: a portrait of Horace Walpole/Morris R. Brownell
       p. cm.
     Includes bibliographical references and index.
     ISBN 0-300-08716-0 (cloth:alk:paper)
     1. Walpole, Horace, 1717–1797 – Art collections. 2. Art – Collectors and collecting – England – London. 3. Title.

N5247.W28 B76 2001
709'.2 – dc21   00-049947

Contents

Acknowledgements

I am primarily indebted to Wilmarth Lewis, editor of the Yale edition of the correspondence, and to Warren Hunting Smith, compiler of 'the index to end all indexes' that unlocked the mysteries of English aristocratic genealogy vital to the student of English portraits. At the Lewis Walpole Library I read the correspondence from beginning to end in Thornton Wilder's copy, which he had annotated with colored pencils marking Walpole's flights of Gibbonian and Ciceronian rhetoric. I am grateful to the Lewis Walpole Library's librarians, Marie Devine and Richard Williams, for expert assistance and generous hospitality, especially to Richard for making arrangements for me to stay in the Root house during my second sabbatical leave at the library. Joan Sussler exercised her magical power to conjure up the right illustrations, and Anna Malicka infallibly found Walpole's manuscripts and annotated books for me, and remembered where they were after I lost track of them.

I am grateful to two anonymous readers for Yale University Press who commented on my proposal for a biographical study of Walpole's life in art. For reading my latest draft with exacting editorial skill and unfailing encouragement, I am particularly grateful to my colleague and friend Elizabeth Francis, an accomplished teacher and editor of legal and judicial writing. My colleague Eric Rasmussen gave me the benefit of his Shakespearian editorial eye. For many years John Riely has listened to the Walpole story I told him as often as the Ancient Mariner's tale.

For advice, encouragement, hospitality, recommendations, and answers to importunate questions, I want to thank the following friends, colleagues, editors, librarians, curators, and keepers (with apologies to any omitted): David Alexander, Paul K. Alkon, Brian Allen, Michael and Delia Ayres, Rosemary Baker, Shelley Bennett, Dwight and Elaine Egbert, Linda Gorelangton, Donald Greene, Jean Hagstrum, John Harris, Anne Becher and Paul Hancock, Catherine Jestin, Loftus Jestin, Clare Lloyd-Jacob, Maynard Mack, Patrick McCoughey, Geri McVeigh, Robert Merrill, Jeffrey Meyers, Valery Meyers, Alice Moorhead, Yvonne Noble, Maxime Préaud, Duncan Robinson, Ann Ronald, Countess Rosebery, Peter Sabor, Elma Schonbach, Jacob Simon, Kim Sloane, Michael Snodin, Barbara Stafford, John Sunderland, Kathleen Thompson, Betsey and Sidney Tyler, Marsha Urban, Clive Wainright, the Countess Waldegrave, Robert Wark, and Steven Zink.

I am indebted to a heavenly host of picture editors, photo librarians, and others who helped me to collect illustrations: Maryan Ainsworth, Rosemary Andreae, Timothy Bathurst, Clare Baxter, Kathryn Bellamy, Lawrence Blackmon, Melanie Blake, Suzanne

Boorsch, Jean Bray, Dr Anthea Brook, Katherine Coombs, Maite Cork, Alessandra Corti, Philippe Couton, Deanna Cross, Jon Culverhouse, Jane Cunningham, Laura Daroca, Nicholas Day, Jacqueline Dugas, Larissa Dukelskaya, Martin Durrant, Tina Fiske, Liz Forster, Burton Fredericksen, Paul Gardner, Estelle Gittins, Melissa Gold, Charlotte Grant, Dr Kate Harris, Sona Johnston. Susanna Kerr, Ivor Kerslake, James Kilvington, Janet Larkin, Emma Lauze, John Laverick, Karen Lawson, Alison Leslie, Mary Lineberger, Anna Marie Logan, Lisa Little, Sarah Lloyd-Davis, Patrice Mattia, Dr Vladimir Matveyev, Marie McFeely, Robert Mills, Lee Mooney, Helen Nicoll, Sandra Powlette, Nancy Press, Sylvie Rabusseau, Antonia Reeve, Charlotte Samuels, Diane Scott, Eileen Simpson, Nancy Stanfield, R.W. Stedman, Emma Strouts, D.J. Taylor, Barbara Thompson, Laura Valentine, Svetlana Vsevolozhskaya, Roger Waine, Helen Walch, the Earl Waldegrave, Tracy Walker, Suzanne Wynn.

For financial support for the research, writing, and illustration of this book I am indebted to David Westfall and the Sabattical Committee of the University of Nevada, Reno, for two sabbatical leaves (spring semesters 1990, and 1998); to the National Endowment for the Humanities for a research fellowship (1990–1); to Ann Ronald, Dean of the College of Arts and Science, University of Nevada, Reno, for a grant-in-aid during the same period; to Stephen Tchudi, Chairman, Department of English, University of Nevada, Reno, for arranging a leave of absence in the nick of time; to John Ryden, Director of Yale University Press, for an illustrations stipend; to Brian Allen, who opened wide the door of the Paul Mellon Centre in London, helped me to obtain illustrations, and came to the rescue at a crucial moment.

Finally, I wish to thank my editors at the Yale Press, John Nicoll and Beatrix McIntyre; David Mannings for allowing me to consult his Reynolds catalogue in proof; Mary Anna Replogle, my capable guide through the underworld of word processing; my daughter Amanda for housing and encouragement in London; and three doctors of medicine who enabled me to complete the task: Kim Bigley, Geoffrey Cecchi, and Robert Rosenquist. My wife Ann and daughter Kate have reminded me that there is a life without Walpole.

'*His Prime Minister Connoisseur in Pictures*':
George Vertue's description of Sir Luke Schaub
(1690–1758), Advisor to Frederick Louis (1707–51),
Prince of Wales

'*I will launch into the world again, and propose
to be prime minister to King George V.*'
Walpole to Anne Liddell (1738–1804), 22 August 1776

CHAPTER I

Introduction, The Trifler Restored

Horace Walpole's career as an art collector is an important but neglected subject, virtually eclipsed by commentary on Strawberry Hill and Walpole's contribution to the Gothic revival.[1] And yet Walpole's art collection – the contents of Strawberry Hill – must surely be a crucial issue for his biography. A biographer of Walpole confronts at the outset a story of mistaken identity as strange as the case of Dr Jekyll and Mr Hyde. Walpole's reputation has been largely determined by Thomas Babington Macaulay's hostile review of an early nineteenth-century edition of his correspondence.[2] Macaulay's brilliant polemic identifies Walpole with an art collection he ridiculed as a collection of curiosities.

Ever since then editors and biographers have laboured to exorcize Macaulay's unforgettable caricature of the trifler. Wilmarth Lewis's Yale edition of the correspondence, completed in 1983, and Ketton-Cremer's 'authorized' biography dedicated to Lewis, represent the culmination of this campaign.[3] In place of Macaulay's caricature of the 'Prince of Cockle Shells' (HWC 14. 170, n. 28), the Yale editors invite us to hang a whole-length Van Dyck portrait of the Doctor of Letters. The new portrait of the sober social historian and connoisseur is magnificent, '[a] very wholsome and comfortable Doctrine,' to quote Henry Fielding, 'to which we have but one Objection, namely, that it is not true'.[4] It is not true because a careful reading of Walpole's correspondence in Lewis's superb edition reveals that Macaulay's caricature of the dilettante is a faithful copy of Walpole's own self-portrait in the correspondence, where he invariably speaks of himself as a trifler and collector of curiosities.

The purpose of this biographical study of Horace Walpole the art collector, therefore, is to restore Walpole's self-portrait, and to reinterpret it without Macaulay's Victorian varnish of political prejudice, moral censure, and ridicule. This study challenges both the traditional view of Walpole as a mere collector of curiosities, and his modern reincarnation as a sober social historian and connoisseur. It argues that Walpole's attitude to the arts throughout his life was that of the courtesy-book gentleman, whose interest in art centered on the philistine genre of portraits. Portraits dominated Walpole's own art collection at Strawberry Hill. Walpole tirelessly inventoried portraits on visits to country seats, and accurately identified portraits of unnamed persons in his annotated catalogues of Royal Academy exhibitions. This study attempts to show that Walpole's passion for the art of portraiture was not the trifling pastime he pretended, but the source of his greatest literary achievement – more than forty volumes of letters containing his record of the dying days of the English aristocracy in a gallery of portraits equal to those of Reynolds and Gainsborough.

Connoisseur Manqué

Although Walpole knew and admired the writings of the leading contemporary authority on the *Science of a Connoisseur*, Jonathan Richardson, it does not appear that Walpole ever adopted Richardson's austere doctrine. In Walpole's apology for Richardson in the *Anecdotes of Painting* he expresses an equivocal judgment of the man and his works. Richardson 'was undoubtedly one of the best English painters of a head', Walpole writes. 'The good sense of the nation is characterized in his portraits, but − [there is almost always a 'but' in Walpole's estimate of artists] − his men want dignity, and his women grace' (2. 273–4). Perhaps Walpole was thinking of Richardson's ungainly portrait of himself (plate 1) when he adds: 'he drew nothing well below the head, and was void of imagination. His attitudes, draperies, and backgrounds are totally insipid and unmeanin.' (2. 274). And while Walpole praises Richardson's *Science of a Connoisseur* (1719), and his guidebook of Italian art, *An Account* (1722), both books in his library − 'full of matter, good sense, and instruction' (2. 275) − he takes pains to point out the 'singularity in his style and expression' (2. 275), and he mentions Hogarth's engraving satirizing Richardson and his son.[5] In spite of 'some affectation in his manner,' Walpole wrote that 'it is impossible not to love the author [Richardson]' (Anecdotes 2. 275, 276, n. 1), but he never joined Richardson's cult of the sublime or became a convert to his doctrine of connoisseurship.

Emulating Joseph Addison's campaign to reform genteel taste in literature, Richardson set out in his *Science of a Connoisseur* to encourage a taste for Italian art, weaning his readers from furniture pictures and portraits to a love of Italian history painting, exemplified by Raphael's cartoons at Hampton Court.[6] In spite of his own doubts about the uncertainties of attribution, and the ubiquity of corrupt agents and dealers, Richardson encouraged the neophyte to believe in his beatitudes of painting: pious belief in the sanctity of originals, the power to distinguish originals from copies, the ability to recognize hands, and the notion that painting is a sublime intellectual art. One imagines that Walpole reacted to Richardson's high-minded ideas of the connoisseur as Rasselas did to Imlac's description of the poet: 'Thou hast convinced me that no human being can ever be a poet.'[7] Richardson earnestly attempts to teach gentlemen to read history painting through the spectacles of the humanist theory,[8] counting the connoisseur's rosary beads of invention, expression, decorum, handling, and the like. Nevertheless, on the Grand Tour we do not hear Walpole exclaiming in the Uffizi like the Richardsons − 'What a luxurious feast for a vertuoso'[9] − because the gentleman's code of *nil admirari* [nothing to be wondered at] precludes such a response.

The Courtesy-Book Gentleman and the Arts

To understand Walpole's attitude to the arts, we must turn from the literature of art to the tradition of the Renaissance courtesy book, which reveals that Walpole's trifler and the courtesy-book gentleman are virtually synonymous. In the correspondence Walpole models his self-portrait as a trifler on the idea of a gentleman in such books as

1.   Jonathan Richardson, Sr.: *Portrait of Horace Walpole. c.* 1735. Oil on canvas, 49½ × 39½ in. Courtesy of the Earl Waldegrave, Chewton Mendip, Bath, Somerset. Photo: Paul Mellon Centre for Studies in British Art.

Castiglione's *Courtier* (1528), and Henry Peacham's *Compleat Gentleman* (1622; Hazen 487). Castiglione refines the idea of 'the perfect virtue of gentlemanliness,' derived from Aristotle's *Ethics*, into an elaborate code of conduct.[10] Thomas Hoby's English translation of Castiglione's *Courtier* (1561) defines the quality indispensable to a true gentleman's character − the quality of *sprezzatura*, an art term denoting 'the seemingly nonchalant and effortless brushwork of a supreme master which expresses his intention perfectly'.[11] Writers of gentlemen's courtesy books appropriated this term to apply to the patron as well as the artist: 'the nonchalance which marks the perfect courtier and the perfect artist'.[12] In Walpole's letters the artist's *sprezzatura* and graceful nonchalance becomes the gentleman's studied pretence of carelessness about any of his pursuits.

'Therefore will I have our Courtier a perfect horseman for everie saddle,' Castiglione writes (1. 41),[13] and remarks 'it is a noble exercise . . . to play at Tenise' (1. 42). Whatever the courtier does, Castiglione will not 'have him to be acknowne that he bestoweth much studie or time about it, although he doe it excellently well' (2. 98). For example, Castiglione gives this warning about playing musical instruments:

> Therefore let our Courtier come to shew his musick as a thing to passe the time withall, and as [if] he were enforced to doe it. . . . And for all hee be skilfull and doth well understand it, yet will I have him to dissemble the studie and paines that a man must needes take in all thinges that are well done. And let him make semblance that he esteemeth but litle in himselfe that qualitie, but in doing it excellently well, make it much esteemed of other men (2. 100).

This practice of dissembling is the basis of Walpole's continual self-deprecation in the correspondence. Castiglione's aristocratic courtier labours tirelessly to reach in every art 'perfect understanding . . . so that every possible thing may be easie to him' (2. 129). But, at the same time, 'though hee perceive himselfe excellent and farre above others, yet [the courtier must] shew that he esteemeth not himselfe for such a one' (2. 129). Elsewhere Castiglione refers to the gentleman's pretence of carelessness about excellence as 'noble shamefastnesse' (3. 194).

It goes without saying that Castiglione's courtier plays tennis or the viola da gamba 'with a grace' (1. 43), and grace, it turns out, means *sprezzatura*: one thing is essential to grace

> and that is to eschue as much as a man may, and as a sharpe and daungerous rocke, too much curiousnesse, and (to speake a new word) to use in everye thing a certain disgracing to cover arte withall, and seeme whatsoever he doth and saith, to doe it without paine, and (as it were) not minding it. And of this doe I believe grace is much derived, for in rare matters and well brought to passe, every man knoweth the hardnesse of them, so that a readinesse therein maketh great wonder. And contrariwise to use force, and (as they say) to hale [haul] by the haire, giveth a great disgrace, and maketh everie thing how great so ever it bee, to be little esteemed (1. 45−6).

Thus the Horatian precept − *ars celare artem* − applies as much to the courtier as to the poet:

> Therefore that may bee said to be a verie arte, that appeareth not to be arte, neither

ought a man to put more diligence in any thing than in covering it: for in case it be open, it looseth credite cleane and maketh a man litle set by. . . . You may see then, how to shew arte, and such bent studie taketh away the grace of every thing (1. 45–6).

Castiglione associates 'bent studie' or pedantry with 'curiosity' which he opposes to gracefulness. He quotes the painter's proverb 'that too much diligence is hurtfull,' and he defines grace as the opposite of curiosity, 'a certaine recklessnesse. . . . which augmenteth the grace of the thing' (2. 99):

> This virtue therefore contrarie to curiositie which we for this time term Recklessnesse, beside that it is the true fountaine from the which all grace springeth it bringeth with it also an other ornament . . . that whoso can so sleightly doe well, hath a great deale more knowledge than in deede he hath: and if he will apply his studie and diligence to that he doth, he might do it much better. . . . Therefore shall our Courtier be esteemed excellent, and in everie thing he shall have a good grace, and especially in speaking, if he avoide curiositie' (1. 48–9).

Pretend to know less than you know, and *mirabile dictu*, you will be thought to know more, according to the self-deprecating precepts of the courtesy-book gentleman. On the other hand, 'curiositie . . . proceedeth of an over great desire to shew much knowledge: and in this wise a man applyeth his studie and diligence to get a most odious vice' (1. 49). Castiglione's spokesman, the count, sums up the gentleman's code of *sprezzatura* thus: 'I trow wee saide that pestilent curiositie doth alwaies give an evill grace unto all thinges: and contrariwise simplicitie and Rechlesnesse a marvailous good grace' (1. 65).

Lord Chesterfield's Vade-Mecum *for the Man of Taste*

Castiglione's *Courtier* is unlisted in the bibliography of Walpole's library, but Walpole certainly knew the book,[14] and he 'devoured' (HWC 28. 146) Lord Chesterfield's *Letters* (1774),[15] which can be considered an eighteenth-century version of Castiglione's *Courtier*. Although Walpole wrote in the margins of the first edition '[t]here is a littleness runs thro all Lord Chesterfield's advice that proves what his life proved, that he was not a great man' (Hazen 436, Letter 178, 1. 529), Walpole's attitude to the arts corresponds exactly to Chesterfield's. Distinguishing between a gentleman's 'liberal and illiberal pleasures,' Chesterfield warns his son against learning to play a musical instrument: 'There are some pleasures that degrade a gentleman. . . . If you love music, hear it; go to operas, concerts, and pay fiddlers to play to you; but I insist upon your neither piping nor fiddling yourself. It puts a gentleman in a very frivolous, contemptible light' (1: 406–7). Chesterfield cautions that 'the minute and mechanical parts' of civil architecture should be left 'to masons, bricklayers, and Lord Burlington [Richard Boyle (1694–1753)] . . . who has, to a certain degree, lessened himself, by knowing them too well' (1: 476).

A taste for classical sculpture and painting is 'as becoming as fiddling is unbecoming,'

Chesterfield allows, provided that the gentleman avoids Castiglione's sin of curiosity:

> I would also have you acquire a liberal taste of the two liberal arts of Painting and Sculpture; but without descending into those *minuties*, which our modern Virtuosi most affectedly dwell upon. Observe the great parts attentively . . . and leave the trifling parts, with their little jargon, to affected puppies (1. 476).

Chesterfield recommends a standard French treatise on painting with the patronizing condescension that marks the gentleman's attitude to scholars:

> It is a part of History, very entertaining, curious enough, and not quite useless. All these sort of things I would have you know, to a certain degree; but remember, that they must only be the amusements, and not the business of a man of parts (1. 476–7).

An amateur's interest in the arts is allowable provided that learning is subordinate to 'good-breeding,' which Chesterfield echoes Castiglione in defining as 'a gentleman-like manner,' 'the ability to be civil with ease'. 'The scholar, without good-breeding, is a pedant', Chesterfield insists. Like Castiglione's courtier, Chesterfield's gentleman conceals his knowledge: 'Wear your learning, like your watch, in a private pocket: and do not pull it out and strike it, merely to show that you have one.' Frivolous subjects like the arts should be reserved for conversation with the beau monde of Paris: 'The point is, to talk well upon the subject you talk upon, and the most trifling, frivolous subjects will still give a man of parts an opportunity of showing them.'

Like Polonious, Chesterfield prescribes a gentleman's proper conduct on the Grand Tour in Italy, and his advice on collecting reflects Walpole's experience. He writes to his son in Italy:

> You are travelling now, in a country once so famous both for arts and arms that (however degenerated at present) it still deserves your attention and reflection. View it therefore with care, compare its former with its present state, and examine into the causes of its rise, and its decay. Consider it classically and politically, and do not run through it, as too many of your young countrymen do, musically, and (to use a ridiculous word) *knick-knackically*. No piping nor fiddling, I beseech you; no days lost in poring upon almost imperceptible *Intaglios* and *Cameos*: and do not become a Virtuoso of small wares. Form a taste of Painting, Sculpture, and Architecture, if you please, by a careful examination of the works of the best ancient and modern artists; those are liberal arts, and a real taste and knowledge of them become a man of fashion very well. But, beyond certain bounds, the Man of Taste ends, and the frivolous Virtuoso begins (1. 466).

Chesterfield collected old master paintings until his dying day,[16] but he never would have considered himself a connoisseur or virtuoso, characters inconceivable to an aristocrat and statesman who believed politics the supreme art: 'I have done buying pictures, by way of virtu,' he wrote late in life, 'yet there are some portraits of remarkable people that would tempt me'. When Chesterfield encouraged his son to learn the art of portraiture he meant something different from a Grand Tourist's lessons in sketching landcape:

> [. . .] I hope you will be as good a portrait painter [student of human nature], which is a much more noble science. By portraits, you will easily judge, that I do not mean the outlines and the colouring of the human figure; but the inside of the heart and mind of man. This science requires more attention, observation, and penetration than the other [landscape sketches]; as indeed it is infinitely more useful. Search, therefore, with the greatest care, into the characters of all those whom you converse with (1. 225).

Searching human character is the political art that Chesterfield's letters inculcate. 'I could wish you to be *omnis homo, l'homme universel*' (1. 278, 445). 'Let the great book of the world be your principal study . . . Turn over men by day and women by night' (1. 397). 'Your destination is political,' Chesterfield writes to his son: 'First, it is absolutely necessary to speak in parliament' (1. 516), and a political career depends upon knowledge of the characters of men: 'The reading of ten new characters is more your business now, than the reading of twenty old books . . . The great usage of the world, the knowledge of characters . . . is all you now want' (1. 408).

In 1756 Sir Joshua Reynolds painted Walpole's portrait (frontispiece) as the debonair gentleman leaning gracefully on a table that bears an engraving of a classical antiquity Walpole had collected on the Grand Tour.[17] Reynolds's depiction is surprising because a careful study of Walpole's collection shows that he was not a collector of Italian art but of English portraits. Shortly after he sat to Reynolds, when Walpole wrote in the third person that the arts 'assumed an entire empire over him' in mid life,[18] he was not referring to classical antiquities or Italian old-master paintings, but English portraits from Holbein to Reynolds.

This study of Walpole's art collection attempts to explain the contradiction between Walpole's pose as virtuoso, and his passion for portraits. Part I, 'The Making of a Portraitist,' demonstrates that Walpole was no connoisseur on the Grand Tour (chapter 2), less than enthusiastic about his father's collection of Italian pictures (Chapter 3), and a disciple of George Vertue, England's leading portrait engraver (Chapter 4). Part II, 'Portraits at Strawberry Hill' (Chapters 5–7), shows that Walpole's collection was dominated by portraits valued for anecdotes attached to them rather than for aesthetic reasons. Part III, 'Portraits in Walpole's Letters' (Chapters 8–17), discusses portraits Walpole was drawing in his letters, a gallery rivalling the portraits Reynolds and Gainsborough were exhibiting at the Royal Academy. The book concludes with a chapter on the Prime Minister of Taste, Walpole's self-portrait in the correspondence.

PART I
The Making of a Portraitist

CHAPTER 2

No Connoisseur: Collecting on the Grand Tour

Shortly after his return to London, Horace Walpole began to unpack the artworks he had collected on the Grand Tour. 'I write to you,' he begins a letter to Horace Mann dated 19 October 1741, 'up to the head and ears, in dirt, straw and unpacking. I have been opening all my cases from the custom house the whole morning, and, are not you glad, every individual safe and undamaged. I am fitting up an apartment in Downing Street' (HWC 17. 170–1). His philistine first cousin, Henry Seymour Conway, had been eagerly anticipating the spectacle of Walpole's unpacking: 'such cartloads of virtu! medals and pictures; a buckle of one hero and a button of another, things that I am miserably ignorant of, God knows,' Conway admitted, but he promised to listen to Walpole's 'history of it all with great attention, like country people that see the Tombs at Westminster Abbey and admire the profound knowledge of the sexton . . .' (37. 107; 19 September 1741). 'Indeed I heartily wish I had been at the unpacking of your virtu,' Conway added a month later, 'for I love to see pretty things though I don't understand 'em. . . . What closet have you fitted up? Are you in your old apartment or is it t'other charming green closet?' (37. 111–12; 26 October 1741), Conway enquired, referring to rooms in 10 Downing Street, Sir Robert Walpole's state residence.[1] By the end of November Walpole could boast to Horace Mann: 'You can't think what a closet I have fitted up! Such a mixture of French gaiety and Roman virtù! You would be in love with it; I have not rested till it was finished; I long to have you see it!' (17. 213; 26 November 1741). '. . . [V]irtu', the twenty-four-year-old Walpole told Conway at this time, 'is my sole pleasure. – I am neither young enough nor old enough to be in love' (37. 110; 21 September 1741). '. . . I am determined, after the laudable example of the House of Medici, to take the title of *Horace the Magnificent*' (17. 505; 21 July 1742).

Walpole rarely expressed such enthusiasm about collecting on the Grand Tour. The note we normally hear in the correspondence is *nil admirari* 'nothing to be wondered at': 'When I first came abroad, everything struck me, and I wrote its history [in letters to his friends]; but now I am grown so used to be surprised, that I don't perceive any flutter in myself when I meet with any novelties; curiosity and astonishment wear off' (13. 206; 16 April 1740). '[W]e did not cry out "Lord!" half so much at Rome as at Calais, which to this hour I look upon as one of the most surprising cities in the universe' (13. 229; 2 October 1740). He wrote to West:

I don't know what volumes I may send you from Rome, from Florence I have little inclination to send you any. I see several things that please me calmly, but *à force d'en avoir vu* ['because I've seen too much of them'] I have left off screaming, Lord! this! and Lord! that! To speak sincerely, Calais surprised me more than anything I have seen since. I recollect the joy I used to propose if I could but once see the Great Duke's gallery [the Uffizi]; I walk into it now with as little emotion as I should into St Paul's. The statues are a congregation of good sort of people, that I have a great deal of unruffled regard for. The farther I travel, the less I wonder at anything' (13. 199; 24 January 1740). '[I]nstead of being deep in the liberal arts, and being in the Gallery every morning, as I thought of course to be sure I would be, we are in all the idlenesses and amusements of the town. For me, I am grown so lazy, and so tired of seeing sights, that, though I have been at Florence six months, I have not seen . . . so much as one of the Great Duke's villas' (13. 230; 2 October 1740).

'I have made no discoveries in ancient or modern arts' (13. 231), he wrote to West. Three hours were enough to exhaust the sights of Siena, and Walpole warned West 'You must not believe Mr Addison about the wonderful Gothic nicety of the dome [duomo]' (13. 204; 22 March 1740).[2]

From the beginning it is obvious that Walpole was more interested in social amusements – cards, *conversazioni*, theatre and opera (13. 191) – than the antiquities and monuments that fascinated his intellectual travelling companion, the poet Thomas Gray. Gray wrote that Florence was 'an excellent place to employ all one's animal sensations in, but utterly contrary to one's rational powers' (13. 228; 31 July 1740). At the same time, Walpole was revelling in Florentine social life: he appears to have fallen in love, and probably had an affair with Elisabetta Capponi, Madame Grifoni. 'I am younger than ever, think of nothing but diverting myself, and live in a round of pleasures. We have operas, concerts, and balls, mornings and evenings. . . . one rises at eleven in the morning, goes to the opera at nine at night, to supper at one, and to bed at three!' (37. 78; 25 September 1740). For the rest of his life Walpole remembered his Florentine idyll, 'enjoying the delicious nights on the Ponte di Trinità at Florence in a linen nightgown and a straw hat with *improvisatori*, and music and the coffee houses open with ices' (11. 287; 8 June 1791). Gray found the same pleasures of Florence annhilating: 'I have struck a medal upon myself: the device is thus O, and the motto *Nihilissimo*. . . . Here you [West] shall get up at twelve o'clock, breakfast till three, dine till five, sleep till six, drink cooling liquors till eight, go to the bridge till ten, sup till two, and so sleep till twelve again' (13. 228; 31 July 1740).

Judging from Walpole's ironical reference to Gray as 'a great virtuoso here [Rome]' (13. 219, 1740), Gray's conscientious notes on monuments and antiquities clearly irritated the *bon vivant* Walpole: 'By a considerable volume of charts and pyramids, which I saw at Florence, I thought it threatened a publication,' he wrote to West. 'His travels have really improved him,' he added with a hint of *mauvaise honte*: 'I wish they may do the same for any one else' (13. 219, 28 May 1740). Anyone else, that is, except Walpole, who composed a burlesque travel journal in Rome, mischievously listing all the sights 'I did not go to see' – the view from the top of St Peter's; the fountain of Egeria; the jewel of Medusa in the Strozzi collection; the ruins of the Septizonium Severi and Michaelangelo's Last Judgment in the Vatican (14. 239–40).

'. . . [Y]ou seem a little tired of seeing sights', West wrote (13. 235; 10 November 1740), and Walpole admitted in old age that:

> [i]n fact I was so tired of *seeing* when I was abroad, that I have several of those pieces of repentance on my conscience when they come into my head – and yet I saw too much, for the quantity left such a confusion in my head, that I do not remember a quarter clearly. Pictures, statues and buildings were always so much my passion, that for the time I surfeited myself, especially as one is carried to see a vast deal that is not worth seeing (11. 357; 25 September 1791).

Of course Walpole is exaggerating; he reveals his extraordinary visual memory and passion for Roman architecture in a note on the Colosseum he wrote in Gibbon's *Decline and Fall* (Hazen 3188; 1776–88), a remark that appears to be deliberately emulating Gibbon's famous description in his autobiography about his inspiration for writing the *Decline and Fall*:

> When I [Walpole] was at Rome, the first time I went into the Coliseum it was still so stupendous that though a company of strollers were acting on a temporary stage and though their audience were sitting on benches, the whole spectacle was so very inconsiderable that it seemed remote and not to be noticed in that vast area of which it occupied a most trifling space – yet as ancient Romans were not taller than modern, it struck me that the gladiators and actors must have appeared still more diminutive to the original spectators from the elevated arches. They must have been like thousands of flies gazing at mites from an immense height (13: 209–10, n. 15).

A second example of Walpole's genuine interest in antiquities can be found in his description of excavations at Herculaneum, 'perhaps one of the noblest curiosities that ever has been discovered' (13. 222; 14 June 1740).

'Dear West, have pity on one, who have done nothing of gravity for these two years' (13. 238; 4 December 1740). Walpole's appeal to West at the end of his Grand Tour sounds like a contrite schoolboy appealing to his tutor. The courtesy-book gentleman is also contrite in a later confession he made to William Mason about his blame for the quarrel with Gray on the Grand Tour: 'I often disregarded his [Gray's] wishes of seeing places, which I would not quit other amusements to visit, though I offered to send him to them without me' (28. 68; 2 March 1773).

Despite these moments of insight and eloquence, Walpole's collecting indicates how closely he conformed to the courtesy-book gentleman's code of *nil admirari*. Three representative examples are worth treating in some detail to challenge the prevailing modern idea of Walpole as connoisseur, and to show how haphazard, casual, and amateur his collecting was: first, the eagle in Reynolds's portrait; second, the medallion of a gladiator Walpole coveted in the collection of the great European collector of intaglios, Baron Stosch; and third, Walpole's purchase of a Madonna attributed to Domenichino for his father's collection at Houghton. These purchases prove the young Walpole to have been closer to the Grand Tourist in Pope's *Dunciad* (1743), who returns from his travels '[w]ith nothing but a Solo in his head' (line 324), than to a connoisseur or virtuoso.

'My Glorious Eagle' (19. 430)

In 1756–7 Walpole sat to the newly fashionable Joshua Reynolds for a three-quarter length portrait (frontispiece), 'standing in a pensive posture, by a table, in which is his fine antique eagle in a print' (HWC 1. 64, n. 5).[3] It is surprising to find Walpole posing as a virtuoso and collector of Italian art in 1756 because by that time he had largely abandoned the Grand Tour taste, devoting himself to the collection of English portraits. But the nonchalant, debonair, and graceful pose, the lounging costume with lace cuffs and handkerchief, and the ironic expression bespeak the *sprezzatura* of the gentleman collector rather than the virtuoso soiled with dusty folios.

Walpole's eagle in Reynolds's portrait, purchased by proxy, illustrates the part played by what may be called an Italian Committee of Taste (plate 2) in Walpole's Grand Tour before he purchased Strawberry Hill.[4] The chairman of the committee was Sir Horace Mann (1706–86), British diplomat at Florence, a *marchand d'amateur* who supplemented his income by dealing in art, and two English expatriates on a protracted Grand Tour: John Chute (1701–76), and his inseparable friend Francis Whithed (1719–51). For Walpole as for the tourists Pope wrote of in the *Epistle to Burlington*, 'Artists [connoisseurs] must choose [their] Pictures, Music, Meats' (line 6).[5]

John Chute liked to play the role of Satan, tempting Walpole to purchase objects of virtu. While dangling a 'Raphael' for Robert Walpole's collection at Houghton in front of him in a letter dated 4 June 1743, Chute goes on to say: 'If I mistake not, there are other things in the list [Mann's missing enclosure] you will receive in this packet that would suit you vastly. I am sure they are tempting names, and I know you are no saint' (35. 38). The tempter was again at work in July 1745, when Chute asked Mann to tell Walpole about an antiquity 'found in the gardens of Boccapadugli within the precinct of Caracalla's baths at Rome in the year 1742' (19. 66, n. 10). Mann obliged: 'Mr Chute has pressed me to mention to you a most beautiful antique eagle that has lately been found at Rome in the highest preservation, and as far superior to that of Benvenuto Cellini which Ganimede keeps [in the Uffizi], as that is to the worst that could be made at Hide Park Corner' (19. 65).

Knowing the value of competitive bids to egg on a client, Mann introduces his Roman correspondent, the collector, connoisseur, and art dealer Cardinal Alessandro Albani (1692–1779):

'Cardinal Albani is in love with it, and says it would be a fine present for the new Emperor [Francis I (1708–65), Holy Roman Emperor (1745–65), Grand Duke of Tuscany (1737–65)], but that he would not know its value; he thinks it too dear. The demand is 250 crowns [*c.* £63], but Mr Chute believes, in case the Cardinal will not have it (as it was he who brought him acquainted with it) that he could get it for 100 zecchins [about £50] ready money' (HWC 19. 66).

From the outset Chute represents the eagle simultaneously as a priceless object fit for the new Holy Roman Emperor and a bargain. Almost as an afterthought, Mann mentions that the eagle had been found intact with its pedestal: 'A Roman altar, decorated with masques of satyrs, centre Medusa head, and festoons of flowers and fruit, beautifully

2.   Thomas Patch: *A Gathering at the Casa Manetti, Horace Mann's House in Florence*. Oil on canvas, 40 × 63 in. Courtesy of the Lewis Walpole Library, Yale University. Scene of meetings of HW's Grand Tour Committee of Taste.

sculptured with noble eagles, in high relief, and a curious old inscription in the centre' (19.66, n. 16). 'It treads a sepulchral stone with its inscriptions and bas reliefs entire,' Mann continues, deferring as usual to Chute's aesthetic judgment, but enough of a salesman to warn Walpole of Time's winged chariot: 'Mr Chute thinks you might indulge your taste for antiquities at such an expense. All I am afraid is, that your orders will come late, in case you would have it. I have not time to say half Mr Chute writes in its praise, but by his accounts both the eagle and its pedestal are complete' (19. 66; 13 July 1745).

Walpole could hardly resist such a well-baited hook, but rumours of 'a French expedition against Great Britain in favour of the Pretender' (*Daily Advertiser*, 19. 78, n. 2) made him hesitate: 'I don't know what to say to Mr Chute's eagle; I would fain have it; I can depend upon his taste – but would not it be folly to be buying curiosities now?' (19. 79; 26 July 1745). Imagining Bonny Prince Charlie's highlanders looting his cabinet in Arlington Street, Walpole adds: 'How can I tell that I shall have anything in the world to pay for it, by the time it is bought?' (19. 79). But these objections were merely rhetorical, and Walpole quickly capitulated to Chute, cheerfully consigning himself to financial ruin: 'You may present these reasons to Mr Chute; and if he laughs at them, why then he will buy the eagle for me – if he thinks them of weight, not' (19. 79; 26 July 1745). The man whom Byron called the last of the Romans, *Ultimus Romanorum*,[6] will leave the fate of this morsel of virtu to his 'oracle in taste' (HWC 24. 209).

It was a foregone conclusion that Chute would not take Walpole's weak protests seriously, and he soon engaged 'a little English sculptor' [possibly Simon Vierpyl (1725–1810)] to act as a stalking horse, hoping 'to save some scores of crowns by not appearing in it [the negotiations] himself' (19. 100–1; 7 September 1745). Within a month Chute had closed the sale, and Mann concluded a letter describing 'dreadful matters' of the War of the Austrian Succession and bombardments in Genoa with a report that Chute had bought the eagle for 'two hundred crowns [c. £50] or 100 *ruspi*, which he most willingly had given' (19. 121; 12 October 1745). Knowing Walpole's anxiety about cost, Chute justified his out-bidding Cardinal Albani without boasting that he had come in £10 below the original asking price, comparing Walpole's eagle to other animal antiquities:

> Mr Chute says he considered how charming he [the eagle] was, and thought the 25 more [100 as opposed to Albani's 50 *ruspi*] well bestowed; that he had compared him with his brother at the Villa Mattei [an eagle later placed in the Sala degli animali in the Vatican], the goat at Giustiniani's [a Roman collection], the boar at Florence [in the Grand Duke's collection], and with every bird and beast the ancients have left us, and, finding him both in his own opinion, and that of all connoisseurs, so equal to any and perhaps superior to some of the most renowned, that he determined to lay the odd 50 crowns [£12. 05s] more upon his tail, that he might not fly away (19. 121–2; 12 October 1745).

Mann then describes a diplomatic gesture Chute made to Cardinal Albani:

> As soon as he had agreed he went to the Cardinal to tell him what he had done, offering, however, as he was the first to treat about it, to relinquish his bargain, though the Cardinal had declared he would not go beyond 150 crowns [c. £37. 10s]. Mr Chute knew his man, therefore run no risk in making him that compliment. The Cardinal kissed him, thanked him, and wished him joy of his purchase (19. 122).

This was extraordinarily generous dealing, but Chute had also bought the pedestal without obtaining Walpole's permission in advance, and this required some special pleading from Horace Mann:

> Mr Chute, having gone so far, had determined, at the persuasion of all the connoisseurs, and particularly his Eminence [Benedict XIV (1675–1758), Pope 1740–58)] to buy his pedestal, which is an antique urn, somehow so [Mann's crude sketch is here introduced], he says, with an inscription very perfect (though he does not say what it is) on which he always stood, and everybody pronounced against a modern one which would cost more. The man asked 40 crowns [about £10] and he [Chute] stood to give 35 [£8. 15s].

Besides, according to Chute, it was pretty, and a good bargain:

> It is of white marble like the eagle, has eagles upon it, pateras, vases, rams' heads, festoons, and everything that is pretty in the antique. Mr Chute asks me if he has ven-

tured too far, and I intend to answer by the return of the post, that I think not, as the eagle could not have stood with his bare paws on the ground, and as any other, worthy of him, made in England, would have cost more (19. 122; 12 October 1745).

The Committee of Taste, after congratulating itself on its prize, promptly set about puffing its reputation, inflating its value, and planning for its conveyance to London:

> Everybody talks of that fine bird; crowds go to see it at Mr Chute's [his lodging in Rome]; the Cardinal [Albani] says nobody would refuse to give *mille scudi* [£250] for it. Its reputation is so raised, and the Pope had such a mind to buy it to grace the capital that I am strangely alarmed lest he should take it into his head not to let it go out of Rome (HWC 19. 135).

Now Cardinal Albani, who a month before 'would not go beyond 150 crowns' [c. £37. 10s] seemed to be saying no-one would offer less than six times as much, and the Pope was rumoured to be saving it for the Capitol.

Meanwhile Chute was arranging to have a *pergno* or pivot installed on the eagle's pedestal:

> that all his beauties may be seen. This little additional expense he ventures to make, for all the [Jacobite] rebellion. When all is done, and . . . he is sent off, he will write to you about it, in a full persuasion that you will be delighted with the purchase. I will be attentive to find a proper conveyance for it to England (19. 135; 26 October 1745).

We soon hear (19. 149; 10 November 1745) that Chute is dispatching the eagle to Leghorn. It is still the talk of Rome, but Albani has interceded to foreclose the possibility 'that the Pope might give orders not to let it go out of Rome' (19. 149). And plaster casts have been ordered for Mann and Cardinal Albani. When Mann's gesso arrived he wrote Walpole that '[i]t must be the finest thing in the world' (19. 197). On 4 November the committee hears that its client is 'extremely pleased with the purchase of the eagle and altar, and think[s] them cheap' (19. 155; 4 November 1745), but Walpole had caught Mann's anxiety about transport: 'You put me in pain for my eagle, and in more for the Chutes [Chute and Francis Whitehed], whose zeal is very heroic, but very ill placed. I long to hear that all my Chutes and eagles are safe out of the Pope's hands!' (19. 161; 15 November 1745). 'When my lovely eagle comes,' he writes to acknowledge Chute's assistance, 'I will consecrate it to his Roman memory' (19. 176–7; 29 November 1745).

Floods in Florence and naval engagements in the War of Austrian Succession delayed shipment of 'the finest thing in the world' for more than a year, but finally the eagle and its pedestal were packed in three cases 'like the Irishman's bird, in two places at once' (19. 274; 7 July 1746), arriving in London in June 1747. Walpole welcomed it jubilantly, and placed it in his cabinet at Arlington Street facing the bust of Vespasian (Roman Emperor, A.D. 69–79).

> My eagle is arrived – my eagle *tout court*, for I hear nothing of the pedestal: the bird itself was sent home in a store ship; I was happy that they did not reserve the statue,

3.   Charles Grignion after Samuel Wale: *Eagle found in the Boccapadugli Gardens in Rome.* Line engraving. Courtesy of the Print Collection, Lewis Walpole Library, Yale University.

4.   John Carter: *The Boccapadugli Eagle in the Library at Strawberry Hill.* Watercolour drawing, 8¼ × 9 in. Courtesy of the Lewis Walpole Library, Yale University.

and send its footstool. It is a glorious fowl! I admire it, and everybody admires it as much as it deserves. There never was so much spirit and fire preserved, with so much labour and finishing. It stands fronting the Vespasian; there are no two such morsels [of virtu] in England! (19. 420; 26 June 1741).

Even before the eagle was shipped, Horace Mann started its consecration by sending Walpole an 'intaglio [design in relief] from the finest eagle in the world' (19. 277; 19 July, 1746), which Walpole found unsatisfactory: 'I conceive a good idea of my eagle, though the seal [intaglio] is a bad one' (19. 289; 1 August 1746). In the next decade, after Walpole tried and failed to get a drawing of the eagle from Richard Bentley, he commissioned a drawing from Samuel Wale, engraved in two prints by Charles Grignion (plate 3), which he distributed to Horace Mann and other Italian friends: 'I could not expect that any drawing could give a full idea of the noble spirit of the head, or of the masterly tumble of the feathers; but I think upon the whole the plates are not ill-done' (20. 485; 16 July 1755). He added a Latin inscription on the plate, '*nunc in aedibus Horatii Walpole Londini*' (now in the London house of Horace Walpole) (19. vi). Walpole thought well enough of the engraving of the eagle to make it a conspicuous feature of James MacArdell's print after Reynolds's 1756 portrait of him, where a schematic facsimile of the print partially unrolled lies on a table bearing attributes of '*Horace Walpole, youngest son of Sir Robert Walpole, Earl of Orford*' (1. 64). The books and the pen bespeak

the writer; the eagle says 'Horace Walpole, Virtuoso.' And when Walpole was asked for his portrait in 1788 by Mrs Dickinson, he replied: 'I beg you will accept the prints of my eagle, which are a better memorandum [than James MacArdell's engraving after Reynolds's portrait of Walpole] of Strawberry Hill and of Your most obedient humble servant, Hor. Walpole' (31. 263).

Madame du Deffand was puzzled by the bird in MacArdell's engraving of Walpole's portrait when she wrote in December 1767: 'dites moi qu'est-ce qu'un oiseau qui est dans votre estampe; c'est san doute un emblème, que signifie-t-il?' (Tell me what is a bird doing in your print? It is certainly an emblem, but what does it signify?) (3. 405). Unfortunately Walpole's reply to Madame's reiterated query – 'I beg you don't forget to answer this question' – has been lost with his side of the entire correspondence, but we can surmise that the eagle was emblematic of Walpole's ironic sense of himself as courtesy-book gentleman posing as virtuoso and antiquarian.

The eagle took its place immediately as one of the choicest objects in Walpole's collection. Later it was placed in the library at Strawberry Hill (plate 4), and then in the gallery under Rosalba's pastel portrait of the French financier, John Law (1671–1729; HWC 42. 386–7), where it established itself as a touchstone for statuary added to the collection. When Mann sent a bronze Caligula in 1767 Walpole thanked him by saying: 'It is more a portrait than any picture I ever saw. . . . I do not know whether it is not more exquisite in its kind than my eagle' (22. 522). When a silver bell said to be Cellini's, richly ornamented with fruit and insects, arrived in 1772, Walpole called it 'the uniquest thing in the world. . . . fit to keep company with my eagle and *your* [Horace Mann's] Caligula – can one say more?' (23. 383).

Soon after the marriage of his cousin Anne Seymour Conway to the sexagenarian John Harris (1690–1767) on 10 March 1755, Walpole gave a banquet which illustrates the way his favourite morsels of virtu figured in the social life of Strawberry Hill:

> Last Wednesday I gave a feast in form to the Harrises. There was the Duke of Grafton, Lord and Lady Hertford, Mr Conway, and Lady Ailesbury. In short, all the Conways in the world, my Lord Orford, and the Churchills. We dined in the drawing-room below stairs, amidst the Eagle, Vespasian, etc. You never saw so Roman a banquet; but with all my virtu, the bridegroom seemed the most venerable piece of antiquity (35. 217; 27 March 1755).

A Roman banquet at Strawberry Hill, the Roman household gods translated to the Thames at Twickenham, part of a stage setting for a wedding of the English aristocracy. A mock-heroic bagatelle, an in-joke between the collector and his purchasing agent, an occasion for Walpole's masquerade as the last Roman, the eagle appears to be the outward and visible sign of the courtesy-book gentleman's Grand Tour taste.[7]

'Far Gone in Medals,' Stosch's Gladiator

'I am far gone in medals, lamps, idols, prints, etc. and all the small commodities to the purchase of which I can attain,' Walpole wrote to Harry Conway from Rome on the Grand Tour: 'I would buy the Coliseum if I could' (HWC 37. 57; 24 April 1740). After his return to London Walpole gave a somewhat less sanguine report on his collecting to his Cambridge tutor, Conyers Middleton, a collector of antiquities: 'On opening my boxes, I find what I suspected, that there is little new, or curious enough to deserve your notice; my chief purchases having lain in medals, and pictures' (15. 11; 9 April 1743). He goes on to describe a dozen busts he had acquired including that of Vespasian 'in the finest black marble. . . . allowed in Rome inferior to nothing but the Caracalla [a famous bust in the Farnese collection]' (15. 12; 9 April 1743).[8] Ambitious to buy the colosseum, settling for 'small collections' (13. 232; 2 October 1740), preening himself on a *chef d'oeuvre* – Walpole's equivocations typify his virtuosoship on the Grand Tour.

Surprisingly, it appears that Walpole was as much interested in collecting medals as any other objects of virtu on the Grand Tour, and both George Vertue and Middleton praised Walpole's collection of medals after his return. Walpole's interest in the now unfamiliar art of intaglio engraving is worth discussion primarily because medals introduced Walpole to one of Europe's great collectors, the notorious Baron Philipp von Stosch (1691–1757), whose collection was catalogued by Winckelmann. The story of Walpole's unsuccessful attempt to acquire two medals from his collection illustrates clearly how strange and alien the idea of a virtuoso collector was to the courtesy-book gentleman on the Grand Tour, and how careful Walpole was to disguise his own virtuosoship as trifling. Before arriving in Florence in 1731 Stosch had, like Mann,

5 and 5A.   *Medal of Alexander Severus.* British Museum, Department of Coins and Medals. © Copyright The British Museum.

served Robert Walpole as a spy at the Pretender's court, using art dealing as a screen for espionage.[9] It was inevitable that Walpole would meet Mann's friend 'the old Baron' while he was 'eager about baubles . . . going to Louis [Siries, French silversmith] at the Palazzo Vecchio' (17. 213; 1741), and visiting Stosch's celebrated musum.

Soon after he arrived in Florence Walpole gave Middleton an account of his initiation to the market for medals there:

> One of my medals is as great a curiosity [as the bust of Vespasian]: 'tis of Alexander Severus [Roman Emperor 208–35; plates 5–5A],[10] with the amphitheatre in brass; this reverse is extant on medals of his, but mine is a *medagliuncino*, or small medallion, and the only one with this reverse known in the world: 'Twas found by a peasant while I was in Rome, and sold by him for sixpence to an antiquarian, to whom I paid for it seven guineas and an half: but to virtuosi 'tis worth any sum (13. 233; 2 October 1740).

To judge from this accidental acquisition of the *medagliuncino*, Walpole's collecting of medals on the Grand Tour was casual and haphazard. Walpole is playing the amateur virtuoso, redeeming his extravagance by claiming the rarity of a unique reverse.

Walpole had offered Stosch £50 for a medal of a gladiator while in Italy. As he wrote to Horace Mann in December 1741: 'I find I cannot live without Stosch's intaglia of the gladiator with the vase, upon a granite. You know I offered him fifty pounds; I think rather than not have it, I would give an hundred' (17. 212; 26 November 1741). Then, thinking of the War of the Austrian Succession raging in northern Italy at the time and Stosch's perpetual trouble with creditors, Walpole continues: 'What will he [Stosch] do, if the Spaniards should come to Florence? Should he be driven to straits, perhaps he would part with his Meleager [the legendary Greek

Argonaut who slew the Calydonian boar]' (17. 212–13). Walpole was so 'eager about baubles' that he seriously hoped an invasion of Florence would yield him the gladiator as spoils of war. He noted that the coveted medal 'is engraved in Stosch's book [Hazen 3767 (1760)]: 'it is a gladiator standing, with a vase by him on a table; on an exceedingly fine garnet' (20. 157, n. 24).[11]

Early on Walpole realized that bargaining with Stosch would be difficult, but he told Lord Lincoln he was prepared to take reckless measures about another medal in Stosch's collection, an engraved Cornelian gem of a pastoral figure said to be Virgil: 'I design to visit the Virgil you tell me of, but for getting it, I have no hopes. If I could steal it roundly, I would without any scruple, but for procuring it from so thorough a rogue as Stosch without paying double its value, I despair' (30. 11; 1741).[12]

In January 1742 Mann reported to Walpole on his unsuccessful negotiations with Stosch for the gladiator. Mann may have hoped for a concession from a fellow secret-service agent in Robert Walpole's employ, but he hoped in vain. 'I did all I could to induce that bear Stosch to part with his Gladiator,' but Stosch drove a hard bargain and was more than equal to Mann's blandishments. 'I thought 'twas a joke to hide who 'twas for,' Mann continued, reporting how his gambit to extract a favour for the prime minister's son had failed:

> After having given me a list of all the people that had offered him money for it and the Meleager, particularly Lord George Benting [George Bentinck (1715–59)] £100 for the former, Lord Raymond [Robert, 2nd Baron (1717–56)] as much for the latter, and that he had refused much greater sums, the conclusion was that if I would assure him that they were for Mr Horace Walpole junior Esquire he would part with them both to him for 600 zecchins [c. £300], but to anybody else he would have twice the sum. What impudence! Stay till he dies and then I'll seize them and shall have them for nothing (17. 263–4; 10 January 1742).

Revealing Walpole as the buyer was a clumsy manoeuvre, and Walpole decided the asking price was much too high: '[T]he temptation of having them [the gladiator and the Meleager] at all is great, but too enormous: if I could have the gladiator for about an hundred pounds, I would give it' (17. 302; 22 January 1742), but Walpole was forced to stay his quest.

Reckless schemes abandoned and Stosch destined to live another fifteen years, Mann seized on another opportunity for getting the gladiator when a scandal erupted involving criminal charges against Stosch for pederasty: 'Cyclops the antiquarian [Stosch, apparently blind in one eye] has been too rough with a tender Ganimede, who has been obliged to retire to the hospital for the assistance of the surgeons there. . . . if matters are carried with rigour [Stosch] would be glad to give his Meleager or Gladiator to be well off' (18. 369; 14 January 1744). But sexual perversion proved no more efficacious than rapine or larceny, and Stosch kept a firm grasp on his gladiator and Meleager.

Denied his favourites, Walpole was nevertheless buying other medals from Stosch in the 1740s, although we are unable to say what in particular. Stosch teased Walpole about his debts 'for the carriage of medals from Rome and postage' that amounted to something like £100, and provokingly said that Walpole ought to have sent him a present of Isaac Ware's *Plans of Houghton* (17. 416; 15 May 1742), a suggestion Walpole, perhaps unwisely, dismissed: '[H]e was so extremely well paid for all I had of him' (17. 439; 26 May 1742). Walpole went on to make the frivolous suggestion that he pay the postage with gifts of Maltese cats, which Stosch doted on (17. 452; 10 June 1742).

In March 1749, eight years after Walpole said he could not live without Stosch's gladiator, an opportunity presented itself when Horace Mann forwarded to Walpole a begging letter from the fifty-eight-year-old Stosch asking Walpole's assistance in obtaining the arrears of his civil service pension (20. 36; 21 March 1749), and offering what can only be called a bribe, 'a gold medal [a Galla Placidia (d. *c.* 450), wife of Constantius III] lately found' (20. 53; 3 May 1749).[13] Walpole abruptly refused the bribe chastizing Stosch in his reply to Mann for 'impertinence' about his pension 'which I beg you [Mann] will tell him [Stosch] I have no manner of interest to procure' (20. 53). Disingenuously having refused the *quid*, Walpole asks for the *quo*: 'It is not for myself, but I wish you would ask him [Stosch] the price for a friend of mine who would like to buy it [the Galla Placidia]' (20. 53). Walpole's transparent ruse was doomed to failure. Mann informed Walpole 'that Stosch has got his affair [arrears of his pension] done by the means of Lord Duncannon [William Ponsonby (1704–93)], which will make him less *traitable* about his Galla Placidia, about which I will speak to him the first time I see him' (20. 70; 20 June 1749).

In refusing to use his political influence Walpole was standing on the principle of *nolo contendere* he proudly followed all his life when asked for favours. But the coveted gladiator was the price he paid on this occasion for his scruples. 'Stosch has grievously offended me,' he wrote to Mann 19 May 1750, 'but that he will little regard, as I can be of no use to him: he has sold or given his charming intaglia of the gladiator to Lord Duncannon. I must reprove you [Mann] a little who sent it [to Duncannon]: you know how much I pressed you to buy it for me, and how much I offered. I still think it one of the finest rings I ever saw, and am mortified at not having it' (20. 157; 19 May 1750). The always compliant Mann answered his friend's petulant letter with his usual patient forbearance, explaining that he had carried out a commission for William Ponsonby who 'wrote to me to desire I would take charge of an intaglio which he bought of Stosch, and forward it to him under the Duke of Bedford's cover' (20. 159; 26 June 1750). Tactfully Mann reminded Walpole 'that Lord Duncannon did him great service in obtaining the payment of his arrears, and settling that of his allowance for the future, but still I make no doubt that my Lord has paid very dear for the intaglio, which originally was offered to him for 30 zecchins [*c.* £15] before Stosch bought it' (20. 159; 26 June 1750). How Walpole could have expected Mann *not* to send Stosch's gift or Ponsonby's purchase is astonishing. But the always obliging Mann, ever dutiful to the friend he calls 'My dear child' (20. 158), in this case a spoiled child, assured Walpole 'I am as angry with Stosch as you can be. . . . but intend to abuse him' (20. 159). Walpole had been forced to swallow the pill that Lord Duncannon acquired the coveted ring of the gladiator for £50, the price Walpole had originally offered. But still he had the cheek to blame Mann!

After Stosch died on 6 November 1757 Mann was appointed executor of Stosch's estate, but he was unable to keep the rash promise he had made to Walpole about the gladiator and Meleager: 'Stay till he dies and then I'll seize them and you shall have them for nothing' (17. 264; 10 January 1742). Mann gave Walpole an account of Stosch's last illness, and reported that his collection valued at £200,000 had been bequeathed to 'Stoschino' (21. 384), Walpole's name for Stosch's nephew Heinrich Wilhelm Muzell (1723–82), who was planning to sell it *en bloc*: 'I wish I knew whether there is any part of it that you should like. His cameos and intaglios are very numerous but the value quite arbitrary. The Meleager is the only one of the first class. Lord Duncannon some years ago gave old Stosch 100 zecchins [£50] for his Gladiator' (21. 151; 19 November 1757).

Mann's reminder of the gladiator must have been painful, but Walpole dispatched a want-list of 'some trifles that I wish to purchase from Stosch's collection' (21. 178; 23 February 1758), including some 'bawdy' medals and possibly some 'obscene drawings' (HWC 21. 160, 202).[14] In the estate sale Mann once again had divided loyalties, since he was also acting as purchasing agent for Lord Duncannon, and competing with 'many and great purchasers' (21. 151; 19 November 1757).[15] Nevertheless Mann succeeded in getting Walpole a number of modern medals he wanted, including three of popes – Julius III with a reverse attributed to Michaelangelo, Innocent X, and Gregory XIII – along with a medal satirizing Walpole's father: 'a most ridiculous vulgar brass medal struck by some Irish priest at Rome. On one side is a figure with a halter by which the Devil is leading it to hell, with the words, "Make room for Sir Robert," and at the bottom, "No Excise" ' (21. 202; 13 May 1758).[16]

'Far gone in medals' but no virtuoso we may conclude of Walpole's collecting of engraved intaglios on the Grand Tour and afterwards. Moreover the correspondence indicates he was as much interested in the 'mysterious dingy nature' (17. 420; 6 May 1742) of Stosch's character as in any of his curiosities. Through Horace Mann, Walpole came into some intimacy with Stosch while in Florence, visiting his collection on several occasions, and observing him with a mixture of admiration and disgust. Walpole added this portrait vignette in a note to his transcription of his correspondence with Mann: 'Baron Stosch, a Prussian, virtuoso, and spy for the Court of England on the Pretender. He had been driven from Rome, though it was suspected that he was a spy on both sides; he was a man of a most infamous character in every respect' (17. 164, n. 5).[17] Walpole owned the catalogue (Hazen 3762; 1724) of his collection of seventy gems with artists' signatures which established Stosch as Europe's leading connoisseur of engraved gems, and the catalogue by Johann Joachim Winckelmann (Hazen 3767; 1760), which secured Stosch's posthumous reputation.

Walpole had ample reason to distrust Stosch as an art dealer, and Mann was always prepared to pass on anecdotes about Stosch's questionable conduct, about 'very good antique statues. . . . only fit for my Lord [Robert Walpole]' belonging to the Baron Cerbone del Nero (1671–1746), who 'wanted to employ Stosch to procure the sale of them in England, but has laid aside the thoughts of employing him for reasons you will easily guess [Stosch's unreliable character]' (18. 308; 24 September 1743). On another occasion Mann tells Walpole an anecdote about an ignorant English Grand Tourist visiting Stosch's collection:

We have had a strange pack of English here whose names I don't recollect; they were at Stosch's one day to see his things, and a parson who was among them was made believe that the large picture of Cataline's conspiracy was the Lord's Supper, and was desired to say which was Christ's figure. He instantly pitched upon Cataline's, but confessed it was the first time he had ever seen our Lord and Saviour with a sword by His side (18. 41; 10 September 1742).

Anecdotes about gulling Grand Tourists are commonplace, but Mann's story also illustrates Stosch's free-thinking that had offended Walpole's acquaintance, Humphrey Prideaux (d. 1793). Walpole wrote to Mann soon after his return from the Grand Tour:

> I have been plagued all this morning with that oaf of unlicked antiquity, Prideaux, and his great boy. He talked through all Italy, and everything in all Italy. Upon mentioning Stosch, I asked if he had seen his collection; he replied, very few of his things, for he did not like his company; that he had never heard so much *heathenish talk* in his days. I inquired what it was, and found that Stosch had one day said before him, *that the soul was only a little glue.* I laughed so much, that he walked off; I suppose, thinking that I believed so too (17. 378; 24 March 1742).

On two occasions Mann told Walpole stories about Stosch's thoughts on the human soul: 'Stosch said he had determined what had been hitherto a dispute, where was the seat of the soul – *dans le trou du queue,* as the most sensible part' (17. 112; 21 August 1741).

Walpole took it for granted that Stosch's spying on the Pretender was of dubious value, though the intelligence he provided may have been more valuable than Mann's because of his connections in Rome (HWC 17. xxxiii). 'I don't approve of your hinting at the falsehoods of Stosch's intelligence,' Walpole wrote to Mann in 1743, 'nobody regards it but the King; it pleases him – *e basta*' (18. 225). Walpole commented on Stosch's dispatches after he was expelled from Rome: 'Stosch used to pretend to send over an exact journal of the life of the Pretender and his sons, though he had been sent out of Rome at the Pretender's request, and must have had very bad or no intelligence of what passed in that family' (18. 225, HW's n. 10). In 1752 Mann wrote to Walpole that 'Stosch is still privately of an opinion that he [the Pretender] does not exist, though he is forced to write about him every week!' (20. 333; 31 August 1752).

Inevitably Walpole and Mann exchanged stories about Stosch's notorious sexuality. Walpole recorded in a Commonplace Book one such anecdote: 'Baron Stosch one day standing in the street with another person, a very pretty girl passed by: the gentleman asked him if he knew her? "Know her? Yes! I have lain with her mother, and two of her sisters, and three of her brothers, and tomorrow I shall lie with her"' (17. 164, n. 5).

To sum up, in Walpole's correspondence with Horace Mann Stosch lives up to his reputation summarized by Leslie Lewis as 'a homosexual, an atheist, a blasphemer, a liar, and a thief'. Still it is an exaggeration to call the private exchange of gossip between Walpole and Mann malicious and spiteful, 'jokes in the very worst of taste'.[18] In spite of his references to Stosch as a 'rogue' (30. 11), 'too worthless to be pitied living' (20. 475; 22 April 1755), Walpole's gossip, like Ghezzi's caricatures (plate 6), seems more comical than satirical. Walpole spoke of him as 'a great virtuoso', owned copies of his catalogues, emulated his collecting (plate 7),[19] and most important, paid him the compliment of imitating his career when he became an English antiquarian. In a letter to

6.   Arthur Pond after Pier Leone Ghezzi: *Due famosi Antiquari* [Stosch and Sabbatini]. Courtesy of the Print Collection, Lewis Walpole Library, Yale University. '[H]e [Stosch] was a man of a most infamous character in every respect' (HWC 17. 164, n.5).

7.   Bernard Picart sc. after Epitychanes: *Stosch's Germanicus Caesar*. Intaglio on cornelian. Philipp von Stosch, *Pierres antiques gravées* (Amsterdam, 1724), p. 43, plate XXXII. Line engraving 10 × 6¾ in. Courtesy of the Lewis Walpole Library, Yale University. 'Baron Stosch's . . . Germanicus . . . [is] larger than Mr Walpole's . . . but it is imperfect' (*Works* 2. 486).

Lord Carteret, Stosch wrote 'that Plato had said the world could not be well governed except by philosophers; that I myself [Stosch] was of the opinion that to the word 'philosophers' one should join antiquaries, because at present [*c.* 1721] the greater part of Europe was governed either by Princes or Ministers who were antiquaries, the Emperor, the regent, your excellency [John Carteret, 2nd Baron, 1st Earl of Granville] . . .'[20] When Stosch's hopes for a diplomatic career ended, he wrote to Count Fleming in April 1721 informing him that he had been obliged to resume the study of antiquities 'like a man who in despair made himself a Capuchin. . . . It is true . . . that in politics one can become great and have the pleasure of governing, which men regard as the greatest advantage in the world, as indeed it is. But as an antiquary I shall rule with little danger over Caesars and Scipios, Greeks and Romans, and I shall place them where I like and fear them much less than a politician his cook.'[21] So Stosch ruled the gladiator and Meleager Walpole coveted, as Walpole ruled over portraits of the English aristocracy when he became Prime Minister of Taste.

'Two or Three Pictures'

'I . . . have only bought . . . two or three pictures' (13. 232), Walpole told West in 1740. His undated handlist (26. 7–8; *c.* 1741) of purchases on the Grand Tour records only four pictures attributed to artists who could be called old masters – the eighteenth-century collector's Pablo Picasso, Carlo Maratti (1625–1713); Pietro da Cortona (1596–1669); Francesco Albani (1578–1660); and a copy of a picture by Antonio Allegri (1494–1534), called Correggio; along with pictures by two view-painters – Giovanni Pannini (1691–1765) and Gaspar van Wittel, called Vanvitelli (1653–1736). The handlist suggests that Walpole's Grand Tour pictures were few in number, small in size, and relatively inexpensive. They replicate the conventional taste of his father's collection at Houghton for Italian late Baroque painting. Like Walpole's antiquities, these pictures were acquired for the most part by the initiative of Walpole's Committee of Taste. Bought by chance rather than choice, they were frequently copies, often in poor condition, illustrating in no sense the Richardsonian connoisseur's discrimination.[22]

After his return from the Grand Tour it appears that Walpole put more energy into collecting pictures for his father's collection than his own. In 1743 the Committee of Taste discovered from English dealers in Rome – Dalton, Parker, and Gaven – that a painting attributed to Raphael (1483–1520), *Christ Disputing with the Doctors*, was to be sold out of the collection of Cardinal Cibo. Rumored to be sought after by kings, cardinals, and the Dukes of Beaufort and Marlborough, the 'Raphael' was an irresistible prize for the prime minister's collection. Mann reported on 'an extreme good draft [drawing]' sent to him by Mark Parker, an art dealer in Rome:

> There are in it above 30 figures besides as many more in profile, and at a distance I am at a loss to judge by his account of it whether the draft is of the whole size. This is near three feet long only, and about two high. The creature [Richard Gaven] who has it now asks 1,000 crowns [*c.* £250] for what Parker tells me he sold him for 2,000 crowns. . . . Mr Chute is quite wild about it, thinking how well . . . [it] would have suited your [Houghton's] gallery (18. 239–40; 4 June 1743).

Chute again played the tempter, this time with sexual innuendo in a postscript to Mann's letter:

> He [Mann] says vastly true; I am quite wild about the Rafael; I know the Duke of Beaufort [Henry Somerset (1707–45), 3rd Duke] will buy it. Who would not give all he has sold for fourscore thousand pound [Somerset was expensively divorcing his duchess, Frances Scudamore, at the time] for such a heavenly picture? If I was married to a dozen Duchesses, I would permit the whole Conclave, nay the whole universal Church, linkboys and all, to taste their sweet bodies for it (35. 37; 4 June 1743).

Comparing the supposititious Raphael to the Hampton Court Cartoons and the School of Athens in the Vatican, the delirious Chute asks 'shall it never hang in the gallery at Houghton?. . . . Oh! but once more, my Lord's [Sir Robert Walpole's] gallery, and the Raphael – there's temptation sufficient to give a vandal an erection of virtù' (35. 38).

Primed by his Committee of Taste, Walpole 'painted the Raphael to my Lord almost as fine as Raphael himself could' (18. 254; 20 June 1743). But Sir Robert had the good sense to resist the temptation of a picture excluded from modern catalogues of Raphael's authentic works: '[H]e will not think of it,' Walpole reported to a disappointed committee. '[H]e will not give a thousand guineas for what he never saw' (18.254).

Walpole returned from the Grand Tour with ideas of his own for additions to his father's collection. One of the pictures Walpole asked Mann to pursue was 'by Correggio, in a convent at Parma, and reckoned the second best of that hand in the world.[23] There are the Madonna and Child, St Catherine, St Matthew and other figures: 'tis a most known picture, and has been engraved by Augustin Carracci' (17. 167; 8 October 1741). As usual Chute could not contain his enthusiasm – 'I never saw anything so charming as the Corregio Madonna with St Jerome [whom Walpole had confused with Saint Catherine] at Parma[24]; will Sir Robert never buy it?' (35.5; 22 August 1741). But inquiries to Antonio Cocchi, Walpole's Florentine doctor and friend, indicated the picture 'is by no means to be disposed of' (17. 199; 26 November 1741), and by January of the following year Mann had thrown in the towel: 'None of the many schemes I have put in practice have succeeded with regard to the Corregio; I am only convinced by them that it will be impossible to get it for any money' (17. 268; 16 January 1742).

So the quest for the Correggio rested until the Spanish War in Italy occasioned comment in Mann's letters in 1743 about the collection of the Duke of Modena, Francesco d'Este (Francis III, 1698–1780), who was commanding the Spanish forces in Italy. The Duke's appointment as 'commander-in-chief . . . generalissimo' (18. 222) had prompted Mann to advise Walpole to write to the Duke about his pictures (18. 223; 7 May 1743). By October 1743 Mann wrote to Walpole that the fortunes of war had forced the duke 'to sell all his furniture (pictures excepted) to the Jews of Mantova. . . . If the *Notte* [Correggio's nightpiece in the ducal palace at Modena] had been to be sold, would you not have turned Jew to have got it?' (18. 323). Mann's question was not merely rhetorical since he goes on to say he was prepared to pilfer the duke's pictures with the help of the opposing Austrian commander, Prince Johann Lobkowitz (1686–1753):

> Nobody knows where the pictures are. If I can discover (for which I have many spies in pay) I intend to send Prince Lobkowitz word, upon condition that he shall let me choose two for the discovery. Seriously, if one knew how to go to work, I believe one might get the Germans to run away with the St Antonio Abbate [the church of San Antonio Abbate at Parma where Walpole's Correggio was located]. If once in their hands they would sell it for a butt of beer (18. 323; 15 October 1743).

Despite the *opera buffa* mock-heroics, it does appear that Mann was seriously proposing to appropriate for the Walpole collection as spoils of war two Correggios, rarest of Italian old-master easel paintings.

As early as 19 November, the indefatigable Mann had decided to enlist another German general, the Baron Johann Ernst von Braitwitz (1672–1759), as uniformed purchasing agent in the campaign for the Correggio Madonna at Parma:

> I have been thinking that now if ever one ought to make a push to get the Coreggio.

8.   Anonymous line engraving: *Mons.ᴿ Le. Virtu'*
[Dr Robert Bragge]. 3 November 1771. Courtesy
of the Print Collection, Lewis Walpole Library,
Yale University.

I have spoke of it to General Braitwitz, who has promised to assist towards it as much
as he can. He has an intimate friend who commands the hussars at Parma, to whom
he writes by the first post. I have drawn up instructions for him, and have engaged,
besides giving them a reasonable price for their picture, to get them a good copy for
the use of their convent and old women to pray to, which he is to say will answer
their end as well. General Braitwitz does not know how many kings of France [Marie
de Médici and Louis XIV are possibilities] have offered to cover it with gold, therefore seems to think the commission easy. I can't guess at what they may ask. Tell me
immediately what you think I may give. *Poffar Iddio* ['By God'] if it could be got.
What an addition it would make to the gallery! One loses nothing by trying, and
who can employ better than hussars, though if they succeed it will be the first time
they did people good against their own inclinations (18. 337–8; 19 November 1743).

Mann's renewed optimism encouraged Walpole to reply: 'I am much pleased with the
prospect you show me of the Correggio. My Lord [Sir Robert Walpole] is so satisfied.
. . . that he will go as far as a thousand pound for the Correggio. Do you really think
we shall get it, and for that price?' (18. 351; 30 November 1743). Before Mann could
reply Walpole wrote again (11 December 1743) alarmed by a rumor that the Correggio
at Parma might be a copy:

My Lord has been told by Dr Bragge,[25] a virtuoso [plate 8], that some years ago the monks asked ten thousand pounds for our Correggio, and that there were two copies then made of it: that afterwards, he is persuaded, the King of Portugal bought the original, he does not know at what price. Now I think it very possible, that this Doctor hearing the picture was to be come at, may have invented this Portuguese history: but as there is a possibility too, that it may be true, you must take all imaginable precautions, to be sure it is the very original – a copy would do neither you nor me great honor (18. 355; 11 December 1743).

Walpole's suspicions about the story were justified: the kings of Portugal and Poland had made offers that were rejected, and in 1749 the painting was removed by popular agitation to the Duomo at Parma.

Walpole suspected and Mann disbelieved Bragge's story (for Bragge was not an honorable man), and although Mann advised Walpole to quiz consular officials about the picture, Mann had realized the price for a Correggio would be prohibitive, and the push for the painting lost momentum as quickly as it started not a month earlier.

In 1779, when his father's collection of pictures was sold to Catherine the Great, Walpole ruefully remarked of the inflated prices his father had paid for them: 'purchasers are not perfect connoisseurs at first' (HWC 2: 168). The same might be said about Walpole's purchase of a picture he had seen on the Grand Tour for his father's collection. The story of this acquisition, told in Walpole's correspondence with Horace Mann from 1741 to 1743, illustrates a kind of connoisseurship very different from the discipline Jonathan Richardson had introduced with evangelical zeal in his *Science of a Connoisseur* (1719; Hazen 310). Even though Walpole read Richardson's works, and sat to him in about 1734 for a portrait (plate 1) before taking the Grand Tour, this episode shows that he had no faith in the connoisseur's creed according to Richardson's gospel, and that his taste in Italian art had more to do with fashion than aesthetics.

Because of Sir Robert's remarriage, Walpole's relations with his father were strained when he embarked on the Grand Tour in March 1739, but pictures helped to reconcile father and son after his return in September 1741. At this stage his father's collection was all but complete, numbering over 450 pictures distributed between houses in London, Chelsea, Richmond, and Houghton Hall, Norfolk. Upon his return, Horace Walpole became, in effect, the curator of his father's collection; he helped to design and hang the gallery at Houghton with pictures brought from 10 Downing Street after his father's resignation, and completed a catalogue of the Houghton pictures by August 1743. Like his older brother Edward, Walpole kept an eye out on the Grand Tour for pictures his father might want and came back eager to pursue three fashionable 'hands' the collection was lacking, namely the Raphael and Correggio just discussed, and a picture by Domenico Zampieri (1581–1641), called Domenichino (plate 9).

The Domenichino is mentioned in a letter to Horace Mann dated 8 October 1741:

'a Madonna and Child by Dominichino,[26] in the palace Zambeccari at Bologna . . . . Mr Chute knows the picture. . . . If you can employ anybody privately to inquire about these pictures [the Domenichino and Correggio], be so good to let me know: Sir Robert would not scruple almost any price, for he has of neither hand. The con-

9. Giovanni Battista Salvi, called Sassoferrato, after Pierre Mignard: *Madonna and Child*. Hermitage Museum, St. Petersburg (Inv. 1506). Oil on canvas, 30 × 23⅝ ins. Photo: State Hermitage Museum. 'Don't you laugh at those wise connoisseurs who pronounced it a copy?' (HWC 18. 79).

vent is poor: the Zambeccari collection is to be sold, though when I inquired after this picture, they would not set a price' (17. 167).

Mann employed the English artist at Bologna, Edward Penny (1714–91), to bargain for the picture, and from the beginning John Chute enthusiastically supported the project: 'How charming it would be if Mr Mann can succeed in procuring . . . [the Correggio and Domenichino] for Sir Robert! I'd give the tip of my little finger to see them arrived safe hither [Florence]' (35. 12; 15 November 1741).

By mid-December Mann had received a report from Edward Penny indicating that Monsignore Francesco Zambeccari was prepared to sell the picture for the equivalent of £225: 'I suppose it's cheap,' Mann added. 'Did not you say they would ask much more?' (17. 227; 17 December 1741). On Christmas Eve Mann wrote to report that Chute and Whitehed had returned from Bologna without the picture 'but 'tis surely Sir Robert's' (17. 241; 24 December 1741). They had not concluded the bargain because 'Pennee has great hopes of getting it for 100 crowns [about £25] less, and that, as there's no danger of losing it, is worth saving' (17. 241). Mann concludes the letter by shower-ing praise on the Committee of Taste, reminding Walpole that Penny had tried to save him money, and that Chute had risked a dangerous trip in winter across the Appenines between Florence and Bologna, heroics Walpole acknowledged with a reference to the fate of his black spaniel crossing the Alps: 'If I was to tell it here [London], it would be believed as little as the rape of poor Tory by a wolf' (17. 257; 29 December 1741).

At year's end the picture had apparently been secured for the Walpoles with record despatch by the skillful bargaining of the Committee of Taste with the Monsignore. Into this happy state of affairs the incubus of doubt about the picture's originality entered when Chute wrote to say he was planning to suspend negotiations for the Domeni-chino because connoisseurs in Bologna, including the painter Donato Creti (1671–1749), had questioned the attribution: '. . . [T]here is such vehement suspicion of its not being Dominichino's,' he writes, 'I could not but think it proper to refer the con-clusion of the bargain to your farther deliberations upon it. . . . I will endeavour to manage so as to have the purchase in our power, in case you should determine to have the picture. . . . [Edward Penny's letter] certainly makes it very doubtful whether it be of the hand we imagined' (35. 17; 1 January 1742).

The deal for the Madonna in jeopardy, the nimble Penny immediately found anoth-er Domenichino for Walpole to pursue, possibly the *Persian Sibyl* now in the Wallace collection.[27] Mann wrote:

> Nobody could ever have managed the thing better than Mr Pennee has done, He has spoke much of a picture that is undoubtedly a Dominichino and the only one at Bologna; 'tis the figure of a sibyl. . . . [Penny] . . . wondered Mr Walpole had not rather chose the sibyl which was so much finer than that they were then about and then thought an original. He has since wrote to me about it and says he believes it may be had for a little more than that of Zambeccari (17. 267–68; 16 January 1742).

Walpole says nothing about pictures in his next letter, instead describing parliamentary debates preceding his father's resignation on 9 February 1742, and when Mann takes up the subject again he retreats from statements in his last letter that could be construed as ques-tioning Walpole's connoisseurship, while repeating Penny's advice to pursue the sibyl.

Unfortunately Walpole's reply (*c.* 14 January) to Chute's letter on suspicions about the pic-ture is missing (possibly he suppressed it). It could not have been a retort courteous to the connoisseurs because Chute pleads *nolo contendere* in order to ingratiate himself with Walpole:

> I own the pleasing cloud of my own ignorance was so thick as to indulge me with as delightful a degree of admiration of this charming imposter, the third visit I made it, as either of the former, and till the disgusting term, copy, saluted my ears, I should, without hesitation, have determined exactly as you do in your last letter, but as the matter stands, I'm sure of nothing but that it fits not me to decide the contest (35. 18–19; 13 February 1742).

In a quarrel between Walpole and the connoisseurs Chute prefers to play the loyal sen-ator: '[T]here are Gods [connoisseurs] against us,' Chute continues, 'that's certain; nevertheless, when I remember (as I do, because I was vastly happy) the approbation and delight with which I saw you behold it, I must confess I have an impious mind which inclines me to my own little Cato's [HW's] side' (35. 19).

Chute then offers the argument of provenance to support the attribution to Domenichino – 'Monsignor Zambecari . . . I verily believe sincerely esteems it *originalissimo*' – before going on to urge again pursuit of the 'picture of a Sibyl, of so notorious Domenichinality as to be even superior to all *fedes* [testimonials] and subscriptions, which Mr Pennee writes me word he could, after all, have procured for our dear Madonna' (35. 19). This leads Chute to a Ciceronian pun which can be paraphrased: 'Woe to those who trust Gods [connoisseurs] or men in attribution.' 'Pennee will return from Venice,' he continues, 'perhaps by the time I can receive your answer, and I think to make him take a little sketch of the Sibyl, which one may send you by the post, because I believe in all your journeys to Bologna you never got a sight of it, as it is in a certain Casa Ratta, which is never shown to strangers' (35. 19). Chute finishes his letter by disclaiming Walpole's thanks to him 'for fishing out a nasty doubt, which perhaps deprives you of a real satisfaction' (35. 19).

Walpole adamantly resisted the attempts of the Committee to interest him in Domenichino's Sibyl, one of several Domenichino painted of this subject,[28] and he refused to tell his father about it, discouraging the zeal of the Committee to add to Sir Robert's collection: '. . . [H]e will not care, I believe, to buy more pictures, having now so many more than he has room for at Houghton' (17. 339–40; 18 February 1742). Matters remained at this inconclusive stage for six months until Walpole decided in July 1742, to ignore the 'nasty doubt,' and buy the picture, insisting he was prepared to pay three times the price he had paid for any of the pictures he had bought for his own collection on the Grand Tour: 'I forgot to mention the Dominichin last post,' he wrote to Mann:

> as I suppose I had before, for I always was for your buying it; it is one of the most engaging pictures I ever saw. I have no qualms about its originality; and even if Sir Robert should not like it when it comes, which is impossible, I think I would live upon a flitch of bacon and a bottle of ink, rather than not spare the money to buy it myself – so, my dear Sir, buy it (17. 496; 14 July 1742).

In October Mann notified Walpole that the picture had safely arrived in Florence, and congratulated him on his purchase, prompting Walpole's triumphant reply: 'Well! Was I not in the right to persist in buying the Dominichin? Don't you laugh at those wise connoisseurs who pronounced it a copy? If it is one, where is the original? Or who was that so great master that could equal Dominichin?' (18. 79; 16 October 1742).

The triumph was short lived, for Mann's next letter brought a more stringent test of Walpole's confidence in his own taste, which he once defined as 'extemposed Judgment'.[29] Mann had discovered virtually indisputable evidence that the picture was not a Domenichino:

> I must not conceal to you a strong suspicion of the Dominicallity of your Madonna. Not from the beauty, for nothing can exceed it, but on my unpacking it I found on the back *Sasso-Ferrato*, whose name is not to be found in the *Abecedario pittorico* or in

any lives of the painters that I have seen; but I find his name is well known in Florence as a famous painter of Madonnas (18. 93–94; 6 November 1742).

Indeed Sassoferrato is not listed in Pellegrino Orlandi's dictionary (1704; Hazen 2082) or in Richardson's *Theory* (1715),[30] and Mann has no difficulty exorcizing this unknown and unfashionable artist: '. . . [N]obody can tell me where or when he lived, but there is a little place somewhere in Italy called *Sasso ferrato*' (18. 94; province of Ancona). Francis Haskell points out that Mann's non-entity was a respectable artist, Giovanni Battista Salvi (1605–85), called Sassoferrato, who had come to Rome during the reign of Urban VIII, where he painted:

> restrained and archaising devotional pictures which were long taken to be by some follower of Raphael. . . . he confined himself almost exclusively to pictures of the Holy Family, basing himself on three or four prototypes which he varied from time to time. His models were Raphael, Annibale Carracci and Domenichino at his most austere, and his simple pictures, which at their best are very beautiful, appear to be almost polemical in their opposition to the current Baroque style.[31]

This brings us to the scandal in the story, Mann's suggestion that the name on the back of the painting be expunged or concealed: 'I would willingly erase these words [Sasso-ferrato],' he continued, 'but am afraid that ink or anything else I should use might in time eat into the picture. If I were you I would line it; the canvas is rather too dry so that a lining would both preserve it and remove this scandal' (18. 94; 6 November 1742). Mann is playing Lady Macbeth: 'A little water clears us of this deed' (*Macbeth*, II, ii, 66), and he offers to send Walpole 'a little Madonna and Child' attributed to Sassoferrato in his collection for comparison, tactfully equivocating: 'It is as much inferior to yours as is possible, but it cannot be denied that there is a great resemblance in the manner of painting' (18. 94; 6 November 1742).

When transcribing the Mann correspondence (1754–5) Walpole apparently suppressed the passage in one of his letters in which he had approved of Mann's idea for removing Sassoferrato's name (18. 133, n. 5), but Mann got the message, replying 7 January 1743: 'I am glad you approve of my hint about the Dominichin; I'll get it done, but don't know well how to set about it, as it will be difficult to conceal the motive from the person employed in doing it. However it's better people should talk here than there' (18. 133; 7 January 1743). The scandal of falsifying a picture intended for the prime minister's collection would be less damaging in Florence than in London, but Mann's hesitation shows that he was beginning to realize, as Walpole remarked to him about buying a copy of the Correggio for Sir Robert, that the deception 'would do neither you nor me great honour' (18. 355, 11 December 1743).

Amidst talk about the difficulties of transporting the picture during the War of the Austrian Succession, Mann wrote to tell Walpole he had erased the name of Sassoferrato from the picture despite his earlier misgivings: 'I have scratched out the odious name myself so well that nobody can have the least suspicion, so that on this account you may be quite at peace' (18. 162; 18 February 1743).

After a delay of two months the 'Dominichino' was shipped aboard a man-of-war, the *Pembroke*, on 6 April 1743 (18. 214–15), arriving at Gravesend late in June. Soon Walpole was preparing to go to London to pick up the picture and take it back to Houghton where '[t]he Dominichin has a post of honour reserved in the gallery' (18. 250; 10 June 1743): 'Now I tremble!' he wrote melodramatically from Houghton: 'If it should not stand the trial among the number of capital pictures here! – but it must: it will' (18. 267; 11 July 1743). Mann had no doubts because of its provenance, purchaser, cost, reputation, and the obsequiousness of connoisseurs:

> Well!, You have by this time seen your Dominichin again; my Lord can't have seen it. I make no doubt but it will stand the trial. The connoisseurs won't dare to criticize it; it is really fine. Then, it came out of the Zambeccari collection; an hundred English have seen it under the denomination of a Dominichin – in short, it cost a vast deal, and is to stand in my Lord's collection. What would they have more? (18. 285; 13 August 1743).

One could not ask for a more telling list of an eighteenth-century dealer's criteria for attribution, standards that might have satisfied Joseph Duveen, but not Bernard Berenson.

Writing from Arlington Street in London on 19 July 1743 Walpole was in holiday mood, exclaiming 'Here am I come a-Dominichining!' (18. 275), but the *Pembroke* was required to perform quarantine throughout July, and he fretted about 'Pictures and statues belonging to Horace Walpole, Esq.' mentioned in the Quarantine Orders (18. 282, n. 2), tantalized by delays at the port, and still trembling: '. . . the things were brought up; then they were sent back to be aired; and still I am not to have them in a week. I tremble for the pictures, for they are to be aired at the rough discretion of a master of a hoy [a Thames cargo sloop], for nobody I could send, would be suffered to go aboard' (18. 282; 31 July 1743).

At last the well-travelled picture, a belated trophy of Walpole's Grand Tour (see HWC 26, Apps. 1 and 18), having survived warfare, quarantine, and rough handling by English tars, reached No. 5 Arlington Street in London the night of Saturday 13 August 1743. Walpole borrowed a phrase from Mme de Sévigné's *Letters* (Hazen 949, 1738) to express his thanks to Mann for the consignment: '*Voilà . . . un présent passant tous les présents passés et présentes!*' (18. 291; 14 August 1743). He insists that his confidence in the attribution to Domenichino survived comparison to Mann's Sassoferrato: 'I cannot think it of the same hand with the Sasso Ferrati you sent me. This last is not so *maniéré* as the Dominichin, for the more I look at it, the more I am convinced it is of him' (18. 292; 14 August 1743). Later in the same letter he clinches the argument about attribution by reporting the judgment of William Cavendish, 3rd Duke of Devonshire (1698–1755): 'I was interrupted in my letter this morning by the Duke of Devonshire, who called to see the Dominichin. Nobody knows pictures better: he was charmed with it, and did not doubt its Dominichinality' (18. 292; 14 August 1743).

In Walpole's mind this opinion of the ducal collector who married his son into the family of Lord Burlington settles the matter of attribution. To Walpole, attribution was not a matter to be left to connoisseurs, Italian or English, or even to his own Committee of Taste. The duke 'knows pictures' as an aristocratic collector; likewise Walpole 'knows pictures' *ex officio* as Prime Minister of Taste, and he never wavered from this attribution.

In all four eighteenth-century editions of the catalogue of his father's collection, *Aedes Walpolianae* (1747, 1752, 1767, and 1798)[32] he lists the Sassoferrato as 'a most beautiful, bright, and capital picture by Dominichino' (*Works* 2: 278). In 1784 when John Boydell published an engraving of the painting [by Valentine Green after a drawing by George Farington (32. 142; plate 10)] the Latin inscription placed on either side of the Walpole arms reads: 'Domenichino pinxit'. Walpole committed another falsification when he carefully excised the name of the artist from an engraving of it that he pasted into his extra-illustrated *Aedes Walpolianae* (1747) in the Metropolitan Museum, writing in ink in the same space – 'Dominichin pinx'.[33]

Walpole's extra illustration, an engraving of the Virgin and Child by François de Poilly (1622–93; plate 11), dated about 1656, provides another surprise in this intrigue of falsified attributions because the excised name of the artist on the print – 'P. Mignard Pinxit Roma' – turns out to be neither Zampieri/Dominichino nor Salvi/Sassoferrato but the French portrait painter, Pierre Mignard (1612–95), who succeeded Le Brun as the king's painter in 1690.[34] Art historians have recently shown that Salvi, Mignard's contemporary at Rome, used engravings of three of Mignard's famous Madonnas, including the one from Walpole's mutilated print, as models for his own pictures: 'He repeated these *Mignardes* with the same fidelity as he did the *Virgins* of Raphael and Perugino, to the point where posterity has almost forgotten that they were created by

10. Valentine Green after Domenichino and George Farington: *The Virgin and Child*. Mezzotint, 10 × 7⅞ in. 1 October 1774. Yale Center for British Art, Paul Mellon Fund. '[A] most beautiful, bright and capital picture by Dominichino' *Works* (2. 278).

11. François de Poilly after Pierre Mignard: *Madonna and Child*. Line engraving, 12½ × 9⅞ in. With Mignard's name excised by HW. HW's extra-illustrated *Aedes Walpolianae*, The Metropolitan Museum of Art, New York, Harris Brisbane Dick Fund, 1925. 'I have . . . [cut] out the odious name myself so well that nobody can have the least suspicion' HWC (18. 162).

12. *A Connoiseur Admiring a Dark Night Piece*. Anonymous line engraving dated 12 November 1771. Courtesy of the Print Collection, Lewis Walpole Library, Yale University.

Mignard and has regarded them as Salvi's own.'[35] Thus Walpole's attribution to Domenichino assisted in eclipsing both Mignard and Sassoferrato, the original artist and copyist. Oddly enough it appears that Walpole wilfully ignored the unequivocal attribution of the picture in a life of Mignard that he owned (Hazen 998; 1731) and annotated with 'numerous marginal markings':

> *La sainte Vierge* en demi figure, portant entre ses bras l'Enfant Jésus, gravée à Rome par François de Poilly d'après le tableau peint à Rome. 'The Holy virgin at half length, holding the infant Jesus in her arms, engraved by François de Poilly, after the picture painted at Rome (It is one of the Madonnas called the Mignardes).[36]

Walpole does not emerge from this incident looking anything like a connoisseur, except perhaps in Hogarth's pejorative sense of an ignorant English patron of Italian art (plate 12). Walpole's selling of a fake to his father appears *prima facie* to be a discreditable episode, and manuscript suppressions suggest Walpole was embarrassed by this exploit, though not enough to remove it entirely from the correspondence, unlike his quarrel with Gray. Walpole had passed up an opportunity to buy a genuine Domenichino, and recklessly settled for Sassoferrato's copy of Pierre Mignard's picture that could have fetched no more than a few guineas on the market in Italy or London, while the fraudulent Domenichino cost his father a 'vast deal' (18. 285). It may fairly be said that Walpole closely resembles one of the pretenders, charlatans, and 'jeunes fanfarons' (young boasters) Richardson describes in the *Science of a Connoisseur* who attribute unknown pictures to celebrated names 'par choix, ou par ignorance, ou suivant son avarice, sa vanité, ou son caprice' (by choice, or ignorance, or following their avarice, vanity, or caprice). Was Walpole then one of those 'Courtiers de Peinture' Richardson describes who 'tirer tout l'avantage qu'ils peuvent de la crédulité des autres . . . [assurant] pour véritable, ce qu'ils savent en conscience être faux' (take every advantage they can of others' credulity, professing true what they know to be false?).[37] If so, this deception was practiced by the man who wrote twenty years later that his *Anecdotes of Painting* (1762) were intended 'to assist gentlemen in discovering the hands of pictures they possess' (HWC 1. 25). Must we therefore conclude that Walpole's caper amounts to one more proof of Macaulay's nasty trifler?

I hope not, since I am attempting to write an apology for the trifler, and there are mitigating circumstances. First of all, Walpole was young, scarcely twenty-five, and spoiled, as he later admitted in acknowledging his blame for the quarrel with Gray. Second, the cover-up was not Walpole's idea: his advisors, Mann and Chute, each ten years older, led him on, and humoured every whim of the prime minister's son. Third, Walpole, like Reynolds himself, thought of art collecting as an amusing game, and Walpole's quest for the Domenichino has the flavour of a schoolboy's lark involving a charmed circle of close friends, conspiracy, and gleeful defiance of authority.

Finally, in mitigation, we must remember that in spite of Richardson's rules eighteenth-century connoisseurship remained a hucksters' carnival. The catalogues teem with mis-attributions, many of them deliberate, by corrupt dealers, connoisseurs, and auctioneers (witness Christie's notorious 'Godfathers' called in to christen pictures for auction). According to Richard Spear's catalogue (1982), many pictures attributed to Domenichino in eighteenth-century English collections appear to have been copies or wrong ascriptions. In 1715 the Earl of Burlington paid 1500 crowns (*c.* £375) for his most expensive purchase on the Grand Tour, Domenichino's *Madonna della Rosa*, a picture he believed to be an original, but it turned out to be a copy involving 'the intervention of a second hand'. In 1722 the French collector, Pierre Crozat, sold to the second Duke of Devonshire, father of Walpole's oracle, an 'unfinished' copy of Domenichino's *Rebuke of Adam and Eve*.[38]

CHAPTER 3

Keeper of the Prime Minister's Pictures

Walpole returned from the Grand Tour to find himself effectively the keeper of his father's collection. He had embarked on the Grand Tour disgusted with his father's remarriage to his mistress Maria Skerrett (1702–38), and remembered the resentment 'with deep shame . . . I felt for him at twenty-two [1739], when he stood before me' (24. 507). Sir Robert Walpole fell from power in February 1742, and the father who had neglected his son while engrossed with politics was drawn into greater intimacy with him in retirement, largely through mutual interest in pictures. 'What I know of him, I could only learn from his own mouth in the last three years of his life.' Walpole later admitted, chiding himself as usual: 'when, to my shame, I was so idle and young and thoughtless that I by no means profited of his leisure as I might have done' (16. 19; 21 October 1758).

Having contributed one questionable picture to his father's collection, Walpole was to witness the removal of many pictures from Downing Street,[1] and others from his father's London houses, to Houghton House in Norfolk, the family's country residence (plate 13), where he helped to design and hang a picture gallery, and compiled a catalogue of his father's Houghton collection (1743–7). Walpole wrote to Mann 10 June 1742 that his father was building a new gallery in what had been a greenhouse in the north wing: 'Sir Robert who begins to talk seriously of Houghton, has desired me to go with him thither, but that is not at all settled. Now I mention Houghton, you was in the right to miss a gallery there, but there is one actually fitting up, where the greenhouse was, and to be finished with the spoils of Downing Street' (17. 452; 10 June 1742). Walpole contributed a design he had obtained on the Grand Tour for the ceiling of the new gallery (18. 63, n. 22).

Since the majority of Robert Walpole's pictures had been collected during the two decades following Walpole's birth in 1717, the Houghton collection amounts to the nursery of his taste in the arts. It will therefore be appropriate to begin this chapter with an account of the genesis and reputation of the Houghton collection, then to turn to Walpole's catalogue of the collection, *Aedes Walpolianae*, and finally to the fate of the Houghton collection sold to Catherine the Great in 1779. This chapter will atttempt to demonstrate that Robert Walpole (plate 14) was no more a connoisseur than his son, who in turn valued his father's pictures not as works of art, nucleus of the Hermitage collection in St Petersburg, but rather as signs of his father's power and his family's glory. Walpole's catalogue of his father's collection, *Aedes Walpolianae* (1747), glorifies the Walpole family at the expense of Italian art and Italian artists.

Contemporary political opposition to Robert Walpole did not hesitate to pronounce

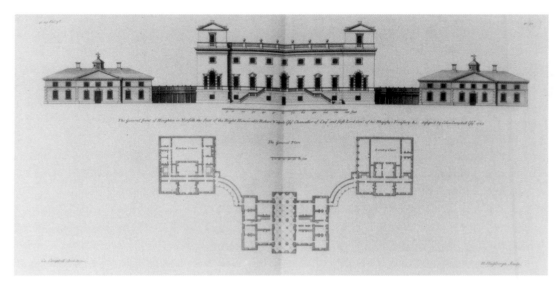

13.   Pierre Fourdrinier after Isaac Ware: *West Front of Hougton House, Norfolk*. Line engraving, from Isaac Ware, *The Plans . . . of Houghton in Norfolk* (1735). By permission of the British Library. 'Not a picture here but recalls a history' (HWC 9. 348).

Sir Robert a philistine, as in the epigram 'To Sir R. W. . . . spick and span new out of Mr Pope's shop':

> Walpole, be wise, let each man play his part,
> You mould the state, let others judge of art;
> What though by either Andrew often bit,
> You scarcely know a Jervas from a Tit[ian];
> Blush not, great Sir, you cannot know it less,
> Than we (God help us) if it's war or peace. [30. 4–5]

On the other hand, Robert Walpole's biographer, J. H. Plumb, speaks of him as 'one of the greatest connoisseurs of his time'.[2] But an analysis of extant records of acquisitions from about 1717 until Horace Walpole became curator of the collection, supported by comparison with other contemporary collections, indicates that in fact Robert Walpole cannot properly be considered a connoisseur. There is no evidence that Sir Robert was a discriminating judge of Italian art with a knowledge of 'hands,' an ability to distinguish originals from copies, and an appreciation of the sublimity of history painting.

Accumulating Capital Pictures

Robert Walpole's collecting cannot be documented in any detail before 1722, when the foundation stone of Houghton House was laid, after he had made a fortune in the South Sea shares, and began to enjoy the emoluments of political office. Orford House

14.   Jonathan Richardson, and John Wootton: *Portrait of Sir Robert Walpole. c.* 1727. Private Collection. Photo: Bridgeman Art Library, London. 'My father is ever before my eyes' (HWC 24. 507). 'Oh! how unlike him I am!' (HWC 23.522).

15. John Hall after Carlo
Maratti: *Clement IX*.
Mezzotint, $20^{13}/_{16}$ × $13^{3}/_{4}$
in. 29 September 1780. Yale
Center for British Art, Paul
Mellon Fund. 'A most
admirable portrait. . .
Nothing can be finer than
this' (*Works* 2. 252).

in Chelsea became his official residence as paymaster in 1714, and '[t]he need to adorn
Chelsea first led him to indulge his taste in pictures' (Plumb, 1: 206). Before 1717 we
have few references to Robert Walpole's activity in the sale room,[3] but from the outset
the motive of the art collector was the customary one of his class and his period – to
furnish houses fashionably. Throughout a busy political career Sir Robert bought pictures by proxy – the purchase of the 'Domenichino' by his son Horace was the rule
rather than the exception – and there are few signs that aesthetics or connoisseurship
played any significant role. Robert Walpole was in no way unusual in regarding pictures
as furniture, and it is anachronistic to suppose that art and aesthetics mattered much to
members of the Whig oligarchy.

The first artist known to have bought pictures for Robert Walpole in Italy was the
English painter of fans and ladies, Charles Jervas (1675–1739), the prime minister's
protégé who painted some dozen portraits of the Walpole family, pictures his son
referred to in the *Anecdotes* (2: 270) as 'wretched daubings'. Studying in Italy Jervas
gained notoriety when the Pope stopped his purchase of Raphael drawings (GVN 3.

93), but he did buy a large number of pictures for Sir Robert by Carlo Maratti
(1625–1713). In commissioning Jervas to buy Maratti, Robert Walpole was following
aristocratic fashion for 'the divine Carlo', a near contemporary Italian painter. Grand
tourists sat to Maratti for their portraits, and Sir Robert's son, Edward Walpole
(1706–84), brought back from his Grand Tour in 1722 Marratti's *Judgment of Paris* for his
father's collection.[4] Sir Robert never lost his enthusiasm for Maratti, now regarded as a
mediocre late-baroque artist, and he devoted an entire room at Houghton to pictures
by this artist and his school. As late as 1737 a dealer was offering him Maratti's *History
of Rebecca*, by 'your favourite painter',[5] and Jervas returned from a second visit to Italy
in the same year with Maratti's 'fine picture of Pope Clement IX . . . which he sold to
Sir Robert Walpole for 200 guineas' (GVN 3. 96; plate 15).

Connoisseurs ranked portraits below history paintings, but in the early 1740s when
the portrait of Clement IX was being moved from Downing Street to Houghton,
George Vertue thought the picture important enough to describe in detail, and made a
thumbnail sketch of it in his notebooks. In the same passage Vertue makes the important points that Sir Robert's picture was the original, which had been commissioned in
1669 for Heneage Finch, second Earl of Winchilsea, and that Richard Boyle, 3rd Earl of
Burlington, the dedicatee of Alexander Pope's *Epistle on Taste*, 'has another such picture
of this Pope [Clement IX], which he bought in England'(GVN 5. 14) – evidence that
emulation of his peers was an important motive for Sir Robert's collecting.[6]

In 1723 Sir Robert purchased fourteen full-length portraits by Van Dyck from the
spendthrift Duke of Wharton for £1500 (GVN 3. 11–12). Vertue 'twice [took] the
opportunity to see these pictures out of the frames at Mr Howard's [framemaker]',
examined them carefully, but gave them something less than the highest praise: 'I looked
into them, and perceive they are all-right pictures, but not the most curious or finished;
but done in a free masterly manner, not studied or laboured; many parts, especially the
heads, though well disposed and graceful [are] not determined. The jewels, hair, trees,
flowers, lace though loosely done appear well at a distance' (GVN 1: 109).

About a year later, in 1723–4, the industrious chronicler of collections, George Vertue,
described Robert Walpole's acquisition of four market scenes by the Flemish artist Franz
Snyders (1579–1657), once again examples of a Dutch genre the connoisseurs held in dis-
repute (GVN 3. 18). Two documents about these pictures indicate the extent to which Sir
Robert Walpole and his contemporaries regarded old master pictures as furniture. The first
document consists of two undated drawings of wainscot frames for Snyders' pictures
hanging at Downing Street, commissioned by Sir Robert from William Kent. According
to Andrew Moore, the designs show that 'a decorative effect achieved by a symmetrical
arrangement was the overriding factor to be considered. In this respect, picture frames
played as important a role in furnishing the walls as the paintings themselves.'[7] The second
document is a letter from George Vertue's patron Edward Harley, who criticized the hang
of the same pictures on a visit to Houghton dated 19 September 1732:

> In the saloon are a great many fine pictures, particularly the famous Markets of Snyder,
> but I think they are very oddly put up, one is above the other and joined in the middle
> with a thin piece of wood gilt. It is certainly wrong because as these pictures of the
> markets were painted to one point of view, and to be even with the eye, they certainly

ought not to be put one above another, besides that narrow gold ledge that is between the two pictures takes the eye and has a very ill effect' (Moore, p. 14).

On two occasions accident rather than connoisseurship determined the pictures Sir Robert acquired. In a note to *Aedes Walpolianae*, Walpole refers to 'two pictures [that] were in [Grinling] Gibbons's house when it fell' – a mishap that enlarged Sir Robert's collection.[8] Similarly about 1723 Sir Robert seized an opportunity when General Wade discovered that an enormous (3.2 m × 6.4 m) and damaged cartoon for a tapestry of *Meleager and Atalanta* (plate 16) by Rubens would not fit in the elegant Palladian town house the Earl of Burlington had designed for him in Cork Street, London. Walpole explained the circumstances in a letter to George Montagu:

> I went yesterday to see Marshal Wade's house, which is selling by auction: it is worse contrived on the inside than is conceivable, all to humour the beauty of the front. My Lord Chesterfield said, that to be sure he could not live in it, but intended to take the house over against it to look at it. It is literally true, that all the direction he gave my Lord Burlington was to have a place for a large cartoon of Rubens that he had bought in Flanders; but my Lord found it necessary to have so many correspondent doors, that there was no room at last for the picture; and the Marshal was forced to sell the picture to my father: it is now at Houghton (HWC 9. 56; 18 May 1748).

Wade's single-minded architect, Richard Boyle, 3rd Earl of Burlington, stubbornly refused to compromise classical designs to accomodate a picture, and the painting eventually took its place in the gallery at Houghton House. This outcome recalls the 'large historical family piece' commissioned by the Primrose family in the *Vicar of Wakefield*, that proved 'so very large, that we had no place in the house to fix it'.[9]

It must not be overlooked that a significant fraction of Sir Robert's collection consisted of gifts from family, friends, diplomats, and even spies; gifts that perfectly mirror conventionally orthodox eighteenth-century taste in painting. J. H. Plumb's account of this dimension of the collection cannot be improved upon:

16.   Richard Earlom after Rubens and George Farington: *Meleager & Atalanta*. Mezzotint, 20½ × 34¾ in. 1 January 1781. Yale Center for British Art, Paul Mellon Fund. 'Ten feet seven inches high, by twenty feet nine and a half wide... [T]here was no room for the picture [in General Wade's house]'. *(Aedes, Works* 2. 268–9).

Friends remembered his passion [Sir Robert's for pictures] when they wished to demonstrate their loyalty or good fortune. General Churchill gave him a couple of antique busts from Cardinal Albani's collection as well as a picture by Romano. Ambassadors and consuls knew their duty. Waldegrave, as well as buying pictures for Sir Robert, sent a present of a Bassano; Benjamin Keene in Madrid offered a Murillo; Tyrawley at Lisbon had the lucky chance to discover a Holbein of Edward VI. Horace Mann, who owed his consulship at Florence to his eminent cousin, marked his deep sense of obligation by sending a magnificent bronze by John of Bologna. Naturally, rich sycophants added their quota – the Dukes of Montagu and Chandos sent pictures, the Earl of Pembroke the fine bronze by John of Bologna which still stands in the well of the great staircase [at Houghton] (Plumb 2: 86).

Long before Horace supplied the falsified 'Domenichino' for his father's collection, the entire Walpole family, including Sir Robert's brother and eldest son, were scouring France and Italy to build the collection. Walpole's uncle Horatio (1678–1757) wrote from Paris on 5 August 1724 about negotiations for a 'Titian': 'I am glad you are satisfied in your pictures and I am sensible that the Titian was the worst of the kind but when I proposed an abatement of the price, my friend Nocé who is very particular and humoursome, had like to have broken off the whole bargain and it was with great management that I brought him to temper again' (Plumb 2: 87 n. 1). 'Two years later,' Plumb writes, 'Horatio was still doing what he could to increase his brother's collection. "As to the pictures," he wrote on 5 June 1726, "the Raphael was sold two days before I received your letter; for 1900 livres which is now about £950 sterling. There remains still the Guido, the Paul Veronese and there is an old Palma that is an excellent picture"' (Plumb 2: 87 n. 1).

Edward Walpole employed the bankrupt impresario Owen MacSwinney, whom Walpole regarded as 'a buffoon' (17. 296, n. 19), to buy antiquities for his father (Plumb 2: 86). MacSwinney introduces us to the motley crew of art dealers that supplied the prime minister with pictures over a period of two decades. The Scottish artist turned dealer and agent, Andrew Hay (d. 1754), has been described by Iain Pears as 'a new figure in the English art world. . . . the full-time professional'.[10] Hay travelled six times to Italy collecting pictures to trade in London. At his 1725/6 sale Robert Walpole purchased half a dozen pictures, including Velasquez's portrait of Innocent X for eleven guineas (Washington, National Gallery), a sale where rival aristocratic collectors included the Duke of Devonshire, and the Earl of Burlington. Hay's clients included Thomas Coke, Earl of Leicester, and Edward Harley, Earl of Oxford; his acquaintance with Robert Walpole is proved by a letter to him asking a favour when 'under suspicion of being a Jacobite agent'.[11]

George Vertue records a vivid anecdote about another of Sir Robert's advisors on pictures, Marcellus Laroon the younger (1679–1772). Laroon's attribution to Van Dyck of a picture he had bought for Sir Robert was challenged in 1729 at a meeting of a socety of artists called the Rose and Crown Club:

Captain Marcellus Laroon having recommended and bought for Sir Robert Walpole a painting of the Madonna and Child with St. Elizabeth which he judged to be painted by Van Dyck, several painters and judges did not think so (particularly Mr. Dahl [Michael 1656–1743]). Much offended at them Laroon came on purpose to a

Tavern Club when he said much in praise of himself and at last this following . . . extempore: 'I challenge any or all of your Tip Top Top-most Connoisseurs, Professors, and Judges in the Art of Painting (besides all pretenders), From the Highest to the Lowest, of every degree whatsoever, Chafferers, bidders, and buyers of pictures, their Bullies, Bawds and Panders, from the great great Sir Hugh [Hugh Howard, 1675–1737], Director and Privy Councillor to Noblemen and Gentlemen that purchase Pictures, down to the lowest scrub, even to *Nunis* the jew (a little ugly fellow, a picture jobber), all I do solemnly Challenge, and every one of them defy to compare with me in Judgment and Art, witness *my hand* with sword and pencil [paint brush], given at our Court Club, August 1729' (GVN 3.40).

This mock-heroic challenge vividly describes the new fraternity of dealers who were vying to serve and profit from the conspicuous consumption of the Whig oligarchy. Jonathan Richardson's *Science of a Connoisseur* (1719) had given birth to a race of connoisseurs very different from his Apollonian ideal. In particular Richardson thought Howard a charlatan: 'Hugh Howard, by means of his name, and affecting to be of the Norfolk family, a small Estate of a Gentleman, a solemn Air and slow Discourse, with a very moderate swathing of polite Knowledge, covered so well his extreme Ignorance and Illiteracy, that he easily passed for a leading virtuoso with the Nobility.'[12]

In about 1736 Sir Robert Walpole sent the dealer and art student John Ellis (1701–57) to Holland to buy from the Princess of Friesland Van Dyck's *Virgin and Angels* for the colossal sum of £1400. It is significant that Ellis, the purchasing agent for the most expensive painting in Sir Robert's collection, was a mere copyist (GVN 3. 38) who owned a share in a tapestry business, and who was rewarded by Sir Robert Walpole with an unusual sinecure: Master Keeper to the Lions in the Tower. 'In these circumstances,' Walpole wrote in the *Anecdotes*, 'he was not very assiduous in his profession'.[13]

French collections with aristocratic provenance yielded pictures to Houghton throughout Sir Robert's collecting career. Bassano's Winter and Summer pieces were 'in the collection of Monsieur de la Vrillière [Louis Phelypeaux, Duc de la Vrillière (1705–77)]'.[14] A magnificent pair of Guidos, allegorical figures of Europe and Africa, came from 'the collection of the Countess de la Verrue at Paris' (*Aedes* 77). The collection of the Comte de Morville (1686–1732) in Paris supplied Guido's *Adoration*, a Rubens *Magdalen* (*Aedes* 52), and French landscape paintings. The dealer appears to have been Mr Charles Edwin (1699–1756), MP, whom Horace Walpole nicknamed 'Mr Perceive-nothing' (HWC 17. 272). Edwin acquired one of two handsome Claudes from the Comte de Morville, and offered Sir Robert pictures by Gaspard Poussin in a transaction recorded in Walpole's annotated *Aedes*:

Mr. Edwin of whom Sir Robert Walpole bought these two Gaspards for £300 at the Halifax sale [1739–40], had two more, but shew'd Sr. Robert only these two at first, and afterwards the others, one of which was the finest of all, & the companion the best of these. Sir Robert offer'd him the worst back with another hundred paid in exchange for the best, but he insisted on the same price for the other two. Since his death [Sir Robert's in 1745] the Prince of Wales has bought the fine one. It is *Jonah in the Storm*, I believe the only Sea piece known of the hand (*Aedes*, p. 84).

What kind of a collection finally emerged from this haphazard process of accumulation? We could hardly expect consistency of taste, or coherent principles of collection considering that most of these pictures were bought by proxy, following canons of fashionable aristocratic taste, a significant fraction of them gifts, with the usual percentage of false attributions. We can get a clue from the inventories of the most meticulous student and cataloguer of collections in the first half of the eighteenth century, George Vertue, who visited Sir Robert's collection at its early stages in London in 1723 (GVN 3. 9), and again at Houghton in 1739 (GVN 5. 121) when the collection was virtually complete. In 1723 he lists (probably at Downing Street) roughly equal numbers of Italian and Flemish pictures, their subjects by no means confined to history painting. These included 'a large picture said to be Titian's painting,' a 'fine large picture . . . by Marco Ricci,' a 'fine great picture in the manner of Borgognone,' and an equal number of Dutch and Flemish artists including 'a large picture painted by Rubens damaged'. He reserves the epithet 'extraordinary' for a Poussin, probably the *Holy Family* bought at the Halifax sale. Vertue's repeated epithets referring to size ('great' and 'large') suggest a collector like Charles Montagu (1661–1715), Earl of Halifax, determined to buy capital pictures, who told his purchasing agent Giuseppe Chiari he wanted 'pleasant subjects and large pictures as most proper for furniture'.[15]

When Vertue revisited Houghton in 1739 most of Sir Robert's collection remained in London houses but Vertue wrote that 'the great collection of noble original pictures exceeds all others in number and variety. . . . Many fine busts . . . many rare pictures [and] statues require time to view well and review several times to conceive their great merit and beauty' (GVN 5. 121). Vertue is talking about the number and variety of pictures, not connoisseurship. Sir Robert modelled his collection on those of the noble-aristocratic class, like the Earls of Burlington and Pembroke, not those of professionals like Dr Richard Mead, gentlemen-connoisseurs like Sir Luke Schaub, or virtuosi like Sir Hans Sloane or Sir Andrew Fontaine.[16] For political reasons Sir Robert delayed his arrival in the House of Lords until 1742 after resigning his ministry in the House of Commons, but he saw to it that his eldest son Edward was elevated to the peerage, and throughout his political career he dedicated himself to the establishment of his family in the aristocracy. The building of Houghton House, and the furnishing of it with a collection of capital pictures and statuary were important means to this end. The Palladian architecture of Houghton House, and the 450 pictures decorating Houghton, Downing Street, Arlington Street, Orford House in Chelsea, and Richmond Park Lodge were calculated to display the aristocratic status of the Walpole family.

Aedes Walpolianae: *Putting Down Italian Painters*

'Only think what a vile employment 'tis, making catalogues!' (HWC 13. 192), Walpole crossly remarked of Thomas Gray's conscientious inventories of art works on the Grand Tour. When Walpole set himself the task of cataloguing his father's collection of pictures at Houghton, his model was the *Aedes Barberinae*, [1642; Hazen 3725; plate 17], an elaborate folio volume glorifying the collection of Cardinal Antonio Barberini (1607–71).[17] Walpole considered such Italian catalogues 'pompous' (*Aedes* 2. 225), but the purpose of

17.   Tetius Hieronymus, *Aedes Barberinae*
(Rome, 1642), front. By permission of the British
Library. '. . . [T]he most pompous works of this
sort are the Aedes Barberinae' (*Aedes Walpolianae,
Works* 2. 225).

his own catalogue was identical: to glorify his father's power and his family's glory by a
description of the pictures in his palace. As he remarks in the dedication to the catalogue, the pictures, 'ornaments of the house . . . are panegyrics on your nobility . . . as
you are the fountain of it in our family. . . . Your power and your wealth speak themselves in the grandeur of the whole building' (2. 223). Panegyric more accurately
describes Walpole's catalogue than Francis Taylor's inflated estimate of it as 'the out-
standing piece of English art criticism of the eighteenth century before Sir Joshua
[Reynolds's Discourses]'.[18] In the *Aedes* Walpole is not talking primarily about art and
artists, but about his father as patron and owner of 'capital' pictures.

By August 1743 Walpole had completed a catalogue, embellished with his 'Sermon on
Painting' dated 1742, and an estate poem by his Cambridge tutor, John Whalley. The *Aedes
Walpolianae* listed less than half of Sir Robert's pictures then distributed between his country
and town houses. The catalogue was Walpole's first book – 'one should have thought a very
harmless performance' (HWC 20. 41; 23 March 1749) – printed anonymously and privately
in 1747 in a small edition of 200 copies, of which he distributed eighty-three to friends, rel-
atives, and correspondents,[19] presumably providing the rest as guidebooks for visitors to
Houghton House. Several copies of the *Aedes* annotated by Walpole are extant,[20] which
gives us some idea how Walpole responded to his father's pictures throughout his life.

Modern estimates of Walpole's *Aedes* have gone to extremes. Opposing Taylor's comparison to Reynolds's *Discourses*, Walpole's biographer writes that 'the general standard of performance can best be judged by the paragraph of resounding nonsense with which it closes'.[21] Iain Pears makes a more accurate estimate in his remark that 'the *Aedes* is primarily a tribute to Robert Walpole'.[22] In truth there is precious little art criticism in Walpole's catalogue which is not the work of an art critic, but of a courtesy-book gentleman who returned from the Grand Tour with a disgust for European connoisseurs, sceptical of the art trade, convinced that Italian art collections were degenerate and decaying, that art was something no self-respecting MP should take too seriously, and that artists deserved no more than patronizing condescension.

Many of Walpole's attitudes are apparent in the 'Introduction' after Walpole boasts that his father's collection 'excells' most Italian ones, because it contains 'most of the chief schools and . . . most of the chief hands' (*Works* 2. 226). 'Knowledge of this sort [art history] is only to be learnt from pictures themselves,' the sophomoric gentleman writes with the callow confidence of a twenty-six-year-old, magisterially dismissing the art history of De Piles (Hazen 351), Félibien (Hazen 1294), Richardson (Hazen 310), and others:

> The numerous volumes wrote on this art have only served to perplex it. No science has had so much jargon introduced into it as painting: the bombast expression of the Italians, and the prejudices and affectation of the French, joined to the vanity of the professors, and the interested mysteriousness of picture-merchants, have altogether compiled a new language. 'Tis almost easier to distinguish the hands of the masters, than to decypher the cant of the virtuosi. Nor is there any science whose productions are of so capricious and uncertain a value (2. 226).

Thinking perhaps of the history and intrigue of his father's acquisitions and his own collecting on the Grand Tour, Walpole laments the absence of standards:

> As great as are the prices of fine pictures, there is no judging from them of the several merits of the painters; there does not seem to be any standard of estimation. You hear a virtuoso talk in raptures of Raphael, of Coreggio's grace, and Titian's colouring: and yet the same man, in the same breath, will talk as enthusiastically of any of the first masters [predecessors of Raphael the eighteenth century regarded as barbaric], who wanted all the excellencies of all the three (2. 226).

Then Walpole makes the comment about Andrea del Sarto (1486–1531) 'whose colouring was a mixture of mist and tawdry' (2. 226) which upset the Prince of Wales when he received a presentation copy of *Aedes Walpolianae* (HWC 9. 89; 5 July 1749).

It is clear from these remarks that the courtesy-book gentleman substitutes iconoclasm and positive opinions for the cant of the virtuosi. The remainder of his 'Introduction' to the catalogue enumerates the faults of almost all the Italian schools and their masters: 'There was something in the Venetian school, especially in Paul Veronese, which touches extremely upon the servile imitation of the Dutch' (2. 227). Of Raphael's predecessors, Cimabue and others are 'only curious for their antiquity, not for their excellence' (2. 230). Walpole concedes that Mantegna's *Triumphs of Julius Caesar* at Hampton Court exhibits 'admirable style' (2. 230), but he damns 'Raphael's superior genius' (2. 230) with faint praise, and dwells on the faults of the Roman school, remarking that 'Michael Angelo was. . . . much too fond of muscles, as afterwards Rubens was of flesh' (2. 231). Strangely enough Andrea Sacchi (1599–1661) earns higher praise than Raphael or Michaelangelo for 'harmony of colours' (2. 231), but Pietro da Cortona's faults outweigh his virtues: 'No collection can be complete without one picture of his hand, and none wants more than one' (2. 231). Robert Walpole's favourite painter, 'the famous Carlo Maratti', receives a bouquet and a brickbat. Credited with grace, beauty, and lightness, he is censured as 'one of the destroyers of painting, by introducing that very light style of colouring, which in less skilful hands has degenerated into glare and tawdry' (2. 231).

In a similar manner the courtesy-book gentleman continues to lay waste to the schools of Italian painting. Of the Venetian painters 'Titian and Paul Veronese [were] by far the best. . . . Pordenone and Tintoret were dark and ungraceful. The Palmas were stiff, and the Bassans particular' (2. 231). Next the Prime Minister of Taste disposes of the Florentine school in a sentence: 'Their drawing was hard, and their colouring gaudy and gothic' (2. 232). Leonardo da Vinci (1452–1519), 'that universal genius' (2. 232), may be the only Italian painter who escapes whipping while Correggio, 'for grace and sweetness confest the first of painters', is censured for 'bad drawing' (2. 232). 'The Neapolitan school has produced little good', he asserts unequivocally, pointing the finger of blame at Giovanni Lanfranco (1572–1647), one of the artists pursued by his own Committee of Taste: 'If Lanfranc was a great master, which in my own mind I do not think, he was bred up in the school of Caracci. His manner was wild, glaring, and extravagant. . . . His genius was like Ovid's, flowing, abundant, various, and incorrect' (2. 232–3).

More at home with the French school, Walpole practices his usual rhetoric of praise and blame, warming to Eustache Le Sueur (1616–55), whose twenty-two history-paintings of the life of St Bruno he had admired in the convent of Chartreux in Paris on the Grand Tour (13. 169–70). But Le Sueur, like all French artists, has shortcomings: 'His fault was in his draperies; the folds are mean and unnatural' (2. 234). And so it is with Nicolas Poussin (1594–1665), 'a perfect master of expression and drawing, though the proportion of his figures is rather too long' (2. 234). Only Gaspard Poussin (1615–75), and Claude Lorrain (1600–82) emerge unscathed, 'the latter especially was the Raphael of landscape-painting' (2. 234). It is significant that Sir Robert was quite content to have copies after Claude in his collection executed by the flower-painter Jacob van Huysum (GVN 1. 80 n. 7).

Considering the importance of the Netherlandish schools in his father's collection, Walpole's account in *Aedes* is dismissive, abrupt, and prejudiced against the Dutch school in particular. Rubens alone escapes Walpole's censure of the Flemish school, but he is dismissed in a *praeteritio*: 'I shall not enter into any detail of the Flemish painters, who are better known by their different varnishes, and the different kinds of utensils they painted, than by any style of colouring and drawing' (2. 235). 'One great man they had, who struck out of the littlenesses of his countrymen, though he never fell into a character of graceful beauty: but Rubens is too well known in England to want any account of him' (2. 235). Sir Anthony Van Dyck, whose portraits and history paintings were among the glories of Houghton, receives even shorter shrift than Rubens. '[He] contracted a much genteeler taste [than Rubens] in his portraits,' but miscarried in his models: 'his Madonnas, which he probably drew from some mistress, are most remarkable for want of beauty' (2. 235). No portrait painter more gloriously achieved Walpole's own ambition of illustrating the English aristocracy, but Walpole does not hesitate to cut Van Dyck down to size.

Walpole reserves for last the Bolognese school – 'as little inferior to the Roman as it was superior to all the rest' (2. 235) – that his father's generation regarded as the glory of Italian art. Overruling critics, he thinks the drawings of Annibale Carracci (1560–1609) equal to Michelangelo's: 'They talk of his faults in drawing, but those figures [Farnese ceiling] and lord Orford's little Venus are standards of proportion for men and women' (2. 235). Guido Reni (1575–1642) has the 'grace and delicacy of Coreggio, and colouring as natural as Titian's. I cannot imagine what they mean, who say he wanted knowledge in the chiaro-oscuro; it was never more happily applied and diffused than in lord Orford's Adoration of the shepherds' (2. 235).

It is almost as if Walpole has been holding his breath in praising the Bolognese school, because his final paragraph recapitulates the faults of Italian artists, including Correggio, Titian, Poussin, Le Sueur, Albano, and Domenichino: 'In short, in my opinion, all the qualities of a perfect painter never met but in Raphael, Guido, and Annibal Caracci' (2. 236). Nevertheless, he is honest enough to burst his bag of spleen over the head of sweet Domenichino, the subject of his deception and special pleading: 'Dominichini, whose communion of saint Jerome is allowed to be the second picture in the world, was generally raw in his colouring, hard in his contours, and wanted a knowledge of the chiaro oscuro' (2. 236). It is difficult to resist the suspicion that this paragraph of 'resounding nonsense' is merely a rhetorical gesture, perhaps a satirical parody of his model, *Aedes Barberinae*. Instead of the pomp and bombast of Italians puffing their painters, Walpole, the patriot virtuoso, puts Italian artists in their place, reserving his accolades for English patrons and collectors whose collections now excel the Italians.

Aedes Walpolianae: *Panegyrical Pictures*

If the introduction to the catalogue proves Walpole's distaste or indifference for the Italian art and artists that comprised his father's collection, the catalogue itself demonstrates the social and political values Walpole attached to the pictures in place of aesthetic appreciation or connoisseurship. 'Your power and your wealth speak themselves in the grandeur of the whole building', he had declared in the 'Dedication' of the catalogue. In the catalogue entries he shows how his father's pictures, the furniture of his house, are 'panegyrics on your nobility' (2. 223).

Let us follow Walpole, accompanied perhaps by Patapan, his 'little Roman dog' (30. 287, n. 1; plate 18),[23] on a tour of a couple of rooms in the house to experience the choreography of pictures advertising the nobility of Walpole and his family. We enter the small breakfast-room hung with ten pictures, half of them family portraits, four animal pieces, and one Italian master, Pordenone's *Prodigal Son*, from one of the great seventeenth-century English collections, that of George Villiers (1592–1628), Duke of Buckingham.[24] The hang of pictures in this room introduces a characteristic pattern at Houghton: the juxtaposition of family portraits with pictures of aristocratic provenance, combining pedigreed portraits with pedigreed pictures. Thus a portrait of Edward Walpole (1621–68), Sir

18.   John Wootton: *Patapan*, 'a Roman dog, belonging to Mr Walpole' (*Works* 2. 452). 1743. Oil on canvas, 40 × 38 in. Private Collection. Photo: © Christie's Images Ltd. 2000. 1743. 'Patapan sits to Wootton tomorrow for his picture' (HWC 18.220–1).

Robert's grandfather, who was created knight of the bath at the coronation of King Charles II and made a great figure in Parliament, hangs in the same room as a *Prodigal Son* painted by Giovanni Antonio Licino (1483–1539), called Pordenone. 'A very dark picture by Pordenone,' Walpole writes of it in the catalogue, 'the architecture and landscape very good. It is five feet five inches high, by eight feet eleven and half wide. This picture belonged to George Villiers, the great Duke of Buckingham' (2. 238). The name of the artist hardly matters. What counts is the ducal provenance of the Pordenone which speaks the nobility of the Walpole family as clearly as its titles and offices do. Buckingham's was one of the three most important seventeenth-century English collections in addition to Charles I's, and Thomas Howard, Earl of Arundel's.

The same deliberately eclectic pattern prevails in the supping parlour in the southeast corner of the house where ten family portraits by Jervas, Richardson, Kneller, and others are accompanied by '*The Battle of Constantine and Maxentius*, a copy, by Julio Romano, of the famous picture in the Vatican, which he executed after a design of Raphael' (2. 239). The picture's dimensions are provided because 'the measures . . . will contribute to ascertain their originality, and be a kind of pedigree to them' (2. 225). Typically, Walpole is prepared to claim a royal provenance for this copy after Raphael: 'There was one of these [copies] (probably this very picture) in the collection of James the second' (2. 239 n.).

Throughout *Aedes Walpolianae* provenance appears to be a primary standard for evaluating pictures in his father's collection: 'Such well-attested descent,' Walpole wrote in the 'Preface' to the catalogue of his own collection, the *Description of Strawberry Hill* (1774–98), 'is the genealogy of the objects of virtu – not so noble as those of the peerage, but on a par with those of race-horses' (2. 396). All the provenances recorded in *Aedes*, like the attributions, require verification, but even the mistakes witness Walpole's enthusiasm for royal and aristocratic provenance. For example, Walpole takes the benefit of the doubt about a cast of the statue of a gladiator by Jehan de Boulogne (1529–1608) standing in the well of the great staircase at Houghton House: 'I should imagine that this is the statue mentioned in the catalogue of king Charles the first, and which was sold for £300 . . . . it stood in the garden at saint James's palace' (2. 242, n.). Walpole is on stronger ground about Van Dyck's *Holy Family*, 'a most celebrated picture': 'It belonged originally to king Charles the first, and is mentioned in the Catalogue of his pictures, p. 171' (2. 250; Hazen 2478).[25] Of course royal portraits proclaim Robert Walpole's nobility even more powerfully than provenance, for example 'King Charles I, a whole length, in armour, by Vandyck' (2. 247; plate 19), and Kneller's whole length of 'king George I, in his coronation-robes, the only picture for which he ever sat in England' (2. 246). Royal portraits and provenances of Sir Robert's pictures declare clearly in the words of Pope's *Epistle to Burlington*: 'These are Imperial Works, and worthy Kings.'[26] So the parade of provenance marches through Walpole's catalogue as pedigree turns pictures into aristocratic icons, creating 'capital' pictures.

The name of Philip, Duke of Wharton (1698–1731), as we have already observed, was attached to fifteen full-length portraits (plate 20) in the collection,[27] and the ducal provenance bespeaks Sir Robert's nobility despite the fact that Walpole wrote of Wharton's disreputable character in *Royal and Noble Authors* (1758). Wharton had been 'seized by the guard in saint James's park, for singing the Jacobite air, *The King shall have his own again*' (*Works* 1. 443). Walpole writes that 'the frolic lord' threw away 'the brightest profusion of parts on witty fooleries, debaucheries and scrapes' (*Works*

19.   Josiah Boydell after Sir Anthony Van Dyck:
Charles I. 2 March 1778. Mezzotint, 20^{13}/$_{16}$ × 13^{3}/$_{4}$
in. Yale Center for British Art, Paul Mellon Fund.
'By a mistake, both the gauntlets are drawn for the
right hand' (*Aedes, Works* 2. 247).

1. 443), the very qualities that caused him to sell the pictures to Sir Robert.

Another great seventeenth-century collection, that of Thomas Howard, 2d Earl of
Arundel (1586–1646), yielded a small picture said to be '[t]he last supper by Raphael': 'It .
. . is mentioned in the catalogue of those pictures', Walpole writes in *Aedes* (2. 277), but
Walpole later voiced doubts about its authenticity (HWC 2. 169). Arundel is only the first
and most famous of the Earls of Creation whose pictures hung at Houghton. Jordaens's
painting of the Rubens family (2. 257) had belonged to William Bentinck (1709–62), Duke
of Portland; Rubens's 'moon-light landscape with a cart overturning' (2. 273) came from
the collection of William, 1st Earl of Cadogan (1671–1726); and *Venus Bathing* (2. 243) by
Andrea Sacchi (1599–1661), an artist Walpole thought tawdry, is redeemed by the fact that
'it was Lord Halifax's' (Charles Montagu's, 1st Earl [1661–1715]).

Corollaries of provenance, gifts from distinguished and titled donors, all attest to the
nobility of the Walpole family, and Walpole is careful to establish the status of the givers in
the catalogue. Le Sueur's *Moses in the Bullrushes*, was 'a present to Lord Orford from the
duke of Montagu' (John, 2d Duke [1690–1749]; 2. 276). The painting *Bathsheba* by Adriaen
van der Werff (1659–1722) was the 'gift of James Brydges, Duke of Chandos' ([1674–1744]
2. 261). Elsheimer's *Saint Christopher* was 'a present from sir Harry Bedingfield' ([1685–
1760]; 2. 262), a descendant of the Arundel family, 'a most bigoted Papist in Norfolk'
(HWC 20. 532). The pedigree of 'James earl of Waldegrave [1684–1741], knight of the
Garter, and embassador at Paris' (2. 260) signifies as much or more to Walpole than the art-
historical fact that Bassano's '*Christ Laid in the Sepulchre*. . . . is a fine design for a great altar-

piece which he has painted at Padua' (2. 260). In Walpole's catalogue, therefore, capital pictures are partly determined by the status of the donors: *Ex dono* and *ex aedibus* add cachet to the pedigree of pictures as aristocratic icons.

Besides the provenance of pictures and pedigree of donors, Walpole attaches value to his father's pictures by comparing them to originals and copies in other collections. Thus he says Quintin Matsys's 'Usurer and his Wife. . . . was painted for a family in France; it differs very little from one at Windsor, which he did for Charles the first' (2. 272). Walpole adds '[t]here is a copy of this picture at Hinchingbrooke [Huntingdonshire, seat of John Montagu [(1718–92), 4th Earl of Sandwich], and another at Boughton House [Northamptonshire, seat of George Brudenell (1712–90), 2d Duke of Montagu]'. This effectively tells us that Sir Robert's picture is the equal of a painting in Charles I's collection, and superior to copies in collections of an Earl and a Duke. Likewise, he compares in detail Sir Robert's *Abraham, Sarah, and Hagar* by Pietro da Cortona (1596–1669) to the 'small sketch' in the collection of Francis I (1708–65), Grand Duke of Tuscany (1737–65), that he had seen in the Grand Duke's gallery (the Uffizi) at Florence: 'The Great Duke has a small sketch of this, but reversed, and with the Sarah and other figures at a distance. The Hagar is much fairer than in this' (2. 273). Walpole's remark reveals his extraordinary visual memory, but it also serves to put the Houghton House collection on speaking terms with the Uffizi.

Similarly, Walpole carefully links Sir Robert's so-called Michaelangelo, *The Eagle and Ganymede*, to King George II, the Queen of Hungary (Maria Theresa [1717–80]), and the collection of Emilio Altieri, Pope Clement X (1590–1676), patron of Sir Robert's favorite Carlo Maratti. '[Michaelangelo's *Eagle and Ganymede* is] a subject he has often repeated, but with alterations. The king has one larger, and the Queen of Hungary another, printed in Teniers gallery [Hazen 3633]: there is another in the Altieri palace at Rome' (2. 278). It does not matter that the attribution has not passed the test of time: a picture attributed to Michaelangelo in the Walpole collection had belonged to an English king, the queen consort of the Grand Duke of Tuscany, the Holy Roman Emperor, and a Pope of the Roman Catholic Church. This is the kind of company the Walpole family pictures keep. Ye shall know them by their pictures.

Another important index of value in Walpole's catalogue consists of numerous prints and engravings after Sir Robert's pictures, which advertised the pictures' and sometimes the collector's importance. For example the letterpress of Bernard Baron's enormous engraving of Le Sueur's *Moses in the Bullrushes*, dated 1720 (2. 276), celebrates with ornate arms and flattery John Montagu (1690–1749), the second Duke who later gave the picture to Sir Robert: 'Keeper of his Majesty's Horses, most noble knight, Maecenas of good arts and excellent culture'. At least fourteen pictures are so distinguished in Sir Robert's collection.[28]

Although such social and political values are paramount attributes of the *Aedes*, Walpole's catalogue does contain symptoms of connoisseurship that show he was not as idle on the Grand Tour as he pretended. Of Rubens's *Bacchanalian*, 'not a very pleasant picture', Walpole remarks: 'There is a small design for this picture reversed, in the great duke's tribune at Florence' (2. 243). If this is not evidence of connoisseurship, it certainly indicates again Walpole's remarkable visual memory. Likewise he observes of Cignani's *Nativity* that '[t]he thought of this picture is borrowed . . . from the *Notte* of Coreggio at Modena, where all the light of the picture flows from the child' (2. 243). Another

remark on Francesco Albano's *Christ Baptized* illustrates Walpole's keen powers of observation: 'There is one of the same design in the church of san Giorgio at Bologna, with an oval top, and God the father in the clouds, with different angels; two are kneeling, and supporting Christ's garments' (2. 250). He recognizes a source for Guido's *Simeon and the Child*: 'The design is taken from a statue of a Silenus with a young Bacchus, in the villa Borghese at Rome' (2. 251), and he identifies two pictures of the Virgin by Luca Giordano (1632–1705) as 'finished designs for two large pictures, which he painted for the fine church of Madonna della Salute at Venice' (2. 255).

On three occasions Walpole offers the kind of iconographical analysis common in modern art catalogues. First, Girolamo Mazzola's *Christ Laid in the Sepulchre*: '[t]he figure of Joseph of Arimathea is Parmegiano's [Mazzola's] own portrait; there are two drawings in the grand duke's collection for this picture, but with variations from what he executed: in one of these, Joseph has his hands extended like Paul preaching at Athens, in the cartoon of Raphael' (2. 258). Second, he observes of Giuseppe Chiari's *Bacchus and Ariadne* in the Carlo Marat Room: '[T]he Bacchus seems to be taken from the Apollo Belvedere [in the Uffizi], as the ideas of the Ariadne, and the Venus, evidently are from the figures of Liberality and Modesty in the famous picture of Guido, in the collection of Marquis del Monte at Bologna. There are four pictures about the size of these in the Spada palace at Rome, by the same hand' (2. 254). Finally, we clearly hear Walpole speaking in the accents of Richardson's connoisseur in his account of Poussin's *Holy Family*: 'It is one of the most capital pictures in this collection; the airs of the heads and the draperies are in the fine taste of Raphael and the antique; Elizabeth's head is taken from a statue of an old woman in the villa Borghese at Rome' (2. 257).

But such comments are rare in the catalogue. Normally the courtesy-book gentleman, who 'knows pictures' as his birthright, never hesitates to evaluate pictures *ex cathedra* with commonplace epithets: 'pleasing', 'agreeable'; 'fine', 'exceedingly fine', 'wonderfully fine'; 'capital', 'very capital', 'most capital'; 'bright', 'very bright', and 'brightest'. The Prime Minister of Taste follows the Walpole family motto – '*Fari quae sentiat*' (say what you think); he speaks positively and unequivocally. Thus Kneller's portrait of the woodcarver Grinling Gibbons (1648–1720) who worked for Sir Robert at Houghton, and carved a cravat in boxwood that ended up in Walpole's collection at Strawberry Hill, is pronounced to be 'a master-piece, and equal to any of Vandyck's' (*Works* 2. 242). It is clear that Walpole's epithetical superlatives in the catalogue replace the fault-finding and sophomoric iconoclasm of the 'Introduction,' and there is nothing in the catalogue to annoy Frederick, Prince of Wales, who complained 'that I [HW] had abused his friend Andrea del Sarto' in the 'Introduction' to the *Aedes* (HWC 9. 88–9; July 1749; *Works* 2. 226). Walpole largely limits fault-finding in the catalogue to anachronism, a quibble possibly derived from the humanistic doctrine of the learned painter.[29]

In the catalogue entries, in short, Walpole occasionally speaks the language of the connoisseur without being a connoisseur. There is no sign that Walpole shares Richardson's enthusiasm for the sublimity of the Italian religious history painting that dominated his

20.   Sir Anthony Van Dyck: *Philip 4th Lord Wharton*. 1632. Oil on canvas, 52$\frac{1}{2}$ × 41$\frac{7}{8}$ in. Andrew W. Mellon Collection; © Board of Trustees, National Gallery of Art, Washington. '. . . [T]he fine collection of Vandyck's . . . were . . . sold to sir Robert Walpole' (*Aedes, Works* 2. 248).

יהוה

THE DOCTORS OF THE CHURCH
consulting upon the Immaculateness of the Virgin
in the Gallery at Houghton

father's collection. Instead he dutifully attaches long Latin quotations from Zosimus and Livy to explain the stories of classical and religious history paintings by Romano (2. 239–40), Mola (2. 269–70), and Poussin (2. 274–5), but his heart is not in it. Van Dyck's portrait of Sir Thomas Chaloner (1561–1615) excites him more than Guido Reni's *Doctors of the Church Consulting on the Immaculateness of the Virgin* (2. 266; plate 21), and it is easy to see why from Walpole's biographical note on the lives of the Chaloner family. Chaloner's grandfather 'was a celebrated wit, poet, and warrior, having served in the expedition against Algier under Charles the fifth; where being shipwrecked, and having swam till his arms failed him, he caught hold on a cable with his teeth and saved himself' (2. 244, n.). Sir Thomas Chaloner's translation of Erasmus's *Prayse of Follie* was in Walpole's library (Hazen 195 [1577]). His son Thomas (1595–1661) wrote a treatise on Moses's tomb (Hazen 210.4, 1657), served as a witness against Archbishop Laud, and died in exile. His son James, an antiquary, 'poisoned himself with a potion prepared by his mistress, on an order for taking him into custody' (2. 244, n.). The portrait of Chaloner is Walpole's passport to dynastic family history, opening up the life stories of several generations.

Walpole gives an equally detailed account of Philip Lord Wharton (1613–96) who:

sided with parliament. . . . narrowly escaped being excepted in the general act of indemnity, though he expended some thousand pounds to make a figure in the cavalcade at the king's restoration, in particular having diamond buttons to the mourning which he was then wearing for his second wife. He was committed to the Tower in the company of the duke of Buckingham and lord Shaftesbury, on their asserting the dissolution of the long parliament; but his chief merits were a patriot fraud, by which he procured the passing of the habeas corpus act, being one of the tellers in the house of lords, when he outwitted his partner and gave in a false majority (2. 247–8).

Springing from family memoirs (Hazen 1608. 20. 1 [1715]), these are the kind of anecdotes Walpole loved to attach to portraits.

The author of *Aedes Walpolianae* is a master of aristocratic English genealogy and pedigree, and Walpole's passion for genealogy supports his preference for portraits. Walpole added this note to Maratti's portrait of Clement IX (1600–69), citing two genealogical sources for an anecdote:

He was a poet. . . . He was nuntio at Madrid, when the six royalists, who had murdered Ascham [Roger (1515–68)], the parliament's resident, were taken out of sanctuary, and insisted on their being re-delivered, which he prevailed on the bigoted king to order. Five of them, catholics, were suffered to escape; the sixth, a protestant, was so watched, that he was retaken on his flight and put to death (2. 252).

Walpole surrounds Velasquez's portrait of Pope Innocent X with similar anecdotes: the old chestnut about how Velasquez refused to take payment for the portrait from anyone

21.   William Sharp after Guido Reni and George Farington: *The Doctors of the Church*. Engraving, 24¾ × 17 in. 1 September 1785. Yale Center for British Art, Paul Mellon Fund. 'Over the farthest chimney [Houghton House Gallery] is that capital picture, and the first in this collection' (*Aedes, Works* 2. 266).

but the Pope; his legendary ugliness, 'reckoned the ugliest man of his time'; and his hatred of the French, a story about his ancestor, a Cardinal who was beaten by a Frenchman for stealing a book from his library (2. 259, and n.).

Walpole added this anecdote to the description of his father's equestrian portrait by John Wootton: 'He is upon a white horse called the Chevalier, which was taken in Scotland in the year 1715, and was the only horse the Pretender mounted there' (2. 241). Similarly, Van Dyck's portrait of Charles I allows Walpole to retell a story about the printer Jacob Tonson, Pope's publisher, who had commissioned the Kit-Cat portraits from Kneller:

> By a mistake, both the gauntlets are drawn for the right hand. When this picture was in the Wharton collection [at Winchendon House, Buckinghamshire], old Jacob Tonson, who had remarkably ugly legs, was finding fault with the two gauntlets. Lady Wharton [Lucy Loftus (1670–1717)] said, Mr. Tonson, why might not one man have two right hands, as well as another two left legs? (2. 247, and n.).

And he tells this harrowing tale of William Dobson's portrait of Abraham Van der Doort (d. 1640), keeper of King Charles's pictures, 'who, on having mislaid a fine small picture, and not being able to find it when asked for it by the king, hanged himself' (2. 259, n.). This story, worthy of the most melodramatic tour-guide, Walpole derived from Sir William Sanderson's *Graphice* (1658, Hazen 251). Thus it is clear that from the beginning the Prime Minister of Taste valued his father's pictures as much for anecdote as for art's sake.

'The Shipwreck of my Family': Sale of the Houghton House Collection

Social and political considerations therefore, appear to outweigh the artistic and aesthetic in Walpole's catalogue of his father's collection. This is also true of the lay-sermon Walpole composed on the Houghton collection and added to *Aedes Walpolianae* to swell a slender volume: 'In the summer of 1742,' he writes in *Short Notes*, 'I wrote "A Sermon on Painting," for the amusement of my father in retirement. It was preached before him [Sir Robert] by his chaplain [possibly Thomas Deresley], [and] again before my eldest brother [Robert Walpole (1701–51)] at Stanno [Stanhoe, near Houghton House, Norfolk]' (HWC 13. 13). Walpole referred to this sermon as 'a slight memorial to Houghton', and described it as 'a sort of essay on [Lord Orford's] collection of pictures' (HWC 13. 13, n. 84). Walpole takes his text from *Psalms* 115, a passage attacking pagan idols: 'They have Mouths, but they speak not: Eyes have they, but they see not: neither is there any Breath in their Nostrils' (2. 279). Walpole's sermon amounts to a Protestant apology for painting, part anti-clerical polemic, part panegyric of his father and his collection. Walpole concludes his sermon with an allegorical reading of Poussin's *Moses Striking the Rock* (plate 22), supplying a note alerting us to his eulogy of Robert Walpole: 'The allusion to lord Orford's [Robert Walpole's] life is carried on through this [Moses's] whole character' (2. 286 n.).

> Examine but the life of that slighted patriot: how boldly in his youth he undertook the cause of liberty! Unknown, without interest, he stood against the face of Pharoah!

22.   Nicolas Poussin: *Moses Striking the Rock*. The Duke of Sutherland Collection, on loan to The National Gallery of Scotland. 'The allusion to lord Orford's [Robert Walpole's] life is carried on through this [Moses's] whole character' (*Aedes, Works* 2. 286).

[Louis XIV and the Pretender]! He saved his countrymen from the hand of tyranny . . . . how patiently did he bear for a series of years the clamours and cabals of a factious people. . . . exasperated by ambitious ringleaders [Oxford and Bolingbroke]! . . . . See him lead them through opposition, through plots, through enemies, to the enjoyment of peace, and to the possession of *a land flowing with milk and honey*! (2. 287).

Walpole belabours the compliment, which is as artificial as the whole sermon, a command performance that probably deserves his own disclaimer as 'a very harmless' one (HWC 20. 41).

Walpole preached a far more eloquent sermon on the Houghton collection in his correspondence as he watched the improvident management of the estate by his father's heirs throughout the century. This lay-sermon in the letters illustrates the extent to which Walpole identified the pictures with the fortunes of his family, and the tenuous hold of the aristocracy on landed property in the eighteenth century.[30] Walpole's text for this sermon comes from Pope's lines on the winged estate wasted by spendthrift heirs in the *Imitations of Horace*:

> The Laws of God, as well as of the Land,
> Abhor, a *Perpetuity* should stand:
> Estates have wings, and hang in Fortune's pow'r
> Loose on the point of ev'ry wav'ring Hour;
> Ready, by force, or of your own accord,
> By sale, at least by death, to change their Lord.[31]

Only three years after Sir Robert Walpole's death in 1745, and one year after publication of the first edition of *Aedes* (1747), Robert Walpole's eldest son and heir, Robert Walpole (1701–51), 2d Earl of Orford, and Walpole's brother Edward (1706–84) employed the disreputable art-dealer, Dr Robert Bragge, to disguise the origins of the first sale of pictures in the Orford collection. The auction dated 5 to 6 May 1748 was conducted by Christopher Cock in London. Two days before the sale the antiquary Reverend William Stuckley visited the auction rooms and moralized the sale in his journal (4 May 1748) as a *Mirror for Magistrates*: 'Dr Milward carried me to Cock's auction room where is a most magnificent show of paintings to be sold by auction . . . [T]hey are the pictures of Sir Robert Walpole, under the fictitious name of Mr Robert Bragge. I have seen 'em at Sir Robert's house. Thus fares it with power and grandeur.'[32]

According to Iain Pears another sale of Sir Robert's pictures 'took place in 1748/9', but the first sale to register in Horace Walpole's correspondence occurred after his brother Robert's death 31 March 1751 which made him fear the worst: 'It is no small addition to my concern to fear or foresee that Houghton and all the remains of my father's glory will be pulled to pieces!' (20. 239; 1 April 1751). The sale at Langford's, Covent Garden, was announced in the *Daily Advertiser* on 13 June 1751: 'The genuine collection of Italian, Dutch, and Flemish pictures of . . . the Earls of Orford . . . brought from the Exchequer [10 Downing Street] and Richmond Park' (20. 261, n. 28). The sale went forward after Walpole and John Chute failed to persuade the reckless 3rd Earl George Walpole to marry an heiress, Margaret Nicoll (1735–68). The would-be matchmaker lamented this *marriage à la mode manqué*: 'Lord Orford has refused to marry her: why, nobody can guess. Thus had I placed him in a greater situation than even his grandfather [Robert Walpole] hoped to bequeath to him, had retrieved all the oversights of my family [Robert Walpole's entailed estate], had saved Houghton and all our glory! – now all must go!' (20. 257; 30 May 1751).

A week after the June sale Walpole moralized the outcome in terms of the passage in Pope's estate poetry, referring to Francis Bacon's Twickenham Park and the Duke of Buckingham's Helmsley, Yorkshire:

> Shades, that to Bacon could retreat afford,
> Become the portion of a booby Lord;
> And Hemsley once proud Buckingham's delight,
> Slides to a Scriv'ner or a City Knight.[33]

Compare Walpole's letter dated 18 June 1751:

> We have already begun to sell the pictures that had not found place at Houghton: the sale gives no great encouragment to proceed (though I fear it must come to that!) the large pictures were thrown away; the whole length Vandykes went for a song! I am mortified now for having printed the catalogue [*Aedes* (1747)]. Gideon the Jew, and Blakiston the independent grocer have been the chief purchasers of the pictures sold already – there, if you love moralizing! (20. 261).

Walpole is expressing the anti-Semitism common to his class in this comment on Sampson Gideon (1699–1762), a financial advisor to his father in the 1740s. Sir Matthew Blakiston (1702–74), Alderman, Lord Mayor of London, and 'a violent party man,' 'had been caught in smuggling, and pardoned by Sir Robert Walpole' (20. 261, HW's n. 32).

George Vertue gives what may be an eye-witness account of the Langford sale and the disappointing prices realized by Sir Robert's pictures, particularly the Wharton Van Dycks which fetched less than half what Sir Robert had paid for them. Vertue refers to a conversation with Walpole about the sale before he goes on to point a moral in the manner of Stuckley:

> These pictures that were bought from Lord Wharton's family cost Sir Robert it was said with some others 1500 pounds most certainly. Mr Horace Walpole told me his father actually paid 100 pounds for each picture. In some part the occasion for lowering prices was the advanced season of the year, persons of distinction out of town 13–14 June 1751, and the suddeness of the disposal, after the death of the last lord Orford [2d Earl, Robert Walpole (1701–1751)] by the want of money in this young present lord the grandson [George Walpole, 3rd Earl of Orford (1730–91)]. Such a strange turn of fortune and grandeur is hardly to be paralleled in any family. To be sure these will not amount to any great sum (GVN 5. 86).

These early sales of pictures from his father's collection inspired in Walpole an anxiety about the Houghton pictures that never ceased until they were sold to Catherine the Great in 1779. With every legacy to his spendthrift nephew he allowed himself to hope 'the Houghton pictures may still be saved!' (20. 418; 28 March 1754). The proceeds of every picture sale prompted his or Mann's speculations about what the Houghton pictures might realize. After Sir Luke Schaub's profitable sale in April 1758, Walpole wrote: 'You would have been amazed, had you been here at Sir Luke Schaub's auction of pictures. . . . I want to paint my coat and sell it off my back. . . . I am mad to have the Houghton pictures sold now' (HWC 21. 199–200; 10 May 1758).

The *sic transit* theme echoes through Walpole's correspondence during the decades leading up to the sale of the Houghton collection in 1779. The most moving expression occurs in a letter to George Montagu dated 30 March 1761, which Walpole begins with an allusion to Gray's *Elegy* before he composes his own prose elegy for his father's estate. Anticipating his own burial in the crypt of Houghton's church in the park about a half mile from the house, he writes:

Here I am, at Houghton! and alone! in this spot, where (except two hours last month) I have not been in sixteen years! Think, what a crowd of reflections! – No, Gray and forty churchyards could not furnish so many. Nay, I know one must feel them with greater indifference than I possess, to have patience to put them into verse. Here I am, probably for the last time of my life, though not for the last time – every clock that strikes tells me I am an hour nearer to yonder church [chapel in the park at Houghton] – that church, into which I have not yet had courage to enter, where lies that mother on whom I doted, and who doted on me! There are the two rival mistresses [Catherine Shorter (1682–1737), HW's mother; and Maria Skerrett (1702–38), HW's stepmother] of Houghton, neither of whom ever wished to enjoy it! There too lies he [Robert Walpole] who founded its greatness, to contribute to whose fall Europe was embroiled – there he sleeps in quiet and dignity, while his friend and his foe, rather his false ally and real enemy, Newcastle [Thomas Pelham-Holles (1693–1768), Duke of Newcastle-Upon-Tyne] and Bath [William Pulteney, Earl of (1684–1764)], are exhausting the dregs of their pitiful lives in squabbles and pamphlets! (9. 348; 25 March 1761).

Then Walpole describes his reaction to the Houghton pictures after sixteen years of visiting auction sales and building his own collection at Strawberry Hill: 'The surprise the pictures gave me is again renewed – accustomed for many years to see nothing but wretched daubs and varnished copies at auctions, I look at these as enchantment' (9. 348). He thinks of his catalogue, *Aedes Walpolianae*, then in a second edition (1752), with disgust as he realizes his own taste has changed: 'My own description of them [Houghton's pictures] seems poor – but shall I tell you truly – the majesty of Italian ideas almost sinks before the warm nature of Flemish colouring!' (9. 348). Although he can no longer see the pictures with 'the poetic eyes' of his youth, he admits his love for painting, for once without an ironic disclaimer: 'In one respect I am very young; I cannot satiate myself with looking', contrasting his response to that of a party of tourists who were visiting Houghton at the same time:

[T]hey come, ask what such a room is called, in which Sir Robert lay, write it down, admire a lobster or a cabbage in a market-piece [Snyders' markets], dispute whether the last room was green or purple, and then hurry to the inn for fear the fish should be over-dressed – how different my sensations! Not a picture here, but recalls a history; not one, but I remember in Downing Street or Chelsea, where queens and crowds admired them, though *seeing* them as litle as these travellers! (9. 348).

The remainder of Walpole's elegiac letter to Montagu introduces us to Walpole's history of the collection, as opposed to anecdotes about individual pictures, a history he writes as the decline and fall of the Walpole family. He refers to these thoughts as 'fine meditations dictated by pride' (9. 349), and 'moral reflections on commonplaces . . . the livery one likes to wear, when one has just had a real misfortune [his first cousin Henry Seymour Conway's going to war in Germany (1761)] . . . I was glad to dress myself up in transitory Houghton, in lieu of very sensible concern' (9. 350). Transitory Houghton comes to mind when Walpole walks in the garden 'now called *the pleasure ground* – what a dissonant idea of pleasure – those groves, those *allées*, where I have passed so many charming moments, are now stripped up, or overgrown' (9. 349). This reminds him of his attitude towards Houghton when leaving for the Grand Tour: 'In the days when all my soul was tuned to pleasure and vivacity . . . I hated Houghton and its solitude – yet I loved this garden; as now, with many regrets, I love Houghton – Houghton, I know not what to call it, a monument of grandeur or ruin!' (9. 349). He then thinks of the ambitious John Stuart (1713–92), 3rd Earl of Bute, who became prime minister two years later (1763), and Robert Woods's architectural conspectus of *The Ruins of Balbec* (London, 1757; Hazen 3547): 'How have I wished this evening for Lord Bute! How I could preach to him! For myself, I do not want to be preached to – I have long considered, how every Balbec must wait for the chance of a Mr Wood' (9. 349).

Walpole then describes the gloomy night-thoughts that haunted him when '[t]he servants wanted to lay me in the great apartment [the Green Velvet Bedchamber in the principal story of Houghton, *Works* 2. 255] – what to make me pass my night as I have my evening!' (9. 349). The Green Velvet Bedchamber, where Francis I, Grand Duke of Tuscany and Holy Roman Emperor, slept on a visit to Houghton (*Works* 2. 257), was a pompous room of state, some twenty-by-twenty feet square, with a 'bed . . . of green velvet, richly embroidered and laced with gold, the ornaments designed by [William] Kent; the hangings are tapestry, representing the loves of Venus and Adonis after Albano' (*Works* 2. 255). Walpole expresses his disgust for sleeping in the state bedchamber and his alienation from Houghton with an allusion of surprising intensity to the daughter of Sir Thomas More: 'It were like proposing to Margaret Roper [1505–44] to be a Duchess in the court that cut off her father's head, and imagining it would please her' (9. 349). Instead Walpole takes refuge in a small room on the other side of the house, where he resumes the theme of Pope's estate poetry, alluding to William Cecil (1521–98), builder of Burghley House, Northamptonshire, whom Walpole claimed as an ancestor (33. 505):

> I have chosen to sit in my father's little dressing-room [*Works*, 2. 255–6], and am now by his scrutoire, where, in the height of his fortune, he used to receive the accounts of his farmers, and deceive himself – or us, with the thoughts of his economy – how wise a man at once and how weak! For what has he built Houghton? For his grandson [George Walpole] to annihilate, or for his son [HW] to mourn over! If Lord Burleigh could rise and view his representative [James Cecil (1713–80), 6th Earl of Salisbury, passionate about stagecoaches] driving the Hatfield stage, he would feel as I feel now – poor little Strawberry! At least it will not be snipped to pieces by a descendant! (9. 349).

The decline and fall of the Walpole estate continued throughout the decade of the 1770s, and Walpole wavered between strenuous efforts towards 'salvation of the family' (23. 496; 13 July 1773) and resignation to ruin. 'It will be mine to try to repair the havoc of three generations', he told Mann: 'My father, excellent and wise as he was, ruined . . . [the family] by pushing this vanity too far' (23. 497). '[T]he shipwreck of my family,' Walpole believed had been 'brought on inadvertently . . . by the mistaken love for it [Houghton] by the best and wisest of men [Sir Robert], pushed on by a thoughtless man [Walpole's brother Robert

(1701–51), 2d Earl of Orford] and completed by a poor man [George Walpole 3rd Earl of Orford (1730–91)], who I doubt, not only is, but always was mad' (23. 489–90).

Walpole writes several vignettes of the impending fate of Houghton that might have come out of Pope's satires. In 1773 Walpole tells of a visit of John Manners (1730–92), one of Lord Orford's creditors, the bastard son of Lord William Manners (1697–1772), who 'came civilly yesterday morning to ask me if he might not seize the pictures at Houghton, which he heard were worth threescore thousand pounds, for nine thousand he has lent Lord Orford. The vulture's throat gaped for them all – what a scene is opened!' He adds melodramatically, 'Houghton will be a rookery of harpies' (32. 121; 11 June 1773). Walpole exorcized Manners with a lawyer, only to be set upon by Mr Richard Vernon (1726–1800), a founding member of the Jockey Club, who 'offered to vouchsafe to live in it [Houghton], if he might have the care of the game' (28. 93; 28 June 1773). '[W]hat vicissitudes have I seen in my family! I seem to live upon a chess-board; every other step is black or white. A nephew [George Walpole] mad and ruined, a niece [Maria Walpole, Duchess of Gloucester], a princess; Houghton, the envy of England' (28. 93), about to slide to 'the jockey' whom Walpole does not mention was an MP.

Without having ever mastered the multiplication table, Walpole found himself an estate agent at Houghton whilst his nephew was committed: 'I am got upon the turf. I give orders about game, dispark Houghton, have plans of farming, vend colts, fillies, bullocks and sheep, and have not yet confounded terms, nor ordered pointers to be turned to grass' (23. 497; 13 July 1773). When Walpole visited Houghton in the summer of 1773 he found his father's monument of grandeur a ruin.

> How can I describe the devastation I found? A new debt contracted by Lord Orford of above £40,000 added to those of his grandfather [Robert Walpole] and father [Edward Walpole]! The estate overwhelmed by mortgages, the livings sold, the glorious house dilapidated, and open in many parts to the weather; the garden destroyed by horses, the park half unpaled, and overgrown with nettles and brambles, a crew of plunderers quartered on all parts, and the house and park mortgaged to my Lady Orford – so that if my Lord were to die, my brother [Sir Edward (1706–84)] would have an empty title, with no estate to come to, and no house to live in (23. 510–11; 2 September 1773).

A similar description written to Lady Ossory in 1773 specifically mentions the pictures which John Boydell was beginning to engrave:

> You know, Madam, I do not want a sufficient stock of family pride, yet perhaps do not know, though I think it far from a beautiful place, how very fond I am of Houghton, as the object of my father's fondness. Judge then what I felt at finding it half a ruin, though the pictures, the glorious pictures, and furniture are in general admirably well preserved. All the rest is destruction and dissolution! The two great staircases exposed to all weathers; every room in the wings rotting with wet; the ceiling of the gallery in danger; the chancel of the church unroofed; the water-house, built by Lord Pembroke, tumbling down; the garden a common; the park half covered

with nettles and weeds; the walls and pales in ruin; perpetuities of livings at the very gates sold; the interest at Lynn gone; mortgages swallowing the estate, and a debt of above forty thousand pounds heaped on those of my father and brother. A crew of banditti were harboured in the house, stables, town and every adjacent tenement (32. 140–1).

The only consolation Walpole found on this visit was the prospect of John Boydell's *Houghton Gallery* (Hazen 3572), engravings of the Walpole collection by subscription: 'I stole from the steward and lawyer I carried with me, to peep at a room full of painters, who you [Anne Liddell] and Lord Ossory will like to hear, are making drawings from the whole collection, which Boydell is going to engrave' (32. 142).[34]

When George Walpole recovered his sanity and began 'dispersing . . . by handfuls and pocketfuls the savings of a whole year' (23. 549; 2 February 1774), Walpole prepared himself for the inevitable, watching auction prices and speculating on what the Houghton pictures would fetch '[i]f they could be sold in proportion' (23. 569; 1 May 1774). The strain of moralizing about 'the vanity of restoring my family' (23. 497) becomes more frequent: 'Mine has been a chequered life of very various scenes! But it has taught me some temper, which I was not born with; and the best of all lessons, to do right, because others do wrong. . . . Alas! we are ridiculous animals! Folly and gravity equally hunt shadows. The deepest politician toils but for a momentary rattle' (24. 301; 4 May 1777). By 1778 negotiations for the sale of the Houghton pictures to Catherine the Great were nearly concluded:

> What I have long apprehended is on the point of conclusion, the sale of the pictures at Houghton. The mad master has sent his final demand of forty-five thousand pounds for them to the Empress of Russia, at the same time that he has been what he calls improving the outside of the house – *basta!* – thus end all my visions about Houghton, which I never will *see*, though I must go thither at last [to be interred]; nor, if I can help it, think of more (24. 427–28; 18 December 1778).

Two months earlier Walpole had politely responded to his nephew's invitation 'to revisit your Penates [household Gods] again, and to see the alterations I am making in both fronts [removing the staircases]' (36. 163), referring to 'my [HW's] duty . . . to promote your service and benefit, to reestablish the affairs of my family, and to conform myself to the views of the excellent man, the glory of human nature [Robert Walpole], who made us all that we are' (36. 164; 5 October 1778). In August 1779 Walpole disclosed his bitterness about:

> the sale of the pictures at Houghton to the Czarina. The sum stipulated is forty or forty-five thousand pounds. . . . a miserable bargain for a mighty Empress!. . . . Well! adieu to Houghton! – about its mad master I shall never trouble myself more. . . . he has undermined every act of my father that was within his reach, but having none of that great man's sense or virtues, he could only lay wild hands on lands and houses; and since he has stript Houghton of its glory. . . . The happiness my father entailed on this country . . . has been thrown away (24. 502–3; 4 August 1779).

Houghton and its pictures are constantly on Walpole's mind at this time: 'I have been told today that they are actually sold to the Czarina – *sic transit*! – mortifying enough, were not everything transitory' (2. 158; 23 April 1779). 'I still retain partiality for the mansions of ancient families,' he writes a friend undertaking improvements: 'though I have so recently swallowed a dose that, one would think, would cure any man of genealogic pomps and vanities!' (30. 275; 4 October 1779). Thinking of the plunder of Houghton, he writes in 1781: '[h]ow weak are these visions about ancestors and descendants! And how extraordinarily weak am I to harbour them, when I see that a madman, a housemaid, and an attorney can baffle all the views Sir Robert himself had entertained! Could he foresee that his grandson would sell his collection of pictures. . . . how transitory are all the glories in the imagination' (25. 133; 26 February 1781). Walpole is being forced to accept reluctantly the lesson that England's 'chief houses . . . dispersed like great rarity plums in a vast pudding of a country' (18. 316), are no more than child's play, destined to fall to ruin like every Roman building: 'I am the more willing to play with local and domestic baby-houses, as the greater scene is still more comfortless – though what is one's country but one's family on a larger scale? What was the glory of immortal Rome, but the family pride of some thousand families?' (25. 133; 26 February 1781).

The coincidence of the sale with the loss of the American colonies invited Walpole to compare 'the shipwreck of my family' (23. 489) with the decline of the British Empire. 'You and I have lived long enough,' he wrote in a Gibbonian tone to Horace Mann, 'to see Houghton and England emerge, the one from a country gentleman's house [Sir Robert Walpole's father's 'plain homely dwelling' (*Works* 2. 224) at Houghton] to a palace, the other from an island to an empire; and to behold both stripped of their acquisitions, and lamentable in their ruins' (25. 133; 26 February 1781). In 1777 the rumour of the impending sale of the Houghton collection prompted John Wilkes to propose the founding of a national gallery in the British Museum, of which Walpole was a trustee.[35]

A few years later the spendthrift heir, George Walpole, was commissioning pictures from Giovanni Battista Cipriani (1727–85),[36] one of the artists who had appraised the pictures for sale to Catherine the Great, and tacking his own sketches on the wall to replace the old masters of his grandfather's collection. Walpole describes another of his nephew's invitations to visit Houghton's improvements with bitter irony:

It [the letter of invitation] was to desire the favour of me to go and see a large picture that Cipriani has painted for him for the salon at Houghton – a most engaging sight to me to be sure!. . . . He has now bespoken another piece, frantic enough, for the subject is both indecent and shocking. Perhaps you have forgotton the story; it is that of Theodore and Honoria, from Dryden's fables, where the naked ghost of a scornful mistress is pursued by demons and worried by bloodhounds. The subject, were it endurable, could only be executed by Salvator or Spagnolet [José di Ribera, called Spagnoletto (1590–1652)] – imagine it attempted by modern artists, who are too feeble to paint anything but fan mounts! I believe I never told you, that since his Lordship [George Walpole] sold his collection of pictures, he has taken to design [draw] himself, and his scratches are pinned up about the stripped apartments – But I am foolish to repeat instances of his deliriums – though indeed the nation is so lunatic that my nephew is no phenomenon (25. 247; 25 February 1782).

Walpole's prejudice against 'modern artists' heightens the bitterness of this sequel to the sale; Walpole's description recalls the black comedy of the famous auction scene in Sheridan's *School for Scandal* (IV i).

The *ubi sunt* motif continues to sound in the last decade of Walpole's life. When the Ossories' Ampthill-Houghton Park House in Bedfordshire was condemned in 1782, he responded nostalgically and elegiacally, hoping to rescue relics from its ruins:

> Poor *Houghton*-Ampthill! – but what is permanent? and what does not present morality and mortality to my old memory! and what a string vibrates on a *Houghton* demolished! – pray, Madam [Anne Liddell], don't I remember in the condemned mansion busts of the Earl of Pembroke and of the Countess of Arcadia, his wife? I think they were of plaster, and therefore, as they cannot be melted for cannon, may not they be exempted from the levelling decree? – you see how the arts and antiques lie in my head, though so many lessons ought to have cured me – but I am here in the cradle where I sucked in so many of those fond visions, and still find them fluttering round my second childhood! Though who knows how soon my playthings may fall under Mr Christie's [James Christie (1730–1803), auctioneer] hammer! (34. 183–4; 16 July 1793).

The collector's appetite for virtu has survived the shipwreck of his family, but the futility of collecting, the inevitable sale of his 'playthings,' has colored the 'fond visions' inspired in his youth by the pictures at Houghton.

How to endure this bitter lesson? The late letters continue to highlight the moral, particularly the sale and demolition of country houses.

> It is very natural for an old man to moralize on events, and still more so for me who have seen Houghton plundered. Claremont [Surrey, Duke of Newcastle's seat] has just now been sold in parcels, and bought on speculation. Sir Gregory Page's [Wricklemarsh, Blackheath], which you [Maria Walpole] once inhabited, Madam, is pulling down. Canons [Edgware, Middlesex, seat of James Brydges, 1st Duke of Chandos] was demolished a few years ago. Such is sublunary grandeur – my morality is, that if everything is transient, misfortunes must be so; and if magnificence is transient, unhappiness is so too. No cup is unmixed (36. 246; 9 July 1787).

A fire at Houghton in 1789 prompted another memory and ironic reflection: 'In my father's time one of the cellars was on fire, but only a door was destroyed. As the gallery is burnt, the glorious pictures have escaped – or are reserved, to be consumed in a wooden palace [the Hermitage] on the first revolution at Petersburg' (34. 88; 12 December 1789).

When Walpole assumed his title as fourth Earl of Orford in 1791 he expressed no delight 'to have outlived all my family, its estate, and Houghton, which, while it was *complete*, would have given me so much pleasure – now it will only be a mortifying ruin, which I will never see' (34. 136; 18 January 1792). In 1794 he wrote to Lady Ossory about an intended visit to Houghton:

> I am not sorry, Madam, that you did not visit the ruins of Houghton and the relics of my poor nephew's madness, and what his friends and plunderers had yet left to him.

You would have found no flight of steps to the front of the house, which one of his counsellors [William Henry Fortescue (1722–1806), Earl of Clermont] had advised him to remove, and then begged for a villa of his own. You say you went to another scene of desolation and could not help moralizing: I hold it better to forget than to reflect: what is permanent? What has lasted but the pyramids, and who knows the builder of them? Moralizing is thinking, and thinking is not the road to felicity. I am even of opinion that a line meant as severe, contains the true secret of happiness.

> In Folly's cup still laughs the bubble, joy

—What signifies whether it be foolish or not, as long as the bubble does not burst? A property which the most eminent sages have not dared to ascribe to wisdom (34. 206; 6 October 1794).

Here endeth Walpole's lesson from Pope's *Essay on Man*.[37]

Walpole's last word on the Houghton collection is *à propos* of Napoleon's assault on Bologna 23 June 1796:

I was so silly as to be shocked at their plundering my favourite school, the Bolognese, though I should never have seen it again, when I recollected that I have lost my own pictures at Houghton! What signifies whether Verres [Caius (d. 43 BC), Roman magistrate] or Catherine Slay-Czar has a fine collection under the Pole or on the Place de la Guillotine? (34. 217; 12 July 1796).

CHAPTER 4

George Vertue: Walpole's Privy Councillor for Portraits

The portrait of Walpole by John Eccardt (plate 23) dated 1754 depicts a seated, smiling figure in Van Dyck costume leaning on a fictitious quarto catalogue of his father's collection, *Aedes Walpolianae*, with a view of his gothicised villa at Strawberry Hill in the background.[1] It would be a mistake to interpret this portrait as an emblem of Walpole's dependency on his father's taste because Walpole was then furnishing his house with English historical portraits as zealously as his father had pursued Italian religious history paintings. '. . . I have done with virtu, and deal only with the Goths and Vandals' (9. 144; 14 December 1752), he proudly delared to George Montagu in 1752. We have seen that the Grand Tour taste did not stick, and that Walpole's catalogue of his father's collection reveals little enthusiasm for old masters. Where then did his passion for English portraits originate? I would like to propose in this chapter the hypothesis that George Vertue (1684–1756) was the dominant influence on Walpole's taste for portraiture. He was the evangelist who attempted and almost succeeded in converting the courtesy-book gentleman into an antiquarian portraitist. Vertue appears to have functioned as Walpole's tutor and his bear-leader on what became an English Grand Tour rummaging for portraits in country houses. Vertue served as Privy Councillor for Portraits to the Prime Minister of Taste.

In 1743, not long after returning from the Grand Tour, Walpole made the acquaitance of George Vertue, England's leading portrait engraver, and assiduous compiler of facts about the history of English art. Throughout the 1740s until Vertue's death in 1756 contacts between Vertue and Walpole continued – conversations, exchanges of visits and information, collaboration on research. After Vertue's death Walpole purchased on 22 August 1758, from his widow, forty volumes of manuscripts which Walpole digested and edited to produce 'a sort of history of the arts in England' (22. 10), the *Anecdotes of Painting* (1762–70). Even though records of the relationship are fragmentary, evidence is sufficient to argue at least an extraordinary coincidence of interests if not a determining influence on Walpole's taste in art. Vertue's single-minded devotion to historical English portraits, his career of copying and engraving illustrious British heads, appears to have been a model and inspiration for Walpole's lifelong passion for portraiture. This chapter will sum up Vertue's career as a portraitist, trace Walpole's relations with Vertue, demonstrate how Vertue's notebooks served as a *vade-mecum* for Walpole's collection of portraits, show that Walpole's visits to country seats were modelled upon Vertue's tours, and finally demonstrate how Walpole transformed Vertue's note-books into his *Anecdotes of Painting*.

23.   John Giles Eccardt: *Horace Walpole*. 1754. Oil on canvas, 16 × 13 in. By courtesy of the National Portrait Gallery, London. Photo: NPG Picture Library.

24.   George Vertue: *Self-Portrait*. 1741. Pen, ink, and chalk drawing, 9¼ × 5½ in. By courtesy of the National Portrait Gallery, London. Photo: NPG Picture Library. 'Ambitious to distinguish himself, he took but one method, application' (HW, 'Life of George Vertue', *Works* 4. 128).

'The First and Chiefest of his Profession'

George Vertue wrote two drafts of a short autobiographical account of his life in the third person which Walpole summarized in the *Anecdotes of Painting*.[2] Vertue's accounts tell the story of an industrious apprentice of English portrait engraving. Born in London to 'parents rather honest than opulent' (GVN 1. 1), he was apprenticed first to a silver-smith who went bankrupt, and subsequently to the copperplate engraver Michiel Van der Gucht (1660–1725). Vertue's father's death in 1711 'left the care of the family on his shoulders . . . which added circumspection in his affairs then as well as industry to the end of his life' (GVN 1. 2). After serving an extended apprenticeship, 'our young Tiro. . . . was encouraged . . . to begin for himself' (1. 15–16), and the Lord Chancellor, John Somers (1651–1716), commissioned him 'to engrave the famous picture [by Kneller] of arch Bishop [John] Tillotson [(1630–94), Archbishop of Canterbury]', a performance that 'had all the approbation imaginable, for at that time no portrait had been done in

England of late so well esteemed' (GVN I. 16). Vertue was recommended to Kneller's Academy where he studied 'with great assiduity' (I. 2), and engraved many portraits after Kneller, Jervas, Richardson, and others, until the accession of George I, when fortune smiled again on Vertue. On a large sheet-plate he engraved the first portrait of the new monarch by Kneller, which was 'shown at court by Sir Godfrey and much approved on several thousands being sold' (I. 2), leading to commissions for other royal portraits. His reputation established by 1715 'as the first and chiefest of his profession in his time' (I. 2), he was called on to engrave 'many pictures of noblemen . . . statesmen, [and] learned men' (GVN 1.16).

At the same time Vertue was practicing limning – portrait drawing in watercolours – copying 'portraits of prime value' (GVN I. 2), and beginning his lifelong researches into the history of English art and artists that filled forty manuscript notebooks at the time of his death. His ingratiating and deferential manners attracted aristocratic patrons such as the collector Edward Harley (1689–1741), second Earl of Oxford, who 'gave him great reputation and advantage over all other professors of the same art in England' (I. 3). Vertue drew 'by his own hand from the life . . . well done and like him' (I. 3) a portrait of Heneage Finch, 5th Earl of Winchelsea (d. 1726), President of the Society of Antiquaries, which led to his appointment as Engraver to the Society, and commissions of engravings for the Oxford almanacs, replacing 'insipid emblems' with 'views of public buildings and historic events' (*Works* 4. 122). He began in the 1720s to accompany aristocratic patrons on tours of country seats, taking inventories of portraits, copying and engraving portraits and antiquities in private collections, and preparing accounts and collections of his engraved portraits for his patrons. In 1728 he visited Knole, Kent, to draw 'some of the Poets' heads' (GVN I. 4) from pictures in the possession of the Duke of Dorset [Lionel Sackville, 1st Duke (1688–1765)], which led to the publication in 1730 of his first series, twelve heads of poets including Chaucer, Milton, and Shakespeare (GVN I. 18). This series was followed in 1736 by Vertue's heads of English Kings for Rapin's *History* (Hazen 3663), contributions to John Birch's *Illustrious Heads* (Hazen 3637; 1743–51), and 'portraits of King Charles I and about twenty noble friends, royals that had suffered their lives or fortunes in his cause' (I. 18).

On his tours Vertue proved himself to be a tireless student and collector. This Autolycus of English portraits goes to Oxford to inventory and copy portraits of the founders, and presents to the Bodleian a collection of his prints; he travels to Gloucester to draw an effigy of Edward II from his monument; he visits Burford to see a picture of Sir Thomas More's family; he interviews Milton's daughter to verify the likeness of a portrait of her father he is copying; he visits Cornbury to see 'a noble collection of portraits' (I. 18), as well as Ditchley, Blenheim, Welbeck and many other country houses.

Vertue drew his self-portrait twice: first, in his prime at the age of thirty-six, wearing a sword, on his wedding day 17 February 1720 with his wife, Margaret Evans, 'in the very habits they were married'. The newlyweds stand holding hands in a wain-scotted room hung with framed engraved portraits and miniatures.[3] The second, a pen-and-ink sketch dated 1741 (plate 24), shows him seated at a table, left hand holding a miniature of his patron, Edward Harley, 2d Earl of Oxford, his right resting on a pile of engravings surmounted by Vertue's engraving of the Chandos Shakespeare for his capital series of the poets. 'On the wall are books and pictures; the table is covered with engraver's tools, a palette, medals and a miniature; on an open cupboard is his bust of Charles I.'[4] This picture, perhaps occasioned by the death of his patron Lord Oxford, shows the self-made portrait engraver with the tools of his trade, surrounded by his heroes. In his autobiography, Vertue adds:

> '[a] description of his person . . . rather of a middle size than short, of shape regular, neither grave nor light, his behaviour respectfully decent to all that knew him, and ever the most humble servant to his acquaintance, always most adapted to this natural character timorous:
>
> > Spare to speak, Spare to speed,
> > In him was true indeed' (1. 6).

Vertue's autobiographical sketch is modest but not self-effacing; he knows his own merits. Walpole's paraphrase of Vertue's short account of his life in the *Anecdotes* emphasizes deference and humility, qualities Walpole valued above all as a patron of artists. '[T]he highest praise he ventures to assume,' Walpole writes approvingly, 'is founded on his industry,' a virtue Walpole thought lacking in the intellectual arrogance of the literary world: 'such book-wights [as Scaliger, who] have mistaken the drudgery of their eyes for parts' (*Works*, 4. 119). He admires Vertue's modesty about supporting his family after his father's death: 'how little the false colours of vanity gave a shining appearance to the morning of his fortune' (4. 120). He is equally impressed by Vertue's account of the publication of his print of Archbishop Tillotson: 'The print will speak for itself. It was the ground-work of his reputation, and deserved to be so' (4. 120). But Vertue attributed the success of the print to the lack of competition owing to the death of European rivals: ' "It seemed," says he himself, "as if the ball of fortune was tossed up to be a prize only for Vertue." One cannot estimate success at a lower rate, than to ascribe it to accident; the comparison is at once modest and ingenious. Shade of Scaliger [Giulio Cessare (1484–1558)], which of your works owed its glory to a dearth of genius among your cotemporaries?' (*Works*, 4. 120–1). Finally, Walpole is touched by Vertue's acknowledgments to his patron, Lord Oxford, who Vertue says ' "gave me great reputation and advantage over all other professors of the same art in England." Another lesson of humility!' (*Works*, 4. 121), a quality Walpole found in few of the artists he patronized.

After quoting two flattering verse epitaphs, Walpole wrote Vertue's epitaph in prose, one of the highest tributes he ever paid to an artist:

> These [verse epitaphs] are well-meant hyperboles on a man who never used any. He was simple, modest, and scrupulous; so scrupulous, that it gave a peculiar slowness to his delivery [speech]; he never uttered his opinion hastily, nor hastily assented to that of others. As he grudged no time, no industry, to inform himself, he thought they might bestow a little too, if they wished to know. Ambitious to distinguish himself, he took but one method, application. Acquainted with all the arts practised by his profession to usher their productions to the public, he made use of none. He only lamented he did not deserve success, or if he missed it when deserved. It was some merit that carried such bashful integrity as far as it did go (*Works* 4. 128).

25.   Hans Eworth: *Lady Mary Neville and her Son Gregory Fiennes, 10th Baron Dacre*. 1559. Oil on panel, 19¾ ×
27¾ in. Walpole's painting at Strawberry Hill, now in a private collection, on loan to the National Portrait
Gallery, London. Photo: NPG Picture Library. 'There is a tradition, that when this great lady [called the Duchess
of Suffolk] made this second match with a young fellow who was only master of her horse, queen Elizabeth
said, "what! has she married her horse-keeper?"' (*Anecdotes, Works* 3. 114).

'Mr Walpole Told Me': Meetings with George Vertue

In 1740 George Vertue inventoried the pictures at Robert Walpole's in Downing Street,
and noted in the closet a portrait of 'young Horace, Sir Robert's son' by Jonathan
Richardson (GVN 5. 126; plate 1). Walpole was then on the Grand Tour, but Vertue's
regular visits to Sir Robert's houses in London and Norfolk raise the possibility that he
had met Walpole before the 1740s, when the first documented references to meetings
occur. In about May 1743 George Vertue wrote in his journal this note about a double
portrait by Hans Eworth (fl. 1540–74) sold the previous year on 8 March 1742 (lot 11)
at the sale of his patron, Edward Harley, Earl of Oxford: 'Frances Duchess of Suffolk
[Lady Frances Brandon (1517–59)] and her husband Adrian Stokes [1533–85] together
painted [plate 25], which picture was bought at the Earl of Oxford's sale by Horace
Walpole junior and lent me to engrave' (GVN 5. 21; plate 25A). This appears to be the
earliest of about a dozen references in Vertue's notebooks to personal relations between
himself and Walpole, and because this portrait illustrates so clearly their mutual passion
for English portraiture, it is worth describing in detail. Vertue first saw the picture on 1

25A.   George Vertue after Walpole's painting [plate 25] attributed to Lucas de Heere. *Called Frances Brandon, Duchess of Suffolk, and her second husband Adrian Stokes.* Line engraving, $17^{3}/_{4} \times 21^{3}/_{4}$ in. No. IV of a set of Tudor prints published by the Society of Antiquaries. Courtesy of the Print Collection, Lewis Walpole Library, Yale University. '. . . [The] picture was bought at the Earl of Oxford's sale by Horace Walpole junior and lent me [George Vertue] to engrave' (GVN 5. 21).

February 1727 at an auction sale in Covent Garden when it was purchased for Vertue's patron, Edward Harley. The picture of the thirty-six-year-old dowager duchess and her twenty-one-year-old husband appealed to Vertue, and he took meticulous notes at the sale, no doubt for the benefit of his patron as much as for himself:

> At a sale of Mr. Collevous' pictures at Covent Garden 1 February 1727: two heads paint-ed on board, something less than life [size]: on the right a lady richly dressed in black, jewels over her head inscribed Aetatis XXXVI; the other a young gentleman with red short hair, very lively and well drawn, inscribed over his head Aetatis XXI; inscribed between on the ground at top MDLIX. On the back of this picture is wrote . . . the Duchess of Suffolk; on one corner of the ground at top this mark . . . HE (GVN 2. 23).[5]

At this point Vertue adds a page reference to a book on Dutch art, adding: 'This picture was bought by Mr Manning in the sale for the Earl of Oxford. In the catalogue this is said to be the Duke and Duchess of Suffolk by Holbein. It is indeed in his manner and done by a master very neatly and curious, but he was dead before that date' (GVN 2. 23). Later on (1731–6) Vertue remarked of a portrait of the first Duke of Dorset owned by John Lord Carteret (1690–1763) that 'this picture is painted in the manner but not so well as that of Frances Duchess of Suffolk and Adrian Stokes at Lord Oxford's' (GVN 4. 70), and he was prepared on the basis of style to attribute it to the same 'poetic [allegorical] painter Lucas de Heere if the time of his being here in England will allow it. Query?' (GVN 4. 72).

In 1736 Vertue recorded notes on the dating of the picture:

I engraved Frances Brandon Duchess of Suffolk (died December 1559). . . . her picture and Adrian Stokes her second husband are painted together by Lucas de Heere; then this picture must have been painted before her death and probably soon after they were married, being plump and jolly in all her gay attire. . . . Her first husband, Henry Grey, [Duke of] Suffolk died 23 February 1554, consequently her picture was painted 1555 or 1556, between or before 1559 by de Heere' (GVN 4. 113).

After the Earl of Oxford's death in 1741 Vertue was asked by his widow to take an inventory of his pictures, and he listed the double portrait of the 'Duchess of Suffolk, *aetatis* 36, 1549, and Adrian Stokes, aetat 21, HE, de la Heere pinx on board' among 'remarkable portraits left in the collection of Edward Earl of Oxford' (GVN 4. 193).

Soon after that sale Vertue visited the cabinet in Arlington Street, which Walpole had fitted with 'French gaiety and Roman Virtù' (HWC 17. 213; 26 November 1741). Vertue ignored Walpole's antiquities, and whatever Walpole meant by 'French gaiety,' but he dutifully recorded three English portraits in Walpole's collection: a portrait attributed to Rubens of George Villiers, first Duke of Buckingham (1592–1628); a watercolour miniature by John Hoskins of Sir John Maynard, a judge (1602–90); and finally, the picture Vertue had been keeping track of for fifteen years: 'The picture of the Duchess of Suffolk and Adrian Stokes bought at Lord Oxford's sale . . . in his [HW's] possession with many other curious pictures, limnings, bronzes, &c.' (GVN 5. 20).

The fortunes of Walpole's double portrait in George Vertue's notebooks nicely illustrates Walpole's character of the engraver in his *Anecdotes of Painting*:

The indefatigable pains of Mr. Vertue left nothing unexplored that could illuminate his subject. . . . [H]e conversed and corresponded with most of the virtuosi in England. . . . he minuted down every thing he heard from them. He visited every collection, made catalogues of them, attended sales, copied every paper he could find relative to the art, searched offices, registers of parishes and registers of wills for births and deaths, turned over all our own authors, and translated [foreign ones]. . . . He wrote down every thing he heard, saw, or read. . . . [T]he integrity of Mr. Vertue . . . exceeded his industry . . . No man living, so bigoted to a vocation, was ever so incapable of falsehood. He did not deal even in hypothesis, scarce in conjecture. He visited and revisited every picture, every monument, that was an object of his researches; and being so little a slave to his own imagination, he was cautious of trusting to that of others. In his memorandums he always put a quaery against whatever was told him of suspicious aspect; and he never gave credit to it till he received the fullest satisfaction (*Works* 3. 4–5).

Walpole passed on the news of his purchase of Eworth's important portrait in a letter to Horace Mann, his *cicerone* in Italian art. Mann probably did not realize what it signified: the effective end of Walpole's interest in Italian pictures as a collector: 'I have made a few purchases at Lord Oxford's sale. . . . an old picture of the Duchess of Suffolk, mother of Lady Jane Gray, and her young husband' (HWC 17. 373–4; 22 March 1742). Walpole's priced copy of the sale catalogue shows that he bought the double portrait on Monday 8 March 'for £15 14s and 6d'. If he attended the sale himself he might have seen George Vertue in the sale room. Twenty years later when Walpole described the portrait in his *Anecdotes*, he listed it among pictures of Lucas de Heere discovered by 'the indefatigable industry of Mr. Vertue':

> a picture in my possession, well known by the print Vertue made from it. It contains the portraits of Frances duchess of Suffolk, mother of lady Jane Grey, and her second husband Adrian Stoke. Their ages, and De Heere's mark HE are on the picture, which is in perfect preservation, the colouring of the heads clear, and with great nature, and the draperies, which are black with furs and jewels, highly finished and round, though the manner of the whole is a little stiff. This picture was in the collection of lord Oxford. There is a tradition, that when this great lady made this second match with a young fellow who was only master of her horse, queen Elizabeth said, 'What! has she married her horse-keeper?' – 'Yes, Madam,' replied my lord Burleigh, 'and she says your majesty would like to do so too.' – Leicester was master of the horse. The date of this picture is 1559 (*Works* 3. 114).

This anecdote about Queen Elizabeth I exemplifies the kind of lively embellishment that Walpole's audience appreciated.[6] Walpole was determined to relieve the dryness and aridity of antiquarian researches: 'I do not see why books of antiquities should not be made as amusing as writings on any other subject' (16. 52; 20 March 1762). The picture, now on loan to the National Portrait Gallery, London, is highly regarded by historians of Renaissance portraiture who recognize in it the 'great nature' Walpole remarked upon. Roy Strong praises Eworth's imagination, tenderness, and sympathy: 'Eworth catches this ill-sorted couple for all time, the corpulent Duchess and the smooth young man fingering the gold chains at his neck. In these characterizations Eworth takes his place within the main stream of European renaissance painting.'[7]

Walpole's loan of Eworth's double portrait to George Vertue occasions the first of several references to personal relations with Walpole in Vertue's notebooks during the 1740s. Soon after he borrowed Walpole's picture, Vertue records a conversation in which Walpole told him about the sale of an important historical picture attributed to Holbein: 'a large picture painted of the battle of Spurrs, Henry VIII, in the possession of . . . Sir John Norris. . . . [information from] Mr Horace Walpole' (GVN 5. 30). There is no evidence that Walpole was personally acquainted with Sir John Norris (1670–1749), Knight, Admiral, and MP. Still, Walpole reports in his correspondence on Norris's campaigns against the French in the 1740s, remarking that Norris 'was called by the seamen *foul weather Jack*' (HWC 18. 423, n. 6). One assumes that Walpole was *au courant* with the art collection of a fellow MP, and thus enabled to pass on information about the picture of one of Henry VIII's battles (1513).[8]

Vertue recorded notes on several visits to Walpole's Arlington Street collection. Some time after September 1745 he refers to miniatures 'amongst the most curious cabinet of limnings and enamels in the possession of Mr Horace Walpole junior' (GVN 5. 49). In the same year Vertue revisited Walpole's collection, when he recorded notes on Walpole's medals, and started to sketch

> a medal in silver of King Philip [Philip II, King of Spain (1527–98)] on one side and Queen Mary [Mary Tudor, Queen of England (1516–58)], the other side very well done in high relief in the possession of Horace Walpole, Esquire; many silver and gold English coins and medals, but of foreign medals and coins a very great collection of the Popes – Italian Princes, Kings and Queens . . . besides a collection of Greek and Roman, his curious cabinet of limnings, enamels, and his collection of English heads &c. (GVN 5. 53; *post* September 1745).

In June 1746 Vertue records Walpole's visit to his own house in London, perhaps in Brownlow Street, near Drury Lane (GVN 6. 126). Vertue gives us a tantalizing summary of their conversation, and a hint about the nature of their relationship: 'In June 1746 Horace Walpole Esq. came to me. After I had shown him many works I was then about, he asked me, Query, "whether I had not some other work in hand besides those." It surprized me because I had not mentioned any thing about the painters' heads, history &c. Query, "if Pond is not about that"' (GVN 6. 139). We cannot determine what Vertue was working on at this time, but the passage suggests Vertue's reserve, and his uneasiness about rival engravers.[9] Elsewhere in his journal Vertue remarks of his rivals in 1745–6: 'So many undertakers, painters, designers, cause much work to be done by interloping on the engravers' honor and interest, and serves them to puff and publish their works and names' (GVN 6. 201; *c.* 1745). In the same passage Vertue expresses his chagrin about Hogarth's work: 'Marriage à la mode, finished 1 June 1745, six sheet plates by Hogarth, employed three French engravers to the obscuration of my reputation' (GVN 6. 201). In 1746 Vertue was further distressed by Hogarth's bringing over Simon Ravenet (1706–74), the French engraver, whom Vertue referred to in May 1747 as 'my most powerful antagonist set forward by Pond' (GVN 6. 202). This record of Walpole's conversation with Vertue is too fragmentary to draw definite conclusions, but it appears to have none of the intimacy Vertue enjoyed with his other patrons, Lord Oxford and the Prince of Wales.[10]

Nevertheless, the record indicates that conversations between Walpole and Vertue continued during the 1740s, and that Walpole took an interest in Vertue's work as a portrait engraver. Walpole is referring to continuing conversations in the correspondence when he mentions 'spurious or doubtful heads [Thomas Birch, *Heads of Illustrious Persons*, 1743; Hazen 3637]. . . . of which honest Vertue often complained to me' (HWC 1. 207; 20 December 1770). Indeed about 1749 Vertue refers to a particular portrait in Birch's *Heads* from an "original limning [owned by] Mr. H. Walpole" (GVN 5. 71). The remaining traces of personal interrelations between Walpole and Vertue appear to date from June–July 1751. One reported conversation refers to Walpole's antiquarian collaboration with Vertue in an effort to trace a picture from the collection of Charles I (Hazen 2478), a collection Vertue was cataloguing that Walpole helped to publish posthumously. Vertue wrote in about 1751:

> After many years inquiry from the description and inventory of King Charles I's [collection of] . . . pictures . . . is mentioned a piece of tapestry . . . representing the Marriage of Prince Arthur [1486–1502], son of King Henry VII, to Katharine of Spain [Catherine of Aragon (1485–1536) m. 1 (1501) Arthur, Prince of Wales; m. 2 (1509) Henry VIII of England], for which I have long inquired at Windsor, Hampton Court, and others of the King's palaces but never could hear of it. Lately, speaking about this affair [the marriage portrait] in the presence of Mr. Lowe, the King's [George II's] gardener at Hampton Court now living there, he observed that he had frequently seen such a piece hanging in some of the lower apartments, under the care of Mrs. Cole [housekeeper at Hampton Court], a person who is now there and has been one of longstanding, and the oldest house [keeper] living. Mr. Lowe has promised by some means to let me know, and Mr. Horace Walpole Esq. will go and see it soon (GVN 5. 87).

After Walpole acquired Vertue's MSS he added a note on this passage – 'could not find it' (GVN 5. 87, n. 6). Nevertheless, this entry provides a documented record of collaboration between Walpole and Vertue searching for an historical portrait, a search that marks the beginning of Walpole's quest for royal-marriage portraits (see Chapter 5).

Only two more facts complete this parsimonious and fragmentary record of the relations between Walpole and his privy councillor for portraits. Firstly Vertue's name appears on Walpole's list (1747–56) for presentation copies of *Aedes Walpolianae* (1747).[11] Secondly, Vertue was one of Walpole's sponsors when he was elected a Fellow of the Society of Antiquaries on 19 April 1753 (HWC 13. 28, n. 188). In addition, it is worth noting that Walpole commissioned copies of portraits from Vertue for his own collection, and collected a large number of his prints.[12]

'Now Mr Walpole's'

Repeatedly Walpole marked references to portraits in Vertue's MSS with the annotation: 'now Mr Walpole's' (GVN 5. 22), or 'bought by Mr Walpole' (GVN 5. 71), or 'now at Strawberry Hill' (GVN 4. 167). A score of such references are sufficient evidence to suggest that Walpole was using George Vertue's notebooks as a *vade-mecum* for his own collection of portraits, both paintings and engravings. When Walpole compiled his digest of Vertue's notebooks in the early 1760s he was also writing a progress report on his own collection, enumerating portraits mentioned by Vertue that he had added to his own collection. After he purchased Vertue's manuscripts Walpole had an unrivalled guidebook for locating English portraits in royal and country-house collections.

The portrait of the remarkable Anne Clifford (1590–1676; plate 26) provides a typical example of Walpole's use of Vertue's notebooks in his search for portraits. In an

26.   Attributed to Nicholas Dixon: *Called Lady Anne Clifford*. Watercolour miniature on vellum, 3 × 2³/₈ in. Courtesy of the Lewis Walpole Library, Yale University. '. . . She was governess to K. Charles 1st's children, and wrote memoires of her own life' (HW's inscription on back of frame).

27.   Gilbert Jackson: *Anne Clifford, Countess of Dorset*. 1637. Woburn Abbey, Bedfordshire. Photo: By courtesy of the National Portrait Gallery, London. 'I have been bullied by an usurper, I have been ill-treated by a court, but I won't be dictated to by a subject' (HWC 9. 125).

undated entry Vertue described a portrait medallion of Anne Clifford in the collection of his patron, Edward Harley, Earl of Oxford. As usual Vertue's note on the portrait is dense with chaotically disorganized detail listing her titles, the name of her father, describing 'the widow's dress' on the face of the medal, and a standing woman holding a cross on the reverse, dating it 'about the latter end of King James's time' (GVN 2. 73). After Lord Oxford's sale in 1742 Walpole proudly wrote in the margins of Vertue's manuscript 'now Mr Walpole's' (GVN 2. 73, n.4).[13] Walpole bought the miniature at Lord Oxford's sale, and we can infer that he located this portrait with the help of Vertue's notebooks, which contain at least two other references to Anne Clifford's portraits. On 2 September 1728 Vertue visited Knole, Kent, where he noted a portrait of 'Richard Sackville, Earl of Dorset, and his Lady Anne' (GVN 2: 50). On a later visit in 1737 he adds an attribution and a qualitative judgment: 'At full length, Anne, daughter and sole heir to George Clifford . . . painted by Cornelius Johnson [1593–1664], a fine, graceful, easy posture, face and hands well drawn, a picture well nigh as good as one of Van Dyck's' (GVN 4. 123).

In contrast to Vertue, Walpole concentrates on collecting biographical facts about the sitter, virtually ignoring the picture and painter. Evidently Walpole is in search of something that transcends fact, namely ideas of human nature expressed in the countenance. Walpole first mentions Anne Clifford in a letter dated 1751 describing the pictures at Woburn, Bedfordshire. He had decided to send his host John Russell, 4th Duke of Bedford, a thank-you gift of a portrait related to one in Woburn's 'purgatory of antiquities':

> I am going to send them [the Russells] a head of a Countess of Cumberland [Lady Margaret Russell (1560–1616), probably Scharf, No. 32], sister to Castalio and Polidore [Walpole's nicknames for portraits of the sons of Francis Russell (1527–85), 2d Earl of Bedford], and mother of a famous Countess of Dorset [Anne Clifford, Scharf 157; plate 27], who afterwards married the mad Earl of Pembroke [Philip Herbert, 4th Earl of Pembroke and Montgomery (1584–1650)]. . . . She was an authoress, and immensely rich. After the Restoration, Sir Joseph Williamson [1633–1701], the Secretary of State [1674–8] wrote to her, to choose a courtier at Appleby: she sent him this answer; 'I have been bullied by an usurper, I have been ill-treated by a court, but I won't be dictated to by a subject; your man shall not stand:/Anne Dorset, Pembroke and Montgomery' (HWC 9. 124–5, 8 October 1751).

This *bon-mot* was too good to limit to a single letter, and Walpole retells it with gusto in a letter to Richard Bentley, describing a visit to Knole with John Chute the following summer of 1752:

> The first little room [Woburn's Brown Gallery] you enter has sundry portraits of the times; but they seem to have been bespoke by the yard, and drawn all by the same painter [once attributed to Holbein, now to John Van Bellcamp (d. 1653)]: one should be happy if they were authentic; for among them there is . . . another good head of the Clifford Countess of Dorset, who wrote that admirable haughty letter to Secretary Williamson, when he recommended a person to her for member for Appleby [Westmorland]: 'I have been bullied by an usurper, I have been neglected by a court, but I won't be dictated to by a subject: – your man shan't stand. Anne Dorset, Pembroke and Montgomery'" (HWC 35. 132–3; 5 August 1752).

Eight months later, writing under the pseudonym Adam Fitz-Adam Walpole decided to use the letter to illustrate an essay he contributed to *The World* (Thursday 5 April 1753; Hazen 911) on the superiority of female letter-writers. Walpole contrasts Anne Clifford's letter with a pompous and long-winded epistle from the Holy Roman Emperor Maximilian I (1459–1519), who wrote to his daughter Margaret a letter dated 18 September 1518 asking her assistance in his campaign to be named Pope, a letter in 'very bad old German French' Walpole considered a 'scrap of imperial folly'. In Walpole's judgment, the Emperor's missive was no match for Anne Clifford's 'reproof valiant'. He writes in *The World*:

> [T]he brave countess, with all the spirit of her ancestors, and with all the eloquence of independent Greece, returned this laconic answer [to Sir Joseph Williamson, Secretary of State to Charles II]. 'I have been bullied by an Usurper, I have been neg-

lected by a Court, but I will not be dictated to by a Subject; your man sha'n't stand./ANNE DORSET, PEMBROKE and MONTGOMERY' (*Works* 1. 168).

'The spirit of her ancestors' must refer to her father, George, 3rd Earl of Cumberland (1558–1605), Queen Elizabeth's favourite, a naval commander against the Armada and captain of ten privateering expeditions, a gambler, spendthrift, and unfaithful husband. Walpole owned at least four portrait engravings of George Cumberland, including one by Robert White 'dressed as for a tournament . . . a beautiful print'.[14]

Walpole transcribed the letter once more in *Royal and Noble Authors* (1758), where he includes Anne Clifford as a noble 'author' tendentiously on the basis of unpublished memoirs of her husband, sundry memorials extant in the British Museum:

[a]nd the following letter to sir Joseph Williamson, secretary of state to Charles the second, who having sent to nominate to her a member for the borough of Appleby, she returned this resolute answer, which though printed in another place [*The World*, No. 14], is most proper to be inserted here. 'I have been bullied by an usurper, I have been neglected by a court, but I will not be dictated to by a subject: your man sha'n't stand./ ANNE DORSET, PEMBROKE and MONTGOMERY' (*Works* 1. 486).

Modern commentators have questioned the authenticity of the resolute countess's single-sentence letter because the original has never been found, the diction is anachronistic (the verb 'bully' is first recorded in 1723), and the dates of elections do not correspond to Sir Joseph Williamson's term of service (1674–78).[15] Sources Walpole cites from his own library (Hazen 9 and 1610) do not record the 'spirited answer' for which 'this remarkable woman [is] best known in the present day' (DNB 4. 512). Is it possible that Walpole made up the quotation? The fact that the wording of the 'letter' continually changes adds to suspicions about its authenticity; the text's mutability suggests anecdote, hearsay, or oral transmission. We have seen in Chapter 2 that Walpole was capable of inventing the name of an artist; we will see in the next chapter that he christened imaginary portraits in his own pictures. It seems quite possible that he may have put words into the mouth of Anne Clifford to embellish her portrait.

More than a score of portraits marked 'now Mr Walpole's' found their way to Strawberry Hill with the help of George Vertue's notebooks. Pictures so annotated include a portrait of the Ladies Percy by Van Dyck (GVN 5. 35); a portrait of Caius Gabriel Cibber by Richter (GVN 5. 62); a portrait of Sir Anthony Shirley by Oliver (GVN 5. 22); and a portrait of Lord St Albans after Lely (GVN 5. 55). Many of these Vertue had discovered in tours of country houses, and Walpole followed in his footsteps on his visits to country seats in search of portraits to add to his collection.

Rummaging Country Houses for Portraits

Referring to Wilton House, Wiltshire, famous for the Earl of Pembroke's collection of classical statuary, Walpole speculates that Vertue shared his own contempt for Pembroke's broken classical busts, and preferred the English portraits at Wilton. 'Wilton he probably saw with only English eyes', Walpole writes of Vertue's visit to the Earl of Pembroke's seat famous for the architecture of Inigo Jones, and for portraits by Van Dyck and Holbein. 'Amid legions of warriors and emperors, he sought Vandyck and Rubens, Holbein and Inigo Jones' (*Works* 4. 122). At Gorhambury 'he made a drawing from the picture of sir Francis Bacon' (*Works* 4. 122). Vertue anticipated Walpole's love of Welbeck Abbey, Nottinghamshire, for its portraits: 'one of the ancient seats of the Countess of Oxford [Henrietta Cavendish Holles (1694–1755)], where after the earl's death she assembled the portraits of her ancestors to a prodigious number, the heroes of many an illustrious race' (*Works* 4. 123). It seems clear that Walpole is projecting his own passion for portraits on to Vertue's pursuit of 'his favourite erudition' when he describes these visits as 'pilgrimages': 'for the love of antiquity is a kind of devotion, and Mr. Vertue had different sets of saints' (*Works* 4. 123).

Describing one of his favourite seats, the Duke of Dorset's Knole, Kent, Walpole imagines Vertue responding as he did himself:

> Humble before his superiors, one conceives how his respect was heightened at entering so venerable a pile, realizing to his eyes the scenes of many a waking vision. Here he drew several of the poets [for his series of engravings]. But he was on fairy ground; Arcadia was on the confines; could he resist an excursion to Penshurst? One may judge how high his enthusiasm had been wrought, by the mortification he expresses at not finding there a portrait of sir Philip Sidney (*Works* 4. 123).

Here we have, full-blown, Walpole's own enthusiasm for pilgrimages to country seats, and waking visions of English history brought to life in portraits.

In 1780 Walpole reports his own waking vision on a pilgrimage to Knole, where Anne Clifford's portrait was hanging. He had just visited Deane House, Kent, the deserted country seat of an office-holder in his father's administration, Sir George Oxenden (1694–1775).

> One place struck me much, but more for recollection of old passages, than from any curiosity in itself. This was Deane, a *trist* old seat of the Oxendens, now deserted – but it was long the residence of Sir George, who in my very youth was the fine gentleman of the age – extremely handsome, a speaker in Parliament, a lord of the Treasury, very ambitious, and a particular favourite of my father – till he became so of my sister-in-law [Margaret Rolle (1709–81) wife of Robert Walpole, HW's brother] – That and a worse story [that Oxenden impregnated and then murdered Arabella Dunch, his sister-in-law], blasted all his prospects, and buried him in retirement – /For when a courtier's out of place,/The country shelters his disgrace (HWC 33. 222–3).

This poetic mood of nostalgic melancholy remembering an old friend and political crony of his father's in the 1720s and a scandal that destroyed Oxenden's career, was nourished by portraits at Deane House:

> Portraits of him, and some heroines of the time – now totally forgotten, but fresh in my memory, seemed a waking vision – it was like Aeneas's meeting Dido in the shades – I could not have conceived that scenes in which I was not in the least interested, could have made so strong an impression – yet they really affected me as if I was

beginning the world again. I could not shake off the sensations till I came to Knowle – and that was a medley of various feelings! (HWC 33. 223; 1 September 1780).

'. . . [A] waking vision . . . like Aeneas's meeting Dido in the shades' (HWC 33. 223). The power of emotions evoked by a family portrait and the memory of a scandal are not suprising, but Walpole responds with similar intensity to the dynastic portraits at Knole, a response very different to that of the antiquarian. Memories evoked by old portraits stir Walpole's historical imagination as powerfully as Aeneas's meeting with the ghost of Dido in the underworld: 'Some pious tears the pitying hero paid,/And follow'd with his eyes the flitting shade' (Dryden's *Aeneid* Book 6, 641–2).

The melancholy Georgian reverie at Deane House prepared Walpole for another waking vision at Knole, a panoramic daydream sweeping from the Elizabethan era to the reign of George II on the wings of portraiture accompanied by a mixture of emotions:

Elizabeth [Queen (1533–1603)] and Burleigh [William Cecil, Baron Burghley (1521–98) and Buckhurst [Thomas Sackville (1536–1608), Baron Buckhurst and Earl of Dorset] – and then Charles [Charles I (1600–49)], and Anne Dorset and Pembroke [Anne Clifford (1590–1676)], and Sir Edward Sackville [(1590–1652), 4th Earl of Dorset] – and then a more engaging Dorset [Charles Sackville, 6th Earl (1638–1706)], and Villiers [George, 2d Duke of Buckingham (1628–87)] and Prior [Matthew (1664–1721)] – and then the old Duke and Duchess [Lionel Cranfield Sackville (1688–1765), and Elizabeth Colyear (d. 1768)] and Lady Betty Germaine [Elizabeth Berkeley (1680–1769)] and the court of George II! (HWC 33. 223–4; 1 September 1780).

Walpole mentions Woburn Abbey, Bedfordshire, another country house he admired for its portraits, in a conversation George Vertue recorded in the 1740s: 'Mr Horace Walpole much commends the old pictures at Wooborn [seat of the] Duke of Bedford [John Russell, 4th Duke (1710–71)], where is the ancient and true picture of Edward Courtney last Earl of Devonshire [d. 1556]' (GVN 5. 87). Vertue had visited Woburn on tours with Lord Oxford in 1727 and 1732, and admired 'in the gallery a great number of ancient portraits of the family and others' (GVN 2. 37).

Vertue's conversation with Walpole probably post-dates Walpole's first visit to Woburn early in October 1751, a tour he describes in a letter to George Montagu dated 8 October, and in his journal of visits to country seats (*Visits* 17–20). Walpole's enthusiasm for the portraits at Woburn, quite unlike his response to Italian pictures, is apparent in his description of the old gallery:

You would be charmed as I was with an old gallery, that is not yet destroyed [Russell was then remodelling the house to the designs of Henry Flitcroft] – it is a bad room, powdered with little gold stars, and covered with millions of old portraits. There are all the successions of Earls and Countesses of Bedford, and all their progenies – one Countess is a whole-length dancing in the drollest dress you ever saw; and another picture of the same woman leaning on her hand, I believe by Cornelius Johnson, is as fine a head as ever I saw.[16] There are many of Queen Elizabeth's worthies, the Leicesters, Essexes, and Philip Sidneys, and a very curious portrait of the last Courtney [Edward

28.   George Vertue: *Mary Tudor and Charles Brandon. c.* 1748. Line engraving, 18 × 21½ in. © Copyright The British Museum. '[H]er face [in the painting] is leaner and longer than in the print; her eyes blue, like her sister's [Margaret Tudor (1489–1541)], and her hair rather more dark' (HWC 40. 365).

Courtenay (1526–56)] Earl of Devonshire who died at Padua; have not I read some-where that he was in love with Queen Elizabeth, and Queen Mary with him? He is quite in the style of the former's lovers, red-bearded and not comely (*HWC* 9. 123).[17]

In his journal of visits to country seats Walpole records these details about Courtenay's portrait: 'Edward Courtney last Earl of Devonshire, poisoned at Padua; he was a Painter, & it is said, Queen Mary was in love with him, & He with Queen Elizabeth. There is a ruined tower behind him, & Latin verses' (*Visits* 20).

   'He was a painter' – this surprising fact of which Vertue gives no hint, accounts for Walpole's inclusion of Courtenay himself in the *Anecdotes of Painting*, because while imprisoned in the tower for nearly twenty of his thirty years, Courtenay had

   a happiness peculiar to him to be able to amuse himself with drawing. . . . [W]e find that queen Mary no sooner delivered him from his captivity than she wished to marry him; and . . . he, conscious of his great blood and yet void of interested ambi-tion, declined a crown, and preferred the younger sister, the princess Elizabeth. For this partiality . . . the princess and he were committed to the Tower, and accused by Wyat [Sir Thomas (1521–4)] as his accomplices. Our historians all reject this accusa-tion [Holinshed, Heylin, and Burnet, Hazen 597, 740, 1105]. . . . Courteney asked leave to travel [after his second release from the Tower by Philip II], and died at Padua, not without suspicion of poison. . . . There is a very good portrait of him at the duke of Bedford's at Woburn, painted, I should think, by sir Antonio More; on the back ground, a ruined tower (*Works* 3. 111–12).

Walpole's authority for Courtenay's proficiency in painting is John Strype's *Ecclesiastical Memorials* (1721; Hazen 883). In the *Anecdotes* (*Works* 3, fc. 111) Walpole reproduces an engraving of the Woburn portrait he attributes to Sir Antonio More; Scharf attributes it to Courtenay himself.

The record of Walpole's relations with George Vertue, fragmentary though it is, sug-gests a remarkable coincidence of interests if not Vertue's decisive influence on Walpole's taste. Lest there be any doubt about how much Walpole learned from Vertue about English portraits, consider the letter he wrote in 1764 to the poet and literary critic, Thomas Warton, responding to Warton's enquiry about the iconography of Mary Queen of Scots:

> My knowledge is extremely confined and trifling; but such information as I can give you, will always be at your service. The most authentic picture of Margaret Queen of Scotland [Margaret Tudor (1489–1541)] is a whole length at Hampton Court. I have a small copy of the head by Vertue [after Daniel Mytens, n. 2]. She has a round face, blue eyes, and brown hair, not light.

Walpole continues, referring to a portrait of Mary Tudor (1495–1533):

> The original of her sister Mary (with her second husband, Charles Brandon [plate 28]), which Vertue engraved while Lord Granville's [John Carteret (1690–1763), 1st Earl], is now mine; her face is leaner and longer than in the print; her eyes blue, like her sister's, and her hair rather more dark. Vertue believed that the small head by Holbein, which I have, and was Richardson's [Jonathan Richardson Sr.(1665–1745)], and which is engraved among the *Illustrious Heads* for Catherine Howard [d. 1542] is the portrait of this Queen Mary; but it has no resemblance to the large one, which is unquestionably of her. In the two first pictures I mentioned, Margaret is much superior to Mary in point of beauty, though I think neither of them handsome; nor is any sense in either face. The picture supposed of Catherine Howard has much expression, but little beauty; the print resembles it very imperfectly (*Works* 40. 365–6; 9 October 1764).

This virtuoso display of portraitist erudition was apparently nourished both by Vertue's notes and conversation. On two other occasions Walpole responded with equal erudition informed by George Vertue to Sir David Dalrymple and Sir Joseph Banks.[18]

No Antiquary: Ghost-Writing English Art History

When we turn to Walpole's *Anecdotes of Painting*, the history of English art Walpole compiled from Vertue's notebooks bought in 1758 from Vertue's widow, it is immediately obvious how far Vertue remained from turning the courtesy-book gentleman into an antiquarian. Throughout the *Anecdotes* Walpole speaks for the patron and collector, not for the artist and antiquarian, as Vertue does.[19] Walpole's ghost-writing exchanges the artist's point of view for that of the patron. In 1753 Vertue had sponsored Walpole for membership in the Society of Antiquaries, and while writing the *Anecdotes*, Walpole told Hogarth in 1761 that he was writing 'an antiquarian history of [painting]' (HWC 9. 366; 5 May 1761).

Although Walpole refers to himself repeatedly as an antiquary, it is clear that the mask of antiquarian does not fit the courtesy-book gentleman. '[W]e antiquaries, who hold everything worth preserving, merely because it has been preserved', he writes disparagingly in the *Anecdotes* (*Anecdotes* 1. 87). Walpole found most antiquarian studies dull, pedantic, and ridiculous, especially publications of the Society of Antiquaries that criticized his books. He was particularly annoyed by scholarly argument:

> Curious facts are all I aim at relating, never attempting to establish an hypothesis. . . .
> The passion for systems did not introduce more errors into the old philosophy, than
> hypothesis has crowded into history and antiquities. It wrests all arguments to the
> favourite point. . . . But the truths we antiquaries search for, do not seem of impor-
> tance enough to be supported by fictions (*Anecdotes* 1. 27–8).

Walpole refuses to attempt a history of primitive architecture, inviting a purge of antiquarian literature on the subject, a history that 'would annihilate fables, researches, conjectures, hypotheses, disputes, blunders, and dissertations, that library of human impertinence' (*Anecdotes* 1. 115).

The author of the *Anecdotes* appears to be an anti-intellectual, an amateur who would never dream of identifying himself with William Camden, John Dart, Thomas Hearne, or with George Vertue, the author he serves as ghost-writer. From the start, the author of the *Anecdotes*, smarting from critical reviews of *Royal and Noble Authors* (1759), was 'sick of the character of author' (16. 29; 14 May 1759), frustrated by the dull duty of an editor, and intimidated by Vertue's chaotic manuscripts. He struggled with Vertue's 'indigested' memoranda (42. 159), a 'farrago' of scattered, unindexed notes, 'a heap of immethodic confusion . . . writtten in so very diminutive a hand . . . I was often forced to use a magnifying glass' (16. 299). He complained of darkness and difficulties at the start of his task, and, when compiling a third index while working on the fourth volume in 1770, he lamented: 'What pains one takes to be forgotten!' (10. 307).

How was he to organize his materials, and was the task worth the trouble? Walpole found several reasonably coherent short articles on individual artists and engravers which probably inspired his '*Vasari-hood*' (35. 207), his plan to organize the book into lives of the English painters, but '[u]nluckily he [Vertue] had not gone far and could not write grammar' (16. 26). Walpole called on antiquarian friends like Gray and Dalrymple for help and encouragement, and he wrote to Henry Zouch: 'I have by no means digested the plan of my intended work. . . . As our painters have been very indifferent, I must to make the work interesting, make it historical; I would mix it with anecdotes of patrons of the arts. . . . I think it capable of being made a very amusing work, but I don't know whether I shall ever bestow the necessary time on it' (16. 27; 15 March 1759).

The courtesy-book gentleman kept careful track of the process of composition in *Short Notes* (HWC 13. 33–8), preening himself *con sprezzatura* on his rapidity of composition: 'It was an easy task when I had the materials collected; and I would not have the labours of forty years, which was Vertue's case, depreciated, in compliment to the work of four months, which is almost my whole merit' (16. 51–2; 20 March 1762). Walpole regularly plays the editor, as opposed to author, in parrying compliments and dismissing criticisms. When Lort praised his redaction of the notebooks, Walpole characteristically belittled his own work: '[H]ow little merit I have in the share I have taken of Vertue's labours . . . how imperfect they are' (16. 156; 16 March 1762). And to the young Christopher Wren, Walpole writes: 'I must here . . . do justice to Vertue, whose merit in the *Anecdotes* is real, while mine is only trifling and ornamental' (40. 354). '[N]o share but in ranging his materials' (15. 72), he tells another flatterer. When answering critics like James Barry, Walpole writes that he would welcome a more satisfactory account 'than Mr Vertue could collect, and I have published, from his researches, not my own, which are indeed very idle' (34. 244). It was also convenient to give Vertue credit when critics pointed out errors: 'I cannot tell now whether Vertue's mistake or my own' (HWC 1. 25; 19 August 1762).

Walpole's antiquarian readers were the first to congratulate him on not writing like an antiquarian.[20] In his dedication of the *Anecdotes* to Mary Lepell, dowager Baroness Hervey of Ickworth, Walpole assumes the attitude of the courtesy-book gentleman determined to conceal his antiquarianism at any cost: '. . . [I]f I could write any thing really deserving your acceptance, I should not prefix your name to such trifles as the following sheets . . . though in the present case I am rather an editor than an author . . . I am forced to pay my debts to your ladyship with Mr. Vertue's coin. If his industry has amassed any thing that can amuse one or two of your idle hours . . . I shall think his life was well employed' (*Works* 3, sig. B1). Snobbery is not mere rhetoric in the dedication; Walpole's patronizing attitude to artists including Reynolds earned him the reputation of being the worst of patrons, and would have been particularly galling to an artist like Vertue who lived on terms approaching friendship between equals with Edward Harley and the Prince of Wales.

Throughout the *Anecdotes* Walpole assumes a patronizing attitude towards English art and artists, speaking of the history of early English art as 'tracing the progress of barbarism' (*Anecdotes* 1. 23), 'mere herald's painting' (1. 36), 'less known minutiae' (2. 52), and 'trifling circumstances' (2. 126). Seventeeth-century English artists as 'the herd of our painters in oil' (3. 1); his own lives of English painters 'brief or trifling articles' (2. 133), 'trifling notices . . . to assist families in finding out the portraits of their ancestors' (2. 237).

The patron's attitude to English artists as well as art history can be clearly seen by comparing Vertue's with Walpole's accounts of Sir Godfrey Kneller, Vertue's teacher. 'Noble' is the key word in Vertue's panegyric (GVN 2. 119–22). Kneller's noble style, manner, and genius had resulted in knighthood: 'glories and honours heaped on him he lived in splendour', purchased a country house, and was praised by Dryden and Pope.

'He has been the morning star for all other portrait painters in his time' (*Anecdotes* 2. 121), Vertue writes. 'No painter perhaps ever had the reputation of drawing portraits more like' (2. 120), and his sittings were so entertaining 'that people go away with more sprightliness than they came' (2. 122). Walpole transforms Vertue's portrait of the artist as hero into a portrait of the mercenary opportunist: 'Where he offered one picture to fame, he sacrificed twenty to lucre' (2. 202).[21] Walpole finds most of Kneller's work mediocre – 'too great a sameness in his airs, and no imagination at all in his compositions' (2. 204), but his criticism is more a judgment of his character than of his art: '[H]e united the highest vanity with the most consummate negligence of character' (2. 202). Dismissing Pope's epitaph comparing Kneller to Raphael as 'a silly hyperbole' (2. 208), Walpole catalogues anecdotes about Kneller's vanity: '"Painters of history," said he [Kneller], '"make the dead live, and do not begin to live themselves until they are dead. I paint the living, and they make me live."' (2. 202, n. 2).

Another sign of the patron in the *Anecdotes* is to be seen in Walpole's frequent mention of pictures in his own and his father's collection. For example, 'a most curious picture of . . . [Henry V]', 'now at Strawberry-hill' (1. 31, and n. 2); *The Marriage of Henry VI* – 'a remarkable piece', '[i]n my possession' (1. 34); 'I have two portraits . . . of singular merit [by Cornelius Jansen]' (1. 212); Peter Oliver's miniature of Lady Lucy Percy, 'perhaps the finest and most perfect miniature in the world' (1. 224); the same artist's large miniature of Sir Kenelm Digby and his family after Van Dyck, 'the most beautiful piece of the size that I believe exists' (1. 223, n. 1.). He includes a similar list of portraits at Houghton (1. 143). And Walpole cries up his own collection of portrait engravings almost as fervently as his paintings: '. . . I am possessed of the most complete collection of his [Hogarth's] prints that I believe exists' (3. 13); the family of James I engraved by William Pass, a 'beautiful and curious print . . . now in my possession' (3. 142–3, n. 2); and Oliver Cromwell, a 'very scarce print . . . in my possession: I never saw another proof of it' (3. 193).

'. . . [H]ad not Waller been a better painter, Sacharissa [Dorothy Sidney] would make little impression now' (1. 318). With this remark Walpole introduces another important idea in the *Anecdotes*: the superiority of literary to painted portraits – *ut pictura poesis*. Waller's poetic character of the countess excels in value Van Dyck's portrait, just as Clarendon's *History* excels Van Dyck's double portrait of Thomas Wentworth, first Earl of Strafford (1593–1641) and his secretary (plate 29):

> I have reserved to the last, the mention of the finest picture, in my opinion, of this master. It is of the Earl of Strafford and his secretary, at the Marquis of Rockingham's, at Wentworth-house, in Yorkshire. I can forgive him any insipid portraits of perhaps insipid people, when he showed himself capable of conceiving and transmitting the idea of the greatest man of the age. There is another of these pictures at Blenheim, but infinitely inferior (*Anecdotes* 1. 327).

Strafford, 'the greatest man of the age,' was MP, Lord Lieutenant of Ireland, and a moderate royalist who supported King Charles against parliament. He was tried for treason in Westminster Hall 22 March 1641, and executed in May on the scaffold, where he stated his political credo: 'parliaments in England . . . be the happy constitution of the kingdom, and the best means under God to make the king and his people happy.'[22] Charles

29.   Sir Anthony Van Dyck: *Sir Thomas Wentworth, Earl of Strafford, and Sir Philip Mainwaring.* 1640. Oil on canvas, 48½ × 55 in. Private Collection. Photo: By courtesy of the National Portrait Gallery, London. '. . . the finest picture, in my opinion, of this master [Van Dyck]. . . capable of conceiving and transmitting the idea of the greatest man of the age' (*Anecdotes* 1. 327).

I had not supported his loyal subject so that among his final words were 'Put not your trust in princes.' Strafford died gallantly, 'refusing to bound his eyes; after prayer he spread forth his hands as a signal to the executioner, and the axe ended his life'. Strafford had not always been Walpole's hero; he is called a 'perjured patriot' in Walpole's satirical verses (1744) on the House of Lords (18. 357–8 line 22). Walpole's note on these manuscript lines summarizes the political career of Strafford, who had been ennobled 12 January 1640: 'Wentworth Earl of Strafford set out a great patriot in the beginning of Charles I's reign, but was bought off by the Court, and made a peer; and at last put to death by the House of Commons for his arbitrary proceedings' (HWC 18. 358, n. 23).

On a visit to Wentworth Woodhouse, Yorkshire, the earl's ancestral estate in August 1756, Walpole gave Strafford a more favourable character:

> Amidst all this litter and bad taste [of the inhabited part of the house], I adored the fine Vandyck of Lord Strafford and his secretary, and could not help reverencing his bed chamber. With all his faults and arbitrary behaviour one must worship his spirit and eloquence: where one esteems but a single royalist, one need not fear being too partial. When I visited his tomb in the church (which is remarkably neat and pretty, and enriched with monuments) I was provoked to find a little mural cabinet, with his figure three feet high kneeling. Instead of a stern bust (and his head would furnish a nobler than Bernini's Brutus) one is peevish to see a plaything that might have been bought at Chenevix's [Paul Daniel, a London toyshop keeper]. There is a tender inscription to the second Lord Strafford's wife, written by himself [Lord William Wentworth (1626–95), 2d Earl of Strafford] – but his genius was fitter to coo over his wife's memory, than to sacrifice to his father's (HWC 35. 267–8).

Walpole's sacrifice to Strafford's memory provides another example of Walpole's impulse to 'monument' portraits in country houses. He continued to pay homage to the 'great Lord Strafford' by visiting another of his houses at Ledston, Yorkshire (HWC 35. 269). Two years later, rummaging through the attics of the Earl of Hertford's seat at Ragley, Warwickshire, he found 'three letters of the great Strafford' in an old chest brimful of papers 'part rotten, another gnawed by rats' (9. 224; 20 August 1758).

Finally, Walpole mentions Strafford's letters in an entry of his *Royal and Noble Authors* (1758), where he strains to justify inclusion of an unpublished author:

> Thomas Wentworth, Earl of Strafford, is not recorded here for his speeches and letters [Hazen 446, *Letters and Despatches* (1739)], those chef-d'oeuvres of sense, of nervous and pathetic eloquence; but on occasion of an elegy with some affecting lines, said to have been composed by him the night before his execution. . . . Most probably it was not genuine: that hero had other ways of venting his scorn than in sonnets and madrigals. When the lieutenant of the Tower offered him a coach, lest he should be torn to pieces by the mob in passing to execution; he replied, 'I die to please the people, and I will die in their own way.' With such stern indifference to his fate, he was not likely to debase his dignity by puerile expressions of it (*Works* 1. 468–9).

Walpole's research on Strafford nicely illustrates the difference between Vertue and Walpole as antiquarians: Vertue avidly collects facts about English portraits and portrait-painters; Walpole collects anecdotes about the lives of English aristocrats. Art history is incidental to Walpole's passion for portraits. He wishes to illustrate his hero's character. And this interest in character predominates in his discussion of portraits throughout the *Anecdotes*. Witness his comparison of Samuel Cooper's miniatures to Van Dyck's full-length portraits:

> [I]t would be an amusing trial to balance Cooper's Oliver [Cromwell] and Vandyck's Lord Strafford. To trace the lineaments of equal ambition, equal intrepidity, equal art, equal presumption, and to compare the skill of the masters in representing the one

[Cromwell] exalted to the height of his hopes, yet perplexed with a command he could scarce hold, did not dare to relinquish, and yet dared to exert; the other [Strafford], dashed in his career, willing to avoid the precipice, searching all the recesses of so great a soul to break his fall, and yet ready to mount the scaffold with more dignity than the other ascended the throne. This parallel is not a picture drawn by fancy; if the artists had worked in competition, they could not have approached nigher to the points of view in which I have traced the characters of their heroes (*Anecdotes* 2. 145).

Tracing the lineaments of character is precisely what preoccupies Walpole in his own collection of portraits at Strawberry Hill.

PART II
A Little Castle Adorned with Portraits

CHAPTER 5

Portraits at Strawberry Hill – I

It is the purpose of Part II to demonstrate that Walpole was not a whimsical collector of curiosities, but a lifelong collector of portraits, which he valued for the sake of anecdote rather than art.

In the preface to the catalogue of his collection at Strawberry Hill, Walpole speaks of it as 'an assemblage of curious trifles' (*Works* 2. 395) unworthy of being compared to his father's at Houghton. He goes on to say something that Macaulay and other students of his collection have studiously ignored: 'The most considerable part of the following catalogue consists of . . . portraits of remarkable persons' (2. 396). It turns out that many of the most notorious trifles were gifts: 'the red hat of cardinal Wolsey' (2. 455), 'the spurs worn by king William' (2. 502), Henry VIII's clock with an obscene pendulum (2. 444–5; HWC 29. 39, n. 6), various locks of royal hair (Edward IV's, *Works* 2. 477), the seal of Hugh O'Neal, King of Ulster (2. 483), the case for the pipe which Van Tromp smoked (2. 502), Dr Dee's conjuring stone (2. 501), Grinling Gibbons's wooden cravat (2. 483), and James I's gloves (2. 499). Of course Walpole also dismissed the portraits he collected as trifling curiosities throughout the correspondence because the courtesy-book gentleman cannot admit to taking antiquarian pursuits seriously. But portraits were serious trifles for Walpole, the heart and soul of his collection, as the following chapters will demonstrate. He collected portraits for reasons he eloquently expressed to George Montagu: 'I almost think there is no wisdom comparable to that of exchanging what is called the realities of life for dreams. Old castles, old pictures, old histories, and the babble of old people make one live back into centuries that cannot disappoint one' (HWC 10. 192; 5 January 1766). Selected representative portraits in his collection will be discussed in roughly chronological order by sitter: mainly sixteenth-century pictures in Chapter five, seventeenth-century portraits in Chapter six; and French portraits of the *ancien régime* in Chapter seven.

Anne Liddell and Walpole's Dream of Portraits

By way of introduction to Walpole's collection, consider the rare occasion in Walpole's correspondence when he dropped the mask of the courtesy-book gentleman for a moment to reveal the real importance of the portraits at Strawberry Hill. Walpole wrote a scolding letter to Anne Liddell (1738–1804) who had removed a portrait of herself from the blue breakfast room at Strawberry Hill without his permission. The picture was a crayon portrait by Hugh Douglas Hamilton (1739–1808)[1] that had been painted for him in 1772:

30.   Hugh Douglas Hamilton: *Anne Liddell*. 1773. Pastel. Private Collection. Photo: Courtesy of the Lewis Walpole Library, Yale University. 'I was in a monstrous passion at your taking away your picture' (HWC 33. 17).

31.   Right. Antonio Canal, called Canaletto: *Richmond House, London.* 1747. Oil on canvas, 41¾ × 46¼ in. Photo: The Trustees of the Goodwood Collection. '. . . your [Anne Liddell's] figure at the Duke of Richmond's masquerade, when you looked like the Empress of the Universe' (HWC 33.17).

32.   Far Right. Samuel Wale: *Lord Ferrers Shooting His Servant. c.* 1768. Pen and ink drawing, 6¼ × 3⅞ in. Courtesy of the Lewis Walpole Library, Yale University. 'The poor creature . . . was shot and lived twelve hours' (HWC 9.272).

I was in a monstrous passion at your taking away your picture [plate 30], and so I am sure will my ghost be, if it is ever removed out of this blue room while poor Strawberry exists. One is an artificial being: I and my friends and this place compose but one idea in my mind, and it is lopping a limb to touch any of the constituent parts – so, how I should not have been angry, I don't know (33. 17; 3 June 1778).

When Walpole says 'one is an artificial being,' he appears to mean that his sense of himself as a social being is composed of portraits like Anne Liddell's, capable of summoning such vivid memories.

Once he recovered his temper Walpole admitted that the alteration she had the artist make in the headdress was an improvement on the original which 'certainly recalled nothing of your figure at the Duke of Richmond's masquerade [6 June 1763, Richmond House, Privy Gardens, London, plate 31], when you looked like the Empress of the Universe, and your Majesty's eyes – but I can draw them no more than if I was a painter' (33. 17–18). Walpole is remembering her appearance at the age of twenty-five in masquerade costume 'as Cleopatra, and such a Cleopatra!' (22. 148). More than 600 of the nobility attended the masquerade with fireworks and music, and 10,000 spectators had watched from barges on the Thames:

The whole garden was illuminated and the apartments. An encampment of barges decked with streamers in the middle of the Thames, kept the people from danger and formed a stage for the fireworks, which were placed too along the rails of the garden.

The ground rooms lighted, with suppers spread, the houses covered and filled with
people, the bridge [Westminster Bridge], the garden full of masks, Whitehall crowded
with spectators to see the dresses pass, and the multitude of heads on the river, who
came to light by the splendour of the fire-wheels, composed the gayest and richest
scene imaginable; not to mention the diamonds and sumptuousness of the habits
(HWC 22. 149; 7 June 1763).[2]

Walpole paints the scene as brilliantly as Canaletto, but it is the portrait of Anne Liddell
that enlivens his landscape.

An equally revealing passage from Walpole's unpublished journals helps to explain his
enthusiasm for historical portraits. The journal entry describes Walpole's dream the night
of 1–2 May 1760, shortly after the trial for murder (16–18 April, 1760) of Lawrence
Shirley, 4th Earl Ferrers (1720–60; plate 32), in Westminster Hall, which Walpole had
attended in his friend Lord Lincoln's box.[3] Significantly, Walpole had the dream while he
was editing George Vertue's *Catalogue of the Collection of Charles I*, and composing his
Anecdotes of Painting from George Vertue's notebooks. Furthermore, the dream was
prompted by an unidentified engraving of Westminster Hall: 'I thought somebody
shewed me a print of the trial of some Lord Chancellor of Scotland before Charles 2d
in Westminster hall. . . . I soon thought myself there. . . . but it did not last a minute. The
King [Charles II], with his crown, black wig and purple robe ermined,' as Walpole
remembered his portrait, 'passed out of the court at a little door on the right hand of the
great gate'.[4] Walpole then finds himself standing at the door next to:

a man in a light brown coat with a plain gold lace, tied wig and garter. . . . I wondered he did not follow in the procession, for I fancied it was the Duke of York [the future James II (1633–1701)]. I was very near him, and examined him narrowly, and said to myself, 'Is it the Duke of York? Is he like the wax-head which George Selwyn [wit, friend, and correspondent of HW (1717–91)] has of him, that was taken off after he was dead, from the mould at Paris?'

Walpole ruminates about the likeness of Selwyn's portrait, saying aloud to himself twice more '"Is it the Duke of York?"', a question overheard by Charles II who sends 'the present Lord Gower (Master of the Horse) to call me [HW]'.[5] Surprised, but determined not to be intimidated by royalty, Walpole enters 'a small low room, where the King was standing in the middle with his back to the chimney, and six or seven persons about him'. Lord Gower gives Walpole a chair back to lean on saying '"that is the way of talking to the King"'. Walpole converses briefly with Charles II 'with great ease and familiarity', and after the king leaves the room, Walpole worries 'he did not like me enough'. Collecting himself, he notices:

> that the room was covered with pictures – 'Oh! thought I in a rapture, this is the collection of Charles 1st. I will examine them [Charles I's pictures] carefully, for they will be burnt in Whitehall [in a fire 1698] (where I thought I now was). I can never see them again; and then I will go home and look in the catalogue of King Charles's pictures [Hazen 2478; plate 33] to see which I can find of them there.'[6]

Still dreaming, Walpole looks at a picture in a lacquered frame of 'Adam and Eve with several beasts round them by old Franks [Sebastiaen Vrancx (1573–1647)]', and wonders why the king had bought two pictures of the same subject. Walpole then remembers that he is keeping the Duke of York waiting, but realizes that he 'did . . . [not] seem to take it ill. Still I was determined to see all I could, as I could never have another opportunity. . . . Thought I, "they will think me very impertinent, but I am resolved to gratify my curiosity"'. Accordingly he enters an adjoining room that turns out to be the Duke of York's bedchamber, of which he draws a crude plan showing two doors, window, bed, and chimney.

> I took down a candle and examined the pictures – and then turned peevishly to George Selwyn and said: 'You pretend to love King Charles 1st,[7] here is his collection, why don't you look at it, you never can have another opportunity, for it will be burnt.' . . . In the recess dotted. . . . thus, I was struck with something which I immediately concluded were the small miniatures by Holbein of which I have often regretted the loss. I ran to them eagerly, but was excessively disappointed to find them little sconces of false coloured stones.

Walpole next visits another adjoining picture gallery 'which I can now recollect was much like Mr Bentley's [Richard Bentley (1708–82)] drawing for my own gallery (plate 34).[8] It was of old unpainted wainscott too, and covered with pictures, which I examined attentively, but could not recollect them when I waked'. Like Alice in Wonderland Walpole enters:

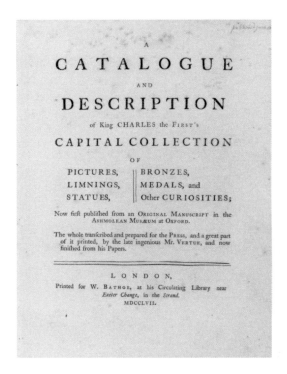

33.   George Vertue, and HW ed. *Catalogue of Charles I's Collection* (London, 1757), title-page. Courtesy of the Lewis Walpole Library, Yale University.

34.   Richard Bentley: *Sketch of the Gallery at Strawberry Hill.* Pencil, ink, and wash drawing, 9¹⁄₈ × 6⁷⁄₈ in. Courtesy of the Lewis Walpole Library, Yale University.

another like gallery. At the end was a very odd picture; it seemed a young King in his robes to the knees, sleeping as on one hand thus [HW's rough drawing of a recumbent figure]. I immediately knew it to be Richard the 2d. He waked, and came out of the frame, and was extremely kind to me, and pressed me to stay with him – 'no, thought I, I know the assassins are coming to murder you; it is not in my power to save you, and I cannot bear to see it – I will make you some excuse & get away.' Still he pressed me earnestly to stay with him, but I made some excuse and slipped out of a door opposite to his frame.

In a passage reminiscent of the *Castle of Otranto*, Walpole finds himself on 'a great stone staircase' leading to 'a vaulted high passsage, where were several cases, as of pictures, with straw and packing lying about', and finally makes his way to 'a porter's lodge . . . [where] somebody spoke to me, I went out at the gate, and waked'.[9] Stylistically Walpole's account of his dream of portraits is a rather wooden document, but it vividly illustrates his enthusiasm for portraits. In the dream he is quite literally on speaking terms with portraits, and we shall see him conversing with portraits throughout his career. As he told Horace Mann, 'I am indefatigable in collecting English portraits' (HWC 23. 423; 23 July 1772).

The Marriage of Henry VI, *and 'The Sagacity of My Guesses' (2.31)*

During alterations to Strawberry Hill in the early 1750s Walpole bought from his architect William Robinson (1720–75), Secretary to the Board of Works, a fifteenth-century painting on wood supposed to represent the marriage of Henry VI (1421–71) to Margaret of Anjou (1430–82). This picture (plate 35) along with another called *The Marriage of Henry VII* appears to have been the first of a series of royal portraits Walpole purchased, concluding with family pictures of Henry V and Henry VIII bought at the sale of James West (1703–72), President of the Royal Society of Antiquaries, in April 1773. 'The first [Henry V] cost me £38,' he told William Cole, 'and the last [Henry VIII], 84; though I knew Mr West bought it for six guineas. But in fact, these two with my marriages of Henry VI and VII compose such a suite of the House of Lancaster, and enrich my Gothic house [Strawberry Hill] so completely, that I would not deny myself' (1. 305; 7 April 1773). If the Holbein chamber at Strawberry Hill indicates the extent of George Vertue's influence on Walpole's collection, the royal marriage pictures demonstrate the limits of Vertue's influence, clearly marking the difference between an antiquarian portrait collector, and a Prime Minister of Taste in love with imaginary portraits.

Walpole asked the poet Thomas Gray to help determine the subject and identify the portraits in both paintings. Gray promised to collect 'what I can about the two marriages' (HWC 14. 68; 15 February 1754), then plunged into antiquarian archives and medieval chronicles at Cambridge. Within two weeks he produced a long letter signed 'by the paynful hand and symple engyne of Your Honour's pour bedesman' (14. 80; 3 March 1754). 'I could tell you many small particulars' (14. 75), Gray wrote. 'If these [details] suit your palate, you may see them all' (14. 76). 'Particulars' and details Gray provides, a cornucopia of facts in three languages that Walpole could use to support his hypothesis that the first royal picture depicted the *Marriage of Henry VI*. 'Now you,' Gray writes to Walpole, 'are to determine whether the picture represent the marriage at Tours' (14. 72), where Henry VI was married by proxy. 'I can tell you exactly who they were [courtiers accompanying Margaret of Anjou], and what they did there . . . If it is nothing to your purpose, you may pass it over' (14. 72).

Gray knew exactly what Walpole's purpose was – to read a picture filled with unknown portraits as the *Marriage of Henry VI* – but he could not help stumbling over stubborn facts. 'I am sorry Duke Humphrey [Duke of Gloucester (1390–1447)] could not be there [at the actual wedding at Southwick, Hants], but you see he did not meet her [Margaret of Anjou] till after the marriage in her way to London' (14. 74). 'The King was barely 23 years old. (What shall we do with this stubborn date?)' (14. 76). Assuming the scene of the picture to be Tours, Gray obligingly offers a way out of difficulty: 'Henry VI may be introduced [in the picture], though not there in person' (14. 72). 'If the scene of the picture lies in England, you may pick and choose' (14. 74), Gray wrote, supplying a likely candidate for the presiding prelate, Henry Beaufort (1375–1447), Bishop of Winchester and Cardinal. 'The Cardinal Beaufort, then at least seventy years old, one would think should have the honor of joining their hands, especially in his own diocese; but I recollect no marks of a cardinal . . . so it may be John Stafford [(d. 1452], Archbishop of Canterbury' (14. 75).

Walpole's reply to Gray's letter about the picture is lost, but Gray's acknowledgment of

35. Flemish, Anonymous: *Marriage of a Saint* HW called 'The Marriage of Henry VI.' Oil on wood panel, 37¼ × 34⅞ in. 1475–1500. Toledo Museum of Art, Purchased with funds from the Libbey Endowment, Gift of Edward Drummond Libbey. 'In my possession is a remarkable piece, which so many circumstances affix to the history of this prince [Henry VI] that I cannot hesitate to believe it designed for him' (*Anecdotes* 1. 34).

the missing letter suggests that Walpole responded to doubts about the *dramatis personae* in the *Marriage of Henry VI* as he had done to doubts about his father's 'Domenichino' on the Grand Tour. 'I am very glad', Gray writes, 'my objections serve only to strengthen your first opinion about the subject of your picture' (14. 81; 11 April 1754). In Walpole's description of the picture in the *Anecdotes of Painting* we discover how whimsically Walpole picked and chose among Gray's possibilities, finessing the difficulties. Walpole nonchalantly confronts the awkward circumstance of the Queen's pregnancy in the picture thus: '. . . [She] is far from being a lovely bride, and . . . the painter seems satirically to have insinuated, by the prominence of her waist, not to have been so perfect a virgin as her flowing hair denotes' (*Anecdotes* 1. 34). For Cardinal Beaufort and Archbishop Stafford, Walpole unhesitatingly substitutes John Kemp (1380–1454), Archibishop of York and Canterbury, who is nowhere mentioned in Gray's letter. Behind the king Walpole insists on seeing Humphrey, Duke of Gloucester, whom Gray had stated 'could not be there' (HWC 14. 74). Even more far-fetched, Walpole places in the foreground Margaret Beaufort (1443–1509), Countess of Richmond, mother of Henry VII, who 'was only two years old at the time of the marriage' (14. 70, n. 12). Near Archbishop Kemp Walpole 'certainly' supplies Henry Beaufort, Gray's candidate for the mitred figure: 'The face is very like the image on his tomb at Winchester' (*Anecdotes* 1. 35).

For more than thirty years Walpole clung to this flimsy hypothesis, clutching at straws of corroboration in defiance of his own caution to antiquaries in the *Anecdotes of Painting*: '. . . the world in general thinks our studies of little consequence; they do not grow more valuable by being stuffed with guesses and inventions' (1. 28). Ignorant of the fact that the effigy on Henry Beaufort's tomb in Winchester Cathedral 'was not placed there until the reign of Charles II,' Walpole writes to Richard Bentley: 'His figure confirms me in my opinion that I have struck out the true history of the picture that I bought of Robinson; and which I take for the marriage of Henry VI' (HWC 35. 250; 18 September 1755, and n. 5).

One of Walpole's motives in buying the Bury St Edmunds altar doors in February 1777 was to confirm his hypothesis about the portraits in the *Marriage of Henry VI*: 'The possession of these boards, invaluable to me,' he wrote William Cole, 'was essential. They authenticate the sagacity of my guesses, a talent in an antiquary coequal with prophecy in a saint' (2. 31; 20 February 1777). Walpole claimed to see on the altar doors portraits of three persons he wanted to find in the picture: '[E]vidently Archbishop Kempe,' he wrote to William Cole, 'or the same person with the prelate in my Marriage of Henry VI – and you will allow from the collateral evidence that it must be Kempe' (2. 31). Another outside figure on the doors 'I believe [to be] Cardinal Beaufort . . . [although] [h]is face is not very like nor very unlike the same person in my picture'. Finally – 'now comes the great point' – he discovered on the altar doors 'Humphrey Duke of Gloucester, kneeling – not only as exactly resembling mine as possible, but with the same almost-bald head, and the precisely same furred robe' (2. 31). Walpole's remarks on the Duke of Gloucester clearly leave the impression that his mania for corroboration of his guesses about the identification of portraits amounts to a parody of antiquarian practices. 'I used to say, to corroborate my hypothesis, that the skull of Duke Humphrey at St Alban's was very like the form of head in my picture, which argument diverted the late Lord Holland [Henry Fox (1705–74)] extremely – but I trust now that nobody will dispute any longer my perfect acquaintance with *all Dukes of Gloucester*' (2. 31; 20 February 1777).

A letter from Walpole to Michael Lort in 1779 thanks him for a manuscript that helped to identify portraits on the Bury doors 'which are incontestably the portraits of Duke Humphrey, Cardinal Beaufort, and the same Archbishop [John Kemp] that is in my "Marriage of Henry VI". . . . The Duke of Gloucester's face is so like, though younger, that it proves I guessed right at his figure in my "Marriage"' (HWC 16. 184; 4 June 1779). After the doors were returned from the restorer, Walpole consulted William Cole about the last figure left to identify, boasting his skill in identifying the others:

> Three are indubitably Duke Humphrey of Gloucester, Cardinal Beaufort and Archbishop Kemp. . . . The Duke and the Archbishop agree perfectly with their portraits in my Marriage of Henry VI and prove how rightly I guessed. The Cardinal's is rather a longer and thinner visage – but that he might have in the latter end of life; and in the Marriage he has the red bonnet on, which shortens his face. On the door he is represented in the character he ought to have possessed, a pious contrite look, not the truer resemblance which Shakespeare drew – 'He dies, and makes no sign!' [*2 Henry VI* III. iii. 29] – but Annibal Caracci [1560–1609] himself could not paint like our Raphael-poet! (2. 219–21; 30 May 1780).

Walpole's hypothesis about the *Marriage of Henry VI* was exploded in the nineteenth century as a 'fantastic theory' by John Gough Nichols:

The picture is really one of those which were not uncommon among the works of painters of religious subjects, intended to represent the marriage of Saint Joseph and the Blessed Virgin, and termed by connoisseurs a *Sposalizio*. The nimbus round the head of the bridegroom, the inscription on the hem of the bride's robe, and the evident indication of her approaching maternity, are all in conformity with the usual conventionalities of the subject, and put out of question Walpole's most fanciful and gratuitous hypothesis. The picture is probably Flemish, and nearly half a century later in date than the marriage of Henry the Sixth.[10]

The Marriage of Henry VII *and the Pleasure of Imaginary Portraits*

Soon after he heard of the death of Thomas Fermor (1698–1753), first Earl Pomfret at Easton Neston, Northamptonshire, where part of the Arundel collection was housed, Walpole calculated the spoils of the estate. '[T]he seat must be stripped,' he told Mann. 'There are a few fine small pictures, and one very curious of Henry VII and his Queen [Elizabeth of York (1466–1503)] with Cardinal Morton [John Morton (1420–1500), Bishop of Ely and Archbishop of Canterbury] and I think the Abbot of Westminster [Jacopo Pasarella, Bishop of Imola (d. 1495)]. Strawberry casts a Gothic eye upon this [plates 36 and 36a], but I fear it will pass our revenues' (20. 390; 21 July 1753). The picture was expensive, but Walpole presents it as a bargain in a note to the Mann correspondence: 'This curious picture was purchased by Lady Pomfret [Henrietta Louisa Jeffreys (1700–61)] for £200. The Earl of Oxford offered her £500 for it. Mr. Walpole bought it at Lord Pomfret's sale for 84 guineas, and it is now at Strawberry Hill' (20. 390; n. 10; 21 July 1753). In the same note Walpole identifies the subject and *dramatis personae* of the picture: 'It is the marriage of Henry VII and Elizabeth of York. The two other figures are probably St Thomas and the Bishop of Imola, the Pope's nuncio, who pronounced the nuptial benediction' (20. 390).

Walpole's identifications of portraits in the picture appear to derive from claims made by the Pomfrets at the sale, the advice of the poet Thomas Gray, and the notebooks of George Vertue. Thomas Gray, the most distinguished member of Walpole's antiquarian Committee of Taste, responded to Walpole's query about the picture early in February 1754 with an apology for finding little 'to your purpose' (14. 78), but in fact we have seen how well Gray served Walpole's purpose by populating a picture of unknown figures with an interesting cast of characters. So it was appropriate for Gray to make a suggestion in one sentence that he withdraws in the next: 'This [Thomas Otterbourne's *Chronicles of English Kings* (*post* 1420)] seemed to account for St Thomas' attending Elizabeth of York as the future annointed Queen of England. But alas! on second thoughts these words must mean St Thomas Becket' (14. 79; 3 March 1754). Similarly, Gray gives Walpole a choice of identifications for King Henry's attendant to the spectator's right: 'If you are sure the person who accompanies the King is a cardinal, it must be Bourchier [Thomas (1404–86), Archbishop of Canterbury 1454–86]. . . . but I take

36.   Before restoration, attributed to Jan Gossaert, a *sposalizio* HW called *The Marriage of Henry VII*. Oil on panel, 25 × 40¾ in. Fifteenth century. Private Collection. Photo: Artemis Fine Arts Ltd., London. 'Strawberry casts a Gothic eye upon this [picture], but I fear it will pass our revenues' (HWC 20. 390).

36A.   After restoration, attributed to Hugo van der Goes, *Virgin and Child with Saints* HW called *The Marriage of Henry VII*. Oil on wood, 44 × 55⅛ in. *c.* 1472. Private Collection on loan to the Metropolitan Museum of Art, New York. '. . . I fear we may multiply conjectures, and yet not ascertain the specific person intended' (HWC 16. 234).

the person there represented to be James, Bishop of Imola [Jacopo Pasarella], who granted the dispensation for this marriage' (14. 79).

When Walpole made his identifications in the letter to Mann (20. 390; 21 July 1753) he had not yet purchased Vertue's notebooks; later he annotated Vertue's report on the picture with his collector's halleluiah 'now Mr Walpole's' (GVN 4. 38). On a visit to Easton Neston in 1732 Vertue stated unequivocally: 'This picture is called by Lady Pomfret the Marriage of King Henry VII to Elizabeth of York' (GVN 4. 38). But Vertue's agnostic description of the picture allows room for doubt whether the picture portrays Henry VII's marriage: 'a picture representing a King, sceptre in his hand, and a Bishop with a crosier; on the right of the picture [spectator's left] is an old grave man with a young lady in white attire, and the perspective of a church, all very neat and curious. The King is called King Henry VII, the Bishop Moreton [John Morton]' (GVN 4. 38). Vertue's scepticism shines through the repeated use of the verb 'called,' and he is full of uncertainty about the identification of the attendant figures. Vertue remarks that 'the Hermit or Bishop' accompanying Elizabeth of York is 'unknown,' and he cites three authorities challenging the identification of John Morton.

Walpole's research on his *Marriage of Henry VII* is predictably less scholarly and cautious than Vertue's. He relies as usual on his Committee of Taste, making sure the members know what they are expected to find; and once again he depends upon 'the sagacity of my guesses' (2.31). In November 1762 Walpole wrote to another member of his anti-quarian committee, the reverend William Cole, to arrange a visit to Christ College, Cambridge, to compare portraits of Henry VII on glass at the college 'to see how far . . . [they] agree with his portrait in my picture of his marriage' (1. 32; 13 November 1762).

When Walpole wrote his chapter on the 'State of Painting to the End of Henry VII' in the *Anecdotes of Painting*, he decided, on unknown evidence, to attribute the picture to Jan Gossaert (1478–1535), called John Mabuse. He supplies an illustration (*Works* 3, facing p. 54), reiterates his boast about his bargain at eighty-four pounds, and admits that the church is 'an imaginary one', not Westminster Abbey 'where those princes were married' (*Anecdotes* 1. 54). Walpole accepts one of Gray's identifications, the king's attendant, the Bishop of Imola. However, for the queen's attendant, Walpole adopts St Thomas whom Gray rejected. Finally Walpole describes the royal portraits: 'His Majesty [Henry VII, "extremely like his profile on a shilling" (HW's n. 4)] is a trist, lean, ungracious figure, with a downcast look, very expressive of his mean temper, and of the little satisfaction he had in the match. Opposite to the bishop [Imola] is the queen [Elizabeth of York], a buxom well-looking damsel, with golden hair' (*Anecdotes* 1. 54).

When Walpole presented his *Anecdotes of Painting* to the lawyer and 'ostrich of an antiquary' (HWC 36. 38–9), Andrew Ducarel (1713–85), he received in reply on 23 February 1762 an 'anecdote,' an iconoclastic statement George Vertue had sent to Ducarel 28 January 1754 dismissing the so-called *Marriage of Henry VII* as a fake sold to the Pomfrets by a corrupt picture dealer, William Sykes (1659–1724). In the twenty or more years since Vertue had visited Easton Neston, his scepticism about the portraits had grown from mere suspicion to a conviction that the picture was a fraud. According to Ducarel's summary (HWC 40. 215–16; 23 February 1762), Vertue told him:

> [t]hat Lord Pomfret bought his picture of one Old Sykes above 30 years ago [*ante* 1724] . . . [that] Sykes dealt in pictures and was a noted tricker – that he (Sykes) gave it that name [*Marriage of Henry VII*], well knowing how to give names to pictures to make them sell – that George Vertue had carefully examined that picture, Lord Pomfret having once a design that he should engrave it, which was not done because Vertue could not spare time to go to Easton for that purpose – that Lord Pomfret had often promised him to send it to London to be engraven which he never did – that upon the strictest examination Vertue could never be convinced that the man was Henry VII, the face not appearing to him like any of the pictures he had seen of that king – that as to the woman, she had pomegrantes upon her clothes, which certainly did not belong to her – that the church in which they are married, as represented in the picture, did not appear to be any English church, and that, upon the whole, it was suspected, at the time that Lord Pomfret bought it, that Old Sykes, who was a rogue, had caused the figures and representation of the marriage, to be added to the representation of the inside of a church, Old Sykes having before been guilty of many pranks of that sort (HWC 40. 215–16; 23 February 1762).

Walpole replied the next day, vehemently dismissing Vertue's doubts as 'a heap of ridiculous contradictions' (HWC 40. 219; 24 February 1762). He questions the suggestion of Sykes's fraud by quibbling about a contradiction in Vertue's story: 'He [Vertue] said, *Sykes knowing how to give names to pictures to make them sell*, called this the marriage of Henry VII and afterwards, he said, Sykes had the figures inserted in an old picture of a church'. As if Sykes could not have christened pictures fraudulently as easily as having figures inserted in an architectural interior, Walpole the prosecutor concludes triumphantly: 'He [Sykes] must have known little indeed, Sir, if he had not known how to name a picture that he had painted on purpose that he might call it so!' (HWC 40. 219). Walpole offers nothing to extenuate Sykes's reputation for dishonesty, but he is on firmer ground when he challenges Vertue's doubts about the portraits: 'That Vertue . . . could not be convinced that his man was Henry VII,' Walpole writes ironically, '[u]nluckily he is extremely like the shilling, which is much more authentic than any picture of Henry VII' (40. 219).[11] But Vertue reported Sykes's adding the figures as a rumor ('it was suspected, at the time'), and the ineptitude of a confidence man is no argument for authenticity. Walpole concludes with harsh words about 'honest' George Vertue (HWC 1. 207), whom he had previously repeatedly remarked was incapable of falsehood (14. 107): 'If Vertue had made no better criticisms than these, I would never had taken so much trouble with his MSS' (40. 219).

Ducarel quickly capitulated to Walpole's countercheck quarrelsome: 'As to the remarks contained in my last,' Ducarel wrote contritely a few days later:

> if any of them have given you the least uneasiness, I am very sorry for it – Vertue's note about your picture of Henry VII I sent you just as Vertue gave it me – for I was so far from laying any stress upon it, and from believing it not to be Henry VII's marriage that I went twice to Easton on purpose to see that picture, and was long since convinced that it is not only what you say, but likewise one of the finest English historical pictures I ever yet beheld (40. 222; 27 February 1762).]

Walpole's outburst at Vertue shows that the Prime Minister of Taste was prepared to overrule his privy councillor for portaits when a picture Strawberry Hill had cast its Gothic eye upon was in question. Walpole had little patience with nay-saying antiquaries who spoiled his game of make-believe. Witness his comment on those antiquaries who denied the identity of a statue of Henry VII that turned up in the rebuilding of Ely cathedral. Walpole wrote to William Cole:

> Pray what is become of that figure [statue] you mention of Henry VII, which the destroyers, not the builders, have rejected? and which the antiquaries, who know a man by his crown better than by his face, have rejected likewise? The latter [sceptical antiquaries] put me in mind of characters in comedies, in which a woman disguised in a man's habit and whose features her very lover does not know, is immediately acknowledged by pulling off her hat and letting down her hair, which her lover had never seen before (HWC 1. 279; 28 August 1772).

Walpole's pictures of medieval royal marriages were the perfect furnishings for a Gothic castle, and in acquiring them Walpole did not hesitate to set aside the scholarly ideal he stated in a letter to the antiquary Sir John Fenn (1739–94) about identifying English portraits in the time of Henry VII:

> In short, Sir, I fear we may multiply conjectures, and yet not ascertain the specific person intended, as there are only marks enough to furnish guesses, and we have not lights from that age sufficient to identify the person. I wish I could have given you better assistance; but I had rather leave obscurities in their darkness, than as most antiquaries do, pronounce rashly. Truth is the sole merit of most antiquities; and when we cannot discover the truth, what value is there in dogmatic error about things that have no intrinsic value? – and such were all our pictures before Holbein, and infinitely the greater part of our pictures since! (HWC 16. 234; 17 September 1774).

On the contrary, imaginary portraits like the *Marriage of Henry VII* had enormous value to Walpole in furnishing a Gothic house with stage scenery.

Recent conservation and restoration reveals that Walpole's painting of *The Marriage of Henry VII* (plate 36A) was a *sposalizio* like his *Marriage of Henry VI*. 'In the early seventeenth century the paint layers on the figures of the Virgin and Child and Saint John the Baptist were scraped off and repainted with a representation of the Marriage of Henry VII and Elizabeth of York'.[12] We can reasonably suspect that Walpole added some of his own imaginary portraits to this palimpsest.

Catherine Parr's Corpse

Late in life Walpole claimed 'I am descended from . . . [Catherine Parr] by her first [husband]' (HWC 12. 165; 1795). He cherished a miniature portrait of Catherine Parr attributed to Holbein in the rosewood cabinet of the Tribune at Strawberry Hill: 'Catherine Parr, by Holbein; a most scarce head, and exactly like the picture of her at the earl of Denbigh's at Nuneham Padox, Warwickshire' (*Works* 2. 476). When Walpole visited Newnham Paddox in September 1768 he was probably comparing his miniature of Catherine Parr to the Earl of Denbigh's full-length portrait, but the family curator did not inspire confidence, and he was still trying to verify the identification in 1794: 'I am much obliged to Lord Ossory [John Fitzpatrick (1745–1818)] for his, though vain, hunt after a portrait of Catherine Parr. I have a small damaged one by Holbein that I believe of her, as it resembles a whole length called hers too at Lord Denbigh's, but his Dutch mother [Isabella de Jong (1693–1769)] or more than Dutch father [William Feilding (1697–1755), 5th Earl of Denbigh] had so blundered or falsified many of the names, though there are many valuable and some fine portraits, that I could depend on few' (HWC 34. 208; 8 December 1794).

Walpole compared the 'passion for portraits of remarkable persons' (*Anecdotes* 1. 192) in the Elizabethan period to his own time, but the zeal of his contemporaries for royal portraits even reached into the tomb. Shortly after the publication of the first volume of James Granger's *Biographical History* (May 1769) George Montagu was inspired to 'rove about' Sudeley Castle, Gloucestershire, in search of the grave of Catherine Parr that Granger located in the chapel there. Montagu wrote Walpole he was sure he had found it: 'I saw in the vault there a Lady Sudely – 'twas Catherine Parr undoubtedly, for I have since found she was buried there' (HWC 10. 285, 25 August 1769). Montagu was mistaken, because the grave was not discovered until 1782 when 'Mr Lucas, a gentleman of fortune and veracity', and 'some ladies who happened to be at the castle in May 1782' unearthed her remains (HWC 42. 112, and n. 5; 8 September 1784).

William Fermor, son of one of Walpole's Twickenham neighbours, interviewed Mr Lucas at Walpole's request, and wrote from his seat in Tusmore, Oxfordshire, describing in loving detail what they had found when they 'opened the grave where Catherine Parr was buried' near the altar rail in the chapel at Sudeley Castle:

> She lay about two feet from the surface of the ground, as it now is, a pavement having been removed some years ago for the purpose of repairs. The following was the appearance of the body – it was of a light brown colour, the flesh soft and moist, and the weight of the hand and arm as those of a living body of the same size. The appearance of the features was rather pleasing than otherwise, Mr Lucas remarking that he had seen many bodies recently dead wearing a much more unpleasing aspect. The teeth were perfect and of the best sort, and the nails in great preservation. She was rather of a low

stature. The body was perfectly sweet and showed no marks of decay. She was clad, one may say, in a leaden doublet, which was made to fit exactly her body, arms, and legs, and entirely covered her face. Between this lead and the body was a thickness of linen cloths, twelve or fourteen double, which appeared to have been dipped in some composition, in order to preserve them, which had answered the end so completely, that it was with difficulty they could be separated with a large knife. There were neither earrings in the ears, nor any ring upon the fingers of the hand they examined; the other hand they did not remove from its leaden case. She had the following inscription in very ill-formed letters on the upper part of the lead over her breast: /Katherine Parr 6th and last wife to Henry the 8th (HWC 42. 113; 8 September 1784).

Walpole may have thought this conscientious report more the work of an owl than a nightingale, but he thanked Fermor for 'such very curious information'. 'I had never heard of that discovery of Queen Catherine Parr's corpse, and am ignorant of its having ever been published. If it was not, it was depriving the public of a very singular event: and it is much pity that no drawing was made of her Majesty's face, nor any precautions taken to preserve the body in the state it was found' (HWC 42. 114; 16 September 1784). Walpole's thank-you note to Fermor had been polite and perfunctory, but it encouraged Fermor to tell more. Ten days later he confided to Walpole his motives for pursuing his '[singular] discovery of Catherine Parr's corpse':

A circumstance so striking in the history of preservation excited my curiosity when in Gloucestershire, and induced me to go to the spot to inquire into the truth of what I had heard asserted by some friends living in that neighbourhood; the result of my inquiries and the testimonies of creditable living witnesses, I had the honour of transmitting to you, and I am happy to find, Sir, they afforded you the least entertainment (HWC 42. 115; 26 September 1784).

The obliging William Fermor transcribed for Walpole a letter dated 1548 from Queen Elizabeth I to Catherine Parr, 'testimonial of the great regard the Queen had for her, and of her then pregnant state, to which the Queen unequivocally alludes' (42. 116). Fermor concludes his letter with a comment on the corpse that would do credit to Jessica Mitford's undertakers at Forest Lawn:

I beg leave to remark here, that we probably owe the high preservation of the body amongst other circumstances to that state she was taken off in, as we may reasonably suppose she was in perfect health; before disorder had destroyed or impaired materially any part of the structure which very probably was committed to the earth, as indeed most of the bodies of Henry VIII's wives were, with little or no blood remaining (HWC 42. 116–17; 26 September 1784).

Walpole could not repress his disappointment that no portrait had been taken of the remains of Catherine Parr's face, but Treadway Russell Nash, who was preparing an article on the discovery for the Society of Antiquaries, sent Walpole a print of 'The Body of Queen Katherine Parr, found at Sudely Castle in Gloucestershire 1782' (HWC 43.

37.   Line engraving: *The Body of Queen Katherine Parr Found at Sudely Castle 1782*. *Archaeologia* (London: J. Nichols, 1789). Courtesy of the Lewis Walpole Library, Yale University. 'I had never heard of that discovery of Queen Catherine Parr's corpse. . . it is much pity that no drawing was made of her Majesty's face' (HWC 42. 114).

385). Nash's 'Observations on the Time of the Death and Place of burial of Queen Catharine Parr' appeared in *Archaeologia* (9 [1789]: 1–9) with the same print as frontispiece (plate 37). The year before he died Walpole encouraged the Berry sisters to visit Sudeley Castle and the remains of his relative: 'I would you had been advertised to say a mass for your great-grandmother' (HWC 12. 165; 12 September 1795).

One could not ask for a more vivid illustration of Walpole's mania for royal portraiture. Iconic portraits ornamented with arms, cyphers, mottos, impresa, and inscriptions all signify the pomp and circumstance of royalty. But how can icons compare to the body itself? Here the atavistic, Egyptian zeal for preserving Pharaonic ancestors in the Pyramids makes common cause with eighteenth-century ladies and gentlemen poking through the ruins of Sudeley Castle. In their enthusiasm the amateur antiquarians did not understand the science of mummification or embalming. Two years after the first opening of Catherine Parr's grave, Nash reports another visitation of connoisseurs of corpses: 'In May 1784 some persons having curiosity again to open the grave, found that the air, rain, and dirt, having come to the face, it was entirely destroyed, and nothing left but the bones.' (HWC 42. 113, n. 7).

CHAPTER 6

Portraits at Strawberry Hill – II

'Monumenting' Portraits

Walpole's miscellaneous records of royal portraits can best be described by the verb 'monumenting', which he applies to the Countess of Oxford's care of portraits at Welbeck, Nottinghamshire. Walpole visited Welbeck within a year of her death on 5 December 1755, and he went into a rapture:

> Oh! portraits! – I went to Welbeck – It is impossible to describe the bales of Cavendishes, Harleys, Holleses, Veres, and Ogles: every chamber is tapestried with them; nay, and with ten thousand other fat morsels; all their histories inscribed; all their arms, crests, devices, sculptured on chimneys of various English marbles in ancient forms (and, to say truth, most of them ugly). Then such a Gothic hall, with pendent fretwork in imitation of the old, and with a chimney-piece extremely like mine in the library [at Strawberry Hill]! Such water-colour pictures! such historic fragments! In short, such and so much of everything I like, that my party thought they should never get me away again. . . . But it is impossible to tell you [Richard Bentley] half what there is. The poor woman [Henrietta Cavendish (1694–1755), Countess of Oxford] who is just dead, passed her whole widowhood . . . in collecting and monumenting the portraits and reliques of all the great families from which she descended, and which centered in her (35. 270–71; August 1756).

'Monumenting' portraits means to inscribe their histories, arms, crests, and devices. Walpole's idea of monumenting portraits resembles the portrait engravings of George Vertue, which literally surround the illustrious heads of subjects with a monumental frame, frequently an oval medallion surmounting a pedestal ornamented with attributes of the life and works of the subject. How Walpole builds his literary correlative to Vertue's frames as a collector of portraits can be conveniently introduced by his apology for a catalogue of the portraits at Woburn Abbey, Bedfordshire, which he had rashly promised in old age to Francis Russell (1765–1802), 5th Duke of Bedford. We will then consider the way he monuments the portraits of three countesses at Strawberry Hill.

Suffering from gout and failing memory in June 1791, Walpole began to annotate an existing list of the portraits at Woburn, possibly one of George Vertue's inventories (GVN 2. 37–8, 40–1). Walpole's apology for his catalogue of the Woburn portraits gives us a clear insight into what he meant by monumenting English portraits. '. . . I can neither lift nor turn over folios of genealogies, for though I used to know who begat whom, like a chapter in Genesis, my memory is not so triflingly circumstantial now, and I might create scandal backwards two centuries ago' (HWC 34. 115–16).

The Woburn portrait of Christian [Christina] Bruce (1595–1675), Countess of Devonshire, illustrates Walpole's method of monumenting 'by collecting scattered incidents and putting them together' in what he calls a 'kind of assemblage' (HWC 34. 128). Walpole compiled his character of the countess from at least three different books in his library. From William Herbert (1580–1630), 3rd Earl of Pembroke's *Poems* (1660; Hazen 207) and from Thomas Pomfret's *Life* (1685; Hazen 3900), he learned that Christina 'was the platonic mistress of William, earl of Pembroke'. From Elijah Fenton he discovered the countess's house was 'Mr Waller's chief theatre'.[1] Walpole admired her practical ability as an estate manager as much as her patronage of poets: 'Upon the whole, her ladyship seems to have been a fair model of our ancient nobility, a compound of piety, regularity, dignity, and human wisdom, so discreetly classed, as to suffer none of them to trespass on the interests of its associates.'[2]

Walpole's model for his literary character-portraits here and elsewhere is Edward Hyde (1609–74), Earl of Clarendon, whom he praises for his character of William Herbert, 3rd Earl of Pembroke (1580–1630), Christina's platonic lover, and compares to Van Dyck in the *Royal and Noble Authors*:

His [Pembroke's] character is not only one of the most amiable in lord Clarendon's History, but is one of the best drawn: not being marked with any strong lines, it distinguishes the delicacy of that happy pencil [paint-brush], to which the real pencil must yield of the renowned portrait-painter of that age. – Vandyck little thought, when he drew sir Edward Hyde, that a greater master than himself was sitting to him. They had indeed great resemblance in their manners; each copied *nature* faithfully. Vandyck's men are not all of exact height and symmetry, of equal corpulence; his women are not Madonnas or Venuses: the likeness seems to have been studied in all, the character in many: his dresses are those of the times. The historian's fidelity is as remarkable; he represents the folds and plaits, the windings and turnings of each character he draws; and though he varies the lights and shades as would best produce the effect he designs, yet his colours are never those of imagination, nor disposed without a singular propriety. Hampden is not painted in the armour of Brutus, nor would Cromwell's mask fit either Julius or Tiberius (*Works* 1. 347–48).[3]

Admiration for Clarendon's characters coexists in Walpole's mind with a gentleman's sceptical attitude towards the value of historical inquiry:

Genealogy and pedigrees . . . become useful in the study of history, if the study itself of history is useful, which I doubt, considering how little real truth it communicates, and how much falsehood it teaches us to believe. Indeed considering how very little truth we can gain from the study of anything, I question whether there is any other good in what is called learning, than its enabling us to converse on an equal foot with those who think they possess knowledge because they have acquainted themselves with the imperfect scraps of what passes for science (HWC 34. 128; 26 October 1791).

But Walpole's scepticism about history does not represent a settled philosophical conviction. Less than a month later he is comparing two contemporary historians in terms that imply some faith in the humanist's creed. William Robertson (1721–93) falls short of Edward Gibbon (1737–94) because 'he cannot melt his materials together, and make them elucidate and even improve and produce new discoveries – in short, he cannot like Mr Gibbon make an *original* picture with some bits of mosaic' (HWC 34. 131–32; 23 November 1791). Such an 'original picture' clearly defines the concept underlying Walpole's process of 'monumenting' portraits throughout his career as a collector. He is constantly composing in his mind an imaginary museum of portraits, each one an original picture made of a mosaic of antiquarian sources.

Lady Frances Howard (1589–1632) 'Madame l'Empoisonneuse'

Walpole's picture of Frances Howard was a copy of the portrait of an uncertainly identified sitter by an unknown artist, a picture he admired on a visit to 'this purgatory of antiquities' at Woburn Abbey, Bedfordshire in October 1751. Walpole described the picture then as 'Madame l'Empoisonneuse, that married Carr Earl of Somerset – she is pretty' (9. 124). Walpole gives his fullest description of the portrait in 'Notes on the Pictures at Woburn Abbey' (1791):

> Frances Howard, a daughter of the lord treasurer Suffolk [Lord Thomas Howard (1561–1626), 1st Earl], married first to Robert, earl of Essex, and then to Robert Carr, earl of Somerset, favourite of James the first, by a sentence of nullity, that fell bitterly on the under agents, disgraced the prelates who pronounced it, and caused the ruin and discontent of the parties concerned, who, tradition says, grew to live under the same roof with the utmost hatred and estrangement.[4]

Although he allowed her portrait at Woburn no more than an epithet and an adjective in his letter to Montagu, Walpole thought enough of the Woburn portrait to have a copy made by Margaret Smith, Lady Lucan (d. 1814), one of his favourites in his academy of female amateurs. The most authoritative catalogue of the Woburn portraits challenges the identification of the Woburn portrait, asserting that it is not a picture of Frances Howard but her mother, Frances Knyvett (1563–1638), Countess of Suffolk (HWC 9. 124, n. 8).[5] Walpole cannot be faulted for mistaking the identification, an error made by his mentor George Vertue (GVN 2. 41). As usual what mattered to Walpole was not the name of the artist, or proof of the sitter's identity, but the opportunity to 'monument' a character. The scandalous chronicle of Frances Howard, Countess of Essex and Somerset concerned her plot to divorce her first husband, Robert Devereux (1591–1646), 3rd Earl of Essex, and marry Robert Carr, Earl of Somerset (1587–1645). This was against the opposition of Sir Edward Coke (1552–1634), Lord Chief Justice, and Somerset's friend, Sir Thomas Overbury (1581–1613), whom the bridal couple had imprisoned and slowly poisoned in the Tower. Frances Howard and Carr were married on 26 December 1613, tried and convicted on 24 May 1616 for the murder of Overbury, condemned to death, later pardoned by the king, and imprisoned in the Tower from 1616 to 1622.

The melodramatic history of this murder came down to Walpole in manuscripts, histories, state trials, autograph letters, and conversation with antiquarian friends. He contributed his own mite to the narrative in his account of '*my* Lord Northampton' (30. 258), Frances Howard's great-uncle, Henry Howard (1540–1614), whom he characterized in his *Catalogue of Royal and Noble Authors* (1758) as a villain who 'became a chief and shocking instrument in that lord's [Robert Carr, Earl of Somerset's] match with Northampton's kinswoman the countess of Essex, and of the succeeding murder of sir Thomas Overbury' (*Works* 1. 338). Walpole dismisses the panegyrics of genealogists 'who winnow the characters of all mankind, and take due care not to lay up any of the chaff – But what have our historians to say of this man! What a tale to tell of murder' (*Works* 1. 335). Although he was aware of bias and credulity in sources now regarded as collections of gossip, Walpole took what he needed from the heteroglossia in his own library to document Northampton's treachery and blacken his character.[6] He quotes descriptions of Northampton as '*a dangerous, intelligencing man,*' '*a subtle papist,*' and 'one of the grossest flatterers alive' (*Works* 1. 335–6). He relies chiefly on the manuscript of a book published in 1643 that he attributed erroneously to Fulke Greville: *Five Years of the Reign of James I with the Rise and Fall of the Earl of Somerset, Sir Thomas Overbury, &c.* (Hazen 87).

The antiquary Michael Lort supplied him with transcripts of correspondence 'fully explanatory of Northampton's share in that black business' (*Works* 1. 340). 'Northampton, the pious endower of hospitals, died luckily before the plot came to light; but his letters were read in court – not all, for there was such a horrid mixture of obscenity and blood in them, that the chief justice could not go through them in common decency' (*Works* 1. 338). Lort expected the letters to provide 'circumstantial proof of Northampton's guilt. . . . [but] circumstances rather led me to acquit Northampton' (HWC 16. 162; 2 June 1765). Unlike Lort, Walpole was not prepared to let his *bête noir* off the hook, and Winwood's *Memorials* (Hazen 1100) convinced him of Northampton's guilt (*Works* 1. 340, n.).

Characteristically Walpole's antiquarian quest to monument Frances Howard's portraits extended even to her family's house. As early as 1735 he visited Audley End, Essex, the Prodigy House built between 1603 and 1616 by the Countess of Somerset's father, Thomas Howard, 1st Earl of Suffolk (1561–1626). '[W]e saw a great castle belonging to the Counts of Suffolcia,' he wrote in a parody of Joseph Addison's *Travels* (Hazen 1844) to Thomas Gray: ''tis a vast pile of building, but quite in the old taste' (HWC 13. 88; 15 October 1735). While writing the *Anecdotes* in May 1762 Walpole revisited the ruins of the Howards's seat at Audley End, Essex, on the way to Cambridge: '[I]t is only the monument now of its former grandeur. The gallery is pulled down, and nothing remains but the great hall and an apartment like a tower at each end. In the church I found, still existing and quite fresh, the escutcheon of the famous Countess of Essex and Somerset' (HWC 10. 30; 14 May 1762). At the sale of Dr Richard Mead's library in December 1754 Walpole had given an 'unlimited commission' to Josiah Graham, a London bookseller, to buy twenty-four plans and views of Audley End by Henry Winstanley, but was relieved to be outbid at 50 guineas for a book he later acquired more inexpensively (HWC 35. 196–7; Hazen 3480). Writing of the architecture in the reign of James I Walpole describes Audley as 'one of the wonders of that age [deserving] little notice but for the prodigious space it covered,' but he also cites Sir William Dugdale's opinion 'that this house was not to be equalled by any fabric in this realm excepting Hampton-court'. (*Anecdotes* 1. 208 n. 2, and 209).

'Tis pity that in noblemen's galleries the names are not writt on or behind the pictures', John Aubrey wrote.[7] Walpole might have echoed this complaint when he acquired another doubtful portrait called the Countess of Somerset now regarded as the masterpiece of Isaac Oliver (d. 1617) at the sale of 'one of our brother antiquaries' (HWC 1. 265), James West's collection at Langford's in Covent Garden 6 May 1773. Thomas Morgan, a china-merchant living in Arlington Street near Walpole, bought the picture (lot 74) for him at the bargain price of £3 17s 6d. The picture was described in West's catalogue as '[a] large and remarkably fine head of the Countess of Somerset' (plate 38). A collector after John Aubrey's heart, Walpole wrote his identification on a paper label attached to the back of the picture, refining on the catalogue entry: 'Lady Frances Howard, Countess of Essex and Somerset, by Isaac Oliver, from the collection of James West, President of the Royal Society. H.W. 1773.'[8] Walpole had little respect for West as a connoisseur – 'In truth Mr West's authority was not very good. His knowledge, judgment . . . were not to be depended on' (HWC 42. 247; 27 June 1789) – but he was happy to acknowledge the provenance of a president of the Royal Society in the *Description of Strawberry Hill* (*Works* 2. 489). Walpole knew West's collection intimately, and had drawn up in 1760 a list of his pictures (HWC 20. 371, n. 3). He had been disappointed to get 'literally nothing' at West's sale of prints sold for 'frantic' sums (HWC 1. 300; 18 February 1773), and his books sold 'outrageously' (HWC 1. 305; 7 April 1773), but he did get the *Marriage of Henry VI* he coveted, and the miniature now regarded as 'Oliver's most beautiful picture', 'his masterpiece'.

Graham Reynolds comments that Walpole's taste in acquiring this picture 'seems startlingly up-to-date', but Walpole seems to have preferred Lady Lucan's copy of Lady Somerset when young to Oliver's miniature 'when old, original, but faded' (HWC 15. 192). Modern art-historians can hardly contain their enthusiasm for 'the exquisite large miniature', 'an Elizabethan Mona Lisa'.[9] Both sitter and date remain in doubt, but it is speculated that the picture may have been a wedding portrait of Frances Howard in masquerade costume, celebrating her first marriage to Robert Devereux, Earl of Essex in 1606, a marriage which occasioned Inigo Jones's masque *Hymenai*.[10] This appealing hypothesis allows for the possibility that Walpole could have seen in this portrait of the Countess of Somerset one of those 'old pictures . . . [that] walked out of their frames' (HWC 17. 339) at the masquerade he attended as Aurengzebe, a character from Dryden's play, on Wednesday 17 February 1742 in London.

Portrait of Frances Brydges (1580–1663), Countess of Exeter

Walpole takes as much pleasure in monumenting the portrait of a saint, Frances Brydges, Countess of Exeter, as he does in the portrait of a sinner, the Countess of Somerset: 'Whether the Charmer sinner it, or saint it,/If Folly grows romantic, I must paint it.'[11] Few portraits in Walpole's collection illustrate more clearly the difference between his antiquarian interest in portraiture and that of the connoisseurs.

Walpole's catalogue entry in the *Description of Strawberry Hill* for Van Dyck's portrait of Frances Brydges, Countess of Exeter (plate 39), indicates four aspects of his interest

38.   Isaac Oliver: *A Lady Called Frances of Somerset.c.* 1606. Miniature, 5 inches in diameter. Victoria & Albert Museum. Photo: V&A Picture Library. 'Madame L'Empoisonneuse, that married Carr Earl of Somerset – she is pretty' (HWC 9. 124).

39.   Jonathan Richardson, Sr. after Sir Anthony Van Dyck: *Frances Brydges, Countess of Exeter.* From the Burghley House Collection. Photo: Photographic Survey, Courtauld Institute of Art. 'This lady was most falsely accused of many crimes, of which she was entirely innocent, and acquitted' (*Works* 2. 463, n.).

in the portrait: its acquisition from the portrait painter Thomas Hudson; a critical essay by the painter Jonathan Richardson; an anecdote about her husband's tomb; and James Granger's anecdotal account of the sitter's history. Here is Walpole's catalogue entry:

> Frances Bridges, daughter of the lord Chandos, and second wife of Thomas Cecil earl of Exeter, on whose left hand she refused to lie on his tomb in Westminster-abbey. This picture, which is an excellent one of Vandyck, belonged to Richardson the painter, who has written a dissertation of eight pages on it in one of his books. It was purchased of Hudson the painter, son-in-law of Richardson' (*Works* 2. 463).

Walpole adds the note: 'This lady was most falsely accused of many crimes, of which she was entirely innocent, and acquitted. . . . see an account in Granger's Biographical History of English Portraits, vol. i. p. 548' (*Works* 2. 463).

To begin with Walpole's acquisition of the portrait, by about 1755 Reynolds's student and Richardson's son-in-law, Thomas Hudson (1701–79), the portrait painter, had become Walpole's Twickenham neighbour (35. 234). Vertue says that Hudson 'bought much [at Jonathan Richardson's sale, February 1747], many drawings to make a collection, also several of his best paintings that cost good sums' (GVN 3. 135). These circumstances appear to explain Walpole's connection with Hudson and his purchase: 'I bought . . . after the death of Richardson the painter, the picture of the Countess of Exeter, which he has described so largely in one of his treatises' (*Anecdotes* 1. 327).

Turning to Richardson's 'dissertation' on the portrait in *Two Discourses* (1719; Hazen 310), Richardson applies to Van Dyck's portrait of the Countess of Exeter the calculus of sublimity he borrowed from Roger de Piles's *Art of Painting* (1706; Hazen 308). De Piles provided a mathematical grading of the parts of painting derived from Renaissance humanistic theory.[12] Richardson begins by saying that prints like William Faithorne's can tell nothing but the size of the picture, three-quarter length. He goes on to complain that the composition is defective, but he admires the 'extreamly beautiful' colouring, and praises the face and hands as 'a model for a pencil in portrait painting' (*Essay on Painting* 185). Richardson is most impressed by the 'beauty and propriety . . . [of] Van Dyck's thought . . . [depicting] the lady . . . sitting in her own room receiving a visit of condolence from an inferior with great benignity. . . . For by this the picture is not an insipid representation of a face and dress, but here is also a picture of the mind, and what more proper to a widow than sorrow? and more becoming a person of quality than humility and benevolence?' (*Essay on Painting* 186–7).

When he comes to 'expression,' the sixth part of humanistic painting, Richardson praises Van Dyck for the tranquil and decent sadness that appears on her countenance: 'Not Guido Reni, no, nor Raphael himself could have conceived a passion with more delicacy, or more strongly expressed it!' (*Essay on Painting* 187). The attitude of the figure, the negligent air in the fall of the hands, produces a sublimity of expression abundantly compensating for everything the composition lacks. This allows Richardson to award the picture the epithets 'grace and greatness' (*Essay on Painting* 188), accolades for the sublime – a bold claim for a portrait since academic dogma limited the sublime to history paintings.

To De Piles's Catholic calculus of the parts of painting Richardson adds two Protestant categories, 'pleasure' and 'advantage' or 'utility' (*Essay on Painting* 188). The thought of 'pleasure' seems out of character for this formal, earnest, and evangelical artist, but 'advantage' turns out to mean the power of the picture to move an uxorious man: 'there is . . . such a decent sorrow and resignation expressed here, that a man must be very insensible that is not the better for considering it. . . . I confess I am particularly affected with . . . the circumstance of widowhood . . .' (*Essay on Painting* 189). Richardson is finally prepared to add up the point scores in two columns (one for the face; another for the whole portrait) for each of seven categories (*Essay on Painting* 190). On a scale of twenty, the 'face' gets all seventeens and eighteens, except for composition and drawing (ten each), but the whole picture scores all eighteens except for drawing (seventeen); and the bottom line spells out the sought-after epithet 'Sublime,' sixteen for Pleasure, and eighteen for Advantage!

Walpole admired Richardson's 'profound . . . reflections on his art', while recognizing the 'quaintness' of his literary style, and 'the difficulty the author had to convey mere visible ideas through the medium of language' (*Anecdotes* 2. 275). But it is most unlikely that Walpole would have understood Richardson's arithmetical rating system of the same portrait. 'I am a woeful arithmetician' (33. 365), Walpole wrote, and the concept of the sublime was quite foreign to his sensibility. It is equally improbable that Walpole would have appreciated Richardson's conscientious dissertation on the 'statistically significant sublimity' of the Countess of Exeter's portrait,[13] because he was primarily interested in her life rather than Van Dyck's art.

In his teens Walpole had already collected the anecdote about the countess's refusal to be portrayed on the Westminster Abbey tomb of her husband, Thomas Cecil, Earl of Exeter (d. 1623; HWC 9. 7; 30 May 1736). In the Strawberry Hill *Description* Walpole refers to a source he preferred to Richardson's dissertation, James Granger's *Biographical History of England* (1769; Hazen 541), which is a catalogue of English portrait engravings, a work Granger based on Walpole's collection, dedicated to Walpole, and organized by Walpole's method of arranging prints according to reigns and classes (40. 313, n.3). Before the publication of the first volume in 1769, Walpole feared that Granger's 'laborious and curious catalogue of English heads, with an accurate though succinct account of all the persons,' might appeal only to collectors: 'I hope the anecdotic part will make it more known and tasted. It is essential to us, who shall love the performance, that it should sell' (HWC 1. 151; 20 August 1768).

The 'anecdotic part' of Granger's account of William Faithorne's print summarizes the Countess of Exeter's persecution in a conspiracy of her husband's relations, the violent and wicked Ladies Roos and Lake, to wrest lands from the family of her husband, Thomas Cecil, 1st Earl of Exeter, 2d Lord Burghley (1542–1623). On the strength of a false confession, the Countess of Exeter was accused of incest with the impotent Lord Roos, and of attempting to poison his wife. James I, playing Hercule Poirot in the investigation of these fantastic allegations, exposed Sarah Swindon, witness to the false confession taken at the Exeters' Wimbledon House, by showing she would have been visible behind the hangings where she was supposed to have overheard the confession. The king presided at the Star Chamber proceeding in February 1619, comparing himself to Solomon; the flimsy case, inspired by Frances Howard's 1616 trial for murder, collapsed. The plaintiffs confessed, and James I compared Lady Lake to the serpent in Paradise, Lady Roos to Eve, and Lord Roos to Adam: 'the first plot of the first sin in Paradise'. Lady Lake was condemned to a fine and imprisonment. 'Nothing is more awful than the trial of a peer,' Walpole wrote in his *Memoirs*. It seems likely that Walpole responded to the memory of Lady Exeter's scandalous trial, recorded by Granger and others, not the sublimity of Van Dyck's painting.[14]

It even appears that Walpole valued William Faithorne's print of Vandyck's portrait of the Countess of Exeter as much as he valued the original in his own collection. When the antiquary William Cole sent him Faithorne's rare engraving in the summer of 1768 Walpole replied: 'The print of the Countess of Essex is the greatest present to me in the world: I have been trying for years to no purpose to get one. Reynolds the painter promised to beg one for me of a person he knows, but I have never had it' (1. 150). 'I wanted it for four different purposes,' Walpole wrote, thanking Cole: 'as a grandmother-in-law, by the Cranes and Allingtons [HW's supposed relations]; for my collection of heads [Hazen 3636]; for the volume of prints after pieces in my own collection; and above all, for my collection of Faithornes [Hazen 3643], which though fine, wanted such a capital print' (HWC 1. 150; 20 August 1768). Walpole listed Faithorne's print in the *Catalogue of Engravers* in Class I designating fine prints (*Works* 4. 51).

Catherine Fitzgerald (d. 1604), 'My Old Countess of Desmond'

Walpole hung in the Holbein Chamber and later in his bedchamber at Strawberry Hill a portrait he described as a 'drawing of Rembrandt's mother, from the picture at Windsor, called the countess of Desmond . . . by Müntz' (*Works* 2. 453).[15] This portrait illustrates the collector's difficulties not only in identifying sitters – a perennial challenge at a time when every country house was filled with portraits of imaginary ancestors – but in untangling bewildering genealogies. Walpole plunged undaunted into an Irish genealogical labyrinth, writing enquiries in the 1750s about inscriptions on a monument in county Sligo. In 1758 he published the results of this research in *Fugitive Pieces* (Hazen 1881), an article entitled 'An Inquiry into the Person and Age of the Long-lived Countess of Desmond' (*Works* 1. 210–17) introduced by this paragraph:

> Having a few years ago had the curiosity to inform myself of the particulars of the life of the very aged countess of Desmond, I was much surprised to find no certain account of so extraordinary a person; neither exactly how long she lived, nor even who she was; the few circumstances related of her depending on mere tradition. At last I was informed she was buried at Sligo in Ireland, and a gentleman of that place [Charles O'Hara (1705–76)] was so kind as to procure for me the following inscriptions on the monument there; which however soon convinced me of that supposition being a mistake, as will appear by the observations in my letter, in consequence of this which contained the epitaph (*Works* 1. 210).

Walpole's informant had spent many hours on a high ladder transcribing inscriptions on a monument erected in 1624 to the wrong Countess of Desmond, namely Eleanor Butler (1546–1636) who married the 14th Earl of Desmond, Gerald Fitzjames Fitzgerald in about 1568 (HWC 40. 109, n. 11).

Walpole never succeeded in untangling the genealogy of the Countess confused with Eleanor Butler, now believed to be Catherine Fitzgerald (d. 1604), who is thought to have married Thomas Fitzthomas Fitzgerald (1454–1534), 11th Earl of Desmond, sometime between 1505 and 1534.[16] Walpole struggled bravely in his dissertation to answer the unanswerable questions, who was the Countess of Desmond, and how long did she live? More than ten years before he published his *Historic Doubts on Richard III* (1768), Walpole had a special interest in the answers because the long-lived countess of Desmond was to become a star witness in his apology for the King Richard III: 'The great particular (besides that of her wonderful age) which interested me in this inquiry,' Walpole wrote to Charles O'Hara of Nymphsfield Manor, County Sligo, in a letter thanking him for sending the inscriptions, 'was the tradition which says that the long-lived Lady Desmond had danced with Richard the Third, and always affirmed that he was a very well-made man. It is supposed that this was the same lady with whom the old Lady Dacre [Anne Sackville, d. 1595] had conversed, and from whose testimony she gave the same account' (40. 108; 17 September 1757).

Besides uncertainty about the identity of the countess and her age, Walpole was contending with the confusing question of her iconography. The historian of Windsor Castle, Joseph Pote, listed at Windsor 'a painting of the countess of Desmond, who lived as is said, to the age of one hundred and fifty within a few days'. But Walpole noted in his copy of Pote's *History* (1749; Hazen 637): 'This is not the Countess of Desmond, but an old woman by Rembrandt (plate 40), given to King Charles I by Sir Robert Kerr, Earl of Ancram' (HWC 40. 108, n. 4).

Rembrandt's mother in the portrait (if indeed it is she) does look 150 years old, but if Walpole had the wrong monument and the wrong picture, how was he to discover 'who this very old Lady Desmond was, at least whose wife she was?' (HWC 40. 110). Different books in Walpole's library gave different answers. Sir William Temple's essay 'Of Health and Long Life' (*Works* 1740; Hazen 1133) estimated her age at 140, saying '[t]hat she had been married out of England in the reign of Edward the Fourth [1461–83], and, being reduced to great poverty by the ruin of the Irish family into which she married, came from Bristol to London towards the end of the reign of James I to beg relief from Court' (HWC 40. 108). John Lodge's *Peerage of Ireland* (1754; Hazen 660), raised more difficulties: 'I can find no one who married an Englishwoman near the period in question' (HWC 40. 109); Lodge contraverted Catherine Fitzgerald's alleged poverty, since she left 300 pounds to the chapel at Sligo for her tomb. 'But here is the greatest difficulty,' Walpole continued:

> if she was one hundred and forty in 1636 . . . she was born in 1496. . . . She was therefore eighty-seven when she married O'Connor of Sligo [Walpole's confusion with Eleanor Butler's second husband] – that is possible – if she lived to one hundred and forty, she might be in the vigour of her age (at least not dislike the vigour of his) at eighty-seven. The Earl of Desmond's first wife, says Lodge . . . died in 1564: if he remarried the next day, his bride must have been sixty-eight, and yet she had a son and five daughters by him. I fear with all her juvenile powers, she must have been past breeding at sixty-eight (HWC 40. 109).

Of course these accounts exploded Walpole's darling hypothesis that the mysterious Countess of Desmond danced with Richard III and complimented him on his person[17]: '[H]e died in 1485, and by my computation she was not born till 1496' (HWC 40. 109). Even postulating an earlier day or date when the tomb was erected (1624) 'labours with as many difficulties. She could not have been married in the reign of Edward the Fourth, scarcely have danced with his brother; and it is as little probable that she had much remembrance of his person, the point, I own, in which I am most interested' (HWC 40. 109–10). Finally, Walpole concludes his objections to Eleanor Butler's identity as Countess of Desmond in his letter to Charles O'Hara: 'It is very remarkable, Sir, that neither her tomb, nor Lodge, should take notice of this extraordinary person's age' (HWC 40. 110).

Unwilling to let his discredited witness stand down, Walpole added a postscript to his letter to O'Hara almost as long as the letter in his *Works*: 'Since I finished my letter, a new idea has started, for discovering who this very old Lady Desmond was, at least whose wife she was, supposing the person buried at Sligo not to be her' (HWC 40. 110). Studying the Desmond genealogy in John Lodge's *Peerage of Ireland*, Walpole turned up Thomas Fitz John (1386–1420), 5th Earl of Desmond, who had been forced to give up his earldom in 1418 because of 'an imprudent marriage' (HWC 40. 110, n. 21). Here was a way out of Walpole's difficulties:

40.   Rembrandt van Rijn: *Rembrandt's mother, called Catherine Fitzgerald, Countess of Desmond*. Oil on panel, 24⅛ × 18⅝ in. The Royal Collection © 2000 Her Majesty Queen Elizabeth II. Photo: Royal Collection Enterprises, Ltd. 'This is not the Countess of Desmond, but an old woman by Rembrandt, given to King Charles I by Sir Robert Kerr, Earl of Ancram' (HWC 40. 108, n. 4).

[I]t is not improbable that his descendants might use the title, as he certainly left issue' (HWC 40. 111). Voilà! Thomas's grandson John 'being born at least in 1451, would be above thirty at the end of [the reign of] Edward the Fourth [d. 1483]. If his wife was seventeen in the last year of that King, she would have been born in 1466. If therefore she died about 1625, she would be one hundred and fifty-nine. This approaches to the common notice of her age, as the ruin of the branch of the family into which she married, does to Sir William Temple's. A few years more or less in certain parts of this hypothesis, would but adjust it still better to the accounts of her. Her husband being only a titular Earl solves the difficulty of the silence of the genealogists on so extraordinary a person (HWC 40. 111).

Walpole offers two further pieces of tendentious evidence, the first weakening his hypothesis about the titular earl. Walpole discovered that Sir Walter Raleigh's *History of the World* (1614; Hazen 2063) refers to 'the old Countess of Desmond of Inchiquin, who lived in the year 1589, and many years since, who was married in Edward the Fourth's time, *and held her jointure from all the earls of Desmond since then*' (HWC 40. 111). This agrees with Sir William Temple's dating of the marriage, and disagrees with the titular earl theory, but Walpole is quick to dodge this difficulty, 'no such lady being mentioned in the pedigree' (HWC 40. 111):

By Sir Walter's words it is probable that she was dead when he wrote that account of her. His *History* was first printed in 1614; this makes the era of her death much earlier than I had supposed; but having allowed her near one hundred and sixty years, taking away ten or twelve will make my hypothesis agree better with Sir William

Temple's account [i.e., 140 years], and does not at all destroy the assumption of her being the wife of only a titular Earl (HWC 40. 111).

This is a remarkable example of wishful thinking, but Walpole does add apologetically that 'all these are conjectures, which I should be glad to have ascertained or confuted by any curious person, who could produce authentic testimonies of the birth, death, and family, of this very remarkable lady; and to excite or assist which was the only purpose of this disquisition' (HWC 40. 111–12). Walpole next consulted Dr Charles Lyttelton (1714–68), Dean of Exeter, and Bishop of Carlisle, who supplied 'the most positive evidence we have' (HWC 40. 112) from Charles Smith's *Ancient and Present State of the County of Cork* (1750), finally identifying the mysterious Countess of Desmond as Catherine Fitzgerald (d. 1604) of County Waterford, second wife of Thomas Fitzthomas Fitzgerald (1454–1534), 11th Earl of Desmond.

Walpole ends his long letter by telling an apocryphal story about the death of the Countess of Desmond he found in a manuscript that had belonged to Robert Sidney (1595–1677), 2d Earl of Leicester:

I cannot omit an anecdote, though too extraordinary to be given as authentic. . . . It is said that that old countess came to England to solicit a pension at the end of queen Elizabeth's reign, and was so poor that she walked from Bristol to London; her daughter being too decrepit to go on foot, was carried in a cart. 'The countess,' adds Lord Leicester, 'might have lived much longer had she not met with a kind of violent death; for she would needs climb a nut-tree to gather nuts; so falling down, she hurt her thigh, which brought a fever, and that fever brought death' (*Works* 1. 217 n.†).[18]

Walpole told the story in Paris in 1769, where it prompted a *bon mot*: 'I was saying that it had been reported that the old Lady Desmond broke her neck in gathering apples; the Bailli de Chabrillan replied, "*Elle était fort attachée au péché originel*"' (She was strongly attached to original sin)' (7. 370).

This became a favorite story, which Walpole liked to tell *à propos* of old age. When Catherine Hyde, Duchess of Queensberry died in 1777 'of a surfeit of cherries,' he compared her fate to 'my old Countess of Desmond . . . robbing a walnut tree' (32. 366). And on refusing to sit for a portrait miniature to be put in a lady's bracelet in 1794, he exclaimed:

I sit for my picture! I, an unfinished skeleton of 77, on whose bones the worms have left but just so much skin as prevents my being nailed up yet. I am not even a curiosity; nobody takes his doctor's degree in antiquity till past a hundred, and I want a score of wrinkles before I can put in my claim. Old Parr [Thomas Parr (1483–1635); buried in Westminster Abbey under an inscription stating he had lived under ten kings and queens] and old Jenkins [Henry Jenkins (1483–1670), called the 'modern Methusaleh'] would call me a vain impertinent boy for sitting for my picture, and hoping to be ranged amongst prints of remarkable veterans – nay, I don't believe Lady Desmond in the other world would venture to be left alone with such a stripling (HWC 42. 408; 16 July 1794).

Thomas Parr had been brought to London in 1635 by the Earl of Arundel, and exhibited as a curiosity, when John Taylor, the water-poet celebrated him in verse as 'The Old, Old, Very Old Man' (1635). Walpole owned one of several prints under the same title (28. 28, n. 13).

Walpole had already pronounced his opinion that the Windsor portrait of the Countess of Desmond was spurious, when Thomas Pennant decided to use an engraving of a similar portrait of the countess to illustrate the third edition of his *Tour of Scotland* (1774), challenging Walpole's authority as a portraitist. Early on Pennant consulted Walpole's friend and correspondent, Michael Lort, the antiquary and keeper of William Cavendish (1748–1811), the fifth duke of Devonshire's pictures, 'who informed him [Pennant] of your [Walpole's] doubts and proof relating to the Countess of Desmond, and of your dissertation in the *Fugitive Pieces* concerning her, on which account he got an introduction to you and came back very blank . . . on his being convinced that your information destroyed the originality and authority of his print' (1. 332; Cole to HW 2 January 1774). Pennant visited Strawberry Hill on 14 April 1774, when he received a presentation copy of *Fugitive Pieces* lacking the note about the portrait that Walpole inserted in some copies, but Walpole must have explained his 'doubts and proof' (1. 332). What transpired next Cole learned in a lost letter from Lort he summarized in a note on p. 216 of his copy of *Fugitive Pieces*, also a gift from Walpole:

[H]e [Lort] assures me [Cole], that on Mr Pennant's calling at Strawberry Hill to see this picture he was much chagrined at having a print of it engraved for his book, till Mr. Lort revived him by carrying him to a garret in Devonshire House [Piccadilly, London], where there was a picture of this same countess, with her name on it, exactly corresponding to his engraved print (1. fc. p. 332).

Cole remembered another 'tolerable good old picture of her at Mr. Dicey's, Prebendary of Bristol, at Walton in Buckinghamshire' (1. fc. 332).

Walpole's staunchest antiquarian allies – Cole and Lort – were deserting him in the crisis. He could hardly retract the opinion he had stated in a note added to remaindered copies of *Fugitive Pieces*:

Having, by persuasion of his grace the lord chamberlain [William Cavendish (1720–64)], obtained a copy of the picture at Windsor, called the countess of Desmond, I discovered that it is *not* her portrait. On the back is written in an old hand, *The mother of Rembrandt, given by Sir Robert Carr*. In the Catalogue of King Charles's collection of pictures, p. 150, No. 101, is described the portrait of an old woman with a great scarf upon her head, by Rembrandt, in a black frame; given to the king by my lord Ankrom. This was the very sir Robert Kerr, earl of Ancram, mentioned above [in HW's 'Inquiry'], and the measures answer exactly (*Works* 1. 217).

Inscription, catalogue entry, and dimensions: these were the proofs that Walpole tried to impress upon Pennant on 14 April 1774. Pennant ignored all three, as Walpole related to Cole: 'I told him I had discovered and proved past contradiction that it is Rembrandt's mother; he owned it and said he would correct it by a note – but he has not' (HWC 1. 329; 28 May 1774). The 'vulgar head called the countess of Desmond' (HWC 1. 329) appeared in the third edition of Pennant's *Tour of Scotland* (pp. 73–4, plate vi), and fourth edition (1776; pp. 85–6), for reasons disclosed in Pennant's letter to an unidentified correspondent dated 21 October 1774: 'I have examined the Countess of Desmond's picture at Windsor; not a word is there on the back of its being Rembrandt's mother: whose print I have now seen, and am convinced that you and I are right *mal-gré* M. Walpole' (1. 329, n. 12). Who are we to believe? Walpole had no doubt that Pennant was in error: 'This is a brave way of being an antiquary: as if there could be any merit in giving for genuine what one knows is spurious. He is indeed a superficial man, and knows little of history or antiquity' (HWC 1. 329–30; May 1774). An interesting judgment from a man who christened portraits in his own collection 'like children at a foundling hospital' (35. 141), but it is one thing to make light of his own 'antiquarian-ility' (HWC 29. 165), and quite another to have his authority ignored by others.

CHAPTER 7

Portraits at Strawberry Hill – III

Writing in his *Paris Journal* on 15 March 1766, Walpole describes a visit to a famous collection of prints and drawings belonging to the engraver and collector Pierre-Jean Mariette (1694–1774): 'To M. Mariette; saw a *book of portraits* in crayons of the court of Francis I [François I (1494–1547)], like the Holbeins at Kensington, but not near so well done: it was Brantôme's, and the names are written by him' (7. 307; 15 March 1766). Nearly a decade later, on 20 December 1775, Walpole acquired this court album at Mariette's sale (lot 1414), including copies of crayon drawings attributed to François Couet, called Janet, now at Knowsley Hall, Lancashire (Hazen 2357; 32. 282, n. 11). Walpole's attribution of the notes to Brantôme has been challenged in this case,[1] but he bought at the same sale another collection with Brantôme's notes (Hazen 3655), a collection described in the nineteenth century as 'a quantity of villainously bad portraits in the most wretched condition . . . not a single print worth having'.[2]

It seems clear that Walpole collected such court albums to illustrate the memoirs (Hazen 1211 [1699]) of the abbé de Brantôme, Pierre de Bourdeille (1540–1614). This is true despite Walpole's disparaging remark in a letter to Horace Mann about courtiers who like 'so many old Brantômes . . . admired and recorded every proud lord and every lewd lady to whom he had bowed in the guard-room. Laugh at them and you will be happy' (HWC 22. 365–6; 13 November 1765). Walpole excuses one of his own gossiping letters to John Craufurd with a disparaging reference to the French scandal-monger as a yes-man: '*Oh! pour cela oui*, says old Brantôme, who always assents' (HWC 41. 7; 6 March 1766). After returning from Paris in 1775 with nothing but old stories to tell, Walpole tells Anne Liddell: 'The only thing I would ever allow myself to write more, should be like Brantôme; but as everybody's history in these days is written in newspapers or magazines, my trouble is luckily saved' (HWC 32. 281; 4 December 1775). A year before he died Walpole was still comparing himself to Brantôme: '. . . rummag[ing] in the old chest of my memory I found it so full of rubbish . . . I should be writing an *Atalantis* . . . like Brantôme . . . forming a *chronique scandaleuse*' (HWC 34. 220–1; 30 September 1796).

While Walpole disparages his love of court gossip in letters written to Lady Ossory, when he writes to an antiquary he discloses more honestly his attitude to French historical portraiture. After summing up his reading on the coronation of Henry VII in the *Select Papers* of John Ives (Hazen 3476.2 [1773]), in a letter of 1780 to the antiquary William Cole, he states:

In short, I have been gossiping amongst the old nobility like Brantome; but yet such inquiries make one taste history ten times more, than if one only reads a bederoll of names. How one should like to have overheard the conversation of Duchess Cicely [Lady Nevill (1415–95), Duchess of York] and her daughter Suffolk [Elizabeth Plantagenet (1444–1503)], the first time they met after the Coronation [of Henry VII in 1485]! (HWC 2. 365; 26 March 1780).

This is the spirit in which Walpole collected portraits of the French aristocracy, when he assumed what he referred to as his 'Brantôme-hood' (HWC 29. 108; 19 February 1781). We will observe Walpole in this chapter 'gossiping amongst the old nobility like Brantome' (HWC 2. 365), illustrating the *Memoirs of Grammont* and the letters of Mme de Sévigné, then collecting portraits of what he liked to call his 'chapter of royal concubines' (HWC 10. 295).

Walpole's 'Rage for Grammont'

We have no clearer illustration of Walpole's 'Brantôme-hood' than his enthusiasm for the memoirs of Philibert, Comte de Gramont (1621–1707), the courtier of Louis XIV who was banished from France to England in 1662 for making advances to one of the King's mistresses. In England Gramont became an ornament of Charles II's court, made friends with the writer Anthony Hamilton (1645–1719), and married Hamilton's sister. In about 1701 he dictated his memoirs to Hamilton. The memoirs were published anonymously in 1713, and subsequently in several eighteenth-century editions including Walpole's (1772). As early as 1751 Walpole was planning an illustrated edition. As he told George Montagu: '[Y]ou must hear how busy I have been upon Grammont. You know I have long had a purpose of a new edition with notes and cuts [portrait engravings] of the principal beauties and heroes, if I could meet with their portraits' (HWC 9. 118; 22 July 1751; Hazen 2511). Popular throughout the eighteenth century, Gramont's memoirs were Walpole's 'favourite book' (28. 57), which he claimed to know 'by heart' (32. 222). For more than twenty years Walpole, 'Grammont-mad' (9. 124), 'a bigot to Grammont' (35. 146), tirelessly collected portraits to illustrate 'the *dramatis personae* of the *Memoirs*' (42. 90). In July 1751 he wrote to Montagu: 'I have made out [identified] all the people, at all remarkable, except *Milord Janet* [Nicholas Tufton (1631–79), 3rd Earl of Thanet]. . . . This rage of Grammont carried me a little while ago to old Marlbro's at Wimbledon, where I had heard there was a picture of Lady Denham [Margaret Brooke (1646–67)]; it is a charming one' (HWC 9. 118–19; 22 July 1751). In October 1751 among 'entertaining morsels' at Woburn Abbey he found '*le vieux Roussel* [John Russell (1620–81)], *qui était le plus fier danseur d'Angleterre*' (HWC 9. 124; *Memoirs*, Strawberry Hill Press [1772], 126). On a country-house pilgrimage with John Chute in 1752, Walpole caught the scent of Gramont at Leeds Castle, Kent: 'The only thing that at all recompensed the fatigues we have undergone,' he told Richard Bentley, 'was a picture of the Duchess of Buckingham [Mary Fairfax (1638–1704)] . . . who is mentioned in Grammont' (HWC 35. 145). At Hagley, Worcestershire, in 1753, Walpole turned up 'two or three curious pictures, and some of them extremely agreeable to me for their relation to Grammont. . . . [in particular] a portrait of Lord Clifford the treasurer [Thomas Clifford (1630–73), treasurer of the Household], with his staff, but drawn in armour (though no soldier) out of flattery to

Charles II, as he said the most glorious part of his life was attending the King at the battle of Worcester' (HWC 35. 147–8; September 1753).

In 1755 at the auction sale of Martin Folkes (1690–1754), President of the Society of Antiquaries, Walpole proudly announced to Richard Bentley, 'I have lately bought two more portraits of personages in Grammont, Harry Jermyn [(1636–1708), Jacobite Earl of Dover], and [William] Chiffinch [1602–88, closet-keeper to Charles II]: my Arlington Street [No. 5, HW's house in London] is so full of portraits, that I shall scarce find room for Mr Müntz's works [Johann Heinrich (1727–98)]' (HWC 35. 227–8; 10 June 1755). In 1774 Walpole rejoiced to discover that one of his Twickenham neighbours, Dorothy Brudenell (1646–1740), Countess of Westmorland 'was sister of Grammont's Lady Shrewsbury' (HWC 32. 199). As late as 1777 Walpole obtained another copy by John Milbourn (fl. 1773–95) of the portrait of Frances Jennings (1649–1731) 'from the original at lord Spencer's [Althorp, Northamptonshire]' (*Works* 2. 495–6); Walpole used the copy to entice his cousin Francis Conway to visit Strawberry Hill 'to see my new divine closet [Beauclerk Tower] . . . [and] the portrait of *la belle* Jennings in the state bedchamber' (HWC 39. 294; 16 September 1777).

While collecting portraits of these minor players in the memoirs of Gramont, Walpole was on the watch for his leading lady, Elizabeth Hamilton (1641–1709), the Countess of Gramont.[3] Early in 1762 the rumor reached Walpole that Honora Daly (d. 1784), Lady Barnewall of Kingsland, Dublin, had a miniature of the countess by his favourite French miniaturist, Jean Petitot (1607–91). Walpole wrote to his friend George Montagu who was visiting Dublin to tempt Lady Kingsland to sell:

> I have been told that a Lady Kingsland at Dublin has a picture of Madame Grammont by Petitot – I don't know who Lady Kingsland is, whether rich or poor, but I know there is nothing I would not give for such a picture. I wish you would hunt it; and if the dame is above temptation, do try if you could obtain a copy in water-colours, if there is anybody at Dublin could execute it (HWC 10. 4; 26 January 1762).

Montagu replied optimistically: 'I will wait on Lady Kingsland and doubt not but I shall get a copy of Madam Grammont, though the miniature painters here are poor performers' (HWC 10. 9; 6 February 1762).

When Montagu visited Lady Kingsland some ten days later he found that this heiress to the Gramont family owned two miniature portraits, one by Petitot and one by Peter Lely (1618–80). He recommended the Lely to Walpole:

> . . . I have just seen Lady Kingsland's two pictures of Madame Grammont. One [the Petitot] is a small one in water-colours in a snuff-box, the eyes very blue and sweet, brown hair, full-chested, a bust only, a large neck, very French, and full forty.
>   The other is Sir Peter Lely, about sixteen, like Lady Hertford [Isabella Fitzroy (1726–82)] before she was married, in an oval to the waist, about the size of Madame Grignan's at Strawberry, fair hair, very blue eyes, a sweet countenance, and as much beauty as youth, a large shift and tucker, and a drapery like a scarf of blue and gold tissue lined with blue – much the prettiest picture of the two, and would make a figure in your collection if the painter does his part well in enameling and drawing. He

asks twelve guineas, and I have seen some of his work well done. Let me know your decision and it shall be put in his hands immediately after I know which you will have done (HWC 10. 12; 18 February 1762).

Walpole's next letter facetiously suggests to Montagu that he steal Lely's miniature of the countess: 'I am sorry Lady Kingsland is so rich. However if the [Irish] papists should be likely to rise, pray disarm her of the enamel, and commit it to safe custody in the round tower at Strawberry' (HWC 10. 15; 22 February 1762). But when pressed, Walpole, who a month earlier was insisting 'there is nothing I would not give for such a picture' (HWC 10. 4), balked at the price of the miniaturist's copy, equivocating like a Restoration-comedy heroine deciding on a marriage proposal:

> I am disposed to prefer the younger picture of Madame Grammont by Lely – but I stumble at the price; twelve guineas for a copy in enamel is very dear. Mrs Veezy [Elizabeth Vesey (1715–91)] tells me, his [the miniaturist's] originals cost sixteen and are not so good as his copies. I will certainly have none of his originals. *His*; what is his name? I would fain resist this copy; I would more fain excuse myself for having it. I say to myself, it would be rude not to have it, now Lady Kingsland and Mr Montagu have had so much trouble – well – *I think I must have it*, as my Lady Wishfort says,[4] *Why does not the fellow take me*? Do try if he will not take ten. Remember it is the younger picture (HWC 10. 16; 25 February 1762).

In the end Walpole never ordered a copy of Lady Kingsland's portrait of the countess. Instead he commissioned his favourite copyist, John Giles Eccardt, to copy Lely's oil portrait of Madame Gramont (plate 41), probably the picture now at Hampton Court, then at Windsor, for which he paid five guineas (HWC 10. 54, n. 19).

It was not until 1765 that Walpole found in Paris by serendipity a portrait of Philibert, Comte de Gramont (1621–1707; plate 42), a discovery he excitedly reported to Conway (39. 32), Gray (14. 157), and Mary Lepell (1700–68). To Lady Hervey, who had helped him obtain his portrait of Ninon he wrote:

> Oh, Madam, Madam, Madam, what do you think I have found since I wrote my let-ter this morning? I am out of my wits! Never was anything like my luck, it never for-sakes me! I have found Count Grammont's picture! I believe I shall see company upon it, certainly keep the day holy. I went to the Grand Augustins [convent near Place St-Michel] to see the pictures of the reception of the Knights of the Holy Ghost [Order of Holy Spirit]: they carried me into a chamber full of their portraits; I was looking for Bassompierre [François (1579–1646)]; my *laquais de louage* [lackey for hire] opened a door, and said, 'Here are more'. One of the first that struck me was *Philibert Comte de Grammont*! It is old, not at all handsome, but has a great deal of finesse in the countenance. I shall think of nothing now but having it copied (HWC 31. 77–8; 28 November 1765).

On 9 December 1765 Abel-François Poisson (1727–81), Marquis de Marigny, Director General of the King's buildings, granted Walpole permission to have the picture copied

PHILIBERT COMTE de GRAMMONT.

41. Sir Peter Lely: *Elizabeth Hamilton, Countess of Gramont. c.* 1663. Oil on canvas, 49¼ × 40 in. The Royal Collection © 2000 Her Majesty Queen Elizabeth II. Photo: Royal Collection Enterprises, Ltd. 'I am disposed to prefer the younger picture of Madame Grammont by Lely – but I stumble at the price' (HWC 10. 16).

42. Thomas Chambars: *Philibert, Comte de Grammont.* 1772. Line engraving, 5¾ × 4¾ in. Courtesy of the Lewis Walpole Library, Yale University.

by an unknown artist (HWC 7. 283). The picture, presently untraced, was engraved by Thomas Chambars for the frontispiece of Walpole's edition of Gramont (Hazen 2511). The original portrays Gramont's head in armour as one of the 'Knights of the St-Esprit at Paris' (HWC 42. 157).

Walpole reveals the spell that the *Mémoires du Comte de Grammont* (Hazen 2511, 1772) cast upon him in a letter to Anne Liddell dated 1778, describing a musical evening at Hampton Court when Richard Grace Gamon (1748–1818), Baronet and MP, sang songs by Henry Purcell:

> It is the most melodious voice I ever heard. . . . His taste is equal to his voice, and his deep notes, the part I prefer, are calculated for the solemnity of Purcel's music. . . . It was moonlight and late, and very hot, and the lofty façade of the palace, and the trimmed yews and canal, made me fancy myself of a party in Grammont's time – so

43.   Robert Nanteuil: *Marie de Rabutin-Chantal, Marquise de* Sévigné. Oil on canvas, 19¼ × 15⅜ in. Musée Carnavalet, Paris. Photo: Photothèque des Musées de la ville de Paris. 'I am going to build an altar for it, under the title of *Notre Dame des Rochers*!' (HWC 35. 198).

you don't wonder that by the help of imagination I never passed an evening more deliciously. When by the aid of some historic vision and local circumstance I can romance myself into pleasure, I know nothing transports me so much (HWC 33. 41–2; 11 August 1778).

Another cult bestowed on Walpole by Madame du Deffand surrounds Marie de Rabutin-Chantal (1626–96), Marquise de Sévigné. Walpole claimed to know her letters as well as the *Memoirs of Grammont* by heart (HWC 32. 222). They were models for his own letters, and prompted Madame du Deffand to send him 'a [pretended] letter from the Marquise in the Elysian Fields, contained in a snuff box with a miniature portrait [of Madame de Sévigné] on the top' (HWC 3. 51). In addition Walpole collected copies of three of her portraits 'at different ages' (HWC 41. 258; 1773).[5] In 1754 Mary Lepell (1700–68), Lady Hervey, 'made me most happy, by bringing me from Paris an admirable copy [plate 43] of the very portrait that was Madame de Simiane's [Françoise-Pauline de Castellane-Adhémar, Madame de Sévigné's grand-daughter]: I am going to build an altar for it, under the title of *Notre Dame des Rochers*!' (HWC 35. 198). In 1766 Walpole commissioned a view of Madame de Sévigné's town house, the Hôtel de Carnavelet in the Rue-Ste-Catherine, from the artist Jean-Baptiste Raguenet (fl. 1750–75). At Strawberry Hill Walpole hung it near his view of Stoke Poges, Gray's elegy churchyard: '[I]nspired by Gray's own melancholy, I have hung it here [Strawberry Hill] in my favourite blue room, as a companion to Madame de Sévigny's Hôtel de Carnavelet and call them my *Penseroso* and *Allegro*' (HWC 28. 196; 7 May 1775).

In 1779 he acknowledged in a telling way the gift of views of Grignan, the country house of Madame de Sévigné's daughter and principal correspondent in Provence, as he wrote to George Hardinge:

> In short, they are so much more beautiful than I expected. . . . I concluded that the witchery of Madame de Sévigné's ideas and style had spread the same leaf-gold over *places* with which she gilded her *friends* [in her letters]. . . . Grignan . . . shall be consecrated here [Strawberry Hill] among other monuments of that bewitching period [the reign of Louis XIV], and amongst which one loves to lose one's self, and drink oblivion of an era so very unlike (HWC 35. 601–2; 4 July 1779).

Walpole's 'Chapter of Royal Concubines' at Strawberry Hill

In March 1764 Walpole wrote to his cousin, Francis Seymour Conway, then ambassador to France, thanking him 'for your anecdotes relative to Madame Pompadour [Jeanne-Antoinette Poisson, Marquise de (1721–64)], her illness, and the pretenders to her succession [as mistress of Louis XV]. I hope she may live till I see her; she is one of the greatest curiosities of the age, and I am a pretty universal virtuoso' (HWC 38. 357; 27 March 1764). Of course Walpole is making fun of himself as a collector of royal gossip and anecdote, facetiously comparing himself to collectors of natural curiosities like Sir Hans Sloane. Despite the self-mockery, however, 'universal virtuoso' is an apt description of the collector of a group of portraits at Strawberry Hill which Walpole liked to call his 'chapter of royal concubines' (HWC 10. 295).

Soon after returning from a visit to Paris in 1762 Walpole wrote excitedly to George Montagu to tell him he was filling his new picture gallery at Strawberry Hill with portraits of French *femmes galantes*:

> The gallery advances rapidly. . . . I . . . have today received from France a copy of Madame Maintenon [Françoise d'Aubigné (1635–1719)], which with my La Valiere [Françoise-Louise de la Baume le Blanc (1644–1710)], and copies of Madame Gramont [Elizabeth Hamilton (1641–1708)], and of the charming portrait of the Mazarine [Hortense Mancini (1646–99), by Carlo Maratti] at the Duke of St Albans's, is to accompany Bianca Capello [1548–87] and Ninon Lenclos [1620–1705] in the round tower. I hope now there will never be another auction, for I have not an inch of space or a farthing left (HWC 10. 53–4; 25 March 1763).

Except for the Medici Duchess, Bianca Cappello, all of these 'old concubines' (HWC 32. 283) belong to the age of Louis XIV; two (Madame Maintenon and La Vallière) were Louis's mistresses. It will be convenient to begin with the portrait of Bianca Cappello because she is the first of the old concubines Walpole collected (1752), a relic of his Grand Tour. The Cappello sets the pattern he followed in collecting and monumenting his French portraits (in order of acquisition): Ninon Lenclos (1757); Madame de la Vallière (1762); Madame de Prie (1765); Madame de Maintenon (1769); and Madame d'Olonne (1774). We will see that the universal virtuoso collecting French portraits has little interest in the pictures as works of art or in the artists who painted them. He values French portraits, as he does English portraits, for provenance, genealogy, and anecdotes about the sitters and friends who donated them. He reveres such portraits as cult objects to be shared with his intimates. '[O]ld pictures,' he wrote to George Montagu in the passage quoted earlier, 'make one live back into centuries that cannot disappoint' (10. 192; 5 January 1766).

Bianca Cappello (1548–87)

The portrait of Bianca Cappello (*Works* 2. 469; plate 44), after Bronzino, attributed in the eighteenth century to Vasari, introduces us to Walpole's cult of the Medici family. It sums up Walpole's motives as a collector of portraits illustrating the social history of the aristocracy.

While in Florence on the Grand Tour, Walpole had frequently visited and admired Bianca Cappello's portrait at the palace of the Marchese Niccolò Vitelli (1687–1747). Horace Mann bought the portrait for Walpole at an estate sale in Florence in about 1752 (20. 402 n.7). After removing a 'venerable rich frame of a foot broad' (HWC 20. 398), Mann shipped the picture to Arlington Street, commenting on its unsettled attribution:

> I should still tell you that whilst the picture hung in the dark at Casa Vitelli it was always called Bronzino's [by Angiolo Troti, called Bronzino (1503–63), the only portrait now recognized as authentic], but all the connoisseurs now have declared it to be of Vassari [Giorgio (1511–74)], a manner much less stiff and dry than the former. What do you think of it? (HWC 20. 399; 9 November 1753).

Walpole's correspondence indicates quite accurately what Walpole thought of the portrait. Altogether unconcerned about attribution, he thought 'your-my picture' (HWC 24. 16; 8 June 1774), first of all, a token of Mann's friendship when:

> teased to death with all kind of commissions, and overrun with cubs and cubbacionis [Grand Tourists] of every kind, he can for twelve years together remember any single picture or bust or morsel of virtu that a friend of his has ever liked. . . . when it is to be obtained – exactly then this person goes and purchases the thing in question, whips it on board a ship, and sends it to his friend (HWC 20. 402; 6 December 1753).

Second, Walpole saw in the arrival of the portrait at Arlington Street an occasion for a witty parody of the court calender:

> 'Her Serene Highness the Great Duchess Bianca Capello is arrived safe at a palace lately taken for her in Arlington Street [Walpole's No. 5]: she has been much visited by the quality and gentry, and pleases universally by the graces of her person and comeliness of her deportment' – My dear child, this is the least that the newspapers would say of the charming Bianca (HWC 20. 407; 28 January 1754).

Third, although Walpole's picture was undoubtedly a copy, he thought it a masterpiece

44.   Angiolo Troti, called Bronzino: *Bianca Cappello, Grand Duchess of Tuscany*. Pitti Palace, Florence. Photo: Alinari.

– 'The head is painted equal to Titian' (HWC 20. 407) – and admired the likeness 'in the bloom of her wrinkles' (HWC 20. 398; *Works* 1. 170), 'though done, I suppose, after the clock had struck five and thirty, yet she retains a great share of beauty' (HWC 20. 407; 28 January 1754).

Fourth, more important than the quality of the portrait, or the identity of the artist (Vasari or Bronzino) – matters Walpole leaves to connoisseurs – Walpole thought mainly about 'monumenting' the portrait, to borrow the verb he used to describe Lady Oxford's care of family pictures at Welbeck (HWC 35. 270; 1 August 1756):

I have bespoken a frame for her, with the grand ducal coronet at top, her story on a label at bottom, which Gray [the poet Thomas Gray] is to compose in Latin as short and expressive as Tacitus (one is lucky when one can bespeak and have executed such an inscription!) the Medici arms on one side, and the Capello's on the other (HWC 20. 407; 28 January 1754).

Gray's inscription (*Works* 2. 469) tells a story rivalling the Duchess of Malfi's about Bianca Cappello's elopement, the murder of her husband by Francesco de' Medici (1541–87), and her becoming mistress and wife of the murderer, who was Grand Duke of Tuscany (1574–87), until both were allegedly poisoned by the Duke's brother Ferdinand. Bianca Cappello's story was not as short and expressive as Tacitus's, and Gray relied on legend as much as fact. Still Walpole was delighted with Gray's label, and busied himself rummaging through his library for the genealogy of the Medici and Cappello families. In a book of Venetian heraldry (Hazen 2051, 1578) he turned right to the page illustrating the Cappello arms which he marked with an 'x', a piece of luck that occasioned the most memorable word – '*serendipity*' – in Walpole's correspondence. '[T]his discovery I made by a talisman,' he told Horace Mann, 'which Mr Chute calls the *sortes Walpolianae*, by which I find every thing I want *á point nommé* [in the nick of time], wherever I dip for it. This discovery indeed is almost of that kind which I call *serendipity*' (20. 407; 28 January 1754).

In April 1771 Horace Mann reminded Walpole of Bianca Cappello when reporting on the Florentine court's *villeggiatura*: 'This Court removed yesterday [10 April 1771] to a villa called Poggio a Caiano, renowned by the death of Francisco I [Francesco de' Medici] and his Bianca Capello' (23. 296). By this time the portrait had been enlarged in Walpole's mind to 'the episode of Bianca Capello' (20. 403; 6 December 1753).[6] Placed in the Round Tower at Strawberry Hill it became part of the *mise en scène* for Walpole's Horatian reverie on the folly of political ambition, a reverie occasioned by the fall of his friend Étienne-François, Comte de Stainville, Duc de Choiseul (1719–85), the French minister of foreign affairs, who once asked if Walpole would consider being the English ambassador to France (HWC 23. 183; 30 January 1770). Walpole tells Horace Mann:

> I am writing to you in the bow-window, of my delicious round tower with your Bianca Capello over against me, and the setting sun behind me, throwing its golden rays all around. . . . From such a scene one looks down with contempt or pity . . . on Monsieur de Choiseul if he is sorry to be at Chanteloup [his country house in exile that Madame Deffand referred to as Choiseul's 'Strawberry Hill' (4. 261)], yet I, who was born in the cradle of that greatness M. de Choiseul dotes on, thank heaven for having given me no inclination to sacrifice my repose to a chimera! As an acquaintance the world amuses me; it is horrible to be its master or its slave (HWC 23. 315; 19 June 1771).

Thus Walpole turns the Duc de Choiseul into a type of his own father, Robert Walpole, a politician who forfeited the pleasures of retirement. The portrait of Bianca Cappello hovers like a ghost over this carefully rehearsed meditation, opening a window on the past that allows Walpole to enjoy vicariously the romance of power politics.

Ninon L'Enclos (1620–1705), 'Nôtre Dame des Amours'

A courtesan whom Walpole called 'Notre Dame des Amours' (HWC 31. 7) played a role in the *Mémoires de Grammont*, and for nearly forty years Walpole collected portraits to illustrate her memoirs and letters. Walpole catalogues the portrait of Anne Lenclos called Ninon (1620–1705) at Strawberry Hill as 'the only original picture of her; given by herself to the countess of Sandwich, daughter of Wilmot earl of Rochester, and by her grandson, John earl of Sandwich to Mr. Walpole' (*Works* 2. 496). Attributed to Jean Raoux (1677–1734), Walpole's version has not been traced but Walpole commissioned a drawing for an engraving from Thomas Worlidge (1700–66) which is extant (HWC 37. viii, 531; plate 45). This picture entails stories of an acquisition, another cult, and an essay by Walpole about the sitter.

Shortly after the death in Paris (July 1757) of Elizabeth Wilmot, Countess of

45.   Thomas Worlidge, after Jean Raoux
(1677–1734): *Ninon de Lenclos*. Watercolour drawing,
$3^{7}/_{8} \times 2^{13}/_{16}$ in. Courtesy of the Lewis Walpole
Library, Yale University.

Sandwich, Walpole wrote to her executors to inquire about relics of Ninon (portraits and letters in her collection), asking permission to have a copy made of the portrait Ninon had given to her intimate friend and correspondent. Her grandson, the rakish John Montagu (1718–92), 4th Earl of Sandwich, promptly replied, offering Walpole the original 'in the prettiest manner in the world' (HWC 35. 100) Montagu wrote:

> I can very sincerely assure you, I make no sort of sacrifice in giving up a dead mistress, had it been a living one, you would not perhaps have found me so tractable; though the civilities I have received from you, would have laid me under great difficulty to refuse you that, or anything else in my possession (HWC 40. 94–5; 22 July 1757).

The delivery of the picture was apparently delayed by the '*droit d'aubaine*' (31, 6, n. 2), Louis XV's right to property of aliens deceased in France, and Walpole wrote asking assistance of the ardent Francophile Molly Lepell, Lady Hervey, who three years earlier had given Walpole a portrait of Mme de Sévigné (31. 7, n. 9):

> [I]t is a cause Madam in which I know you feel, and I can suggest new motives to your Ladyship's zeal. In short, Madam, I am on the crisis of losing Mlle de l'Enclos's

picture, or of getting both that and her letters to Lady Sandwich. . . . Don't wonder, Madam, at my eagerness; besides a good quantity of natural impatience, I am now interested as an editor and printer: think what pride it would give me to print original letters of Ninon at Strawberry Hill! If your Ladyship knows any farther means of serving me, *of serving yourself good Mr Welldone* as the Widow Lackit says in *Oroonoko* [Thomas Southerne's play (1695), I ii.71], I need not doubt your employing them . . . your Ladyship and I are of a religion, with regard to certain saints [meaning Madame de Sévigné] that inspires more zeal than such trifling temptations as persecution and faggots infuse into bigots of other sects (HWC 31. 6–7; 13 September 1757).

Walpole's committee managed to wrest the portrait of Ninon from Louis XV's agents in spite of the *droit d'aubaine*, and Walpole triumphantly quoted Henry VIII and Mme de Sévigné in a letter to Conway when the portrait arrived at Arlington Street in June 1758:

Mademoiselle de l'Enclos is arrived, to my supreme felicity – I cannot say very handsome or agreeable; but I had been prepared on the article of her charms. I don't say, like Harry VIII, of Anne of Cleves, that she is a Flanders mare, though to be sure she is rather large: on the contrary, I bear it as well as ever prince did who was married by proxy – and she does not find me *fricassé dans de la neige* (HWC 37. 531).

Walpole had joined the cult of Ninon soon after the publication of her memoirs in 1751 (Hazen 988.2). These memoirs inspired Walpole's essay on the secret of happiness for *The World* (No. 28, 12 July 1753; *Works* 1. 169–73) under the pseudonym Adam Fitz-Adam. Walpole, alias Fitz-Adam, mock-seriously imparts his 'mysterious precept', kindred to Benjamin Franklin's, that '"*Young* women are *not* the proper objects of sensual love: it is the MATRON, the HOARY FAIR, who can give, communicate, insure happiness"' (*Works* 1. 170). 'The renowned NINON L'ENCLOS' completes Walpole's catalogue of veteran sirens which included Helen of Troy, Queen Elizabeth I, and Madame de Maintenon whom he describes as 'an old governante' who 'captivated' Louis XIV (*Works* 1. 172). Walpole introduces Ninon as 'a lady whose life alone is sufficient to inculcate my doctrine in its utmost force' (*Works* 1. 172). He then retells apocryphal anecdotes about two of her most scandalous affairs, derived from potboiler editions of her life and memoirs (Hazen 988.2).[7] The first concerns Ninon's natural son, brought up in ignorance of his real parents, who on first seeing Ninon falls in love with her and cannot be discouraged until, in a burlesque of Racine's *Phèdre*, she carries him into her bedchamber determined to disclose the truth of his parentage. Walpole/Fitz-Adam continues:

Here my readers will easily conceive the transports of a young lover, just on the brink of happiness with a charming mistress of near three-score! – As the adventurous youth would have pushed his enterprises, she checked him, and, pointing to a clock, said, 'Rash boy, look there! At that hour, two and twenty years ago [*c.* 1656], I was delivered of you in this very bed!' It is a certain fact, that the unfortunate, abashed young man flew into the garden and fell upon his sword (*Works* 1. 173).

Walpole's 'certain fact' is regarded by one of Ninon's recent biographers as pure fabrication.[8]

The second anecdote inculcating the 'love of elderly women' (*Works* 1. 171) concerns the abbé Nicolas Gédoyn (1677–1744) who 'pressed and obtained an assignation' more than twenty years later [*c*. 1700], five years before Ninon died in 1705 at the age of eighty-five.

> He came and found the enchanting NINON lying on a couch, like the Grandmother of the Loves, in the most gallant dishabille; and, what was still more delightful, disposed to indulge his utmost wishes. After the most charming endearments, he asked her – but with the greatest respect – Why she had so long deferred the completion of his happiness? 'Why,' replied she, 'I must confess it proceeded from a remain of vanity: I did pique myself upon having a lover at past FOURSCORE, and it was but yester-day [b. 15 May 1620/23] that I was EIGHTY complete (*Works* 1. 173).

Voltaire and others expressed scepticism about stories of Ninon's geriatric sexuality, but Madame du Deffand, Walpole's tutor on the *ancien régime*, verified the Gédoyn story from a conversation she had had with the abbé himself when she sent Walpole a second edition of Ninon's *Memoirs*:

> This little work [Antoine Bret's *Memoirs*, 1751][9] is nothing new; I have long had it among my books: I re-read it by chance; and because you love proper names and anecdotes, I thought it would amuse you. There are facts not reported accurately. I learned from the Abbé Gédoyn [d. 1744] himself his love affairs with Ninon ['when she was eighty years of age' (Mary Berry's note)]; I think I have told you about them: the circumstances are different, but the substance is true (HWC 6. 128–9).

Walpole had expected a new life of Ninon, and was disappointed to find 'it is an old book: doubtless the one I drew on for my article in the *World*, and which I know by heart' (HWC 6. 136; 13 January 1775).

Thus the collector of Ninon's portrait exhibits the 'universal virtuoso' at work: Walpole commits Ninon's memoirs to memory, collects her *bon mots*, dreams of pub-lishing her letters at Strawberry Hill, writes an essay about her, and eagerly discusses her career in his correspondence. It is clear that both Walpole and Mme Deffand regarded Ninon, like Madame de Maintenon, as one of their own contemporaries. In 1774, Madame Deffand wrote to tell Walpole that re-reading the correspondence of Ninon and Saint-Évremond had disabused her sense of herself as a wit ('bel esprit'): '– a decid-edly false opinion. . . . No, indeed, I have none of it. Ninon had a great deal, and St-Évremond more than I realized' (HWC 6. 122; 17 December 1774). Here Madame Deffand measures her own wit by Ninon's, just as Walpole more than a decade later compares Ninon to Elizabeth Malyn, Lady Cathcart (1691–1789), who was dancing at the age of ninety-five 'to show her vigour at past fourscore'. He warned Anne Liddell: '– [be]ware an Abbé de Gedoyn!' (HWC 33. 542; 1 December 1786).

'The Sweet Portrait of Madame de Prie' (1698–1727)

The Marquise Marie de Vichy-Champrond (1696–1780), Madame du Deffand, veteran siren born in the age of Louis XIV and mistress of the French Regent, helped Walpole to portraits of the court of Louis XIV. But strings were always attached to gifts from Madame du Deffand, who tormented Walpole in 800 querulous letters playing a game of superannuated coquettry. The story of her gift to Walpole of the portrait of Madame de Prie (Agnès Berthelot de Pleneuf [1698–1727]) in 1765 differs markedly from the gift outright three years earlier from Lady Margaret Cavendish Harley (1715–85), Duchess of Portland. She, Walpole told George Montagu, 'has lately enriched me exceedingly – nine portraits of the court of Louis Quatorze! Lord Portland [Ambassador to Paris 1698] brought them over; they hung in the nursery at Bulstrode [Bulstrode Park, Buckinghamshire], the children amused themselves with shooting at them – I have got them' (HWC 10. 4; 26 January 1762). One of these was probably the portrait of 'the duchesse de la Valiere [Françoise-Louise de la Baume le Blanc (1644–1710)], mistress of Louis XIV given by the duchess dowager of Portland' hanging at Strawberry Hill in the great north bedchamber on the side opposite to the bed (*Works* 2. 496).

On Christmas Eve 1765 Madame du Deffand had offered Walpole a 'beautiful picture of Mme de Prie' (HWC 7. 289), mistress of the Duc de Bourbon [Louis–Henri de (1692–1740)], prime minister in the minority of Louis XV, but Walpole refused to accept the Trojan horse until Madame du Deffand gave it to his cousin Henry Seymour Conway to convey to him. Walpole encouraged Conway to see this picture on his visit to Paris in 1774: 'Oh! make Madame du Deffand show you the sweet portrait of Madame de Prie' (HWC 39. 215; 1774). Walpole mentions the portrait again in a letter to Conway reminiscing about his 1765 Christmas visit to Madame du Deffand's:

> To be sure, you know that her apartment was part of Madame du Montespan's [mistress of Louis XIV], whose arms are on the back of the grate in Madame du Deffand's own bedchamber. Apropos, ask her to show you Madame de Prie's picture, M. le Duc's mistress – I am very fond of it – and make her tell you her history (39. 233–4; 26 December 1774).

In his Paris journal Walpole took notes on the history of the portrait told to him by Madame du Deffand, who had visited Madame de Prie in exile at Courbépine after the duke's disgrace:

> Mme du Deffand told me a great deal of Mme de Prie, the mistress of Duc de Bourbon, and who had governed him absolutely. At first she bore her banishment well [she had been sent to Courbépine 12 June 1726 when the Duke de Bourbon lost favour], but finding no hopes, grew desperate, acted illness, and made them give her emetics and opium, which were bad for fits that she was subject to, and so killed herself. Was very handsome, and but 29 when she died. 'Not clean,' Madame du Deffand [added] who was her great friend, and saw her but the day before she died, telling her that she did not take care of her teeth, she replied, 'I cleaned them but two days ago' (HWC 7.275; 25 November 1765).

Fifteen years later Madame du Deffand was still telling anecdotes about Madame de Prie: 'You are no longer livlier than I am, my friend,' she wrote in 1780, scolding Walpole for neglecting her:

this taste for seclusion, this aversion for society, the boredom conversation causes you, proves to me that truth of a very beautiful and harmonious verse [song] I composed fifty years ago at Courbépine with Mme de Prie, who was exiled there. Here it is; but I must tell you about the whole song and what led up to it. Every morning we used to send each other a stanza; I had received one to a tune whose refrain was *Tout va cahin-caha*; she applied it to my taste. I made up this stanza [couplet]; just like Chapelain's verse [Jean Chapelain 1595–1674], author of *la Pucelle*, to the tune 'When Moses did defend,' etc.:

> Quand mon gôut au tien contraire,
> De Prie, te semble mauvais,
> De l'écrevisse et sa mère
> Tu rappelles le procès.
> Pour citer gens plus habiles,
> Nous lisons dans L'Évangile:
> *Que paille en l'oeil du voisin*
> *Choque plus que poutre au sien.*

'And why beholdest thou the mote that is in thy brother's eye, but considerest not the beam that is in thy own eye?' (HWC 7. 214; 22 March 1780).[10]

Pathetically, in the year of her death, Madame du Deffand goes on to apply these verses about a contest of female vanity to her tiresome obsession with Walpole's alleged neglect of her. One of her bequests to Walpole along with her lapdog Tonton, and a snuff box containing her imitation of a letter by Madame de Sévigné addressed to Walpole, was a commonplace book recording this anecdote, which Walpole annotated:

Mme de Prie was sister of Mme de la Touche, who came to England with the Duke of Kingston. Madame de Prie showed off her wit and elegance, and got only gibberish in return. One day when the beauty of two women was being debated, and wishing to say preference could only be given to the youngest, Madame de Prie said: 'C'est le baptistaire du propriétaire du luminaire qui doit décider' (It is the baptistery of the author of light [God] who must decide it) (HWC 6. 130, n. 6).

Walpole's picture showing Madame de Prie with a bird, sold at Christie's in 1920, has not been traced, but Walpole pasted a print of it in an extra-illustrated copy of the *Description* (HWC 6. 130, n. 6). Hanging in his own bedchamber at Strawberry Hill the portrait opened a window on the Regency in France, his trying friendship with an eyewitness of the ancien régime, French *vers de société*, and the tragic waste of a life at court.

Twenty Pictures of Madame de Maintenon

Walpole's most fully monumented French portrait was that of Françoise d'Aubigné (1635–1719), Madame de Maintenon, who supplanted the Duchesse de la Vallière and the Marquise de Montespan (Françoise-Athénaïs de Rochechouart (1641–1707), as Louis XIV's mistress and then morganatic wife in 1684. Hanging in the Great North Bedchamber at Strawberry Hill (*Works* 2. 496; plate 46), it was probably a copy of the portrait by Pierre Mignard (1612–95; HWC 10. 293, n. 19; plate 47), whose Madonna and Child Walpole had falsified as a Domenichino.

Walpole saw the original of this portrait at St-Cyr in 1769 during a visit to Versailles that he described as a play in two acts in a long letter to George Montagu. In Act I Walpole and his friends watch the Dauphin (the future Louis XVI [1754–93], King of France 1774–93) and his brothers at dinner, and he supplies some epistolary portrait sketches. 'The eldest is the picture of the Duke of Grafton [Augustus Henry Fitzroy (1735–1811)], except that he is more fair and will be taller. He has a sickly air and no grace' (HWC 10. 291; 17 September 1769). Walpole notices particularly the Comte d'Artois [Charles-Philippe (1757–1836)], 'the genius of the family. . . . very fat, and the most like his grandfather [Louis XIV] of all the children . . . [subject of] as many bons mots . . . as of Henry Quatre [1553–1610] and Louis Quatorze' (HWC 10. 291).

46.   John Carter: *Great North Bed-Chamber at Strawberry Hill.* Watercolour drawing. Courtesy of the Lewis Walpole Library, Yale University.

47.   Pierre Mignard: *Françoise d'Aubigné, Marquise de Maintenon*. From HW's collection at Strawberry Hill. Oil on canvas, 25 × 21 in. Witt Library, Courtauld Institute of Art. 'Of Madame de Maintenon we did not see fewer than twenty pictures [at St Cyr]' (HWC 10. 293).

48.   Jacques-Firmin Beauvarlet, after François-Hubert Drouais: *Jeanne Bécu, Comtesse du Barry*. 1769. Line engraving, 8 × 8 in. Bibliothèque Nationale, Département des Estampes, Paris. Photo: Bibliothèque Nationale. 'I have not yet seen Madame du Barri, nor can get to see her picture at the Exposition at the Louvre, the crowds are so enormous that go thither for that purpose' (HWC 35. 121).

Then Walpole looks down from the balcony of the chapel to witness Louis XV [(1710–74; King of France 1715–74)] and Madame du Barry [Jeanne Bécu (1743–93)], the reigning mistress of Louis XV who had succeeded Madame de Pompadour [Jeanne-Antoinette Poisson, Marquise de (1721–64)], at a 'royal mess'. Walpole had been unable to see her portraits as a man and a woman by François-Hubert Drouais [d. 1775] celebrated at the 1769 salon (HWC 35. 121, 30 April 1769; plate 48). 'As royal curiosities are the least part of my virtu, I wait with patience' (HWC 35. 121; 30 August 1769), he wrote philosophically to Chute, but Madame du Barry had been his 'first object . . . to see' (HWC 10. 291; 17 September 1769) at Versailles.

Madame du Barri arrived over against us below, without rouge, without powder, and indeed *sans avoir fait sa toilette*; an odd appearance, as she was so conspicuous, close to the altar, and amidst both court and people. . . . There is nothing bold, assuming or affected in her manner. . . . In the tribune above, surrounded by prelates, was the amorous and still handsome King [Louis XV]: one could not help smiling at the mixture of piety, pomp and carnality' (HWC 10. 291–2; 17 September 1769).

During Act I the 'universal virtuoso' feasts on the spectacle of royalty eating in public, 'almost stifled' in the press of the crowd (HWC 10. 292). Act II takes place at St-Cyr,[11] the convent school founded by Madame de Maintenon three miles west of Versailles. The scene shifts from the court of Louis XV to the 'bewitching period' (HWC 35. 602) of Louis XIV, where the rapt observer of royalty becomes the zealous antiquarian portraitist: 'Our second act was much more agreeable', he continues, describing his tour of St-Cyr: 'We quitted the court and a reigning mistress, for a dead one and a cloister. . . . The first thing I desired to see was Madame de Maintenon's apartment' (HWC 10. 292). Walpole found it disgraced by 'bad pictures of the royal family' (HWC 10. 292–3), but he took careful inventory of the portraits of Madame de Maintenon:

> We did not see fewer than twenty pictures. The young one looking over her shoulder has a round face without the least resemblance to those of her latter age. That in the royal mantle, of which you know I have a copy, is the most repeated; but there is another with a longer and leaner face which has by far the most sensible look. She is in black, with a high point head and band, a long train, and is sitting in a chair of purple velvet. Before her knees stands her niece Madame de Noailles [Françoise-Charlotte-Amable d'Aubigné (d. 1739)], a child; at a distance a view of Versailles, or St-Cyr, I could not distinguish which (HWC 10. 293–4).

Walpole and his company visit the chapel where 'I was placed in the Maintenon's own tribune' (HWC 10. 293). They attend convent classes where performances of Racine's *Athalie* and Madame de Maintenon's homiletic conversations are presented, and they see the archives where Walpole is given relics – the fragment of one of Madame de Maintenon's letters, and a lock of her hair, both preserved at Farmington (HWC 10. 294, n. 23; Hazen 2576). Commenting on the schoolgirls' performances, Walpole remarks that Madame de Maintenon 'was not only their foundress but their saint' (HWC 10. 294). His own pilgrimage, relics, and portrait, like the icon of a cult, suggest that Madame de Maintenon was his saint too.

The 'universal virtuoso' is fascinated by Louis's succession of royal mistresses. It is second nature for Walpole and his circle to compare reigning ones – Comptesse de Mailly (1710–51), de Pompadour, du Barry – to old concubines like Madame de Maintenon. Her mixed character was an enigma throughout the eighteenth century in England and France; she was discussed in Walpole's circle of friends like a contemporary. He read the latest editions of Maintenon's *Memoirs* and *Letters* (Hazen 1255 [1755–6]; Hazen 1280 [1756]), commenting that her correspondence with Cardinal Noailles (1651–1729) 'has persuaded me of the sincerity of her devotion' (HWC 35. 276; 6 June 1756). At a dinner party in 1756 at Blackheath, the fractious Anna Maria Gumley (1694–1758), Lady Pulteney, 'combatted Mrs Cleland on Madame Maintenon's character with as much satire and knowledge of the world as ever I heard in my life' (HWC 35. 94; 8 June 1756). And before a visit to Paris in 1765, Walpole wrote Mary Lepell, Lady Hervey, that he preferred the young Madame de Maintenon, when married (1652–1660) to the poet Paul Scarron, to the old penitent married to Louis XIV: '[H]ad not we both rather go thither [to Paris] fourscore years ago? Had you rather be acquainted with the charming Madame Scarron, or the canting

Madame de Maintenon?' (HWC 31. 43; 3 September 1765).

Clearly the devout Catholic penitent did not appeal to Walpole as much as the *femme galante*. In this his attitude corresponds to Madame Deffand's who thought the unattractive portrait of her in *Memoirs of the Duc de Noailles* (Hazen 3130, 1776) extremely just: 'She [Maintenon] was not at all amiable, because she was sad and aloof; her devotion blunted her wit and spoiled her discrimination. . . . She was not a hypocrite, [but] her piety was petty and minute' (HWC 6. 434; 16 April 1777; my translation). Madame Deffand, and perhaps Walpole, might have preferred a licentious imaginary portrait. This picture attributed to the Marquis de Vallarceaux, a lover whom gossip reported the then Madame Scarron had stolen from Ninon Lenclos, shows Madame Scarron leaving the bath while an ugly brown imp looks on.[12]

Nowhere can we observe more clearly Walpole's delight in visions of royalty than this pilgrimage to St-Cyr, a delight he shares with his friend and correspondent George Montagu because 'the same scenes strike us both, and the same kind of visions [have] amused us both ever since we were born' (10. 291; 17 September 1769). Walpole visited Versailles primarily to see Madame du Barry – '[o]ur first object' (10. 291) – delighting in the comedy of the royal spectacle. He visited St-Cyr to recover the vision of the court of Louis XIV, and to 'monument' another royal mistress. He collected Madame de Maintenon's relics, read her memoirs, treasured anecdotes about her – how Louis XIV used to call her 'Votre Solidité' (HWC 30. 257 n. 7) – and recommended her letters while fearing they might rival 'my adored Madame de Sévigné' (HWC 35. 276).

Mary Granville Delany (1700–88), 'Our Madame Maintenon'

On 14 February 1782 Walpole wrote to William Mason about a new portrait painter he had discovered:

> There is a new genius, one Opy [John Opie (1761–1807)], a Cornish lad of nineteen, who has taught himself to colour in a strong, bold, masterly style by studying nature and painting from beggars and poor children. He has done a head of Mrs Delany [Mary Granville (1700–88), Second Keeper of the Robes to Queen Charlotte] for the King – *oui vraiment*, it is pronounced like Rembrandt, but as I told her, it does not look older than she is, but older than she does (HWC 29. 184–5; 14 February 1782).

At this time Walpole was beginning to take notice of Opie in Royal Academy exhibitions. In his Royal Academy catalogue (1782) he praised ('very well') Opie's portrait of an 'old woman' (RA 82. 371, p. 15), a portrait it is tempting to believe was the king's portrait of Mrs Delany. Earlier in the same catalogue Walpole wrote of the artist: 'a lad of 19 from Cornwall who had taught himself to paint by having poor people and children sit to him. He painted with a strong body of colours, something like Rembrandt, but his colouring dirty. He suceeded best in old heads' (RA 82. 199, p. 10; MS n.).

After Mrs Delany died in 1788, Walpole designed an elaborate gilt frame for a copy of the king's portrait of her that was commisioned by Charlotte Jane Windsor (1746–

1800), Countess of Bute.[13] The framed picture (plate 49) has recently been described by Marcia Pointon:

> Musical instruments surmount the frame in reference to the supposed harmony of her life and her accomplishments as a musician. At the foot is a palette bearing the following inscription [by HW]: 'Mary Granville/Neice of Lord Lansdown/ Correspondent of Dr Swift/Widow of Mr Pendarvis and of/Dr Delany, Dean of Downe/ – Her Piety and Virtues, her excellent understanding/ and her Talents & Taste in Painting and Music/were not only the Merits, Ornaments & Comforts of/ an Uniform life, but the blessings that crowned/and closed the termination of her existence/at the uncommon age of 88/She died April 15th/1788.[14]

Walpole's frame with an inscription amounting to a prose epitaph indicates that Walpole's passion for monumenting portraits extended to contemporary ones and continued to the end of his life. Walpole's design of the picture frame is more than a favour to Lady Bute. It commemorates his own friendship that had begun in the early 1760s when he told George Montagu, 'Mrs Delany I know a little' (HWC 9. 392; 8 October 1761). From the early 1770s Walpole's correspondence records exchanges of visits between Strawberry Hill and Mrs Delany's London house in St James's Place, and a mutual interest in books and manuscripts. Mrs Delany insisted on reading the manuscript of Walpole's tragedy, *The Mysterious Mother* (1768), although 'I knew how it would shock her devout delicacy. She returned it with compliments, but was sorry the subject [incest] would condemn it to oblivion' (HWC 28. 366; 4 March 1778). In 1772 Mrs Delany loaned Walpole the manuscript of William Gilpin's *Forest Scenery*, which remained unpublished until 1791 (HWC 29. 175). Two years later she sent Walpole Chesterfield's *Letters*, of which they both disapproved: 'He mentions . . . adultery as an accomplishment. *Les graces* are the sum total of his religion,' she wrote in her autobiography (HWC 41. 275, n. 3; 7 April 1774). In 1786 Walpole sent her a present of the fourth edition of his *Anecdotes*, adding a note complimenting her artistic talents: '. . . [T]he widow of Doctor Delany and correspondent of Swift; a lady of excellent sense and taste, a paintress in oil, and who, at the age of 75, invented the art of paper-mosaic, with which material coloured, she, in eight years, executed within twenty of a thousand various flowers and flowering shrubs, with a precision and truth unparalleled' (42. 179, n. 2).

In the summer of 1785 George III and Queen Charlotte gave Mrs Delany a furnished house at Windsor and supported her by a pension of £300, favours that prompted Walpole to call Mrs Delany 'our Madame de Maintenon': 'When the new favourite arrived [at Windsor], Louis [George III, playing Louis XIV] himself was at the door to hand her out of the chaise' (HWC 33. 498). The following year, after Mrs Delany recommended Frances Burney (1752–1840) to be a Keeper of the Robes to Queen Charlotte, Walpole wrote: 'My good friend [Mrs Delany] in truth is but a baby of a courtier, or she would not introduce a young favourite [Frances Burney] to supplant herself' (HWC 42. 171; 6 July 1786). Two days before Mrs Delany died on 15 April 1788, Walpole wrote to a mutual friend: 'I hope . . . you may live to Mrs Delany's age and be as much beloved' (HWC 31. 262; 13 April 1788). These details in Walpole's cor-

49.   John Opie: *Mary Granville, Mrs Delany*, in a frame designed by Horace Walpole. 1782. Oil on canvas, 29½ × 24½ in. By courtesy of the National Portrait Gallery, London. Photo: NPG Picture Library. 'Have you [Anne Liddell] heard the history of our Madame de Maintenon?' (HWC 33. 497–8).

respondence monument Lady Bute's portrait of Mrs Delany more sentimentally than Marcia Pointon allows in her remark on Walpole's frame as an 'interpretative gloss': 'At one level the actual frame . . . may flatter the subject, but at another it may serve to appropriate the sitter and, also, to erase the artist' (p. 34). Nevertheless there is no denying the truth of Pointon's conclusion:

> Walpole, having designed the frame and composed the inscription, signed his name prominently on one of the brushes extruding from the palette, inviting viewers to recognize his role as author pre-eminent over artist (in this case a carpenter's son) and subject (in this case female), a claim that operates through the composite materiality of frame and canvas and that demands that the portrait image be read as text (p. 35).

50.   Jean Petitot: *Madame la Comtesse d'Olonne Comme Diane*. Miniature from HW's collection surrounded by a frame of enamelled flowers. Exhibited at Victoria & Albert Museum 1865. Photo: Witt Library, Courtauld Institute of Art.

Possessing Madame d'Olonne

An account of Walpole's French portraits could not be complete without mentioning the miniatures of Jean Petitot (1607–91), an artist whose very name conveniently typifies the pettiness and puerility Macaulay indelibly stamped on Walpole's collection. A detailed account of Walpole's quest for Petitot's miniature of Madame d'Olonne [Catherine-Henriette d'Angennes (1634–1714); plate 50] indicates how mistaken Macaulay's estimate of the collection and the artist was.

On his visit to Paris in 1765 Walpole visited the collection of Pierre-Jean Mariette (1694–1774), where he first saw the portrait he coveted, as he wrote to Thomas Gray: 'Old Mariette. . . . has such a Petitot of Madame d'Olonne! The Pompadour offered him fifty louis [*c.* fifty guineas] for it – Alack! so would I' (HWC 14. 145–6; 19 November 1765). Nearly ten years later Madame du Deffand notified Walpole promptly of Mariette's death, and offered to 'chercher la femme': 'I have already inquired unsuccessfully where his heirs are to be found; if I find out, do you want me to ask if they would consent to sell the enamel portrait, by Petitot, of Madame d'Olonne? In that case, you must tell me what price you wish to put on it' (HWC 6. 95–6, 20 September 1774). Walpole still coveted the miniature, and Madame du Deffand organized a French Committee of Taste – the Marquise Marie-Thérèse Geoffrin (1715–91); Anne-Julie-Françoise de Crussol, Duchesse de la Vallière (1713–

93); Madame Poirier, wife of a china-merchant; Louise-Honorine Crozat du Châtel (1735–1801), Duchesse de Choiseul; the banker Harenc de Presle; and the auctioneer, Pierre-François Basan (1723–97) – to assist in the quest 'de la miniature' (HWC 6. 97; 2 October 1774).

The Committee attempted in vain to arrange a sale by private treaty [*vente particulier*]. Teasing Walpole about his 'fantaisies' (HWC 6. 97), his irrational passion for 'bagatelles' (HWC 6. 140), and his 'vilain petit château [Strawberry Hill]' (HWC 6. 98), Madame du Deffand wrote tantalizingly: 'Do not suppose I forget the miniature, it will not be until after Saint Martin [11 November, Martinmas] that we will know where we stand; I hope we will get it; I hope it won't ruin you' (HWC 6. 111; 30 October 1774). Finally after a year of frustrating delays Harenc de Presle offered the winning bid, and Walpole paid more than three times what Madame de Pompadour had offered, as Madame du Deffand reminded Walpole:

> I resume [letter dated 5 o'clock, 12 December 1775] sooner than I thought, but the reason is a surprise I have just received; I have Madame Olonne in my hands; that's the summit of your joy; but moderate your joy when you realize that gallants would not pay more for her living than you are paying for her dead; she is costing you three thousand two hundred livres [*c.* 133 guineas]. Is it possible you have given such unlimited power to your flea marketer? It is said the Prince de Conti pushed up the price of this jewel so extravagantly (HWC 6. 245).

After a terrible crossing, putting Madame d'Olonne at risk, Colonel Horace St Paul, Secretary to the Embassy of the Court of France, arrived at St James's on the evening of Saturday 9 March 1776, allowing Madame du Deffand a final sexual innuendo: 'Has not the pleasure of possessing Madame Olonne been purchased rather expensively' (HWC 6. 282–3; 10 March 1776).

Like Antony, Walpole was happy to have lost a world for his Cleopatra, as he told Anne Liddell after the auction:

> I am mighty busy about Mariette's sale, where I have been so lucky as to ruin myself. I have got Madame d'Olonne [No. 8 in Basan's catalogue (1775), Hazen 3867]. Madame du Deffand says I have paid dearer for her than any of her lovers did in her lifetime. . . It is droll that even Madame d'Olonne is *en Diane*' (HWC 32. 281–2; 20 December 1775).

Walpole noted in the *Description of Strawberry Hill* that Petitot's Madame d'Olonne was 'a character very different from that given of her in Bussy's *Histoire Amoureuse des Gaules,*' (Hazen 1002 [1731]; HWC 32. 282, n. 13). Walpole had paid a lot, but he consoled himself that he had triumphed over a royal bidder in the Mariette sale:

> A few days before the sale the King of France offered 300,000 livres [12,500 guineas] for the whole collection; it was refused, and has not produced so much, though my correspondent the auctioneer [Pierre-François Basan] says everything sold for three times what it was worth. You may imagine, Madame, I shall be in a fine taking till my old concubin[e] arrives (HWC 32. 282; 20 December 1775).

PART III
Portraits in Walpole's Letters

CHAPTER 8

Identifying Portraits:
Walpole's Catalogues and Letters

Walpole's career as a portraitist began, but did not end, with his collection of historical portraits at Strawberry Hill. It is the argument of Part III that Walpole's passion for collecting portraits culminated in portraits of contemporaries he drew in his letters. His enthusiasm for collecting them was never the absurdity he affected; on the contrary his passion for portraits was the source of his greatest literary achievement. The fashion for public art exhibitions in London in the 1760s coincided with Walpole's maturity as a letter writer; at the same time Walpole was filling his letters with portraits of his contemporaries, and composing characters of public figures in his *Memoirs*. It is appropriate, therefore, to introduce this chapter with a discussion of Walpole's annotated exhibition catalogues, continue with an analysis of his idea of literary portraiture, and then exhibit a representative selection of Walpole's portraits as they appear in the letters.[1]

'I drove about the door', Walpole says of an auction sale at Prestage and Hobbs in London where he had placed a bid on a Petitot miniature in December 1761 (HWC 9. 412). Since the opening of the first public art exhibition a year earlier, Walpole had been driving in his 'chariot decorated with Cupids' (HWC 10. 176) to the door of nearly every art exhibition in London. He appears to have attended most of the ones in London from 1760 until a few years before his death in 1797, and carefully preserved and annotated a nearly complete set of exhibition catalogues of various societies of artists during the 1760s, and the Royal Academy exhibitions beginning in 1769.[2] Walpole made pencilled notes in his catalogues while in the press of spectators peering at pictures. Typically pictures were hung in random order from floor to ceiling at exhibition rooms in Pall Mall, Charing Cross, the Strand, and Somerset House. Walpole often overwrote his pencilled notes in ink many years later when he recollected the exhibitions in the tranquillity of his library at Strawberry Hill. There he added marginalia and footnotes to entries in the catalogues, pasted in the occasional newspaper clipping, bound his catalogues together in portfolios with manuscript title-pages in his print hand, and inserted miscellaneous reviews and commentary. Hugh Gatty writes that Walpole's notes in the Society of Artists' catalogues 'are interesting as the comments of the well-informed connoisseur from whom the Walpole Society takes its name'. He remarks that Walpole's biographical comments on artists 'add considerably to the materials available for the study of the minor artists of the period'.[3]

But Gatty's dictionary of Walpole's exhibition catalogue notes organized alphabetically by artist conceals their true significance. When these annotated exhibition catalogues are read *seriatim* one by one it becomes immediately obvious that it is not a con-

noisseur but a collector of portraits who is writing the notes. More than half the notes
in a typical catalogue identify portraits that the catalogues list anonymously (portraits of
'a lady', 'a gentleman', 'a clergyman', etc.; catalogues named only royalty, actors, and
actresses). Far from the miscellaneous commentary of a connoisseur, representing a
general interest in artists from A to Z, Walpole's annotated catalogues prove him to be a
collector absorbed by portraits of Reynolds, Gainsborough, and a small number of other
portrait painters. The predominance of portraits is the most striking characteristic of
more than fifty extant catalogues of public art exhibitions annotated by Walpole.

Walpole's Society of Artists' Catalogue (1762)

A close look at two of Walpole's annotated catalogues – Society of Artists (1762), and
Royal Academy (1771) – will suffice to characterize Walpole's concentration on portraits in his catalogue annotations, and his experience in the exhibition room. The third
Society of Artists' catalogue (1762) boasted an engraved title-page with a vignette
(Charles Grignion after Samuel Wale; plates 51 and 51a) showing a winged angel bearing a basket of fruits from flourishing trees marked 'architecture', 'painting', and 'sculpture'. The Angel offers the basket to a warlike Britannia festooned with flags and lances,
seated on a cannon, subscribed with a line from Martial: 'If you bring me golden gifts,
you will do less'. On the first page of the 'Preface' (sig. A 1 *recto*, p. iii) Walpole careful-

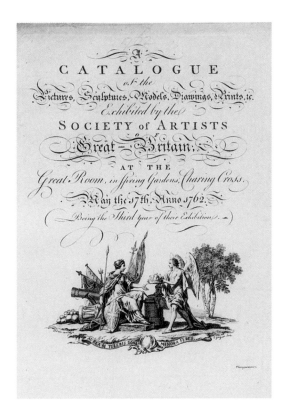

51.   Charles Grignion, after Samuel Wale:
Walpole's annotated *Society of Artists Catalogue*
(1762), title-page. Line engraving. Courtesy of the
Lewis Walpole Library, Yale University. As usual,
Walpole's annotations of portraits predominate:
ten portraits, three landscapes, two architectural
designs, and one history painting.

51A.   Walpole's *Society of Artists Catalogue* (1762),
p. 3, an annotated page typical of HW's exhibition catalogues. Courtesy of the Lewis Walpole
Library, Yale University.

52.   Sir Joshua Reynolds: *Lady Elizabeth Keppel,
Marchioness of Tavistock*. S.A. 1762. Oil on canvas, 93 ×
57½ in. Duke of Bedford, Woburn Abbey. Photo:
Paul Mellon Centre for Studies in British Art. 'He
[Reynolds] has just finished a pretty whole length of
Lady Elizabeth Keppel, in the bride-maid's habit,
sacrificing to Hymen' (HWC 9. 417).

ly wrote in pencil 'by Dr Samuel Johnson'. A committee of the Society of Artists including Reynolds had enlisted Johnson to explain the artists' rationale for charging sixpence
for the catalogue; the catalogue charge being in lieu of an admission charge, which the
sponsoring Society of Arts opposed.[4] Of Walpole's eighteen annotations in this catalogue, more than half identify portraits. The only history painting Walpole notes in this
catalogue, Gaven Hamilton's *Andromache weeping over the dead body of Hector*, he dismisses matter-of-factly as a 'very large piece' (MS *marginalia*, p. 3).

 The parade of portraits begins with Gainsborough's 'whole length of a gentleman with
a gun' (No. 30, p. 3), which Walpole identifies as 'Mr Poyntz'. It is Walpole's usual practice to comment in his catalogues on almost every picture Reynolds exhibited. Here
Walpole identifies two of three portraits (Nos. 87 and 89), and comments on a third,
Reynolds's famous *Mr Garrick, between the two muses of tragedy and comedy* (No. 88, p. 7):
Garrick 'vulgar', comedy 'good'.[5] Reynolds's *whole length of a lady, one of her Majesty's bride
maids* Walpole identifies as 'Lady Elizabeth Keppel, adorning a statue', adding later in a
darker ink 'of Hymen/ There is a print from this picture' (No. 87, p. 6, *marginalia*). The
previous September Walpole had attended the royal wedding of George III and Princess
Charlotte, seeing Lady Elizabeth Keppel (1739–68) in the bridal procession at St James's
Palace – among 'beautiful figures' (HWC 38. 117; 9 September 1761) he thought her
'very pretty' (HWC 21. 530). On 30 December 1761 he had visited Reynolds's studio in

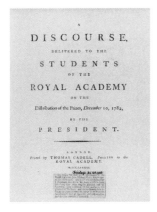 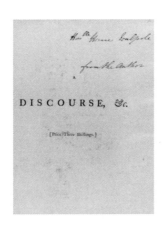  

52 A and B. Sir Joshua Reynolds, presentation copy of *Discourse XI*, 10 December 1782, inscribed to Walpole on the half-title page. Courtesy of Lawrence G. Blackmon, Scottsdale, AZ, USA.

53. Walpole's annotated *Third Royal Academy Exhibition Catalogue* (1771), title-page. Private Collection. Photo: Antonia Reeve Photography, Edinburgh. A Royal Academy catalogue with characteristic annotations by Walpole: twenty-four portraits, twelve history paintings, and four landscapes.

53A. Walpole's annotated *Third Royal Academy Exhibition Catalogue* (1771), p. 16. Private Collection. Photo: Antonia Reeve Photography, Edinburgh. A typical page from Walpole's Royal Academy catalogues, with annotations identifying almost all of Reynolds's portraits.

Leicester Square to see 'the charming picture Reynolds had painted for me'.[6] On that visit he also saw the exhibited portrait: 'He has just finished a pretty whole length of Lady Elizabeth Keppel [plate 52], in the bride-maid's habit, sacrificing to Hymen' (HWC 9. 417; 30 December 1761). Walpole identifies another of Reynolds's fancy pictures, *A lady with her child, in the character of Dido embracing Cupid* (No. 89) as a portrait of his niece, 'Maria [Walpole] Countess of Waldegrave' (No. 89, p. 7, *marginalia*).

These identifications mark Walpole as the complete insider in the social world of the exhibition room. He can only have known of Johnson's authorship of the catalogue's 'Preface' from Reynolds himself, who served on the Society of Artists' committee that had requested it from Johnson.[7] Two years earlier Lady Elizabeth Keppel had joined Walpole in an intimate wedding party in Pall Mall where his niece Maria Walpole was married to James Earl Waldegrave by Elizabeth Keppel's brother, the Reverend Frederick Keppel, Canon of Windsor (9. 235). Needless to say, Walpole has no difficulty in identifying exhibited engravings after Reynolds's portraits. He identifies James MacArdell's mezzotint of 'a young lady with her brother' (No. 160, p. 12) as 'Miss and Master Greville in the characters of Cupid and Psyche' (No. 160, p. 12, *marginalia*). The 'universal virtuoso' (38. 357) knows the details of a design 'for the King' by the royal architect William Chambers, *The North front of a villa* he locates at 'Richmond' (No. 173, p. 13). Walpole tartly corrects the catalogue's description of a second architectural design for James Caulfeild (1728–99), Viscount Charlemont, by Johann Heinrich Müntz, Walpole's difficult protégé whom he had recently dismissed from his patronage at

Strawberry Hill: *A plan, elevation, and section, of a moresque, or Egyptian-room* (No. 192): 'not moresque,' Walpole writes peremptorily, 'corrupted Gothic' (p. 14, *marginalia*). In the last of six annnotations in the Society of Artists' catalogue, Walpole writes after the name of William Marlow (1740–1813): 'scholar of Mr [Samuel] Scott [1702–71]' (p. 5, *marginalia*), a marine painter whose view of Pope's villa was among eight pictures Walpole collected at Strawberry Hill (see below, Chapter 18, plate 101).

Walpole's Royal Academy Catalogue (1771)

Admission charges and premiums sowed the seeds of division in the short-lived union of the Society of Arts and Society of Artists. Throughout the decade until the founding of the Royal Academy and its first exhibition in 1769, societies of artists increased, multiplied, divided, and expired. Walpole's annotated catalogues prove that he attended most, if not all, of these exhibitions in the 1760s, looking at portraits as intensely as he looked at Benjamin Rackstrow's statue at a Society of Arts exhibition.[8] In 1768 Reynolds had been elected president of the Royal Academy, and was beginning to deliver his famous discourses, sending presentation copies to Walpole (plates 52A–B), and inviting him to the annual dinners before the exhibitions were opened to the public.[9] The third exhibition (plates 53 and 53A) will serve to introduce Walpole in the Royal Academy's exhibition room. 'Artists who intend to exhibit with the Academicians,' the *Public Advertiser* announced on 5 April 1771, 'are desired to send their several works on Thursday the 11th of April or before six o'clock in the evening of Friday the 12th after which time no performance will be received'.[10] The third exhibition, which opened on Wednesday 24 April 1771 and closed a month later, was held at No. 125 Pall Mall, premises owned by Mr Lambe, and later by James Christie, auctioneer. On the afternoon of Monday 22 April, two days before the opening, the Royal Family 'honoured the Exhibition of the Royal Academy in Pall-Mall with their Presence. . . . attended by their Royal Highnesses the Prince of Wales, the Bishop of Osnebrug, Prince William, and his Serene Highness Prince Ernest of Mecklenburg Strelitz' (*Public Advertiser*, 24 April 1771, p. 2).

On Tuesday 23 April Walpole was one of the guests at the annual dinner, as the *Public Advertiser* reported on Saturday 27 April 1771 (p. 3):

> Last Tuesday all the Academicians with their associates and the Professors of the Royal Academy dined together in their exhibition room in Pall-Mall.[11] Many noblemen and gentlemen who are distinguished as patrons and lovers of the arts dined with them and had an opportunity of seeing the exhibition more commodiously than when it is open to the public. There were present the Earls of Buckingham, Hardwick, and Besborough . . . the Hon Mr Horace Walpole[12] – Many of the pictures which were to be disposed of were either bought or bespoke by the company present; amongst the rest the picture of Garrick in the Character of Richard III is said to be purchased by Sir Watkin Williams Wynn for £150.[13]

In order to aggrandize the intellectual status of painting, Reynolds appointed two celebrated writers to the faculty of the Royal Academy: Oliver Goldsmith, professor of ancient history, and Samuel Johnson, professor of ancient literature. Both professors attended the dinner. It was probably at this dinner that Reynolds attempted unsuccessfully to introduce Walpole to Johnson, as Walpole informed Mary Berry many years later:

> Johnson's blind Toryism and known brutality kept me aloof, nor did I ever exchange a syllable with him; nay, I do not think I ever was in a room with him six times in my days. The first time I think was at the Royal Academy.[14] Sir Joshua [Reynolds] said, 'Let me present Dr Goldsmith to you'; he did. 'Now I will present Dr Johnson to you.' – 'No,' said I, 'Sir Joshua, for Dr Goldsmith, pass – but you shall *not* present Dr Johnson to me' (HWC 11. 276; 26 May 1791).

Walpole's correspondence preserves in amber another fragment of conversation at the same dinner concerning the controversy about Thomas Chatterton. Walpole's rejection of the Rowley poems as forgeries led to allegations that Walpole had contributed to Chatterton's recent suicide on the night of 25 August 1770: 'Dining at the Royal Academy,' Walpole wrote in 1778 to William Bewley, a reviewer for the *Monthly Review*:

> Dr Goldsmith drew the attention of the company with an account of a marvellous treasure of ancient poems lately discovered at Bristol, and expressed enthusiastic belief in them, for which he was laughed at by Dr Johnson, who was present. I soon found this was the *trouvaille* of my friend Chatterton; and I told Dr Goldsmith that this novelty was none to me, who might, if I had pleased, have had the honour of ushering the great discovery to the learned world. You may imagine, Sir, we did not at all agree in the measure of our faith; but though his [Goldsmith's] credulity diverted me, my mirth was soon dashed, for on asking about Chatterton, he told me he had been in London, and had destroyed himself. I heartily wished then that I had been the dupe of all the poor young man had written to me, for who would not have his understanding imposed on to save a fellow being from the utmost wretchedness, despair and suicide! – and a poor young man not eighteen – and of such miraculous talents – for, dear Sir, if I wanted credulity on one hand, it is ample on the other (HWC 16. 129–30; 23 May 1778).

Portraits predominate in Walpole's notes to the 1771 Royal Academy catalogue, like the Society of Artists' catalogue a decade earlier. Walpole identified more than two dozen portraits, which together suggest that Walpole thought of a Royal Academy exhibition as a National Portrait Gallery. He annotates portraits on every page of the catalogue. Edward Francis Calze's *portrait of a lady* (No. 22) he identifies as 'Miss Kitty Hunter, now Mrs. Clarke', a picture that would have brought to his mind 'the amazement of a new elopement' he describes in the correspondence (see Chapter 11). Mason Chamberlin's full-length portraits of Prince Edward and Princess Augusta he dismisses as 'ugly and bad' (No. 31, p. 6). His note on Richard Cosway's allegorical portrait of *A lady and her daughters, in the characters of Virtue and Beauty, directed by Wisdom to sacrifice at the altar of Diana* (No. 44, p. 7), is illegible, but he annotated a print now in the British Museum, revealing his genealogical expertise: 'The Countess of Carrick, wife of Henry Thomas Butler, and her daughters Lady Henrietta and Lady Margaret Butler, from a picture in the Exhibition of the Royal Academy in 1771 by Cosway.'[15] Richard Crosse's 'Three miniatures' Walpole corrects and identifies: 'Two, Dukes of Gloucester and Cumberland' (No. 52, p. 8; *marginalia*). A close observer of David Garrick's publicity campaign in the exhibition room,[16] Walpole praises Nathaniel Dance's *Mr Garrick in the character of King Richard the Third, act 5*, as 'good and bold' (No. 54, p. 8, *marginalia*). A second portrait by Dance, *A portrait of a lady and children* (No. 56, p. 8), Walpole identifies as 'Mrs Palk', possibly the wife of Robert Palk (1717–98), an MP who succeeded to one of the Walpole family's seats for King's Lynn in 1767 (HWC 39. 192, n. 1).

Lady Palk's is the only one of Nathaniel Dance's six portraits Walpole identifies, but it is typical to find him identifying four of the five that Gainsborough exhibited in 1771. First among them is the picture that appears in Charles Brandoin's drawing (front endpaper) at the center of the left wall, *Portraits of a lady and child*, (No. 74, p. 10), which Walpole identifies as 'Lady Sussex', Hester Hall (1736–77), who married an army officer her family disapproved of in 1758, Henry Yelverton, 3rd Earl of Sussex. Walpole's correspondent William Cole described the dark-complexioned Lady Yelverton and her husband on a visit to Easton-Mauduit in 1763: 'The Earl is a thin little man, of a very plain person, and great hesitation in his speech: my Lady is a black woman of a very good presence' (HWC 10. 339; 21 July 1763).

Walpole was drawing his own portraits in the correspondence concerning Gainsborough's pictures of *A lady in a fancied dress* (No. 75), and *A nobleman with a horse*, full-length portraits he identifies as 'Lady Ligonier,' and 'Lord Ligonier' (p. 10, *marginalia*). Lady Ligonier was then involved in an affair with the poet Count Vittorio Alfieri (1749–1803), which led to a duel and a divorce from her husband, a scandal that Walpole dramatises in his letters (see Chapter 11). The last Gainsborough in the exhibition, a *Portrait of a gentleman* (No. 77) Walpole identifies as Mr Nuthall (Thomas, d. 1775), a treacherous solicitor who was involved in Walpole's unsuccessful attempt to marry his spendthrift nephew, heir to Houghton, to a wealthy heiress.[17]

Next Walpole identifies a portrait by Nathaniel Hone of *A lady in the character of Calista in the Fair Penitent, Act V. Scene I. a three quarters* (No. 100). The sitter is Lady Stanhope, Anne Hussey Delaval (1737–1812), who married Sir William Stanhope, brother of Philip Dormer, the letter-writing 4th Earl of Chesterfield. In May 1767 Walpole describes her 'acting plays' at 'a pretty little theatre' in James Street with Edward Augustus (1739–67), Duke of York, who played Lothario to her 'admirable Calista' (HWC 22. 521). At a later date Walpole added 'There is a print of it' (No. 100, *marginalia* p. 11). He praises a second attractive portrait by Nathaniel Hone *of a boy with a port folio* (No. 104, p. 12) thought to be the artist's son, now in the Aberdeen Art Gallery, as 'very natural'. Angelica Kauffmann's *portrait of an artist* (No. 118, p. 13) Walpole identifies as 'Zuchi,' presumably Antonio Zucchi whom she married in 1781. Walpole next identifies *a portrait, in enamel* (No. 131, p. 14) by the miniaturist Jeremiah Meyer as 'Lord Granby, fine', adding that 'the king bought it'. Writing to Henrietta West in 1762, Walpole joked that John Manners (1721–70), Marquis of Granby, MP, a famous army officer, would not do for the hero of a romance he pretended to be writing: 'My Lord Granby, with a soul as great as Alexander's, and as noble a countenance, thinks too much like that monarch that/Bacchus' blessings are a treasure,/ Drinking is the soldiers' pleasure' (Dryden, *Alexander's Feast Ode*, iii. 56–7; HWC 40. 241–2; 4 May 1762).

54. Sir Joshua Reynolds: *Theophilia Palmer*. RA 1771. Oil on canvas, 29⅛ × 24⅜ in. Private Collection. Photo: Paul Mellon Centre for Studies in British Art. 'Charming, his [Reynolds's] niece ['Offy' Palmer] reading Clarissa' (RA 71. 158, p. 16; HW *marginalia*).

Next Walpole identifies the *bust of a nobleman, in marble* (No. 139) by Joseph Nollekens as 'Lord Holland, very like,' referring to Henry Fox (1705–74), Baron Holland, MP, of whose character he wrote in 1756: 'If I were like common painters, I should give him a ruddy healthful complexion, and light up his countenance with insipid smiles and unmeaning benevolence. But this would not be a faithful portrait' (HWC 30. 333; December 1756). Matthew William Peters' 'portrait of a gentleman, half length' (No. 153) he recognises as an 'imitation of Reynolds' (p. 16, *marginalia*). At last we come to the pictures of Reynolds, always Walpole's star of first magnitude in Royal Academy catalogues, and invariably the most copiously annotated. After dismissing *Venus Chiding Cupid* (No. 156), and *A Nymph and Bacchus* (No. 157) as 'charming but drawing faulty' (*marginalia*), Walpole identifies *A girl reading* (No. 158, p. 16; plate 54), possibly pictured in Brandoin's drawing at upper right, with an epithet and a revealing descriptive detail – 'Charming, his niece reading Clarissa', a book that bored Walpole (HWC 31. 43, n. 6). Walpole spent 'four most agreeable days' at Nuneham Courteney, Oxfordshire, in September 1778 (HWC 33. 54) with Reynolds and his niece Theophila 'Offy' Palmer

(1756–1848), aged fourteen. Walpole praises ('very fine') Reynolds's next portrait, *An old man, half length* (No. 150), identifying the sitter as 'an old beggarman,' adding a note on Reynolds's model, George White the Paviour, whom he keeps track of in half a dozen notes in Royal Academy catalogues: 'This was an old beggar, who had so fine a head, that Sir Joshua chose [him] for the father in his picture from Dante [RA 73. 243, p. 21]; and painted him several times as did others in imitation of Reynolds. There were even busts and cameos of him' (RA 71. 159, MS note, p. 16).[18]

Walpole omits comment on the *Portrait of a Gentleman* (No. 160) that Graves identifies as the poet Samuel Dyer. Richard Baker, author of a critical review of the exhibition Walpole collected, thought this portrait Reynolds's 'best,' complaining about 'marks of . . . hurry' in his other exhibited pictures that 'have no very extraordinary merit' (*Observations*, p. 16). Walpole writes his dissenting opinion in Baker's margin: 'They have great merit' (p. 16).[19]

Reynolds's last portrait, possibly represented in Brandoin's drawing (Plate i, right wall, second from left, upper right), Walpole identifies as 'Mrs Abingdon, actress, easy and very like' (No. 161, *marginalia*, p. 16). Walpole matches this masterpiece with a portrait of the actress he knew well in his letters. Reynolds's painting depicts Frances Barton (1737–1815), Mrs James Abington, in the role of Miss Prue in Congreve's *Love for Love*, a role she had played five times in the 1769–70 season. The portrait shows Frances Barton in character in Act III, Scene 7 when the 'great sea-calf' Ben makes awkward love to the silly country girl: 'Come, Mistress, will you please to sit down? For an you stand astern a that'n we shall never grapple together' (lines 314–16). Biting her thumb, Miss Prue looks as if she is reacting to Ben's insults – 'you cheese-curd . . . Lapland Witch' – preparing to revile him as 'you stinking tar-barrel'.[20]

Walpole's commentary on portraits is not confined to identifications such as George Willison's *portrait of a nobleman in his coronation robes* (No. 218, p. 21), which he calls 'Duke of Queensberry' [William Douglas (1725–1810), 3rd Earl of March, and 4th Duke]. Of John Russell's *Portrait of a child with a dog* (No. 170) he remarks amusingly 'very ugly child' (p. 17, *marginalia*) and he comments on Johann Zoffany's portrait of George III: 'very like, but most disageeable and unmeaning figure' (No. 230, p. 22). It is characteristic to find Walpole commenting on exhibits of honorary exhibitors or amateurs, whom he cares more about than their sitters. Thus he identifies *A portrait of a young gentleman in crayons* as 'Duke of Hamilton' (possibly James Hamilton [1724–58], 6th Duke), describing the artist named 'Miss S. Keck' in the catalogue as 'maid of honour to the Princess of Wales, afterwards married to Mr Charteris' (No. 243, p. 23, *marginalia* and MS n.), a note typical of Walpole's genealogical expertise.

Walpole's twenty-four annotations of portraits in the Royal Academy's 1771 catalogue double the twelve notes concerning history painting, the genre Reynolds was then glorifying in the annual *Discourses* he addressed to students of the Academy in the December preceding each Royal Academy exhibition. Reynolds's fancy pictures in this exhibition – *Venus Chiding Cupid for learning to cast accompts* (No. 156), and *A Nymph and Bacchus* (No. 157) are neither the classical nor the religious histories that the connoisseurs were crying up. Walpole gives the first of these would-be histories a back-handed compliment, and grudgingly concedes that the second is 'better coloured than usual' (No. 157; *marginalia*). Nor was Bartolozzi's drawing of *Venus Embracing Cupid* (No. 13)

more than 'middling' in Walpole's view. Walpole thus opposed Baker's praise in his pamphlet review, *Observations*, where Baker called the drawing 'one of the best pictures in
crayons in this exhibition' (p. 22, *marginalia*). Although Walpole praised ('good')
Nathaniel Hone's *David, when a shepherd* (No. 99, p. 11), the picture can be classified as
a portrait in character of the artist's son, Horace Hone.[21] Significantly, Walpole disapproved of the one undoubted English history painting of the kind the Society of Arts
was encouraging with premiums in the early 1760s. He found 'very little expression' in
Angelica Kauffmann's *The Interview of King Edgar with Elfrida, after her Marriage with
Athelwold* (No. 113; p. 12, *marginalia*).

   If Reynolds is Walpole's paradigm portrait painter in the Royal Academy catalogues,
Benjamin West, the American artist who snatched the perquisite of principal painter to
the king from Reynolds, is Walpole's model history painter. Year after year Walpole never
tires of disparaging West's work. Until 1780 Royal Academy catalogues were organized
alphabetically by artist, and when we reach West in Walpole's annotated 1770 catalogue,
derogatory comments thicken on the page. In 1771 Walpole commented on six of nine
histories exhibited by West. *Hannibal brought, when nine years old, by his father Hamilchar,
to the Altar of Jupiter, where he swears eternal enmity to the Romans* (No. 209, p. 20; plate 55),
the painting Richard Baker regarded as '[t]he picture of the greatest merit in the present exhibition', Walpole thought 'full of faults and bad colouring' (*Observations, margin-*

55.   Benjamin West: *Hannibal and Hamilchar*. RA 1771. Oil on canvas, 88¼ × 119¾ in. The Royal Collection © 2000 Her Majesty Queen Elizabeth II. Photo: Royal Collection Enterprises, Ltd.

56.   James Barry: *Adam and Eve*. RA 1771. *National Gallery of Ireland* (No. 762). Oil on canvas, 91¾ × 73½ in. Photo: National Gallery of Ireland.

alia, p. 14). In the catalogue he wrote, 'very bricky colouring, and the Amilcar very ill drawn' (p. 20, *marginalia*). West's *Continence of Scipio*, a diploma piece of history painters for centuries, Walpole thought 'ill told' (No. 213, *marginalia*). Walpole brackets pictures of *The prodigal son received by his father* (No. 215), and *Tobias curing his father's blindness* (No. 216) with an illegible note in the right margin, probably derogatory because he writes of its companion', the prodigal son, in the left margin 'bad' (No. 215), and of Tobias 'the father's head ridiculous' (No. 216). All West's history paintings are of the 'hard and heavy' sort that Walpole criticized in every exhibition. Still he gave qualified approval to the picture modern art-historians value for its innovative introduction of contemporary dress into classical history painting, *The Death of General Wolfe* (No. 210): 'fine picture, though there is too little concern in many of the principal figures, and the grenadier on the right [is] too tall' (p. 20, *marginalia*).[22]

The most conspicuous picture in the Royal Academy exhibition room in 1771, appearing in the center of Brandoin's drawing, was James Barry's history painting *Adam and Eve* (No. 12, p. 4; plate 56). Barry had sent the picture from Rome to his Irish patron, Edmund Burke, the previous year, requesting 'that Sir Joshua Reynolds . . . procure a good place for it near the sight'.[23] The press made arch and indignant comment about 'insufficiency of drapery', Adam's 'disgusting' expression, and 'the *prudish* part of the spectators, who rather wished the painter had drawn our primogenitors *after* they

had put on their apron of fig leaves'.[24] Walpole contented himself with the comment 'ill drawn' in his catalogue (No. 12, p. 4, *marginalia*). The following year he was less discreet when Barry exhibited *Venus rising from the sea* (RA 1772, No. 12, p. 4; plate 57), a painting 'with some genius', Walpole wrote in the margin, but 'extravagant', 'wild', and again 'ill drawn' (Ibid., *marginalia*). Later Walpole wrote a note on the artist in his catalogue, explaining how Barry's Venus occasioned a quarrel:

> Mr H.W. happened to laugh at this picture at the exhibition [RA 1772, No. 12] when Barry, whom he did not know, was present. Barry resented this so much that not long [after] in a treatise he wrote on painting [*An Inquiry into the Real and Imaginary Obstructions to the Acquisition of the Arts in England* [(1775); Hazen 2793], he satirized Mr W. as an admirer of the Flemish painters [in *Aedes Walpolianae*]. . . . Barry was of a quarrelsome temper, broke with his patron Mr Burke and with the Academy and after some time ceased exhibiting (RA 1772, p. 4, MS n.).

More than ten years later Barry was completing one of his ambitious murals for the Society of Arts, in John Adam Street, Adelphi, London, *The Distribution of Premiums*, part of his *History of Human Culture*. Walpole was preparing to visit the picture, when he explained the occasion of his quarrel with Barry in a detailed letter to William Mason:

> This vision of immortality [*The Distribution of Premiums*] I have not yet seen, but I am dabbing my eyes with euphrasy and rue [Milton's *Paradise Lost*, XI. 414], and propose to treat them with it tomorrow [Thursday 8 May 1783]. I must astringe my mouth too with alum, lest I laugh and be put into purgatory again myself, as I was for the same crime when I first saw Barry's Homeric Venus standing start [sic] naked in front [of the exhibition room], and dragging herself up to heaven by a pyramid of her own red hair. I had never seen nor heard of the man, and unfortunately he stood at my elbow. To punish me for that unwitting crime, he clapped me into his book on painting [*Inquiry* (1775)] as an admirer of the Dutch school, which others have blamed me for undervaluing. I suppose he concluded that if I laughed at bombast-frenzy, I must dote on the lowest buffoonery (HWC 29. 297–8; 7 May 1783).

No anecdote more clearly reveals Walpole's attitude to artists, including Hogarth, Müntz, Reynolds, Bentley, and others, all of whom the Prime Minister of Taste considered born under Saturn: alienated, anti-social, eccentric, even mad.[25] Walpole quarreled with every artist he had to do with, even Vertue and Reynolds, which may be the reason why John Pinkerton, a disappointed seeker of his literary patronage, called him 'the worst of patrons'.

As in the Society of Artists 1771 catalogue discussed above, Walpole's attention to landscapes and topographical views remained subordinate to portraits, and occasionally subordinate (though sometimes equal) to history paintings. Of Gainsborough's two

---

57. James Barry: *Venus Rising from the Sea*. RA 1772. Oil on canvas, 103 × 67 in. Hugh Lane Municipal Gallery of Modern Art, Dublin. Photo: Hugh Lane Gallery.

58.   Thomas Gainsborough: *Coastal Scene*. RA 1781. Oil on canvas, 39½ × 50 in. By kind permission of Her Grace Anne, Duchess of Westminster. 'Gainsborough has two pieces with land and sea, so free and natural that one steps back for fear of being splashed' (HWC 29. 138; RA 81. 94, p. 6).

landscapes with figures, Walpole wrote 'very good, but too little finished' (RA 1771, Nos. 79–80; *marginalia*, p. 10; plate 58).[26] He makes no comment on Charles Brandoin, the Chelsea artist who was exhibiting *A landscape, in water colours* (No. 14, p. 4), and who painted the watercolour of *The Royal Academy Exhibition in 1771* (plate i), now in the Huntington Art Gallery. Walpole appreciated ('good', No. 179, *marginalia*) the first and only exhibit at the Royal Academy of the marine painter Samuel Scott (1702–72), his Twickenham neighbour, *A View of the Tower of London, supposed on his Majesty's birth-day* (No. 179, p. 17). He recognized *A view from the Arcade in Covent-Garden* by the architect Thomas Sandby (1721–98), as 'a perspective drawn for his lectures' (No. 172, p. 17, *marginalia*).[27]

Walpole overlooked three views by Richard Wilson of *Wynnstay, Denbighshire* (No. 221), *Crow Castle, Denbighshire* (No. 222), and *Houghton, Bedfordshire* (No. 223), but he annotated Baker's *Observations* on Wilson's paintings: 'hard as bas reliefs' (*Observations* p. 30). Antonio's Zucchi's *A ruin of an ancient monument, with figures dancing* (No. 234) he criticizes as 'too theatric' (p. 22, *marginalia*). He identifies the artist of a topographical drawing, *A view of the Pont Neuf, at Paris, by a gentleman* (No. 245) as by 'Mr H. Bunbury'

[William Henry (1750–1811)], one of his favourite amateur artists whom he called 'the second Hogarth'.[28] Finally Walpole comments on two landscapes and figures by the Irish artist, G. Mullins 'of Dublin,' bracketing them 'in the manner of Polenburg' (interlineated MS note), labelling them 'good' (No. 266, *marginalia*), and 'better' (No. 267, *marginalia*), adding of the latter in a manuscript note: 'purchased by Mr H. Walpole' (RA 1771, p. 24).

Walpole's identifications in the annotated catalogues frequently provide us with the only extant record of the identity of many portraits exhibited in London from 1760 to 1795. Without his almost obsessive care to document these portraits, a large number would be lost in oblivion. Whitley and others cite some mistakes,[29] but in truth Walpole, trained by 'honest' George Vertue, and steeped in genealogy, was nearly infallible in identifying portraits of his contemporaries. To complain about Walpole's errors in identifying portraits is like complaining about wrong notes in a piano recital by Arthur Rubinstein. Walpole's identifications are valuable for more than proper names: 'What odious portraits, when time shall write proper names under them!' (HWC 19. 460; 26 January 1748), Walpole wrote of William Pulteney (1684–1764), Earl of Bath, leader of the political opposition to his father. In addition to proper names, Walpole's identifications refer us to a portrait gallery of his contemporaries in his own correspondence.

Portraits in Walpole's Memoirs *and* Letters

Throughout his *Memoirs of George II* and *George III* Walpole makes clear his intentions as a literary portraitist: '. . . I am no historian. I write casual memoirs, I draw characters; I preserve anecdotes, which my superiors, the historians of Britain, may . . . pass over'.[30] Elsewhere Walpole writes a courtesy-book gentleman's apology for his self-portrait in the *Memoirs*:

Remember, reader, I offer you no more than the memoirs of men who had many faults, written by a man who had many himself; and who writes to inform you, not to engross your admiration. Had he given you a perfect history, and a flattering picture of himself, his work would be a romance, and he an imposter. He lived with a contempt of hypocrisy, and writes as he lived (1. 3).

Walpole justifies his account by his 'acquaintance with the actors':

It is my part to explain, as far as I could know them, the leading motives of actions and events; and, though the secret springs are often unfathomable, I had acquaintance enough with the actors to judge with better probability than the common of mankind; and where these memoirs are defective or mistaken . . . [they may prompt] sounder materials (1. 162).

Walpole comments on the influence of his opposition politics in Parliament: '. . . it was difficult for me to unravel the windings and turnings of so many minds, who were all my enemies' (2. 1). He reiterates his stance as historian manqué:

It must not be supposed that I would pass off these trifling anecdotes of myself and others for a history of England. But they contain that most useful part of all history, a picture of human minds. They show how little men are, though riding at what is called *the Top of the World*. These and the following scenes were what filled me with disgust, and made me quit that splendid theatre of pitiful passions [the House of Commons from which Walpole resigned in March 1768]; not from having been too good for my company, but ashamed of being one of such *Dramatis Personae* (2. 7).

Inevitably Walpole offers apologies for writing anecdotally about such events as the siege of Bedford House, London, during the weavers' riots in response to the Regency Bill: 'As my [Walpole's] chariot had no coronets, I was received with huzzas [by the mob besieging Bedford House]; but when the horses turned to enter the court, dirt and stones were thrown at it' (2. 113). 'Perhaps,' Walpole concludes, 'I have dwelt too minutely on this episode; perhaps I have done so on many other points equally unimportant. But it must be remembered that I am painting a portrait of the times, rather than writing history. . . . [and particularities] that may serve for the scaffolding, may [later on] be thrown by as no longer of use' (2. 114). Explaining his decision to continue writing political memoirs after resignation from Parliament distanced him from 'the mysterious springs of several events', Walpole confides: 'The honestest answer is the best: it amuses me. I like to give my opinion on what I have seen: I wish to warn posterity (however vain such zeal) against the folly and corruption and profligacy of the times I have lived in' (3. 124–5). Walpole's urge to amuse seems more plausible than his masquerade as Cassandra. Still it is the zeal of a good reporter that motivates his account of John Wilkes and the Brentford election (28 March 1768): 'At night the people grew outrageous; though when Wilkes first arrived in town, I had seen him pass before my windows [No. 5 Arlington Street, London] in a hackney chair, attended but by a dozen children and women; now all Westminster was in a riot' (3. 129). Walpole acknowledges the motive of amusing his reader, the chief imperative of the portraitist in the letters, when he introduces a two-page note on Elizabeth Gunning, the Irish beauty who heroically resisted the rioters: 'These trifling anecdotes may at least be as amusing as the more serious follies committed by and about Wilkes' (3. 131, n. 1; *see* Chapter 17).

Walpole's *Memoirs* seemed 'dry bones' to Romney Sedgwick when compared to Lord Hervey's, but Matthew Hodgart's praise for the portraits in the memoirs is warranted, except for his claim that they surpass the letters.[31] Here is Walpole's 'character' of Sir Charles Wyndham (1710–63), 2d Earl of Egremont:

Lord Egremont was a composition of pride, ill-nature, avarice, and strict good-breeding; with such infirmity in his frame, that he could not speak truth on the most trivial occasion. He had humour, and did not want sense, but had neither knowledge of business, nor the smallest share of parliamentary abilities (1. 215).

A 'character' it is, summary, analytical, but a little dry compared to the letters. Consider this half-length 'character' of Princess Charlotte Sophia (1744–1818) of Mecklenburg-Strelitz before her marriage to George III, a portrait we can compare to Walpole's livlier picture in the letters:

She had been educated in that strict course of piety which in Germany reaches to super-stition. . . . Yet this weakness seemed solely the result of a bad education. Her temper appeared to be lively, and her understanding sensible and quick. Great good-nature, set off by much grace in her manner, recommended all she said. Her person was small, and very lean, but well made. Her face pale and homely, her nose something flat, her mouth very large. Her hair was of a pale brown, and her countenance pleasing (1. 55–6).

The full-length portraits in the *Memoirs* are superb, though they lack the immedia-cy of the letters. Witness Elizabeth Seymour (1716–76), Duchess of Northumberland, well-drawn but lacking the anecdotal dramaturgy of the letters, and the speaking voice of the correspondent:

The Countess of Northumberland was a jovial heap of contradictions. The blood of all the Percies and Seymours swelled in her veins and in her fancy; while her person was more vulgar than anything but her conversation, which was loaded indiscrimi-nately with stories of her ancestors and her footmen. Show, and crowds, and junket-ing, were her endless pursuits. She was familiar with the mob, while stifled with dia-monds; and yet was attentive to the most minute privileges of her rank, while almost shaking hands with a cobbler. Nothing was more mean than her assiduity about the King and Queen, whom she termed her *Master* and *Mistress*; and yet, though indi-rectly reprimanded by the latter, she persisted in following her Majesty to the the-atres with a longer retinue of domestics than waited on the Queen herself. She had revived the drummers and pipers and obsolete minstrels of her family; and her own buxom countenance at the tail of such a procession gave it all the air of an antiquat-ed pageant or mummery. She was mischievous under the appearance of frankness; generous and friendly without delicacy or sentiment (1.333–4).

This is admirable, and can only be criticized by comparison to the more telling likeness in the letters (see Chapter 12). Here is a half-length portrait of the Duc de Choiseul mentioned in the account of Ninon Lenclos (see Chapter 7):

The Duc de Choiseul, the Prime Minister, was a man of excellent parts, but of a levity and indiscretion, which most of that nation [France] divest themselves of before his age, or when they enter into business. Except the hours which he spent with the King, the rest of his life was dissipation, pleasure, profuseness, and *bons mots*. Rash, daring, and presumptuous; good-humoured, but neither good nor ill-natured; quick, gay, and thoughtless, he seemed the Sovereign more than the Minister of a mighty kingdom. . . . Gallantry without delicacy was his constant pursuit. His wife, the most perfect character of her sex, loved him to idolatry; but, though a civil husband, he spared her no mortification that his carelessness could inflict (2. 172).

We do not have space to transcribe a full-length portrait of Charles Townshend (1725–67) from the *Memoirs* that more than equals the letters. Walpole dramatizes the 'incongruities of his character' from a speech in the House of Commons, 8 May 1767, debating a bill for regulating dividends:

. . . [B]efore he sat down, he had poured forth a torrent of wit, parts, humour, knowledge, absurdity, vanity, and fiction, heightened by all the graces of comedy, the happiness of allusion and quotation, and the buffoonery of farce. . . . For myself, I protest it [Townshend's speech] was the most singular pleasure of the kind I ever tasted. . . . It was Garrick writing and acting extempore scenes of Congreve. . . . To solve the contrast of such parts and absurdity in the same composition, one is almost tempted to have recourse to that system of fairy manicheism, wherein no sooner has one benevolent being endowed the hero of the tale with supernatural excellence, but a spiteful hag of equal omnipotence dashes the irrevocable gift with some counter qualification, which serves to render the accomplished prince a monster of contradictions (3. 17–19).

Finally, let us look at this outline of General Pasquale Paoli (1725–1807), a sketch worthy of Boswell:

I saw him soon after his arrival [in London after exile from Corsica], dangling at Court. He was a man of decent deportment, vacant of all melancholy reflection, with as much ease as suited a prudence that seemed the utmost effort of a wary understanding, and so void of anything remarkable in his aspect, that being asked if I knew who it was, I judged him a Scotish officer (for he was sandy-complexioned and in regimentals), who was cautiously awaiting the moment of promotion. All his heroism consisted in bearing with composure the accounts of his friends being tortured and butchered, while he was sunk into a pensioner of that very Court that had proclaimed his valiant countrymen and associates rebels (3. 258).

Whether these characters in the *Memoirs* are 'dry bones' as Sedgwick thought, or 'the glory of the *Memoirs*,' (Hodgart, p. xiii), there is no doubt that they are the work of a portraitist, a writer seized with what he admitted was 'portrait-frenzy . . . I am the head of the sect' (HWC 2. 12; 1 June 1776). It is interesting to discover that despite comparisons Walpole explicitly repudiated Lord Hervey as a model for his own letters. Walpole's reflections on court gossip about Lavinia Bingham's engagement to Lord Althorp (*see* Chapter 10) reveal what Walpole aimed at in his portraits. In a letter dated December 1780 to Anne Liddell, he writes:

. . . [I]f a court is no bigger than an egg-shell, it is equally full of jealousy and treachery. I wish the inhabitants of any court would write comedies – if they could speak truth. They would need but to write down what they have seen and heard – and there would be character with a witness! Lord Hervey [John Hervey (1696–1743), Baron Hervey of Ickworth] did leave a Dialogue of one whole day in the late King's reign [George II], that is, of what commonly passed there.[32] It was not I believe exactly what I mean, but rather a ridicule on the individuals of the *dramatis personae*; I never saw it, but Lady Hervey [Mary Lepell (1700–68)] told me it was the best thing he ever wrote – However, those would be transient ridicules. I would only have general Nature, when it has been refined and strained through the thousand sieves of self-love, ambition, envy, malice, mischief, design, treachery, falsehood and professions, glazed over with perfect ease, good-breeding and good-humour, and the passions

only evaporating through invisible pores, but the angles of the atoms as sharp as nee-
dles, and mortal as diamond dust – but how could one describe smiles that assent
away another's favour, or a bow purposely omitted, and then recollected as designed-
ly to tell a person he is in disgrace, before he knew it himself? Could a pit or a gallery
[at the theatre] comprehend the importance assumed by a bed chamber-woman or a
page of the back stairs in denying some arrant trifle that was a secret in the morning
and is to be in the *Gazette* at night? (HWC 33. 253; 17 December 1780).

Walpole could have known Hervey's posthumously published *Memoirs* only by
hearsay from Mary Lepell, but intuitively he realized that Hervey's Muse of Satire –
'ridicule on the individuals', 'transient ridicules' – 'was not . . . exactly what I mean'. 'I
. . . would write comedies – if . . . [courtiers] could speak truth. . . . [I] would need but
to write down what . . . [I] have seen and heard – and there would be character with a
witness!' (33. 253). True, Walpole shared with Hervey faith in the gospel of trifles – 'accu-
mulated trifles', 'trifling particulars', 'immaterial incidents . . . as can come to the knowledge of few historians' (Hervey's *Memoirs* 2. 622). Like Hervey, Walpole writes 'to those
only . . . who . . . have more pleasure in looking upon those great actors dressing and
undressing than when they are representing their parts on the public stage' (2. 622). But
Hervey adopts the unsparing, satirical point of view of Swift. He is:

> determined to report everything just as it is, or at least just as it appears to me, and
> those who have a curiosity to see courts and courtiers dissected must bear with the
> dirt they find in laying open such minds with as little nicety and as much patience as
> a dissector of their bodies; if they want to see that operation, they must submit to the
> stench (2. 347).

Here he describes the Prince of Orange dressed for his wedding night: 'From the make
of his brocaded gown, and the make of his back, he looked behind as if he had no head,
and before as if he had no neck and no legs' (1. 271).
     Walpole luckily did not read Hervey's satirical accounts of his uncle Horatio,
Baron Walpole of Wolterton (1678–1757), Ambassador to France, and his aunt, Mary
Magdelaine Lombard (1695–1783): 'Horace [Baron Walpole] was envious, revengeful,
inveterate, and implacable', 'a very good treaty-dictionary' (1. 285). His wife is pitilessly
described: 'a form scarce human, as offensive to the nose and the ears as to the eyes, and
one to whom he [Baron Walpole] was kind, not from any principle of gratitude, but
from the bestiality of his inclination' (1. 284–5). Speaking of Walpole's father, Sir Robert,
Hervey expresses surprise at the friendships of 'one who had been so long raking in the
dirt of mankind to be capable of feeling for so worthless a species of animals' (1. 18).
Hervey quotes elsewhere Queen Caroline's caustic description of Sir Robert's relationship with his mistress Maria Skerrett (1702–38), Walpole's step-mother:

> She [Queen Caroline] . . . could neither comprehend how a man could be very fond
> of a woman he only got for his money, nor how a man of Sir Robert's age and make,
> with his dirty mouth and great belly, could ever imagine how any woman would
> suffer him as a lover from any consideration or inducement but his money (2. 421).

Satirical portraits like Hervey's are rare in Walpole's letters. The malice attributed to Walpole in the correspondence is largely a fiction, even in such prejudiced vignettes as that of Lady Mary Wortley Montagu (1689–1762) after her return to London from Italy in 1762: 'I have seen her,' he wrote to George Montagu:

> I think her avarice, her dirt, and her vivacity are all increased. Her dress like her languages, is a galimatias of several countries; the groundwork, rags; and the embroidery, nastiness. She wears no cap, no handkerchief, no gown, no petticoat, no shoes. An old black laced hood represents the first, the fur of a horseman's coat, which replaces the third, serves for the second; a dimity petticoat is deputy and officiates for the fourth, and slippers act the part of the last (HWC 10. 5; 2 February 1762).

Even when Walpole is talking about someone he hates, cheerfulness keeps breaking in because the correspondent remembers his first duty is to draw entertaining portraits. Hodgart may be right about a 'malicious' (p. xiii) strain in the *Memoirs*, but it is easy to exaggerate in the letters if we forget the epistolary context. More often than not the portrait-characters in the letters give us the gold leaf of Sévigné, and the gaiety of Gramont. The portraits in the letters are the work of an artist who is a brilliant witness to character, writing down what he sees and hears: 'Life seems to me as if we were dancing on a sunny plain on the edge of a gloomy forest, where we pass in a moment from glare to gloom and darkness' (HWC 33. 26; 12 July 1778).

CHAPTER 9

Walpole's Portraits in the Letters: Maria Walpole

On the morning of Friday 12 November 1779 Walpole visited the London studio of Johann Zoffany (1733–1810) to see his large conversation piece of Leopold II, the Grand Duke of Tuscany's gallery (the Uffizi) filled with portraits of Grand Tourists and consular officials: 'The first thing I looked for was *you*', he wrote to Horace Mann, '– and I could not find you' (HWC 24. 527). It seems likely that the first thing Walpole looked for in most of the exhibitions he attended were portraits of family and friends. It is accordingly appropriate to begin this survey of Walpole's portraits in the correspondence with paintings of his favourite niece, Maria Walpole (1736–1807), illegitimate daughter of Walpole's brother, Sir Edward Walpole (1706–84), by his mistress Dorothy Clement (fl. 1715–1739).[1] Walpole identified more than half a dozen portraits of Maria Walpole and her family in his catalogues, including several of his own commissions. She is representative of a cult of family portraits that gave Society of Artists and Royal Academy exhibitions a special appeal to Walpole. Maria Walpole's portraits tell a Cinderella story, how the illegitimate daughter of a Covent-Garden seamstress married into the English aristocracy, becoming the Countess Waldegrave, and later Duchess of Gloucester, married to George III's brother.[2]

A Wedding Portrait, Joshua Reynolds px

Walpole identifies the first of Reynolds's four exhibited portraits at the Society of Artists' second exhibition, as 'Lady Waldegrave, in a Turban' (plate 59) adding the footnote: 'Maria Walpole, countess of Waldegrave. There is a print from it. The original is at Strawberry Hill' (SA 1761, No. 81, p. 9). Walpole may have commissioned the portrait from Reynolds, or it may perhaps have been a bequest from his brother Edward (d. 1784). Walpole had played the role of matchmaker for Maria Walpole's first marriage to James, second Earl Waldegrave (1715–63). In March 1759, noticing that the Earl had broken his engagement to Harriet Drax (9. 166, n. 6), Walpole acted quickly: 'In this month I happened to hear that James Earl Waldegrave, Knight of the Garter, liked my niece Maria. . . . I immediately contrived that he should have meetings with her, and in two days less than a month drew him to make his declaration and proposal of marriage' (HWC 13. 31; 17 March 1759). Six weeks later Walpole was anticipating the wedding day, and reconciling friends and relations to the match:

> Our great match approaches: I dine at Lord Waldegrave's presently, and suppose I shall then hear the day. I have quite reconciled my Lady Townshend [Walpole's aunt,

59.   Sir Joshua Reynolds: *Maria Walpole, Countess of Waldegrave*. SA 1761. Oil on canvas, 30 × 25 in. Courtesy of the Earl Waldegrave, Chewton Mendip, Bath, Somerset. Photo: Paul Mellon Centre for Studies in British Art. 'In . . . [March 1759] I happened to hear that James Earl Waldegrave, Knight of the Garter, liked my niece Maria. . . . and drew him to make his declaration and proposal of marriage' (HWC 13. 31).

Etheldreda Harrison (1708–88), known for her wit and anti-matrimonial bias] to the match (saving her abusing us all) by desiring her to choose my wedding cloths – but I am to pay the additional price of being ridiculous, to which I submit: she has chosen me a white ground with purple and green flowers.[3] I represented, that however young my spirits may be, my bloom is rather past; but the moment I declared against juvenile colours, I found it was determined I should have nothing else – so be it!. . . . I shall not come off with them [the Bedford family, related to Waldegrave] by letting them dress me up like Garrick or a shepherd (HWC 9. 231–2; 26 April 1759).

On Tuesday 15 May Walpole, wearing 'juvenile colours', attended the wedding at Sir Edward Walpole's house in Pall Mall, an occasion he describes to George Montagu with the satisfaction of a successful matchmaker:

Well! Maria was married yesterday. Don't we manage well? The original day was not once put off, lawyers and milliners were all ready canonically. It was as sensible a wedding as ever was: there was neither form, nor indecency, both which generally meet on such occasions. They were married at my brother's in Pall Mall, just before dinner, by Mr Keppel [Frederick Keppel, Canon of Windsor]; the company, my brother, his son, Mrs Keppel and Charlotte, Lady Elizabeth Keppel, Lady Betty Waldegrave and I. We dined there; the Earl and new Countess got into their post-chaise at eight o'clock, and went to Navestock [near Chipping Ongar, Essex] alone, where they stay till Saturday night [19 May]: on Sunday [20 May] she is to be presented [at St James's Palace] – and to make my Lady Coventry [a rival Irish beauty, Maria Gunning (1732–60)], distracted (HWC 9. 234–5; 16 May 1759).

Walpole goes on to paint his own portrait of the bride:

Maria was in a white and silver night gown with a hat very much pulled over her face; what one could see of it was handsomer than ever; a cold maiden blush gave her the sweetest delicacy in the world. I had like to have demolished the solemnity of the ceremony by laughing – when Mr Keppel read the words, *Bless thy servant and thy handmaid*, it struck me how ridiculous it would have been, had Miss Drax [Harriet Drax (d. 1786) jilted by James Waldegrave] been the *handmaid* as she was once to have been (9. 235).

Town and Country reported King George saying after the Waldegrave wedding, 'he [George II] had prevented him marrying a W[hore] (Harriet Drax), and now he had wedded a B[astard]' (9. 166, n. 6).

Lady Waldegrave in Mourning; Joshua Reynolds px

At the Society of Artists' 1765 exhibition, Reynolds exhibited another portrait of *A lady*, a *kit-cat*, that Walpole identified as his niece: 'Countess dow[ager] of Waldegrave in mourning' (SA 65. 105, p. 12; plate 60), 'one of his [Reynolds's] best coloured pictures' (*marginalia*). This picture was a memorial to the death of her husband, James 2d Earl Waldegrave (1715–63), whom Walpole was visiting at his house in London every day during his last illness: '. . . I go to Albemarle Street early in the morning, and don't come home till late at night' (HWC 10. 56–7; 6 April 1763). On Wednesday 30 March 1763 Walpole had listened to Waldegrave's symptoms at his club, and prescribed his favourite nostrum, Robert James's fever powder, but learned worse news on Friday 1 April: 'At eight o'clock on Friday night, I was told abruptly at Arthur's that Lord Waldegrave had the smallpox' (HWC 10. 55). Walpole rushed home to Arlington Street. Upon being told that his best friend and first cousin, Henry Conway, had returned from abroad, he hurried to Conway's house in Little Warwick Street, and 'burst into a flood of tears', unable to speak, overcome with '[t]hese two opposite strokes of terror and joy' (HWC 10. 55; 6 April 1763).

The next morning, Saturday 2 April, Waldegrave asked to speak to Walpole alone, and told him 'that the moment he knew it was the smallpox, he signed his will' (HWC 10. 56). Walpole reports the opinion of one of the attending physicians, Dr Edward Wilmot, 'that if anything saves him, it will be this tranquillity' (HWC 10. 56), and is gratified to

60.   Sir Joshua Reynolds: *Maria Walpole, Countess of Waldegrave*. Oil on canvas, 35½ × 27½ in. Private Collection. Photo: Photographic Survey, Courtauld Institute of Art. 'Since the death of Lady Coventry [Maria Gunning] she [Maria Walpole] is allowed the handsomest woman in England' (HWC 22.128).

hear 'that James's powder has probably been a material ingredient towards his recovery' (HWC 10. 56). Hester Lynch Thrale thought differently in annotating this remark in Walpole's letters to Montagu, exclaiming: 'No, no poor fellow! It must have checked the eruption too suddenly, and too violently' (HWC 10. 56, n. 2). Walpole then describes 'the universal anxiety' about Waldegrave, and the surprising devotion of his niece to a husband more than twenty years her senior:

> Her tenderness, fondness, attention and courage are surprising. She has no fears, to become her, nor heroism, for parade. I could not help saying to her, 'My dear child, there never was a nurse of your age had [possessed] such attention' – she replied, 'There never was a nurse of my age had such an object.' It is this astonishes one, to see so much beauty sincerely devoted to a man so unlovely in his person. But if Adonis was sick, she could not stir seldomer out of his bed chamber (10. 56; 6 April 1763).

Walpole reported in his next letter to Montagu some 'glimmerings of hope' on the night of Thursday 7 April when Waldegrave joked with his doctors Wilmot and James:

> He . . . expressed himself in this engaging manner; asking what day of the week it was, they told him Thursday: 'Sure,' said he, 'it is Friday' – 'No, my Lord, indeed it is Thursday' – 'Well!' said he, 'see what a rogue this distemper makes one; I want to steal nothing but a day.' By the help of opiates, with which for these two or three days they had numbed his sufferings, he rested well (HWC 10. 58; 8 April 1763).

On the morning of 8 April, 'worn out with anxiety and attendance,' Walpole returned to Strawberry Hill for lunch, planning to return in the evening: '. . . I had not risen from table, when I received an express from Lady Betty Waldegrave [Waldegrave's sister-in-law], to tell me that a sudden change had happened, that they had given him James's powder, but that they feared it was too late, and that he probably would be dead before I could come to my niece, for whose sake she begged I would return immediately' (HWC 10. 58–9). Waldegrave died at about two o'clock on Friday 8 April 1763, before Walpole could return to London.

Despite the outcome, Walpole kept his faith in James's powder, and faulted the doctors: '– but these are vain regrets! Vain to recollect, how particularly kind he, who was kind to everybody, was to me!' (HWC 10. 59; 8 April 1763). Walpole returned that evening to his brother's house in Pall Mall where Lady Walpole had been married only four years earlier:

> [S]he weeps without ceasing, and talks of his virtues and goodness to her in a manner that distracts one. My brother [Edward Walpole] bears this mortification with more courage than I could have expected from his warm passions: but nothing struck me more than to see my rough savage Louis [Walpole's Swiss servant, d. 1767, who drove Walpole from Strawberry Hill to Pall Mall] in tears as he opened my chaise (HWC 10. 59).

On Sunday 10 April Walpole took his 'poor unhappy niece' to Strawberry Hill. He described the 'terrible scene' (HWC 22. 128) to Horace Mann, mentioning that Waldegrave had not been inoculated like his brother and sister because 'he was the eldest son and weakly', and 'it was early in the practice of that great preservative which was then devoutly opposed' (HWC 22. 127; 10 April 1763). Walpole reiterates his confidence in his cure-all, and his scorn for Dr Wilmot: '. . . I believe James's powder would have preserved him. . . . But James was soon chased away, to make room for regular assassins.' He sizes up Maria's situation on the marriage market pragmatically and elegiacally:

> My niece has nothing left but a moderate jointure of a thousand pounds a year, three little girls, a pregnancy [Walpole was mistaken], her beauty, and the testimonial of the best of men. . . . She loses in him a father, who formed her mind, and a lover whose profusion knew no bounds. From his places his fortune was very great – that is gone! From his rank and consideration with all parties, she was at the summit of worldly glory – that is gone too! Four short years were all their happiness. Since the death of Lady Coventry [Maria Gunning (1732–60), the Irish beauty who married George William, 6th Earl of Coventry in 1752, and died of tuberculosis] she is allowed the handsomest woman in England: as she is so young, she may find as great a match and a younger lover – but she can never find another Lord Waldegrave!' (HWC 22. 128; 10 April 1763).

When Walpole and his family tried in vain to console Maria about the will 'by observing how satisfactory it must be to her to find what confidence her Lord had placed in her sense and conduct, she said, charmingly, "Oh! I wish he had ever done one thing I could find fault with!"' (HWC 22. 128; 10 April 1763). And tears continued to fall at Strawberry Hill, where Walpole gave up his own room to his niece, 'and have betaken myself to the Holbein chamber' (HWC 10. 63; 14 April 1763):

61.   Francis Cotes: *William Henry, Duke of Gloucester.*
RA 1769. Pastel on paper, 24 × 28 in. The Royal
Collection © 2000 Her Majesty Queen Elizabeth II.
Photo: Royal Collection Enterprises, Ltd.

She has such a veneration for her Lord's memory, that if her sisters and I make her
cheerful for a moment, she accuses herself of it the next day to the Bishop of Exeter
[her brother-in-law], as if he was her confessor and that she had committed a crime.
She cried for two days to such a degree, that if she had been a fountain it must have
stopped. Till yesterday [Wednesday 13 April] she scarce eat enough to keep her alive,
and looks accordingly (HWC 10. 62; 14 April 1763).

Only the king failed to send a letter of condolence (Waldegrave had been one of
George III's governors when Prince of Wales) – 'I suppose his childish mind is too much
occupied with the loss of his last governor [Bute, who had resigned 8 April 1763]!'
(HWC 10. 63). More than a year later (July 1764) when Maria was visiting Strawberry
Hill, Walpole was still trying to console her, by reading aloud to her, with the help of
Thomas Gray, the autobiography of Edward Herbert that Walpole was planning to print
at the Strawberry Hill Press: 'We could not go on for laughing and screaming' (HWC
10. 130; 16 July 1764).

William Henry (1743–1805), Duke of Gloucester: 'The Transitory Happiness of Red Liveries': Francis Cotes px

Francis Cotes exhibited a crayon portrait of George III's brother William Henry
(1743–1805), Duke of Gloucester. He had been secretly married to Walpole's niece
Maria Walpole, the Dowager Countess of Waldegrave, on 6 September 1766, a marriage
not publically announced until 1772 after the passage of the Royal Marriage Act.

62.   Sir Joshua Reynolds: *The Ladies Waldegrave*. RA 1781. Oil on canvas, 55 × 65 in. The National Gallery of Scotland. Photo: NGS.

Walpole thought Cotes's portrait 'exceedingly like' (RA 69. 27, p. 5; plate 61), and its melancholy air illustrates the unhappy outcome of a marriage Walpole tried to prevent.

In spite of Walpole's almost Jesuitical equivocations about his attitude toward this clandestine royal marriage, he was telling the truth when he replied to his brother's letter (HWC 36. 62–3; 19 May 1772) informing him of the marriage of his niece:

> . . . I hope in God it will prove as great felicity to her, as it is an honour to her and her family. When I have said this with the utmost truth, it would be below me to

affect much zeal and joy for the attainment of an object, which at the beginning I said all I could to dissuade her from pursuing, on the sincere belief that it was not likely to tend to her happiness (HWC 36. 64; 20 May 1772).

Hence it can have come as no suprise when he received a letter fifteen years later from Horace Mann's nephew about the 'unhappiness', 'mutual discontent', and 'mutual ill will' (HWC 25. 674; 5 April 1787) he noticed of the duke and duchess on holiday in Italy. All this adds a poignancy to Walpole's rueful remark in 1789 about the Prince of Wales George Augustus Frederick's 'two or *three* wives': 'Believe me, who have some cause for knowing, there is nothing so transitory as the happiness of red liveries!' (HWC 11. 50; 6 August 1789).[4]

The Three Ladies Waldegrave: *'Harmony and Acquiescence'. Joshua Reynolds px*

In May 1778 Walpole wrote irritably to his niece, Maria Walpole (1736–1807), Duchess of Gloucester, to answer an 'unjust accusation' (HWC 36. 161) that he had slighted her family by not hanging portraits at Strawberry Hill of her three daughters by her first husband James, 2d Earl of Waldegrave (d. 1763): '. . . I certainly owe no account to anybody on so trifling a subject as the furniture of a house [Strawberry Hill] which I am master to do what I please with, living or dead. . . . I do surely [love] your daughters and nieces, yet have not happened to have their pictures' (HWC 36. 161; 10 May 1778). Walpole was touchy about interference with his collection of portraits at Strawberry Hill, but two years later he commissioned from Reynolds a portrait of the three Ladies Waldegrave – Horatia, Maria, and Laura – who were sitting to Reynolds at his studio in Leicester fields by May 1780, a year before the picture was exhibited at the Royal Academy (1781, No. 187). Walpole wrote playfully to William Mason:

> Sir Joshua has begun a charming picture of my three fair nieces (plate 62), the Waldegraves, and very like. They are embroidering and winding silk. I rather wished to have them drawn like the Graces adorning a bust of the Duchess as the Magna Mater [Roman name of the Goddess Rhea, mother of the Olympian Gods] – but my ideas are not adopted; however I still intend to have the Duchess and her two other children [Princess Sophia Matilda, b. 1773; and William Frederick (b. 1776)] as Latona [mother of Apollo and Diana], for myself (HWC 29. 45–6; 28 May 1780).

Walpole's Roman ideas for portraying the Duchess of Gloucester as the 'Great Mother' or Latona are surely ironic, satiric parodies of pictures Reynolds had been exhibiting at the Society of Artists and the Royal Academy.[5] Walpole had no taste for Reynolds's Grand Style, and disliked his allegorical paintings. He praised ('good') *A lady sacrificing to the graces* (SA 65. 104, p. 12), but he faulted Reynolds's picture of the Montgomery sisters: 'the thoughts old, and flowers too neglected' (RA 74. 216, p. 22; *marginalia*). The picture Reynolds painted for Walpole, perfectly reflecting the character Walpole gives of the Ladies Walpole in the correspondence, suggests that the program for the portrait was Walpole's own. 'I am,' he wrote to the Duchess of

Gloucester, 'as affectionate as if I was their father'. The controlling 'ideas' of the portrait on Reynolds's canvas and in Walpole's letters are the social virtues of harmony and acquiescence, eloquently expressed in Pope's *Epistle to a Lady, Of the Characters of Women* (1735). Such virtues have nothing to do with fancy pictures in the Grand Style.

The Duke of Gloucester had uncharitably said 'he could not live with another man's [James Earl Waldegrave's] children' (*Last Journals* 1. 134; 36. 131, n. 18). Walpole served as surrogate father to his nieces when they were staying at the duke's house at Hampton Court while the duke himself toured Italy for his health. Another of their uncles, Lionel Tollemache (1734–99), 5th Earl Dysart, was treating them 'like Charity Girls' during their parents' absence (HWC 36. 327; 4 January 1777), but Walpole found them delightful company:

> The Duchess's three daughters are by his Royal Highness's goodness lodged in Hampton Court Park [in one of the Pavillions designed by Christopher Wren], which is very near me, and take up most of my time. They are charming girls – I don't mean only their persons, but good, sweet-tempered, admirably brought up, and amiable in every respect. I try to amuse and improve them, though I have little to do on the latter head; and they are so reasonable, and easily contented, even with the company of an old uncle, that even the other [amusement] is not difficult (HWC 24. 315; 17 July 1777).

They visited Strawberry Hill this summer – 'so I have been an old patriarch, as far as an uncle can be so. The weather and my young nieces made the Gallery [at Strawberry Hill] very splendid' (HWC 32. 382; 29 September 1777). The following year Walpole took the memorable moonlight walk at Hampton Court with the Ladies Waldegrave where, 'by the help of imagination I never passed an evening more deliciously' (HWC 33. 42; 11 August 1778). The same summer Walpole danced 'the hays [country dances] . . . with my own charming nieces. . . . [who] laughed a little irreverently, though I told them that I was a very fine dancer before I had the small pox' (HWC 33. 46–7; 29 August 1778). And later that summer Walpole and the Ladies Waldegrave had a narrow escape in a boating accident on the Thames near Ham House, Petersham, Surrey (HWC 39. 310–11; 21 August 1778).

After the happy summer of 1778 Walpole had written to reassure their anxious mother in Italy: 'I have studied my nieces as much as possible in the time, and will answer they are all you can wish. . . . and though they all three are very different, there is the most perfect harmony amongst them' (HWC 36. 149; 27 September 1777). Walpole drew rather dull and dutiful character portraits of each of his nieces. The eldest, Laura (the central figure in Reynolds's conversation piece) was recovering from worry about her step-father's illness:

> The truth is, her sensibility is so great, that with her adoration of you [Maria Walpole] and a turn naturally serious, she cannot easily pass from one extreme to the other. . . . You know Lady Laura best, Madam, and I need not repeat that she has sense, sensibility and tenderness, with a proper pride that will never suffer her to disgrace herself (HWC 36. 149).

To the left of Laura, this pious and compassionate character, Reynolds placed Maria, the Waldegraves' second daughter, whom Walpole regarded as an intellectual:

Lady Maria has the most uncommon understanding I ever saw at near her age [six-teen]. If one did not know her youth and how very little she has seen of the world, one should take it for strong judgment formed by long experience. She makes me start every day by the quickness of her conception, which is delivered with a truth and precision that are astonishing; and sometimes with dry humour that makes one laugh for half an hour (HWC 36. 149).

The youngest, to the right in Reynolds's portrait, had an abundance of good temper and humour, female virtues Pope prized above all in the *Epistle to a Lady*. Walpole wrote: 'Lady Horatia is all life and spirits and cheerfulness, with unbounded good nature, and a great deal of humour. Her vivacity and sweet temper make her the prettiest girl [aged fifteen] in the world, which she is, though her height makes her look a fine woman' (HWC 36. 150).

In concluding his characters of the three sisters, Walpole makes clear the idea which Reynolds was painting in place of a Roman allegory: 'In one thing they are still more sur-prising, which is their perfect cheerful acquiescence to everything that is proposed to or for them' (HWC 36. 150). The sewing circle shows the three sisters absorbed in knotting silk – Horatia concentrating on her tambour, Maria holding a skein of silk for Laura. The painting presents an image of domestic harmony and accord that Walpole hung in the refectory at Strawberry Hill (*Works* 2. 403; now National Gallery of Scotland).

Images of the dance are common in Walpole's intermittent glimpses of the Waldegrave sisters, whom Reynolds idealized like figures on a Grecian urn. After Walpole entertained his nieces with the hays, he 'exhibited' them dancing at Strawberry Hill on Thursday 8 October 1778. 'I gave my nieces a most brilliant assembly. My whole castle was illumi-nated, and the palace of Armida was not more enchanting' (HWC 33. 61; 21 October 1778). Walpole gave a mock-heroic description of this entertainment to William Mason:

I am not of opinion that this *festival of nieces* was absolutely the most charming show that ever was seen. I believe the entertainment given by the Queen of the Amazons to the King of Mauritania in the Castle of Ice, and the ball made for the Princess of Persia by the Duke of Sparta in the Saloon of Roses were both of them more delightful. . . . Though my nieces looked as well as the houris [Muslim virgins in paradise], notwithstanding I was disappointed of the house of North [plain daugh-ters of Walpole's Twickenham neighbour, Lord North] to set them off (HWC 28. 446–7; 11 October 1778).

Three years later, on Tuesday 24 July 1781, when Walpole 'danced three country-dances with a whole set forty years younger than myself!' (HWC 33. 282) at the Earl of Hertford's in Thames Ditton, Walpole finally had his chance to compare his nieces to Lord North, the Prime Minister's daughters, Catherine (1760–1817), and Anne (1764–1832):

All the *jeunesse* strolled about the garden. We ancients with the Earl [Francis Seymour Conway (1718–94), Earl of Hertford] . . . retired from the dew into the drawing room. Soon after the two youths and seven nymphs [including the three Waldegraves, and the North sisters] came in, and shut the door of the hall. In a moment we heard a burst of laughter, and thought we distinguished something like the scraping of a fiddle. My curiosity was raised, I opened a door and found four couples and a half standing up, and a miserable violin from the ale-house. 'Oh,' said I, 'Lady Bel [Isabella Rachel Seymour-Conway (1755–1825), Hertford's unmarried daughter] shall not want a partner' – I threw away my stick, and *me voilà dansant comme un charme*! At the end of the third dance, Lord North, and his son in boots, arrived – 'Come,' said I, 'my Lord, you may dance, if I have' – but it ended in my *resigning my place* to his son . . . (HWC 33. 283–4; 25 July 1781).[6]

Walpole found the dancing rejuvenating, but 'I feel I shall have some difficulty to return to my old dowagers . . . and shall be humming the "Hemp-dressers",[7] when they are scolding me for playing in flush' (HWC 33. 284; 25 July 1781).

Walpole took an avuncular interest in the marriage prospects of the three Ladies Waldegrave, an interest that was as pragmatic as Reynolds's picture is idealized. Walpole carefully calculated their prospects in the marriage market, estimating their dowries, and ranking their beauty:

. . . I once proposed to Lady Walpole [Rachel Cavendish (1727–1805) who married Walpole's uncle, Horatio Walpole] that her son [Horatio (1752–1822)] should marry one of the Duchess of Gloucester's daughters. She said he must marry a fortune. The Duchess's three daughters had each twenty thousand pounds. The eldest and youngest [Ladies Laura and Horatia Waldegrave] were much superior in beauty to Miss Churchill [Sophia (d. 1797)], and the second [Maria Waldegrave], thoroughly handsome' (HWC 25. 132; 26 February 1781).

Walpole was so scrupulous about the prerogatives of the marriage market that he advised George Henry Fitzroy (1760–1844), Earl of Euston, future 4th Duke of Grafton, not to marry his 'favourite niece' (HWC 33. 451), Maria (1761–1808), against the wishes of his father, Augustus Henry Fitzroy (1735–1811), Duke of Grafton and Prime Minister. Walpole urged Lady Maria 'to break off the connection entirely' (HWC 33. 451; 17 November 1784), advice she chose to ignore.

The lively Lady Horatia Waldegrave was luckily spared from marriage to a rakish duke before marrying her first cousin. Robert Bertie, 4th Duke of Ancaster (1756–1779), died on 8 July 1779. Walpole wrote to Horace Mann the following day:

The Duke of Ancaster is dead of a scarlet fever, contracted by drinking and rioting, at two and twenty. He was in love with my niece Lady Horatia, the Duchess's third daughter, and intended to marry her. She is a beautiful girl, like her mother, though not of so sublime a style of beauty. I much doubt whether she would have been happy with him, for though he had some excellent qualities, he was of a turbulent nature; and though of a fine figure, his manners were not noble. Fortune seems to have removed him, to complete her magnificent bounties to one family (HWC 24. 498–9; 7 July 1779).

On 3 April 1786 Lady Horatia married her first cousin once removed, Captain Hugh Seymour-Conway (1759–1801), an intimate of the Prince of Wales. Walpole thought

Conway 'one of the first marine characters' (HWC 25. 632; 16 March 1786), and 'one of the most amiable men in England' (HWC 36. 235; 8 April 1786).

On 5 May 1782 at Gloucester House in London the more sober and serious Lady Laura married her cousin George Waldegrave, Viscount Chewton (1751–89), 'an excellent young man, but very poor,' Walpole wrote to William Mason, 'still we are all much pleased' (HWC 29. 216). Walpole admired Lady Laura's character – 'an extremely good young woman, of a very grave turn and extreme sensibility; she very seldom is in high spirits, but always more affected by sorrow than joy' (HWC 33. 374) – a character that was tested before the end of the decade, when Chewton died 17 October 1789 at the age of thirty-eight. After her husband's death Walpole described Laura's 'great piety' (HWC 36. 273) as a 'female sain[t]' (HWC 31. 394). She acknowledged Walpole's assistance in settling 'many pecuniary affairs. . . . You, my dearest Sir, I reckon one that loved him most' (HWC 36. 270; 23 November 1789).

Walpole called Reynolds's picture of his nieces 'charming' (HWC 29. 45; 28 May 1780) in the studio, while ridiculing the artist's programs for fancy pictures of ladies adorning terms of Hymen. In 1781 when Walpole saw the picture at the Royal Academy dinner at Somerset House, his catalogue note praises it as 'a most beautifull composition, the portraits very like, and the attitudes natural, and easy' (RA 81. 187, p. 9, MS n.). But in 1783, Walpole wrote to William Mason that Reynolds's drawing of hands in the picture was 'abominably bad. . . . [T]hough the effect of the whole is charming, the details are slovenly, the faces only red and white; and his journeyman [probably Guiseppe Filippo Liberati Marchi (1735–1808)], as if to distinguish himself, has finished the lock and key of the table like a Dutch flower-painter' (HWC 29. 285; 10 February 1783). Writing to Mason often draws out Walpole's nastiness, but his fault-finding here seems gratuitous, excessive, and inconsistent; Walpole faults Reynolds for too little and too much finishing. Praise turned to blame appears to characterize most of Walpole's judgments of contemporary artists – Müntz, Bentley, Zoffany, and Barry. He cannot help quarrelling with them, even if it is only to complain about their prices. In his conversations with John Pinkerton, Walpole more than doubled Reynolds's price of 300 guineas for the *Three Ladies Waldegrave*, a fact confirmed by a receipt in Reynolds's hand at the Lewis Walpole Library: ' "Sir Joshua Reynolds gets avaricious in his old age. My picture of the young ladies Waldegrave is doubtless very fine and graceful; but it cost me 800 guineas" ' (HWC 29. 46, n. 22).

CHAPTER IO

Walpole's Portraits in the Letters:
Marriage à la Mode

Lavinia Bingham (1762–1831), Lady Althorp. Joshua Reynolds px

Walpole identified 'one of . . . [Reynolds's] most enchanting portraits' at the Royal
Academy 1782 exhibition as 'Lady Althorpe' (RA 82. 157, p. 9; plate 63).[1] Daughter of
one of Walpole's favourite amateur artists, Margaret Smith, Lady Lucan (d. 1814), whose
miniatures he praised in the *Anecdotes*, Lavinia Bingham was married on 6 March 1781
to George John Spencer (1758–1834), Viscount Althorp. Lady Lucan taught her daughter drawing and hoped that Walpole would 'grant . . . Lavinia the same protection you
have afforded me, as *she* has an original genius' (HWC 41. 419; 5 October 1780). Walpole
thought Lavinia's drawing 'very incorrect' (HWC 41. 419, n. 6), but he collected engravings after her designs (Hazen 3588). One Saturday evening, 14 November 1779, at the
Lucans's house in Charles Street, Berkeley Square, Walpole had to endure hearing the
accomplished Lavinia and her sister Louisa sing 'Jomelli's *Miserere*, set for two voices. . .
. The service lasted near three hours, and was so dull, instead of pathetic, that I rejoiced
that *the worst was over*, and *the two women had left the sepulchre*' (HWC 33. 139; 14
November 1779). Lavinia's engagement to Viscount Althorp, later (1783) 2d Earl Spencer,
was announced on Saturday 9 December 1780 at Devonshire House in London.

Walpole described the comedy of their engagement in three letters; first, mock-heroically when he joked after the death of Maria Theresa, Queen of Hungary and wife of
the Holy Roman Emperor, that 'Miss Bingham is to succeed her' (HWC 33. 249; 11
December 1780).

Walpole's second account in a letter to Horace Mann describes the engagement as a
love match flouting the conventions of *marriage à la mode*:

> The chief event in private life is a match designed and declared but three nights ago [9
> December 1780 at Devonshire House] between Lord Althorpe and Lord Lucan's eldest
> daughter. He is certainly one of the capital *partis* in England. She has no fortune and in
> my eyes no beauty, but the image of her father, but she is very lively, and the birds grew
> so in love that he could not be said nay, though certainly neither his father or mother
> could admire the choice – yet they have yielded (HWC 25. 104; 12 December 1780; a con-
> jectural reconstruction of a passage heavily crossed out in manuscript).

Walpole saved for the *pièce de résistance* a description of a supper at the Lucans's house
in Charles Street, Berkeley Square, on Thursday 7 December two days before the public

63.   Sir Joshua Reynolds: *Lavinia Bingham, Viscountess Althorp, and Countess Spencer*. RA 1782. Oil on canvas, 29 × 24 in. The Collection at Althorp. Photo: Althorp. 'She has no fortune and in my eyes no beauty. . . but she is very lively' (HWC 25. 104).

announcement of the engagement, where sycophants were flattering the earl's rumoured choice, while the family was politely concealing the engagement. 'The crapaudines [toad eaters or sycophants] begin to discover amazing charms in Miss Bingham', he wrote again to Anne Liddell: 'One of them, as Lord Althrop was talking to her, went up to him, and holding up her fan that Miss might not *see* what she said, told him, "She is a *sweet* creature!" Another of them repeated this – and yet I would not swear was not the very person that said it' (33. 253; 17 December 1780).

Walpole then gives an instance of courtly mystification about the engagement, reporting his conversation with Lord Althorp's mother, Margaret Georgiana Poyntz (1737–1814).

I caught Lady Spencer t'other night [Thursday 7 December 1780] – It was two nights before Lord Althrop's match was owned – but I had supped at Lord Lucan's with the whole court of Spencer, and Lord A. had sat at a side-table with the two girls [Lavinia and Louisa Bingham], Miss Molesworth [Frances (1756–1829)] and old Miss Shipley [Anna Maria (1749–1829)]. I knew if I asked directly, I should be answered, 'Upon my word, *I* know nothing of the matter' – so after supper sitting by Lady Spencer on a settee, I said, 'Pray, Lady S., is it owned that Lord A. is to marry – Miss Shipley?' She burst out a-laughing, and could not recompose her face again (HWC 33. 253–4; 17 December 1780).

By New Year's Eve Walpole had composed a burlesque nuptial 'Ode' for Lady Lucan that he hoped would be translated into a quipu [a knotted hieroglyph] to 'stuff a pincushion':

I
Hymen O Hymenaee!
To Althorp and Bingham!
Ye bards come and sing 'em,
And all the bells ring 'em
With ding, ding a dong.
II
To Althorp and Bingham!
But pray do not ding 'em
With this or that thingum
That may call up in Bingham
A blush all day long.
III
Your best wishes bring 'em,
Your best roses fling 'em
O'er the hammock, where Bingham
And Althorp shall swing 'em
With ding, ding a dong.
(HWC 33. 260–1)

After the wedding on 6 March 1781 Walpole printed at the Strawberry Hill Press 250 copies of a more sublime nuptial ode, 'The Muse Recalled', by Lord Spencer's boyhood tutor and the future Orientalist, Sir William Jones (1746–94). Walpole defended it against Anne Liddell's Johnsonian objections: '. . . if the ode is not perfect, still the eighth, ninth and tenth stanzas have merit enough to shock Dr Johnson and such syco-phant old nurses, and that is enough for me' (HWC 33. 287–8; 4 September 1781). Walpole explicates in particular the imagery of a stanza flattering Lavinia Bingham's artistic talent:

> Each morn, reclin'd on many a rose,
> *Lavinia*'s pencil shall disclose
> New forms of dignity and grace
> Th'expressive air, th'impassioned face,
> The curled smile, the bubbling tear,
> The bloom of hope, the snow of fear. (HWC 33. 287, n.5)

In 1785 Walpole was hoping Lavinia's visit to Italy in 1785 would improve her skill in drawing: 'Lady Spencer draws – incorrectly indeed, but has great expression. Italy probably will stimulate her, and improve her attention' (HWC 25. 613; 30 October 1785). Two months later, however, he records that she climbed the erupting Vesuvius with her husband, an athletic rather than artistic achievement: 'Lord and Lady Spencer have ascended the mountain while the lava boiled over the opposite brim: I should have no thirst for such bumpers' (HWC 33. 509; 16 January 1786).

Frances Pelham (1728–1804): 'Poor Miss Pelham'; William Dickinson sc., Joshua Reynolds px

In April 1776, the 'seventeenth year of exhibiting,' Walpole attended the nearly defunct Society of Artists' exhibition 'at their Academy, near Exeter Exchange, Strand'. He identified a mezzotint by William Dickinson after Reynolds of *A whole length of a lady* (SA 76. 204, p. 14; plate 64) as 'Mrs Pelham'. We first hear of Frances Pelham (1728–1804) in Walpole's correspondence at the age of nineteen, subject of gossip about her marriage prospects: 'The Twickenham Alabouches [gossips] say that Legge [Henry Bilson Legge (1708–64), MP] is to marry the eldest Pelhamine infanta [Frances Pelham]. He loves a minister's daughter – I shall not wonder if he intends it, but can the parents?' (HWC 9. 53; 5 October 1747).[2] Legge bided his time until 1750 when he married an heiress instead (HWC 9. 53, n. 8). Walpole's doubts about the Pelhams' approval were well founded, since they appear to have intended Frances for her cousin Thomas Pelham (1728–1805) who was having an affair with an Italian countess on the Grand Tour, as Horace Mann informed Walpole in March 1750.

> Mr Pelham is still here [Florence], though he ought to have been long ago in England, to supply the young lady [Frances] destined for him with the drops she may most stand in need of. It was really an unlucky accident. I have told Mr Pelham that he neglects his future too much, and have done all I could to send him home, but hitherto the Countess Acciajuoli has had the greatest ascendant (HWC 20. 129; 13 March 1750).

64.   Sir Joshua Reynolds: Called *Frances Pelham*
(1728–1804). Oil on canvas, 33 × 27 in. The
Baltimore Museum of Art: The Mary Frick Jacobs
Collection. 'Poor Miss Pelham outgoes her usual *out-
goings.* . . . in short. . . [she] is such an object that one
cannot but be heartily sorry for' (HWC 32. 169–70).

Mann's allusions to the 'accident' and 'drops' refer to an anecdote Walpole told about
Frances Pelham who had been robbed during the celebration of King George II's birthday on 30 October 1749:

> Among the robberies, I might have told you of the eldest Miss Pelham leaving a pair
> of diamond earrings, which she had borrowed for the Birthday, in a hackney chair: she
> had put them under the seat for fear of being attacked, and forgot them. The chairmen
> have sunk them. The next morning when they were missed, the damsel began to cry:
> Lady Catherine [Manners, her mother] grew frightened, lest her infanta should vex
> herself sick, and summoned a jury of matrons to consult whether she should give her
> hartshorn or lavander drops? Mrs Selwyn [Mary Farrington (1690–1777)], who was on
> the panel, grew very peevish, and said, 'Pho! give her brilliant drops.' – Such are the
> present anecdotes of the Court of England!' (HWC 20. 114; 31 January 1750).

At the end of the summer Mann reported that Thomas Pelham was still passionately in
love with the Countess Acciaiuoli – 'I never saw any couple more wrapped up in each
other than they are,' Mann wrote on 21 August: '. . . I have pressed him long to go [to
England] . . . as he is designed for the eldest Miss Pelham, now unmarried, and most probably by that means will be considered as the heir to the Pelham family; views too important to be neglected for any transient attachment' (HWC 20. 172–3; 21 August 1750). But
in 1754, after all this, Thomas Pelham married Anne Frankland (1734–1813), not Frances
Pelham. The Duke of Newcastle gives this description of him: 'Tom Pelham's person is not
very good. He is little and his hair a little too much of Lord Granby's [balding];[3] but he is
lively, well-bred, and has enough to say for himself' (HWC 20. 195, n. 13).

65.   *A Jerboa*, a medal in the collection of William Cavendish (1673–1729), 2d Duke of Devonshire. Line engraving, 8 × 11¾ in. From Niccolò Francesco Haym, *Del Tesoro Brittanico parte prima*, 2 vols. (London, 1719–20), vol. 2, fc. p. 124. By permission of the British Library.

Walpole delighted in the anecdote about Frances Pelham's earrings, but it was her turn to laugh six years later when Walpole had a much more serious accident while walking from Kitty Clive's Little Strawberry Hill back to Strawberry Hill by way of the London–Hampton Court road with his guests the Conways, and 'little' Mary Rich (d. 1769).

> We were returning from Mrs Clive's through the long field, and had gotten over the high stile that comes into the road, that is, three of us [Caroline Campbell (1721–1803), Lady Ailesbury; her husband, Walpole's cousin, Henry Seymour Conway; and HW]. It had rained, and the stile was wet. I could not let Miss Rich straddle across so damp a palfrey [saddle-horse]; but took her in my arms to lift her over. At that instant I saw a coach and six come thundering down the hill from my house [Strawberry Hill, about 400 yards north–east on the London–Hampton Court road]; and hurrying to set down my charge, and stepping backwards, I missed the first step, came down headlong with the nymph in my arms: but turning quite round as we rushed to the ground, the first thing that touched the ground was Miss Rich's head. You must guess in how improper a situation we fell; and you [William Wentworth (1722–91), 2d Earl of Strafford] must not tell my Lady Strafford [Anne Campbell (1720–1785)] before anybody, that every petticoat, etc. in the world were canted – high enough indeed! The coach came on, and never stopped. The apprehension that it would run over my Chloe, made me be where I was, holding out my arm to keep off the horses, which narrowly missed trampling us to death. The ladies [in the coach], who were Lady Holderness [Mary Doublet (1720–1801)], Miss Pelham, and your sister Lady Mary Coke [Mary Campbell (1727–1811)], stared with astonishment at the theatre which they thought I had chosen to celebrate our loves; the footmen laughed; and you may imagine the astonishment of Mr Conway and Lady Ailesbury, who did not see the fall, but turned and saw our attitude. It was these spectators that amazed Miss Pelham, who described the adventure to Miss Pitt [Anne Pitt (1712–81)], and said, 'What was most amazing, there was Mr Conway and Lady Ailesbury looking on!' I shall be vexed to have told you this long story, if Lady Mary has writ it already; only tell me honestly if she has described it as decently as I have (HWC 35. 275–6; 6 June 1756).

Decent, but titillating enough to inspire some ribaldry in a letter from Walpole's cousin, Henry Seymour Conway, who had given his wife, Caroline Campbell, Lady

Ailesbury, a present of a jerboa [mouselike rodent of North Africa] in 1752. Walpole had sent Conway information about the jerboa from a catalogue of the Duke of Devonshire's collection that included a medal of the animal (plate 65).[4] Conway wrote 29 June 1756:

> Your appendix on the subject of Little Mary [Rich] is natural and just what we expected; I wish those who know her figure mayn't take it for a continuation of the history of the jerebo, which considering your familiarity with her [at the scene of the accident] does not sound well for you; she certainly is like in many parts; whether she has a long tail and but one hole for evacuation you know best (HWC 37. 468).

Conway is referring to Niccolò Francesco Haym's description of the jerboa (Hazen 269):

> It had only one hole for evacuation like a bird, thro' which alone he eased nature. . . . the tail was all of one colour inclining to yellow, and the hair upon it very short; but there grew at the end of it, as it were, a white plume with a black list, which divided it in the middle (HWC 37. 468, n. 7).

Walpole seldom mentions Frances Pelham later in the 1750s, except to note her presence at 'an immense assembly' at Chesterfield House in mid-February 1752, and to report rumors of her attachment to William Douglas (1725–1810), 3rd Earl of March, 'Old Q', a rake whom her father forbade her to marry. Conway told Walpole on 1 August 1758 that Frances Pelham was still mooning over him at the age of thirty on a visit to Vauxhall with Mary Coke, her rival for March, and Charles Townshend (1725–67): '. . . [A]fter they had sighed at the moon, and admired the *charming moon* by turns half a dozen times, he [Townshend] said, "*Come, prithee don't both fall in love with the moon too*"' (HWC 37. 557; 1 August 1758).

Walpole described the last chapter of Frances Pelham's unlucky courtships in 1762 when referring to the marriage of Lady Sarah Lennox (1745–1826), who was rumoured to have had an affair with George III:

> Lady Sarah Lenox, I believe, by this time has finished the first volume of her novel [life], and married the swain [Thomas Charles Bunbury (1740–1821)] instead of the monarch [George III]. This season has added very few other tomes to the shelf of romances: whether Miss Pelham's present story will be more than an episode [referring to a quarrel with Lord March], I cannot tell; she has so many *égarements du coeur* and *de l'esprit*,[5] that she is likely to leave her adventures as unfinished as any of Marivaux's;[6] I shall see her tomorrow [Wednesday 2 June 1762] at the ball at Bedford House [Bloomsbury] with all her admirers and *admirées*, Lord Gower [Granville Leveson-Gower (1721–1803), 2d Earl], Lord March and Pam ['the knave of clubs, trump in five-card loo'] (HWC 32. 6–7; 1 June 1762).

Lady Louisa Stuart explains the reason for the desperation sensed by Walpole, opening a sad, second volume of Frances Pelham's life: 'When she and Lord March were young, they had liked each other so well that he would fain have married her; but Mr Pelham [Henry Pelham (1695–1754), MP and prime minister], aware of his libertine character, already established, refused his consent' (HWC 32. 6, n. 11).[7] Lady Northumberland's *Diary* describes the quarrel that occurred at Ranelagh on 24 May 1762 where Frances Pelham met March with his mistress, the Contessa Rena: 'Miss Pelham put herself in a fury with Lord March and Mr George Selwyn and even went so far as to strike the former a blow on the side, because Mr Selwyn had presented the Reyna with a rose which he [March] had had from her [Miss Pelham]' [HWC 32. 6, n. 11).[8]

In 1760 Walpole observed another of Frances Pelham's 'égarements du coeur' on a visit to Magdalen House, a refuge for penitent prostitutes where the Reverend William Dodd preached a sermon: 'He apostrophized the lost sheep, who sobbed and cried from their souls – so did my Lady Hertford and Fanny Pelham, till I believe the City Dames took them both for Jane Shores [heroine of Nicholas Rowe's she-tragedy]' (HWC 9. 274; 28 January 1760). Subsequently in December 1761 Frances Pelham and Walpole beat William Augustus, Duke of Cumberland (1721–65) at cards: '. . . in less than two hours t'other night the Duke of Cumberland lost 450 pounds at loo; Miss Pelham won three hundred, and I the rest' (HWC 9. 412; 23 December 1761). The nickname 'Fanny' and the card-table establish Walpole's friendship with Frances Pelham early in the 1760s. A song Walpole wrote to her entitled 'The Advice'[9] after a conversation at Richmond House on the Thames in March 1763 shows how deeply he understood the plight of an unmarried woman of fashion:

1.

> The business of woman, dear Chloe, is pleasure,
> And by love ev'ry fair one her minutes should measure.
> 'Oh! for love we're all ready,' you cry – very true;
> Nor would I rob the gentle fond god of his due.
> Unless in the sentiments Cupid has part,
> And dips in the amorous transport his dart,
> 'Tis tumult, 'tis loathing and hate,
> Caprice gives it birth, and contempt is its fate.
>
> (HWC 10. 54–5; 25 March 1763)

Walpole's Chloe sounds like a sketch from Pope's *Epistle to a Lady* on the characters of women, but Walpole goes on to offer a touching remonstrance to a highly strung woman who at thirty-five was still pursuing hopelessly the man her father had prevented her from marrying more than ten years before:

2.

> True passion insensibly leads to the joy,
> And grateful esteem bids its pleasures n'er cloy.
> Yet here you should stop – but your whimsical sex
> Such romantic ideas to passion annex,
> That poor men, by your visions and jealousy worried,
> To nymphs, less ecstatic, but kinder are hurried.
> In your heart, I consent, let your wishes be bred;
> Only take care your heart don't get into your head.
>
> (HWC 10. 54–5; 25 March 1763)

66.   James Walker after William Woollett: *Esher Surrey, the Seat of the Right Hon. Henry Pelham.* Courtesy of the Print Collection, Lewis Walpole Library, Yale University. 'I never passed a more agreeable day. . . . it [Esher] was Parnassus as Watteau would have painted it' (HWC 10. 72–3).

One suspects Walpole's advice was as welcome to the desperate Frances Pelham as Clarissa's to Belinda in Pope's *Rape of the Lock* (Canto 5, lines 9–34).

Frances Pelham was delivered from her passions in the spring of the same year when she entertained an elegant company including Walpole at Esher Place, Surrey (plate 66), the stylish seat she had inherited from her father.[10] Walpole's letter describing Esher is often quoted by garden historians, but it belongs to social history too, and it forms a well-painted background to his half-length portrait of Frances Pelham, the genius of the place:

I never passed a more agreeable day than yesterday [Wednesday 18 May 1763]. . . . The day was delightful, the scene transporting, the trees, lawns, concaves, all in the perfection in which the ghost of Kent [William (1686–1748), landscape architect] would enjoy to see them. At twelve we made a tour of the farm [the layout at this date resembled a *ferme ornée*] in eight chaises and calashes, horsemen and footmen, setting out like a picture of Wouverman [Philip Wouwerman (1619–68), Dutch landscape painter]. My lot fell in the lap of Mrs Anne Pitt [(1712–81)], which I could have excused, as she was not at all in the style of the day, romantic, but political.

We had a magnificent dinner, cloaked in the modesty of earthenware: French horns and hautboys on the lawn. We walked to the belvedere on the summit of the hill, where a threatened storm only served to heighten the beauty of the landscape, a rainbow on a dark cloud falling precisely behind the tower of a neighbouring church, between another tower, and the building at Claremont [Duke of Newcastle's seat]. Monsieur de Nivernois, who had been absorbed all day and lagging behind, translating my verses, was delivered of his version, and of some more lines, which he wrote on Miss Pelham in the belvedere, while we drank tea and coffee. From thence we passed into the wood, and the ladies formed a circle of chairs before the mouth of the cave, which was overhung to a vast height with woodbines, lilacs and laburnums, and dignified by those tall shapely cypresses. On the descent of the hill were placed the French horns; the abigails, servants, and neighbours wandering below by the river − in short, it was Parnassus as Watteau would have painted it. Here we had a rural syllabub, and part of the company returned to town; but were replaced by Giardini and Onofrio, who with Nivernois on violin and Lord Pembroke on the bass, accompanied Miss Pelham, Lady Rockingham and the Duchess of Grafton who sang. This little concert lasted till past ten; then there were minuets, and as we had seven couple left, it concluded with a country dance − I blush again, for I danced, but was kept countenance by Nivernois, who has one wrinkle more than I have. A quarter after twelve they sat down to supper, and I came home by a charming moonlight (HWC 10. 72−3; 17 May 1763).

The idyll at Esher was followed by the humiliation of Frances and her sister Mary on Monday 3 December 1764, at 'Pittsburgh' (24. 15), Anne Pitt's house in Berkeley Square, a scene Walpole described to Francis Seymour Conway (1718−94), the Earl of Hertford.

It would have made you shrug up your shoulders at dirty humanity, to see the two Miss Pelhams [Frances and Mary Pelham (1739−94)] sit neglected, without being asked to dance. You may imagine this could not escape me, who have passed through the several gradations in which Lady Jane Stuart [(1742−1828)] and Miss Pelham are and have been; but I fear poor Miss Pelham feels hers a little more than ever I did (HWC 38. 475−6; 3 December 1764).

Remembering the daughter of John Stuart, 3rd Earl of Bute who had resigned the prime-ministership a year earlier, and his own father's fall from power, Walpole understood, as few others could, the situation of Frances Pelham, daughter of a prime minister, Henry Pelham (1694−1754). It is this sympathy that accounts for Walpole's conversations, his lines of 'The Advice', and his readiness 'to walk with Miss Pelham on the terrace [Richmond House, London] till two in the morning, because it is moonlight and her chair is not come' (HWC 31. 36; 11 June 1765). At the same time he had to resign himself ruefully to the futility of his advice: 'Fashionable as I am and *charming*,' he wrote to Anne Liddell from Arlington Street in London, 'my attractions are not great enough to draw Miss Pelham hither. I should neither flatter her nor fret her, and anything is insipid to her, that does not make her temper ferment' (HWC 32. 92; 4 February 1773).

The last chapter of Frances Pelham's life recorded in Walpole's correspondence concerns her well-publicised quarrel in March 1773 with a Mrs Fitzroy, possibly Isabella Fitzroy (1726−82), Lady Hertford. Both were founding members of the Ladies Club in Albemarle Street, and both lived 'gaming rakehelly' lives (HWC 38. 494). They got into an argument at Powys House, Knightsbridge, about 'the reputation of Mr Frere, late master of the Thatched House [tavern] in St James's Street; and words rising very high, Mrs Fitzroy gave Miss Pelham a slap upon the cheek' (HWC 32. 103, n. 32). Remembering a duel when George Townshend had shot a bullet into Lord Bellamont's belly, Walpole turns the cat-fight into a duel in his letter to Anne Liddell: 'I have not heard a more recent duel than that of Chevy Chase or the one between Mrs F. and Miss P. – they have not found the ball in the latter yet' (HWC 32. 103–4; 11 March 1773). Walpole lost no time in seeking particulars about the 'duel', improving on his mock-heroic conceit:

> To the Club [Ladies' Club, Albemarle Street] I shall go tonight [Tuesday 16 March 1773] for the first time; but have not yet seen Thomyris [Thamyris, Frances Pelham as Homer's bard, deprived of sight and power of song after challenging the Muses] or Thalestris [Isabella Fitzroy, as Queen of the Amazons]. I was t'other morning at Lady Powis's [Barbara Antonia Herbert (1735–86), Powis House, Knightsbridge]: her great room is hung with a glorious scarlet damask. She told me it was only silk and worsted: I could not believe my eyes, but insisted it came from Genoa. She vowed it was made in Spitalfields[11] – the sound struck me – I asked if that chamber had not been the scene of battle? and as it was, I have desired it may for the future be called Spittlefields (HWC 32. 106–7; 16 March 1773).

Walpole gives the last word in this mock-heroic anecdote to Lord Chesterfield, who had been uttering *bon mots* on his deathbed: 'Alas!,' Walpole wrote to Anne Liddell, 'I shall have no more of his lively sayings, Madam, to send you. Oh! yes, I have his last; being told of the quarrel in Spittlefields, and even that Mrs F. struck Miss P., he said, "I always thought Mrs F. a striking beauty"' (HWC 32. 112; 27 March 1773). But Walpole found no comedy in 'Miss Pelham's orgies' (HWC 32. 121; 11 June 1773) of gambling, and his last references to her are Hogarthian: 'As to Miss Pelham,' he writes in October 1773, 'she will have neither house nor lares left' (HWC 32. 160). He adapts an expression of Colley Cibber's on the actress Mrs Oldfield in the 'Preface' to the *Provok'd Husband* to paint the final scene of Frances Pelham's progress:

> Poor Miss P. outgoes her usual *outgoings*.[12] She sits up all night at the Club [the Ladies' Club] without a woman [servant], loses hundreds every night and her temper, beats her head, and exposes herself before all the young men and the waiters – in short, is such an object that one cannot but be heartily sorry for (HWC 32. 169–70; 14 December 1773).

Again Pope's lines apply, except that Frances Pelham had a friend in Horace Walpole:

> See how the World its Veterans rewards!
> A Youth of frolicks, an old Age of Cards,
> Fair to no purpose, artful to no end,
> Young without Lovers, old without a Friend,
> A Fop their Passion, but their Prize a Sot,
> Alive, ridiculous, and dead, forgot!
> (*Epistle to a Lady*, lines 243–8; TE 3.2, p. 67)

67.   Thomas Gainsborough: *Augustus John Hervey, 3rd Earl of Bristol*. SA 1768. Oil on canvas, 91½ × 60 in. Private Collection. Photo: National Trust Photographic Library/John Hammond. 'Very good. . . one of the best modern portraits I have seen' (SA 68. 60, p. 5; HW *marginalia*).

68.   R. Brookshaw after R. Pyle: *Elizabeth Chudleigh Countess of Bristol as Flora*. Mezzotint engraving, 14 × 9⅞ in. © Copyright The British Museum. 'I have known her from five years old, and seen her in all her stages' (HWC 28. 260).

Elizabeth Chudleigh (1720–88), Duchess of Kingston: 'Neither Man, Woman, or Androgyne . . . but Everything' Thomas Gainsborough px

The apotheosis of Walpole's marriage theme can be observed in Thomas Gainsborough's portrait of the husband of Elizabeth Chudleigh (1720–87; plate 67). In the 1768 Society of Artists catalogue Walpole identifies 'a sea officer, whole length' (No. 60) as 'Capt. Augustus Hervey [Augustus John (1724–79), naval officer, M.P., and 3d Earl of Bristol (1775)],' remarking it 'very good, and one of the best modern portraits I have seen. It is at Lord Bristol's in St James Square [Hervey's brother Frederick Augustus (1730–1803)]' (SA 68. 60, p. 5, *marginalia*).

Augustus Hervey was the favourite son of Walpole's close friend, Mary Lepell, Lady

Hervey, and a naval hero Walpole liked to call the 'Black Prince' (HWC 31. 13). Walpole collaborated with Hervey in the effort to save Admiral Byng (HWC 35. 97, n. 11). 'I have great satisfaction in Captain Hervey's gallantry . . . he is my friend' (HWC 21. 233), Walpole wrote after Hervey, aboard the *Monmouth*, drove the French ship *La Rose* ashore at Malta 1 July 1758, and set her afire the next day (HWC 21. 225, n. 10). But Hervey figures principally in the correspondence as the first husband of the notorious Elizabeth Chudleigh (1720–88) who was tried for bigamy in 1776 for marrying Evelyn Pierrepont (1711–73), 2d Duke of Kingston-upon-Hull on 8 March 1769. 'I have known her from five years old and seen her in all her stages' (HWC 28. 260; 14 April 1776). 'She and her brother were my play-fellows when we lived at Chelsea' (HWC 24. 198; 24 April 1776). The Walpoles in Orford House, and the Chudleighs in Chelsea Hospital where her father was deputy governor, had been neighbours.

Walpole watched the progress of Elizabeth Chudleigh's career with fascination, and she sat at full length for her portrait (plate 68) in his letters. After her clandestine marriage to Hervey in 1744, kept secret to allow her to continue serving as maid-of-honour to Princess Augusta, she appeared at a subscription masquerade 1 May 1749 as 'Iphigenia, but so naked that you would have taken her for Andromeda' (HWC 20. 49; 3 May 1749).[13] The following year Walpole reports that '[t]he new amour [George II's with Miss Chudleigh] did not proceed' (HWC 20. 212, n. 5):

Two days ago [24 December 1750] at the Drawing-Room [St James's Palace] the gallant Orondates [George II as lover of Statira in Calprenède's *Cassandre*] strode up to Miss Chudleigh, and told her, he was glad to have an opportunity of obeying her commands, that he appointed her mother [Harriet Chudleigh (d. 1756)] housekeeper at Windsor, and hoped she would not think a kiss too great a reward – against all precedent he kissed her in the circle. He has had a hankering these two years. Her life, which is now of thirty years' standing, has been a little historic. Why should not experience and a charming face on her side, and near seventy years on his, produce a title? (HWC 20. 213; 22 December 1750).

Walpole's note on this letter summarises Elizabeth Chudleigh's history and her future bigamous career:

She was, though maid of honour, privately married to Augustus, second son of the late Lord Hervey, by whom she had two children; but disagreeing, the match was not owned. She afterwards, still maid of honour, lived very publicly with the Duke of Kingston, and at last married him – during Mr Hervey's life (HWC 20. 213, n. 14).

Miss Chudleigh makes another entrance in Walpole's correspondence in the early 1760s when she gave a ball Walpole attended on 4 June 1760 to celebrate the twenty-third birthday of the Prince of Wales [George III (1738–1820)] at her newly completed house in Hill Street, Berkeley Square. Walpole wrote to William Wentworth, Earl of Strafford:

You had heard, before you left London, of Miss Chudleigh's intended loyalty on the Prince's birthday. Poor thing, I fear she has thrown away above a quarter's salary! It was magnificent and well-understood [*bien entendu*] — no crowd — and though a sultry night, one was not a moment incommoded. The court was illuminated on the whole summit of a wall with a battlement of lamps; smaller ones on every step, and a figure of lanthorns on the outside of the house. The virgin-mistress [of the Duke of Kingston] began the ball with the Duke of York [Edward Augustus (1739–67), Prince of Wales, George III's brother], who was dressed in a pale blue watered tabby [silk], which, as I told him, if he danced much, would soon be *tabby all over*, like the man's advertisement [a London staymaker]; but nobody did dance much. . . . Miss Chudleigh desired the gamblers would go up into the garrets — 'Nay, they are not garrets — it is only the roof of the house hollowed for upper servants — but I have no upper servants!' Everybody ran up: there is a low gallery with bookcases, and four chambers practised [built] under the pent of the roof, each hung with the finest Indian pictures on different colours, and with Chinese chairs of the same colours. Vases of flowers in each for nosegays, and in one retired nook a most critical couch!

The lord of the festival [The Duke of Kingston] was there, and seemed neither ashamed nor vain of the expense of his pleasures. At supper she offered him tokay, and told him she believed he would find it good. The supper was in two rooms and very fine, and on all the sideboards, and even on the chairs, were pyramids and troughs of strawberries and cherries; you would have thought she was kept by Vertumnus (HWC 35. 299–301; 7 June 1760).

The following year Walpole collected one of Miss Chudleigh's *bon-mots* about the Earl of Bute's alleged affair in a conversation with Princess Augusta: 'They talk of a print in which . . . [she] is reprimanding Miss Chudleigh — the latter curtsies, and replies, "*Madame, chacun à son But* [Bute]"' (HWC 9. 338; 7 February 1761).[14] And Walpole describes another ball with fireworks, intended to flatter the royal family, given by the 'dashing . . . Virgin Chudleigh' (HWC 38. 203) in May 1763. It appears to have taken place at another of her houses in Knightsbridge overlooking Hyde Park:

Oh, that you [Henry Conway] had been at her ball t'other night [Thursday 19 May 1763]! History could never describe it and keep its countenance. The Queen's [Charlotte (1744–1818)] real birthday, you know, is not kept [19 May being too close to George III's 4 June]: this maid of honour kept it — nay, while the Court is in mourning [Friedrich Wilhelm Margrave of Brandenburg Bayreuth d. 26 February 1763]. . . . A scaffold was erected in Hyde Park for fireworks. To show the illuminations without to more advantage, the company were received in an apartment totally dark, where they remained for two hours — If they gave rise to any more birthdays, who could help it? The fireworks were fine, and succeeded well. On each side of the court were two large scaffolds for the Virgin's tradespeople. When the fireworks ceased, a large scene was lighted in the court, representing their Majesties; on each side of which were six obelisks, painted with emblems, and illuminated; mottos beneath in Latin and English.[15] . . . The lady of the house made many apologies for the poorness of the performance, which she said was only oil-paper, painted by one of her servants; but it really was fine and pretty. The Duke of Kingston [Evelyn Pierrepont] was in a frock, *comme chez lui*. Behind the house was a cenotaph for the

Princess Elizabeth [d. 1759, age 18], a kind of illuminated cradle; the motto, *All the honours the dead can receive.* This burying-ground was a strange codicil to a festival; and, what was more strange, about one in the morning, this sarcophagus burst out into crackers and guns. The Margrave of Anspach began the ball with the Virgin. The supper was most sumptuous (HWC 38. 203–5; 21 May 1763).

The next act in the scandalous chronicle of the virgin-mistress occurred in 1768 when Hervey sued Chudleigh for divorce on the grounds of adultery, which she answered by obtaining a ruling from the Ecclesiastical Court (Doctor's Commons) on 10 February 1769 that 'declared her to be free from any matrimonial contract' (HWC 23. 93, n. 9). When Walpole reported these events to Horace Mann on 28 February 1769 he was unaware that Hervey had colluded with Chudleigh to abrogate the marriage.

Well, but to come to goddesses – after a marriage of twenty years, Augustus Hervey, having fallen in love with a physician's daughter at Bath, has attacked his spouse, the maid of honour, the fair Chudleigh, and sought a divorce for adultery. Unfortunately he had waited till all the witnesses of their marriage, and of her two deliveries, are dead as well as the two children. The provident virgin had not been so negligent. Last year [HW's mistake for 1759] she forced herself into the house of the parson [Thomas Amis] who had married them, and who was at the point of death. By bullying and to get rid of her, she forced the poor man to give up the certificate.
   Since that she has appeared in the Doctor's Commons [August–September 1768], and sworn by the Virgins Mary and Diana, that she never was married to Mr Hervey. The Ecclesiastical Court has admitted her corporal oath, and enjoined silence to Mr Hervey. Next week [8 March 1769] this fair injured innocence, who is but fifty, is to be married to the Duke of Kingston, who has kept her openly for almost half that time [since 1750] – and who by this means will recover half his fortune, which he had lavished on her. As a proof of her purity and poverty, her wedding gown is white satin trimmed with Brussels lace and pearls. Every word of this history is extremely true. The physician [Abel Moysey (1715–80), MD, of Bath], who is a little more in his senses than the other actors, and a little honester, will not give his daughter [Mary Moysey]; nay, has offered her five thousand pounds not to marry Mr Hervey, but Miss Rhubarb [Mary Moysey] is as much above worldly decorum as the rest, and persists, though there is no more doubt of the marriage of Mr Hervey and Miss Chudleigh, than that of your father and mother. It is a cruel case upon his [Moysey's] family, who can never acquiesce in the legitimacy of his children, if any come from this bigamy (HWC 23. 92–4; 28 February 1769).

When Chudleigh's first husband's brother, George William Hervey (1721–75), 2d Earl of Bristol, died on 18 March 1775 (HWC 24. 86, n. 7), Walpole immediately recognized the implications for the would-be Duchess of Kingston:

Will her Grace of Kingston now pass eldest [play without the trump card in the game of loo], and condescend to be, as she really is, Countess of Bristol? Or will she come over [from Italy], and take her trial for the becoming dignity of the exhibition in

Westminster Hall? How it would sound! 'Elizabeth Countess of Bristol, *alias* Duchess of Kingston, come into Court!' (HWC 24. 87; 20 March 1775).

Hervey's marriage to Mary Moysey never took place, and it was his first wife, the Duchess of Kingston, who faced charges of bigamy after the death of the Duke of Kingston in Bath on 23 September 1773. 'I have not yet heard the Duke's and Duchess's will', Walpole wrote describing the pomp of her mourning a week later:

> She moved to town [London from Bath] with the pace of an interment, and made as many halts between Bath and London as Queen Eleanor's corpse [Eleanor of Castile, Queen of Edward I, d. 28 November 1290]. . . . Her black crape veil they say contained a thousand more yards than that of Mousseline la Sérieuse [a fairy princess],[16] and at one of the inns where her grief bated, she was in too great an agony to descend at the door, and was slung into a bow window as Marc Antony was into Cleopatra's monument (HWC 32. 146–7; 1 October 1773).

The Duke's will leaving his estates to her was probated in October 1773 (HWC 24. 21, n. 14). The Duke's nephews filed suit in chancery 'to prove her first marriage [to Augustus John Hervey in 1744], and . . . to set the will aside' (HWC 24.21; 10 July 1774). The Duchess responded by taking refuge in Rome; where her friend Pope Pius VI (1717–99) was serving as custodian of valuables she shipped to Italy anticipating prosecution for bigamy, and as her agent to purchase a Roman villa of Sixtus Quintus.[17] On 10 July 1774 when she returned from Italy to Kingston House, Knightsbridge, '[a] prosecution for bigamy was ready to meet her. She decamped [at 3 am, returning to Italy] in the middle of the night; and six hours after [9 am, 11 July 1774], the officers of justice were at her door to seize her. This is but an unheroic catastrophe of her romance. . . . What will be the issue of the suit and law suit I cannot tell. As so vast an estate [c. £16,000] is the prize, the lawyers will probably protract it beyond this century' (HWC 24. 24–5; 3 August 1774).

Elizabeth Chudleigh was indicted for bigamy on 9 January 1775 by the General Quarter Sessions of the Middlesex Court, and she was summoned 'to answer to some questions . . . concerning her first marriage' in order to avoid outlawry and confiscation of her estates (HWC 24. 83; 11 March 1775). Horace Mann, who spoke to her in Florence, reported that 'she is resolved to stand to any trial, and seems persuaded that she shall defeat at last all the efforts of her prosecutors' (HWC 24. 84).

Later in the summer the playwright Samuel Foote submitted to the Lord Chancellor his farce, *A Trip to Calais* (1776) ridiculing the Duchess of Kingston as Lady Kitty Crocodile (HWC 33. 458, n. 9; Hazen 1810. 28. 5). When the play was refused a license, Foote threatened to publish the scenes. The Duchess replied with a scurrilous letter to *The Evening Post* (13 August 1775), insulting Foote as 'a Merry Andrew' and theatrical assassin, which he answered by graciously agreeing to withdraw the play. Walpole commented on the paper war:

> That heroine of the Doctor's Commons . . . has at last made her folly, which I have long known, as public as her shame, by entering the lists with a Merry Andrew, but who is no fool. . . . She wrote a letter in the *Evening Post*, which not the lowest

of her class, who tramp in pattens, would have set her mark to. Billingsgate from a ducal coronet was inviting – however, Foote with all the delicacy she ought to have used, replied [*London Chronicle*, 15–17 August 1775; Hazen 538] only with wit, irony, and confounded satire. The Pope [Pius VI] will not be able to wash out the spots with all the holy water in the Tiber. I imagine she will escape a trial – but Foote has given her the *coup de grâce* (HWC 24. 125–6; 7 September 1775).

On 11 November 1775 the Duchess of Kingston's petition for a trial in the House of Lords was granted, and a writ of *certiorari* removed the proceedings from the King's Bench to the House of Lords (HWC 24. 143, n. 12). In December:

Lord Mansfield [William Murray (1705–93)] entered the lists as her knight, and contended for a private hearing in the chamber of Parliament, and treated the affair very lightly. This revolted the Chancellor [Henry 2d Earl Bathurst (1714–94)], and he drew her failings in very ungentle colours. A committee was appointed [Friday 8 December 1775] to examine precedents. Her Grace was alarmed, went to St James's chapel at eight in the morning, and was delivered of a scream that roused all the palace (HWC 24. 150; 17 December 1775).

The Daily Advertiser reported that Chudleigh had been 'suddenly seized with a fainting fit during divine service . . . and carried home speechless' (HWC 24. 150, n. 5).

The obdurate Lords committees proceeded. The tide was turned and everybody spoke all they knew. Collusion between the Duchess and Lord Bristol [Augustus Hervey, 3rd Earl] to impose on the Ecclesiastic Court [in 1769], money taken by the Earl, perjury on both sides, the register of their marriage torn out, which is felony, a new certificate said to be forged – in short, nothing but a trial in Westminster Hall could satisfy justice and the public. Screams now ripened to madness, and the Duchess begged a respite for two months (HWC 24. 150–1; 17 December 1775).

Her physicians testified 'great alienation of mind' (HWC 24. 151). She appealed to the king 'begging a *nolle prosequi*,' but:

[t]he committee went on, and have decided [14 December 1775] that she shall be tried in Westminster Hall. . . . What this heroic lady will attempt next is very unknown. If she decamps, outlawry and forfeitures follow. Laudanum she had recourse to formerly on an emergency. If she adheres to frenzy, she must retire to a madhouse. If she braves her fate – I shall not wonder if she escapes. A fair one, more artful, but not of so high rank, nor patronized by a Chief Justice [Mansfield], has just foiled the law, though nobody questions her guilt. This is a Mrs Margaret Caroline Rudd [(1745–79) tried and acquitted for forgery 8 December 1775 at the Old Bailey], whose history would make as large a volume as Madame de Kingston's (HWC 24. 151–3; 17 December 1775).

In spite of the arguments of a 'mob' of fourteen lawyers in Attorney-General Thurlow's chambers 'the *nolle prosequi* will not be granted. . . . The trial is fixed for the end of February' (24. 162; 26 December 1775). The House of Lords granted one more delay and '[t]he trial of the late Pope's [Clement XIV (1705–74)] friend, the Duchess of Kingston, is put off till April' (HWC 24. 175; 28 January 1776). By March '[e]verybody is on the quest for tickets for the Duchess of Kingston's trial' – everyone except Walpole, crippled by the gout, who was anticipating a *coup de théâtre*:

> I am persuaded her impudence will operate in some singular manner. Probably she will appear in weeds with a train to reach cross Westminster Hall, with mourning maids of honour to support her when she swoons at her dear Duke's name, and in a black veil to conceal her not blushing. To this farce, novel and curious as it will be, I shall not go. I think cripples have no business in crowds but at the pool of Bethesda – and to be sure this is no angel that troubles the waters (HWC 24. 187; 22 March 1776).

Although Walpole did not attend the trial, he wrote detailed and vivid accounts to Mann and Mason with the help of newspaper accounts, informants like his friend George 2d Earl Harcourt (1736–1809), and the 'printed trial' published on the last day of the proceedings 22 April 1776 (HWC 24. 192, n. 4). He told Horace Mann:

> You may think of America, if you please, but we think and talk but of one subject, the solemn comedy that is acting in Westminster Hall. Deep wagers had been laid that the Duchess-Countess would decamp before her trial – This with a million of other stories have been so spread, that I am determined to believe no one fact, but what I shall read in the printed trial[18] – for at it I have not been, though curious about so august a mummery, and so original a culprit; but I am too little recovered to encounter crowds (HWC 24. 191–2; 17 April 1776).

William Mason demanded a daily account of the trial from Walpole despite his absence from the proceedings: '[I]f I have not an account of the Duchess of Kingston's trial every day from you I shall die of the pip' (HWC 28. 260; 10 April 1776). Walpole replied the day before the trial, Sunday 14 April, the 'Eve of St Elizabeth of Kingston': '[Y]ou commission me to send you journals of the Duchess's trial, as if I was to be there! . . . Thus you must expect no ocular accounts from me, perhaps nothing better than the newspapers would tell you, except with a little more authenticity' (HWC 28. 260–1; 14 April 1776). Harcourt probably supplied the details of the duchess's appearance that enliven his first report on the trial to Mason:

> The Duchess-Countess has raised my opinion of her understanding, which was always but at low ebb, for she has behaved so sensibly and with so little affectation, that her auditory are loud in applause of her. She did not once squall, scream or faint, was not impudent, nor gorgeous, looked well though pale and trembling; was dressed all in black, yet in silk, not crape; with no pennon hoisted but a widow's peak (HWC 28. 261; 16 April 1776).

Chudleigh acquitted herself decently on the first day of the trial 15 April in the awe-inspiring chambers of Westminster Hall as she addressed the assembled peers: 'My Lords,

69.   John Taylor: *Elizabeth Chudleigh, Duchess Dowager of Kingston*. Mezzotint engraving. From *The Trial of Elizabeth Duchess of Kingston* (1776), front. Courtesy of the Lewis Walpole Library, Yale University.

I, the unfortunate widow of your late brother, the most noble Evelyn Pierrepont, Duke of Kingston, am brought to the bar of this right honourable House without a shadow of fear, but infinitely awed by the respect that is due to you, my most honourable judges' (HWC 28. 261, n. 2). Walpole gives Mann a spare summary of:

> the doubly noble prisoner [who] went through her part with universal admiration. Instead of her usual ostentatious folly, and clumsy pretensions to cunning, all her conduct was decent, and even seemed natural. Her dress was entirely black and plain [plate 69]; her attendants not too numerous, her dismay at first perfectly unaffected. A few tears balanced cheerfulness enough; and her presence of mind and attention never deserted her. This rational behaviour, and the pleadings of her four counsel, who contended for the finality of the Ecclesiastical Court's sentence against a second trial, carried her triumphantly through the first day, and turned the stream much in her favour (HWC 24. 192–3; 17 April 1776).

The second day of the trial, Tuesday 17 April, when the attorney and solictor generals refuted the duchess's counsel:

> was less propitious . . . and seem[s] to have unhinged some of her firmness. She was blooded as soon as she retired, fell into a great passion of tears, and is, or affects to be very ill. However, the Lords have given her and themselves a respite of two days. . . . [I]s not the whole burlesque, when, except the foreigners, there could not be one

person in the Hall who was not as much convinced of the bigamy, as of their own existence? (HWC 24. 193; 17 April 1776).

On Friday the court heard testimony that exploded the duchess's claims: '. . . the capital witness [Ann Cradock, a servant], the ancient damsel who was present at her first marriage and tucked her up for consummation' (HWC 28.263; 20 April 1776). Her cause was disintegrating:

If the Pope [Pius VI] expects his Duchess back [to Rome], he must create her one, for her peers have reduced her to a Countess. Her folly and obstinacy now appear in their full vigour, at least her faith in the Ecclesiastic Court, trusting to the infallibility of which she provoked this trial, in the face of every sort of detection. A living witness of the first marriage, a register of it fabricated long afterwards by herself, the widow of the clergyman [Thomas Amis] who married her, many confidants to whom she had trusted the secret, and even Hawkins [Sir Caesar (1711–86)] the surgeon, privy to the birth of her child, appeared against her. The Lords were tender, and would not probe the Earl's [Augustus Hervey's] collusion; but the Ecclesiastical Court, who so readily accepted their juggle, and sanctified the second match, were brought to shame. . . . The Duchess, who could produce nothing else of consequence in her favour, tried the powers of oratory, and made a long oration, in which she cited the protection of her late mistress [Augusta, Princess Dowager of Wales (1719–72)]. . . . She concluded her rhetoric with a fit, and the trial with rage, when convicted of the bigamy. The Attorney-General [Edward Thurlow (1731–1806)] laboured to have her burnt in the hand [the prescribed penalty], but the judges were hustled into an opinion against it, and it was waived. So all this complication of knavery receives no punishment (HWC 24. 195–6; 24 April 1776).

On Monday 22 April, after the duchess made 'a paltry defence and an oration of fifty pages, which she herself had written and pronounced well,' the Lords unanimously found her guilty of bigamy and 'dismissed her with the simple injunction of paying her fees. . . . So ends that solemn farce! which may be indifferently bound up with the State Trials and the *History of Moll Flanders*' (HWC 28. 266; 23 April 1776).

Thus Walpole sums up the trial of a character whose portrait he had been drawing in his letters for at least twenty-five years, adding this note to his transcription of his letters to Mann on the Earl of Bristol's predicament: 'Augustus John Hervey Earl of Bristol. He had never avowed his marriage with Miss Chudleigh, and was supposed to have connived for a sum of money at her marrying the Duke' (HWC 24. 193, n. 12).

We have noted that Walpole refers to Gainsborough's portrait of Hervey as 'one of the best modern portraits I have seen' (SA 1768, No. 60), and the same might be said for Walpole's epistolary portrait of Hervey's wife. His picture of the 'Duchess-Countess' (HWC 28. 261) is a mosaic, built up like Boswell's Johnson from a multitude of fragmentary vignettes, anecdotes, *bon-mots*, nicknames, and epithets. 'I must go out and learn anecdotes' (HWC 28. 263–4), Walpole writes to Mason from Strawberry Hill in the midst of the trial. It is from his collection of 'Kingstoniana' (HWC 28. 227) that he builds his own vivid portrait of Elizabeth Chudleigh's marriages, entertainments, mourning, and trial. Witness his epithets for her – 'that holy virgin, St Lubrica' (HWC 31. 423); 'Madam of Babylon' (HWC 24. 162); the 'virgin-mistress' (HWC 35. 300); 'Christina' for her 'imitation of that stroller, Queen Christina [Queen of Sweden (1626–89)]' (HWC 24. 14). He compares her story to a scene in *Don Quixote*:

> What think you of that pompous piece of effrontery and imposture, the Duchess of Kingston? Is there common sense in her ostentation and grief, and train of black crape and band of music? I beg you would not be silent on that chapter; it is as comic a scene as that of the Countess Trifaldine in *Don Quixote* (HWC 23. 556–7; 23 February 1774).

Walpole compares the extravagance of the duchess's mourning to a princess in a fairytale (HWC 32. 146, 1773), and transmutes a detail collected from *The London Magazine* (43 [1774]: 455) about her histrionic entrance 'at the window [of a tavern at Salthill, Buckinghamshire], to avoid the vulgar stare of the mob' (HWC 32. 147, n. 14), into a mock-heroic allusion to a stage direction in Shakespeare's *Antony and Cleopatra* (HWC 32. 147, n. 15).

Thus he transforms the leaden prose of the press into the leaf-gold of the letters: 'All my intelligence here [Strawberry Hill] arrives dislocated through dowager prisms' (HWC 32. 147, 1773). Although Walpole discounts his own reports of the duchess as 'perhaps nothing better than the newspapers' (HWC 28. 261), Walpole raises journalism to art in the manner of Boswell's fact imagined.[19] He delights in the *Public Advertiser*'s 'collection of applications to public characters from *Tom Thumb* [Hazen 1818.3]. . . . The last, on the bigamist maid of honour . . . is one of the happiest quotations I ever saw': –

> A maid like me heaven formed at least for *two*;
> I married him – and now I'll marry you.
> (HWC 28. 489)

During the Wilkes' riots he imagines her ravished by the mob: 'if Lord Talbot [William (1710–1782)] had not . . . recommenced bruiser, I don't know but the Duchess of Kingston, who has so long preserved her modesty from *both* her husbands, might not have been ravished in the drawing-room [of Kingston House, Knightsbridge]' (HWC 10. 274; 26 March 1769). As early as 1760 he applies to her the enigmatical Bolognese inscription to AElia Laelia Crispis: '*nec vir, nec mulier, nec androgyna . . . sed omnia* (neither man, woman, or androgyne . . . but everything') (HWC 9. 276 n. 5; 27 March 1760).

Walpole never tires of adding details to his portrait of the duchess from incidental observations. 'There is no keeping off age by sticking roses and sweet peas in one's hair, as Miss Chudleigh does still' (HWC 10. 245; 31 July 1767). He writes in the postscript of a letter to Horace Mann à propos of her confinement during the trial:

> I must add an anecdote of the Duchess-Countess that I heard last night [Tuesday 23 April 1776]. On some altercation between her and Sir Francis Molyneux [1737–1812], Black Rod, under whose custody she was in her own house,[20] she carried him into another room, and showed him a hole in the ceiling or wainscot made

by a pistol ball. I have heard formerly that she used to terrify the Duke of Kingston in that manner, with threatening to murder him or herself (24. 198, 1776).

How are we to interpret Walpole's composite portrait of 'Saint Elizabeth of Kingston' (28. 260)? Is it malicious gossip, verifiable historical biography, or both? It certainly teems with unequivocal judgments (*Fari quae sentiat*) about her guilt, her character – 'that pompous piece of effrontery and imposture' (23. 556); and her false pretences – 'this fair injured innocence' (23. 93). But Walpole keeps an open mind, admitting after the first day of the trial that her behaviour was better than he had expected, and was willing to grant her, a year before her trial, credit for the creation of a remarkable personality: 'I can tell you nothing more extraordinary; nor would any history figure near hers. It shows genius to strike out anything so new as her achievements. Though we have many uncommon personages, it is not easy for them to be superiorly particular' (24. 87). Comparing her to Queen Christina of Sweden, he says she is 'a phenomenon . . . [but] no original' in buying a papal villa (24. 14). 'Extraordinary,' 'uncommon', 'particular', a 'phenomenon' – these words mark Walpole's fascination with the force of Elizabeth Chudleigh's character.[21]

But particularity and factual accuracy do not fully account for Walpole's portrait of the Duchess of Kingston. Sometimes he gets the facts wrong, as when he says 'she forced the . . . [parson] to give up the [marriage] certificate', describing her plea to the Ecclesiastical Court, while insisting that '[e]very word of this history is extremely true' (23. 93). Walpole was constantly aware of the fallibility of his sources, and his own genius for embellishment, determined to believe only 'what I shall read in the printed trial' (24. 192). His 'extremely true history' (23. 93) of her 'historic' life (20. 213), is the product of Walpole's imagination as much as a product of fact. He admits he 'cannot reconcile contradictions' (HWC 28. 246; 18 February 1776) in her story, but he gives us a full-length portrait of Elizabeth Chudleigh that matches Gainsborough's portrait of her husband.

CHAPTER II

Walpole's Portraits in the Letters: Scandal

Sir Henry Bate Dudley (1745–1824), Thomas Gainsborough px

Walpole identified the *Portrait of a gentleman* by Gainsborough in the 1780 Royal Academy exhibition (No. 189, p. 10), as 'Bate, [The Reverend Henry Bate Dudley] author of the *Morning Post*', praising the picture as 'good', something he would not have said of the sitter, the scandal-mongering editor and part-owner of the newspaper from 1772 to 1780 (HWC 32. 331, n. 9; plate 70). On 12 November 1776, Walpole witnessed a raucous demonstration in Piccadilly raised by the Reverend Henry Bate Dudley (1745–1824) against an upstart rival newspaper called the *New Morning Post*. The riot prompted a tirade against the press: 'A solemn and expensive masquerade exhibited by a clergyman in defence of daily scandal against women of the first rank, in the midst of a civil war!. . . . Do you think, Madam [Anne Liddell], that anything can save such a sottish and stupid nation? Does it deserve to be saved?' (HWC 32. 332; 13 November 1776). 'Mr Bates had rather lie than speak truth' (HWC 33. 171; 1 June 1780), Walpole wrote after the *Morning Post* published Bate's libel of Charles Lennox (1735–1806), 3rd Duke of Richmond, 'the hero of his abuse' (HWC 33. 171). In the era of the *School for Scandal* (Drury Lane, 8 May 1777), Bate's favourite subjects were attacks on women of fashion that Walpole deplores in another Ciceronian letter to Anne Liddell:

> We are a virtuous, civilized, sober people! and must be the admiration of all Europe. Our gallantry in truth is not that of the ages of chivalry. Instead of defending oppressed damsels, our newspapers teem with nothing but abuse on all the handsome women in England, who, if you believe those daily biographers, are errant street-walkers. These scandalous chronicles are our diurnal amusements in the midst of a civil war [the American revolution], and at the eve of a war with France – and the principal historian is a divine, and the pensioner of a pious Court! (HWC 33. 30; 22 July 1778).

Of course Walpole the letter-writer and portraitist is also a supreme historian of scandal. Scandal is irresistible to the letter-writer – 'Augustus Hervey, thinking it the *bel air*, is going to sue for a divorce from the Chudleigh' (HWC 39. 105; 9 August 1768), he writes breathlessly to Henry Seymour Conway. But the news he reports in private letters to his friends is different from that of the scandal-mongering press and gossiping dowagers 'who are the first to propagate scandal of one another' (HWC 18. 62; 25 September 1742). Walpole is not blasting reputations, but dramatizing the human comedy for the entertainment of his friends. The half-length portraits in this chapter illus-

70.   Thomas Gainsborough: *Sir Henry Bate-Dudley*. RA 1780. Oil on canvas, 88 × 59 in. Private Collection. Photo: Royal Academy of Arts, London. 'Mr Bates had rather lie than speak truth' (HWC 33. 171).

71.   Francis Cotes: *William O'Brien*. SA 1763. Pastel on paper, 25½ × 21½ in. Private Collection. Photo: Paul Mellon Centre for Studies in British Art. 'You [Francis Conway] will have heard of the sad misfortune that has happened to Lord Ilchester by his daughter's marriage with O'Brien the actor' (HWC 38. 366).

trate Walpole's genius for transforming the lead of press notices into the leaf-gold of his letters.

William O'Brien (d. 1815), 'A Handsome Young Actor'; Francis Cotes px

A portrait of William O'Brien (d. 1815), the actor and playwright, exhibited at the Society of Artists (1763, No. 26, p. 3; plate 71) by Francis Cotes, evokes from Walpole the unequivocal judgment: '[Mr Obrien in crayons] the comedian, the best picture in the exhibition,' adding (probably at a later date) 'there is a print of it' (SA 63. 26, p. 3; *marginalia*) – 'best' not only for artistry, but for the rich fund of social history the picture brought to mind. A year after this picture was exhibited, O'Brien, whom Walpole thought superior to Garrick in the role of a man of fashion (38. 524), was acting off-stage the part of Lovelace in his elopement with, and marriage to, Lady Susan Sarah Louisa Fox-Strangways (1743–1827), daughter of Walpole's friend, Stephen Fox Strangways (1704–76), Earl of Ilchester. Walpole briefly outlines the plot of the play to Horace Mann:

A melancholy affair has happened to Lord Ilchester; his eldest daughter, Lady Susan, a very pleasing girl, though not handsome, married herself two days ago [Saturday 7 April 1764] at Covent Garden church to Obrien, a handsome young actor. Lord Ilchester doted on her, and was the most indulgent of fathers. 'Tis a cruel blow (HWC 22. 218–19; 9 April 1764).

It is worth quoting Walpole's fuller account of this elopement in a letter to his cousin Francis Seymour Conway (1718–94), Earl of Hertford, because the letter brilliantly illustrates Walpole's relish for the social context of eighteenth-century portraits on exhibition:

You will have heard of the sad misfortune that has happened to Lord Ilchester by his daughter's marriage with O'Brien the actor. But, perhaps, you do not know the circumstances, and how much his grief must be aggravated by reflection on his own credulity and negligence (HWC 38. 366–7; 12 April 1764).

What follows resembles a chapter from Richardson's *Clarissa Harlow*. The scene is the house Walpole had visited two summers earlier in July 1762, Lord Ilchester's seat at Redlynch, Somerset:

a comely dwelling, a new stone house with good rooms and convenient. . . . It stands above half way up a high steep hill, cloathed with old trees, commanding a pleasant view. . . . The park is filled with a particular breed of cows. . . . that . . . look as if they had a sheet flung over them, whence they are called, Sheet-cows (*Visits*, p. 44).

'The affair has been in train for eighteen months', Walpole informed Francis Seymour Conway.

The swain [O'Brien] had learned to counterfeit Lady Sarah Bunbury's [Lady Susan's correspondent] hand so well, that in the country Lord Ilchester has himself delivered several of O'Brien's letters to Lady Susan; but it was not till about a week before the catastrophe that the family was apprised of the intrigue (HWC 38. 367; 12 April 1764).

Enter Charles Schaw, 9th Baron Cathcart (1721–76), wounded in the Battle of Fontenoy (11 May 1745), who wears a black patch over the 'Fontenoy' scar on his cheek in Reynolds's portrait of him (plate 72). Cathcart visits the studio in St James's Place of the genteel portrait-artist Katherine Read (1723–79):

Lord Cathcart went to Miss Reade's, the paintress – she said softly to him – 'My Lord, there is a couple in the next room that I am sure ought not to be together, I wish your Lordship would look in'. He did, shut the door again, and went directly and informed Lord Ilchester. Lady Susan was examined, flung herself at her father's feet, confessed all, vowed to break off – but – what a *but*! – desired to see the loved object,

72.   Sir Joshua Reynolds: *Charles Schaw, 9th Baron Cathcart*. 1754. Oil on canvas, 50 × 39 in. © Manchester City Art Galleries. 'Lord Cathcart went to Miss Reade's, the paintress – she said softly to him – "My Lord, there is a couple in the next room that I am sure ought not to be together, I wish your Lordship would look in"' (HWC 38. 367).

73.   Katherine Read: *Lady Susan Fox Strangways*. 1764. Pastel on paper. Private Collection. 'It is the completion of a disgrace – even a footman were preferable. . . . I could not have believed that Lady Susan would have stooped so low' (HWC 38. 367).

and take a last leave. You will be amazed – even this was granted.

The parting scene happened the beginning of the week. On Friday [6 April 1764] she came of age, and on Saturday morning [7 April] – instead of being under lock and key in the country – walked downstairs, took her footman, said she was going to breakfast with Lady Sarah [Lennox (1745–1826)], but would call at Miss Reade's; in the street, pretended to recollect a particular cap in which she was to be drawn, sent the footman back for it, whipped into a hackney chair, was married at Covent Garden Church, and set out for Mr O'Brien's villa at Dunstable [Bedfordshire]. My Lady [Isabella Fitzroy, Countess of Hertford (1726–82)] – my Lady Hertford! what say *you* to permitting young ladies to act plays, and go to painters by themselves? (HWC 38. 366–7; 12 April 1764).

Walpole had seen Lady Susan and Lady Sarah act in a children's performance of Nicholas Rowe's *Jane Shore* at Holland House on 20 January 1761: 'Lady Sarah was more beautiful than you can conceive', he wrote to George Montagu. 'Lady Susan was dressed from Jane Seymour [probably after Holbein's portrait]' (HWC 9. 335; 22 January 1761).

Walpole shared with Johnson a conviction that aristocratic women must marry in their own class. 'The woman's a whore, and there's an end on't', Johnson is supposed to have said of Walpole's intimate friend, Lady Diana Spencer, when she divorced Henry St John to marry Topham Beauclerk.[1] Walpole reaches the same conclusion about Lady Susan's elopement with an actor, but more tendentiously:

> Poor Lord Ilchester is almost distracted; indeed, it is the completion of disgrace – even a footman were preferable; the publicity of the hero's profession [acting] perpetuates the mortification. *Il ne sera pas milord, tout comme un autre*. I could not have believed that Lady Susan [plate 73] would have stooped so low. She may, however, still keep good company, and say, '*Nos numeri sumus*' ['We are mere ciphers', adapting Horace, *Epistles* I, ii, 27] – Lady Mary Deacon, Lady Caroline Adair, Lady Betty Gallini [who married respectively a doctor, surgeon, and dancing master] – The shop keepers of next age will be mighty well born (HWC 38. 367–8; 12 April 1764).

Two years earlier, in 1762, Reynolds had painted another chapter in the gallantries of Lady Susan and Lady Sarah.[2] The painting depicts the thirteen-year-old Charles James Fox (1749–1806), the future Whig politician, standing in the gardens of Holland House beneath a window, holding Latin verses which the infatuated Eton boy had written to Lady Susan Fox Strangways, bidding 'a pigeon to fly to his love Susan, & carry her a letter from him'. Lady Susan is pictured holding the pigeon as Lady Sarah points to it from a window of Holland House.

Elizabeth Catherine Hunter (d. 1795), 'The Amazement of a New Elopement'; Sir Joshua Reynolds for Edward Francis Cunningham, px

At the Royal Academy exhibition of 1771 Walpole noticed a portrait by a now-forgotten artist, Edward Francis Cunningham (1741–93), called Calze. He identified the sitter as 'Miss Kitty Hunter, now Mrs Clarke [wife of Sir Alured Clarke (1745–1832); plate 74]', who had eloped with Henry Herbert, 10th Earl of Pembroke(1734–94; plate 75) early in February 1771, thus creating 'the amazement of a new elopement' (HWC 10. 14, 22 February 1762). The Earl of Pembroke, then twenty-eight, was an associate of Casanova (1725–98) who referred to him as 'the greatest profligate in all England' (HWC 10. 15, n. 13). Elizabeth Catherine 'Kitty' Hunter (d. 1795), daughter of Thomas Orby Hunter (1716–69), MP, and Lord of the Admiralty (HWC 10. 52, n. 5), was 'somewhat above 20 years of age; her person easy, elegant, and showy, her disposition sprightly and vivacious' (*London Chronicle*; 10. 14, n. 8). In his letters Walpole entertained George Montagu and other friends with a story he realized had all the materials of a Richardsonian epistolary romance. The intrigue began at a ball on Wednesday 17 February 1762 at George Brodrick (1730–65) Viscount Midleton's house, where, the *Gentleman's Magazine* reported, 'an escape after the ball was foiled by the vigilance of the lady's mother' (HWC 10. 14, n. 9).

On the following day, however, the lovers decamped, and the earl 'left half a bushel of letters behind him. . . . In none he justifies himself, unless this is a justification! that, having long tried in vain to make his wife hate and dislike him, he had no way left but this!' (10. 15). Walpole thought the elopement stranger than fiction. He asked George Montagu:

> In all your reading, true or false, have you ever heard of a young Earl, married to the most beautiful woman in the world [Lady Elizabeth Spencer (1737–1831), a Lord of the Bedchamber, a general officer, and with a great estate [Wilton House, Wiltshire], quitting everything, resigning wife and world, and embarking for life in a packet boat with a Miss? (HWC 10. 14; 22 February 1762).

Walpole tells another version of the same 'cruel story' to Horace Mann three days later:

> . . . though you are no ways interested for any of the persons concerned, your tender nature will feel for some of them, and be shocked for all. Lord Pembroke, Earl, Lord of the Bedchamber, Major-General, possessed of ten thousand pounds a year, master of Wilton, husband of one of the most beautiful creatures in England, father of an only son [b. 1759], and himself but eight and twenty, to enjoy this assemblage of good fortune, is gone off with Miss Hunter, daughter to one of the lords of the Admiralty, a handsome girl with a fine person, but silly and in no degree lovely as his own wife, who has the face of a Madonna, and with all the modesty of that idea, is dotingly fond of him. . . . It is not yet known whither this foolish guilty couple have bent their course. . . . her story is not so uncommon; but did one ever hear of an earl running away from himself? (HWC 22. 9–10; 25 February 1762).

Walpole had already collected more details, recounted to George Montagu the same day:

> No news yet of the runaways: but all that comes out antecedent to the escape, is more and more extraordinary and absurd. The day of the elopement he [Lord Pembroke] had invited his wife's family and other folk to dinner with her, but said he himself must dine at a tavern – but he dined privately in his own dressing-room, put on a sailor's habit and black wig that he had brought home with him in a bundle, and threatened the servants he would murder them if they mentioned it to his wife (HWC 10. 16–17; 25 February 1762).

Some of these details probably originate from the press, but others are clearly gossip derived from Walpole's intimate social contacts and knowledge of private correspondence.

> He [Pembroke] left a letter for her [Elizabeth Spencer], which the Duke of Marlborough [her brother, George Spencer (1739–1817), 4th Duke] was afraid to deliver to her, and opened. It desired she would not write to him, as it would make him completely mad. The poor soul [Lady Pembroke], after the first transport, seemed to bear it tolerably, but has been writing to him ever since. He desires the King would preserve his rank of Major-General, as some time or other he may serve again (HWC 10. 17).

Walpole puts the finishing touch on this chapter of the story by quoting 'an indifferent epigram' on the elopement attributed to William Mason. The joke depends on the

74.   Sir Joshua Reynolds: *Elizabeth Catherine Hunter*. 1756–7. Oil on canvas, 29¾ × 25 in. Reproduced by permission of the Marquess of Bath, Longleat House, Warminster, Wiltshire, Great Britain. Photo: Photographic Survey, Courtauld Institute of Art. 'Lord Pembroke. . . is gone off with Miss Hunter. . . a hand-some girl with a fine person, but silly and in no degree lovely as his own wife' (HWC 22. 9).

75.   Sir Joshua Reynolds: *Henry Herbert, 10th Earl of Pembroke*. 1763–67. Oil on canvas, 50 × 39¾ in. By kind permission of The Earl of Pembroke, and the Trustees of Wilton House Trust. Photo: Wilton House. 'In all your [George Montagu's] reading. . . have you ever heard of a young Earl, married to the most beautiful woman in the world. . . quitting everything. . . and embarking for life in a packet boat with a Miss?' (HWC 10. 14).

fact that Pembroke had published the year before a book entitled *A Method of Breaking Horses, and Teaching Soldiers to Ride* (1761):

> As Pembroke a horseman by most is accounted,
> 'Tis not strange that his Lordship a Hunter has mounted.
> (HWC 10. 17; 25 February 1762)

The London Chronicle and the *Gentleman's Magazine* published detailed reports by the beginning of March about the lovers' escape on a Dutch ship, her rescue and return to the *Falcon* at Gravesend, Pembroke's pursuit and re-capture of her, and their reunited escape to Holland on a cod smack (HWC 22. 16, n. 8). Walpole gives this ironic summary of their adventures in a letter to Horace Mann:

> Lord Pembroke is quite forgot. He and his nymph were brought back by a privateer who had obligations to her father [Thomas Orby Hunter], but the father desired no such recovery, and they are again gone in quest of adventures. The Earl [Pembroke] was

76.   Thomas Gainsborough: *Penelope Pitt, Viscountess Ligonier*. 1770. Oil on canvas, 94$^{1}/_{2}$ × 62 in. Courtesy of the Huntington Library, Art Collections, and Botanical Gardens, San Marino, California. Photo: The Huntington. 'I wish, when she has run the gauntlet through all the troops on the road to Paris, she may replace Madame du Barry, and prove *la fiancée du Roi de France*' (HWC 30. 256).

77.   Thomas Gainsborough: *Edward, 2d Viscount Ligonier*. 1770. Oil on canvas, 94 × 62 in. Courtesy of the Huntington Library, Art Collections, and Botanical Gardens, San Marino, California. Photo: The Huntington. '. . . [I]t is to be feared that such people as affect to be witty, will say the horse is as good a man as his master' (Baker, *Observations*, p. 17).

so kind as to invite his wife [Elizabeth Spencer] to accompany them, and she, who is all gentleness and tenderness, was with difficulty withheld from acting as mad a part from goodness, as he had done from guilt and folly (HWC 22. 16; 22 March 1762).

A year later Walpole reports the surprising reconciliation of all the principals in this scandal, and the reinstatement of the Earl of Pembroke. By this time Catherine Hunter had given birth on 23 November 1762 to a bastard son named anagrammatically Augustus Retnuh [Hunter] Reebkomp [Pembroke] (HWC 10. 52, n. 6):

Lord and Lady Pembroke are reconciled, and live again together. Mr Hunter would have taken his daughter too, but upon condition she should give back her settlement to Lord Pembroke, and her child. She replied nobly, that she did not trouble herself about fortune, and would willingly depend on her father, but for her child, she had nothing right left to do but take care of that, and would not part with it – so she keeps both – and I suppose will soon have her lover again too, for my Lady Pembroke's beauty is not glutinous (HWC 10. 52; 25 March 1763).

The spirit if not the letter of Walpole's prophecy was fulfilled. A year later Kitty Hunter was involved in another affair, this time with Elizabeth Chudleigh's first husband, Augustus John Hervey (1724–79), 3rd Earl of Bristol, by whom she had another son, before she married the respectable Sir Alured Clarke, K. B., on 7 April 1770. The licentious Earl of Pembroke continued his rakish career. Walpole reports on his reappointment as Lord of the Bedchamber to George III while Pembroke was travelling in Italy: 'Lord Pembroke is not yet returned, though replaced in the King's Bedchamber. As he was turned out for running away with one woman of fashion, I suppose he was restored for carrying off another' (HWC 23. 152; 6 November 1769). Walpole explains the details of the second elopement in his *Memoirs of George III* (HWC 1. 330, n. 2): 'Lord Pembroke was again made a lord of the Bedchamber in 1769, without applying; and exactly at a time when he was said to have carried off another woman, a young Venetian bride. . . . the very night of her wedding' (HWC 23. 152, n. 14).

Lord and Lady Ligonier: 'Madame Messaline' and 'The Generous Husband', Thomas Gainsborough px

Walpole's identifications of Gainsborough's portraits of 'a lady in a fancied dress' (No. 75: 'Lady Ligonier'; plate 76), and 'a nobleman with a horse' (No. 76: 'Lord Ligonier'; plate 77) at the 1771 Royal Academy exhibition tell another scandalous story, this time involving a rakish wife and a cuckolded husband. In the spring of 1771, during the Royal Academy exhibition, the adulteries of the honourable Penelope Pitt (1749–1827), who had married Edward, second Viscount Ligonier (1740–82) in 1766, and whom Walpole nicknamed 'Madame Messaline' (5. 77), were the talk of the town. In May Lord Ligonier fought a duel in Hyde Park with his wife's lover, the Italian poet Vittorio Amadeo (1749–1803), Count Alfieri, and sued her for divorce, granted by Act of Parliament on 7 November 1771. Ligonier's conduct in the duel, which involved swords in Hyde Park inspired an illustrated pamphlet entitled *The Generous Husband* (1771). After the duel, the press avidly reported that John Harding, Lord Ligonier's groom or postilion, was another of her lovers (HWC 35. 453, n. 2). Both affairs are alluded to in William Combe's verse-satire *The Diabo-lady, or, A Match in Hell* (Hazen 3222. 15.9 [1777]):

> The next that rose was wanton [Ligonier]
> With front assured, and dressed *en cavalier*;
> A[lfieri] led her forth, Jack H[arding] followed,
> While grooms and jockeys in full chorus hallooed.
> (HWC 30. 255, n. 6)

By September Lady Ligonier had decamped to Calais, where she was rumored to be having a tryst with the captain of the packet-boat, and 'the whole officerial corps of an Irish Brigade' (HWC 30. 255, n. 7).

Walpole sums up these delectable scandals in a letter to George Selwyn, comparing Lady Pembroke to La Fontaine's tale about a licentious royal fiancée:

Have you heard the last adventure of the *fiancée du Roi de Garbe*? [Hazen 2406 (1762)]. She was seven hours and a half at sea; the captain of the packet-boat is tall, comely enough, and a very shark on such an occasion. He snapped her up at once as voraciously as she did John Harding. They passed a week together at Calais, and he then consigned her over to a marching regiment at Ardres. Alfieri told this story himself to Monsieur Francès [Jacques Bataihe de (1724–88), French chargé d'affaires in London], from whom I had it fresh. Alfieri's sentiments, that had resisted so many trials, could not digest this last chapter; he has given her up. I wish, when she has run the gauntlet through all the troops on the road to Paris, she may replace Madame du Barry [Jeanne Bécu (1743–93), mistress of Louis XV], and prove *la fiancée du Roi de France* (HWC 30. 255–6; 9 September 1771).

In reporting this 'episode . . . proper for an Atalantis' (HWC 25. 538), referring to Mary de la Rivière Manley's novel, *The New Atalantis* (1709), Walpole clearly takes Alfieri's side, revealing a rare streak of misogyny.

The unfortunate cuckold, Edward Ligonier (1740–82), figures in Walpole's correspondence as captain in the Earl of Granby's Royal Horse Guards in the Battle of Minden 1 August 1759. Ligonier was aide-de-camp to Prince Ferdinand, who failed to deliver orders to Lord George Sackville to bring up the cavalry (HWC 30. 157; 29 August 1759). He carried the victory despatch from Prince Ferdinand more successfully, and Walpole describes the happy result:

. . . [E]very house in London is illuminated, every street has two bonfires, every bonfire has two hundred squibs, and the poor charming moon yonder, that never looked so well in her life, is not at all minded, but seems only staring out of a garret window at the frantic doings all over the town (HWC 21. 314; 8 August 1759).

Thereafter, Walpole takes little notice of Ligonier: he mentions his appointment as groom to the Duke of Gloucester in 1764 (HWC 38. 468, n. 34), and describes his service as second to George Townshend (1724–1807) in a duel with Lord Bellamont, 'a brave young Irish lord' (HWC 32. 93, n. 6), when he managed to garble another message (HWC 32. 93, n. 6; 4 February 1773). Richard Baker's *Observations* (1771) finds fault with the equal prominence of the heads of the horse and nobleman in Gainsborough's picture, a comment Walpole annotates 'true'. Baker writes:

Though this piece be very well done, it is liable to one objection. Every picture ought to have some principal object. But the picture has none. The horse, being represented as near to the spectator as the gentleman, and being a large object, and of a light colour, attracts the eye as much as the gentleman does. The eye is equally divided between them: and it is to be feared that such people as affect to be witty, will say the horse is as good a man as his master (*Observations*, p. 17).

Seymour Dorothy Fleming: 'Gallantry that Scorns a Mask'. Joshua Reynolds px

Walpole wrote on the title-page of the Royal Academy catalogue of the twelfth exhibition (1780): 'fine exhibition with excellent pictures by Gainsborough, and several good by Sir Joshua Reynolds. . . . This was the first exhibition at Somerset House'. He identified Reynolds's *Portrait of a lady* (No. 102; plate 78), as 'Lady Worsley,' Seymour Dorothy Fleming (n.d.) who had married Sir Richard Worsley (1751–1805) on 15 September 1775. Lady Worsley embarked on a career of extra-marital affairs soon after sitting to Reynolds in 1776; her gallantry culminated in a civil trial for adultery brought by her husband in 1782. Reynolds's spectacular portrait of Lady Worsley holding a whip in red riding habit, adapted from the uniform of her husband's regiment, colourfully illustrates the character Walpole painted in his correspondence of a woman who recklessly defied the social conventions of her time.

In November 1781 Lady Worsley had eloped with Captain Maurice George Bisset (1757–1821), of the Southern Hampshire militia, of which her husband, Sir Richard Worsley, was colonel. Walpole wrote to Horace Mann in December about an impending suit for divorce:

> After Doctor's Commons [the ecclesiastical Divorce Court at St Bennet's Hill, St Paul's Churchyard, capable of granting legal separations] had lain fallow for a year or two, it is again likely to bear a handsome crop of divorces. Gallantry in this country scorns a mask. Maids only intrigue; wives elope. *C'est l'étiquette.* Two young married ladies are just gone off – no, this is a wrong term for one of them [Lady Worsley], for she has just come to town and drives about London, for fear her adventure should be forgotten before it comes into the House of Lords. It is a Lady Worseley, sister of Lady Harrington [Jane Fleming (1755–1824)]. On hearing she was gone away with a Major Blisset, another young gentleman said at St James's Coffee House, 'I have been very secret, but now I think I am at liberty to show this letter [from Lady Worsley]' – It was couched in these laconic and sentimental terms, 'I have loved Windham [Charles William Wyndham (1760–1828), MP·who testified at the trial he had received a ring from Lady Worsley]; I did love Graham [James, Marquess of Graham (1755–1836)]; but now I love only you [Captain Bisset] by God.' I am a little angry for my nephew Lord Cholmondeley [George James (1749–1827), 4th Earl], who has been most talked of for her, and who is thought to have the *largest* pretensions to her remembrance. If you see him, you may tell him I resent her forgetfulness (HWC 25. 227–8; 28 December 1781).

Walpole's bawdy insinuation about his promiscuous great-nephew's intercourse with Lady Worsley is explained by Walpole's account of Lady Worsley's trial for adultery on grounds of criminal conversation. The civil trial for damages of £20,000 took place on 21 February 1782 at the Court of the King's Bench, Westminister Hall, before William Murray, Earl of Mansfield, Lord Chief Justice.

78.   Left. Sir Joshua Reynolds: *Seymour Dorothy Fleming, Lady Worsley*. RA 1780. Oil on canvas, 93 × 56¾ in. Private Collection. Photo: Bridgeman Art Library, London. 'To save her last favourite [Captain Bisset] she summoned thirty-four young men of the first quality to depose to having received her favours. . .' (HWC 25. 245).

79.   Attributed to James Gillray: *A Peep into Lady W !!!'s Seraglio*. Etching, 9⅜ × 13¾ in., dated 29 April 1782. © Copyright The British Museum. 'Gallantry in this country scorns a mask. Maids only intrigue; wives elope. *C'est l'étiquette*' (HWC 25. 227).

Accustomed as you [Horace Mann] are to our newspapers, you will read in them [*London Courant* 22 February 1782] with astonishment the detail of a late trial for adultery between a Sir Richard Worseley and his wife, sister of the countess of Harrington. To save her last favourite [Captain Bisset] she summoned thirty-four young men of the first quality to depose to having received her favours, and one of them, a Duke's son [James, Marquess of Graham], to having bestowed an additional one on her [a physician testified that Lady Worsley had complaints . . . of a venereal disorder]. The number was reduced to 27, and but a few [six] of them were examined – and they blushed for her. A better defence for her was the connivance of the husband, who was proved to have carried one of the troop [Bisset] on his back to the house-top to view his fair spouse stark naked in the bath [Maidstone, Kent] – The jury was so equitable as to give the plaintiff but one shilling damages (HWC 25. 245–6).

This of course could have been made to order for the press and print shops. In addition to publication of the *Trial . . . between the Right Honourable Sir Richard Worsley . . . and George Maurice Bisset* (1782), two satirical poems appeared, *The Whim*, and *Variety, Or Which is the Man?* with a frontispiece entitled 'Maidstone Whim' showing Bisset 'peeping into the bath window, standing on the shoulder and horns of the cuckolded Worsley' (HWC 25. 245, n. 10). The *pièce de résistance* was *A Peep into Lady W !!!'s Seraglio*, a print attributed to James Gillray (1757–1815; plate 79), that shows a queue of nine lovers waiting their turns outside a cutaway view 'of the insatiable Lady Worsley's bedroom, with a painting of the chaste Lucretia hanging ironically over the door'.[3] Walpole had little respect for Worsley, whose *History of the Isle of Wight* (1781; Hazen 3220), a 'courtier's book' dedicated to George III, he derided (HWC 29. 146–7; 14 June 1781).

CHAPTER 12

Walpole's Portraits in the Letters: Aristocrats

Walpole repeatedly expressed a Whiggish disdain for kings and courts, but he could not resist watching with rapt fascination what he called 'the puppet show' (HWC 9. 311), and filling his letters with portraits of royalty and aristocrats. This mixture of delight and disgust appears in his remarks after showing his collection of portraits at Strawberry Hill to Anthony Morris Storer (1746–99), collector and MP:

> Mr Storer has just left me; I have shown him such hosts of portraits of the dead, that if he retains their names, he would make a good vice-chamberlain to Proserpine on a *Birth-night*, if there were any such fête in the shades below; but as ceremonies are of the essence of all courts, I suppose there they keep death-nights, and then he will be more at home in a ballroom than even Lord Brudenel [Baron James (1725–1811), George III's Master of the Robes] (HWC 33. 273–4, 13 June 1781).

Walpole looks on courts simultaneously as a hell of intrigue, and a theatre of ceremony where the Prime Minister of Taste can observe human nature.

'I don't love courts' (HWC 31. 56; 8 October 1765), Walpole writes to Anne Pitt about the French court at Fontainebleau. We have already quoted his remark on the little court surrounding Lavinia Bingham's engagement to Lord Althorp: '. . . if a court is no bigger than an egg-shell, it is equally full of jealousy and treachery' (HWC 33. 253; 17 December 1780). Writing to Horace Mann about the Grand Ducal court at Florence he remarks: 'I wish . . . your new Court may enliven your life, and not be the cause of any mortification in it' (HWC 22. 365; 13 November 1765), but he thinks it deserves contempt rather than esteem. He consoles his cousin Thomas Walpole, a diplomat in Germany, that 'if little courts are not interesting, their mimicry of grander follies is diverting and various – diverting to anybody but their plundered subjects' (HWC 36. 251; 21 July 1788).

As he ages, Walpole grows weary of courts: 'Courts were not made for old age: it requires all the giddy insensibility of youth not to be struck with such farces. How one should smile if one could look down on a crowd of insects acting importance, dignity, or servility!' (HWC 25. 307; 20 August 1782). He writes a moving letter to the novelist Frances Burney, deploring her decision to serve in Queen Charlotte's household to appease her father:

> . . . Were your talents given to be buried in obscurity? You have retired from the world into a closet at Court – where indeed you will still discover mankind, though not dis-

close it; for if you could penetrate its characters on the earliest glimpse of its superficies, will it escape your piercing eye, when it shrinks from your inspection, knowing that you have the mirror of truth in your pocket! (HWC 42. 294; 20 October 1790).

In this letter to Frances Burney Walpole describes his own achievement: 'still discovering mankind' in courts, seeing through 'superficies', 'penetrating its characters', and 'disclosing' portraits drawn in the correspondence. In a letter warning Mary Berry about the risks of serving in the household of Caroline (1768–1821) Princess of Wales, Walpole again describes his own perspective:

I never was *of* a court myself, but from my birth and the position of my father could but, for my first twenty years, know much of the nature of the beast; and from my various connections since I have seldom missed farther opportunities of keeping up my acquaintance even with the interior (HWC 12. 129–30; 7 October 1794).

Although Walpole despised 'varnishers [who] have slobbered over' (HWC 37. 370, head-note) vices of the nobility, he is no satirist. He does poke fun at aristocratic ignorance: 'For the nobility. . . . are glad to be eased of thinking, which is equivalent to the headache in a man of quality' (HWC 22. 415; 20 April 1766). And he does ridicule the royal family celebrating the embarcation of troops for Ostend in 1742: 'Messieurs d'Allemagne ['The royal family' (HW)] roll their red eyes, stroke up their great beavers, and look fierce – you know one loves a review and a tattoo' (HWC 17. 410; 29 April 1742). And he mocks the royal family's ritual questions asked of visitors: 'Do you love walking?' 'Do you love music?'(HWC 18. 148; 27 January 1743). He belittles his own title, Lord Orford, assumed in 1791, as a mere nickname: 'it is being called names in one's old age' (HWC 31. 364). Nevertheless, despite these symptoms of the satirist, early and late, Walpole's portraits in the letters are primarily in the comic mode – 'general Nature . . . strained through the thousand sieves of self-love' (HWC 33. 253; 17 December 1780).

Sir Hugh Smithson (1715–86), 'Antiquated Duke' and 'Vulgar Countess'. Thomas Gainsborough px

Walpole identified Gainsborough's portrait of Sir Hugh Smithson (1715–86; plate 80), 'Duke of Northumberland', and marked it 'very good, whole length garter robes' (RA 83. 153, p. 9, *marginalia*). He had noted in his correspondence Northumberland's installation on 18 November 1756 as Knight of the Garter, taking the vacant place of Lord Albemarle: 'Three Garters are given to the Duke of Devonshire, to Lord Carlisle, Lord Northumberland, and (to my great satisfaction) to Lord Hertford' (HWC 21. 27; 29 November 1756). After Smithson married Elizabeth Seymour (1716–76; plate 81) of the Percy family in 1750, he assumed his wife's name and title as Earl of Northumberland. Walpole quickly questioned his pedigree in a letter to Horace Mann:

The new Duke of Somerset [Algernon Seymour (1684–1750)] is dead: that title is at last restored to Sir Edward Seymour [1695–1757], after his branch had been most

80.   Thomas Gainsborough: *Sir Hugh Smithson, 2d Earl and 1st Duke of Northumberland*. RA 1783. By kind permission of the Trustees of the Middlesex Guildhall Collection and Trust Fund. Photo: Photographic Survey, Courtauld Institute of Art. 'Antiquated dukes may hobble into and out of golden chariots, if they think their corpses look well in them – I should not like to lie in state before I am dead' (HWC 33. 259).

81.   Sir Joshua Reynolds: *Elizabeth Seymour, Countess and Duchess of Northumberland*. 1757–59. Oil on canvas, 94½ × 58¼ in. Collection of the Duke of Northumberland. Photo: Photographic Survey, Courtauld Institute of Art. 'That great vulgar Countess has been laid up with a hurt in her leg; Lady Rebecca Poulett pushed her on the birthnight against a bench' (HWC 9. 264).

unjustly deprived of it for about 150 years. Sir Hugh Smithson and Sir Charles Windham are Earls of Northumberland and Egremont with vast estates; the former title, revived for the blood of Percy, has the misfortune of being coupled with the blood of a man that either let or drove coaches – such was Sir Hugh's grandfather (HWC 20. 124–5; 25 February 1750).

Walpole was apparently wrong about Northumberland's vulgar ancestor, but the allegation coloured Walpole's scepticism about his opulent way of life and questionable political ambitions.

Walpole disapproved of the earl's project to '[bespeak] at a great price five copies of capital pictures in Italy . . . for his gallery at Northumberland House in the Strand' (HWC 20. 507, n. 7; HW's note). In 1757 Horace Mann arranged for copies of the *School of Athens* and other paintings by Raphael, Guido (*Aurora*), and Carraci (*Triumph of Bacchus*) from Mengs, Batoni, and other artists for the earl, but he never succeeded in overcoming Walpole's prejudice against the idea.[1] Soon after Mann got the commission Walpole wrote to criticize Northumberland's extravagant projects:

> Your brother [Galfridus Mann (1706–56)] tells me that you defend my Lord Northumberland's idea for his gallery, so I will not abuse it so much as I intended, though I must say that I am so tired with copies of the pictures he has chosen, that I would scarce hang up the originals – and then, copies by anything [any artist] now living! – and at that price! – indeed *price* is no article, or rather *is* a reason for my Lord Northumberland's liking anything. They are building at Northumberland House, at Sion [Syon House, Middlesex], at Stansted [Walpole's error for Stanwick Park, Yorkshire], at Alnwic [Alnwick] and Warkworth Castles [both Northumberland]! They live by the etiquette of the old peerage, have Swiss porters, the Countess has her pipers – in short, they will very soon have no estate (HWC 20. 340–1; 28 October 1752).

Walpole 'adjourned [his] curiosity till the gallery . . . [was] thrown open with the first masquerade' (HWC 20. 507), when he approved only of Mengs's copy:

> Lord Northumberland's great gallery is finished and opened; it is a sumptuous chamber, but might have been in better taste. He is wonderfully content with his pictures, and gave me leave to repeat it to you [Horace Mann]: I rejoiced, as you had been the negotiator – as you was not the painter, you will allow me not to be so profuse of my applause. Indeed I have yet only seen them by candlelight. Mengz's school of Athens pleased me: Pompeio's [Batoni's] two [Supper and Council of the Gods] are black and hard; Mazucci's Apollo, *fade* and without beauty; Castanza's piece [*Triumph of Bacchus*] is abominable (HWC 21. 88; 5 May 1757).

The Northumberlands' taste in entertainments appealed to Walpole as little as their taste in paintings. It is clear from his grudging approval of the gallery that by 1757 Walpole was visting Northumberland House (plate 82) and on speaking terms with the earl. The following year he reported on a supper the Northumberlands presented for George II's mistress Amalie von Wendt (1704–65), Countess of Yarmouth, featuring a bizarre confection:

> The Earl and Countess of Northumberland have diverted the town with a supper, which they intended should make their court to my Lady Yarmouth; the dessert was a *chasse* [a hunting scene made of cake?] at Herrenhausen [Electoral palace at Hanover], the rear of which was brought up by a chaise and six containing a MAN with a blue ribband [Order of the Garter] and a lady sitting by him! Did you ever hear such a vulgarism – The person complimented is not half so German, and consequently suffered martyrdom at this clumsy apotheosis of her concubinage (HWC 21. 191; 14 April 1758).

Walpole first glimpsed the countess at a subscription masquerade in the King's Theatre, Haymarket, when he compared her to a character in his favourite memoir of the Age of Louis XIV, Anthony Hamilton's *Gramont* (Hazen 2389): 'Lady Betty Smithson [Elizabeth

82.   Antonio Canal, called Canaletto: *View of Northumberland House, London.* 1752. Oil on canvas, 33 × 54 in. Collection of the Duke of Northumberland. Photo: Photographic Survey, Courtauld Institute of Art. 'They are building at Northumberland House' (HWC 20. 341).

83.   Richard Bentley: *Lady Northumberland's Invitation Card.* 2½ × 3¹³⁄₁₆ in. Courtesy of the Lewis Walpole Library, Yale University. 'That party [cards at Northumberland House] was larger but still more formal than the rest. . . . I played with Madam Emily, and we were mighty well together' (HWC 9. 334).

Seymour] had such a pyramid of baubles upon her head, that she was exactly the Princess of Babylon [Lady Margaret de Burgh (d. 1648) in masquerade costume] in Grammont' (HWC 20. 49–50, n. 29; 3 May 1749). But Walpole delighted in her vulgarity and eagerly collected anecdotes about her pride and ostentation:

> That great vulgar Countess has been laid up with a hurt in her leg; Lady Rebecca Poulett pushed her on the birthnight [George III's birthday 4 June] against a bench: The Duchess of Grafton asked if it was true that Lady Rebecca kicked her? – 'Kicked me, Madam! When did you ever hear of a Percy that took a kick?' I can tell you another anecdote of that house, that will not divert you less: Lord March [William Douglas (1725–1810), 3rd Earl] making them a visit this summer at Alnwic-castle, my Lord received him at the gate, and said, 'I believe, my Lord, this is the first time that ever a Douglas and a Percy met here in friendship' – think of this from a Smithson to a true Douglas (HWC 9. 264–5; 23 December 1759).

By the early 1760s Walpole was being invited to card parties at Northumberland House (plate 83),[2] sending the countess Strawberry Hill Press imprints (HWC 38. 78), instructing her about her ancestors (HWC 40. 178), keeping track of Lady Northumberland's royal appointments in Queen Charlotte's household (HWC 38. 96), and describing lavish entertainments at Northumberland House as well as their Thames villa at Syon House. Walpole played cards with George II's daughter Princess Emily, and 'was surprised at her being so vulgar; as she went away she *thanked* my Lady Northumberland, like a parson's wife, *for all her civilities*' (HWC 9. 334; 22 January 1761).

Walpole describes a party at Northumberland House for the queen's brother Prince Ernst (1742–1814) of Mecklenburg-Strelitz:

> Lady Northumberland made a pompous *festino* for him t'other night; not only the whole house, but the garden was illuminated, and was quite a fairy scene. Arches and pyramids of lights alternately surrounded the enclosure; a diamond necklace of lamps edged the rails and descent, with a spiral obelisk of candles on each hand; and dispersed over the lawn were little bands of kettledrums, clarinets, fifes etc., and the lovely moon, who came without a card (HWC 10. 34–5; 8 June 1762).

Walpole gives a comical account of 'my disaster' (HWC 38. 529), a dinner at Northumberland House on 2 April 1765 that the countess delayed until the end of debates in the House of Lords on a bill 'for the better relief and employment of the poor' (HWC 38. 528, n. 16):

> I was to dine at Northumberland House, and went a little after four: There I found the Countess. . . . At five, arrived Mr Mitchell [Sir Andrew (1708–71), MP], who said the Lords had begun to read the Poor Bill, which would take at least two hours, and perhaps would debate it afterwards. We concluded dinner would be called for, it not being very precedented for ladies to wait for gentlemen: – no such thing. Six o'clock came, – seven o'clock came, – our coaches came, – well! we sent them away, and excuses were we were engaged. Still the Countess's heart did not relent, nor uttered a syllable of apology. We wore out the wind and the weather, the opera and the play, Mrs Cornelys's and Almack's,[3] and every topic that would do in a formal circle. We hinted, represented – in vain.
>
>   The clock struck eight: my Lady, at last, said, she would go and order dinner; but it was a good half hour before it appeared. We then set down to a table for fourteen covers, but instead of substantials, there was nothing but a profusion of plates striped red green and yellow, gilt plate, blacks and uniforms! My Lady Finlater [Lady Mary Murray (1720–95)], who had never seen these embroidered dinners, nor dined after three, was famished. The first course stayed as long as possible, in hopes of the Lords: so did the second. The dessert at last arrived, and the middle dish was actually set on when Lord Finlater [James Ogilvy, 6th Earl (1714–70)] and Mr Mackay [probably John Ross Mackye (1707–97), MP] arrived! – would you believe it? – the dessert was remanded, and the whole first course brought back again! – Stay, I have not done: – just as this second first course had done its duty, Lord Northumberland, Lord Strafford, and Mekinsy came in, and the whole began a third time! Then the second course and the dessert! I thought we should have dropped from our chairs with fatigue and fumes! When the clock struck eleven, we were asked to return to the drawing-room, and drink tea and coffee, but I said I was engaged to supper, and came home to bed. My dear Lord [Francis Seymour Conway], think of four hours and a half in a circle of mixed company, and three great dinners, one after another, without interruption (HWC 38. 529–30; 7 April 1765).

Walpole is complaining about more than the tedium of a movable feast, but the rites of 'civil pride' Pope satirizes at Timon's Villa in the *Epistle to Burlington*:

> Is this a dinner? this a Genial room?
> No, 'tis a Temple, and a Hecatomb.[4]

In a letter to Lady Northumberland Walpole signs himself 'Your Ladyship's most obliged and obedient humble servant and tenant' (HWC 40. 179; 2 April 1760). Strawberry Hill was in the manor of Syon House, Islesworth, the duke's villa near Brentford; and Walpole referred to the duke as 'Lord Paramount of Strawberry' (HWC 33. 109). Walpole visited Syon House on several occasions and claims to have advised on the design of the Gallery:

> I have been this evening [Monday 27 August 1764] to Sion, which is becoming another Mount Palatine. Adam [the architect Robert Adam (1728–92)] has displayed great taste, and the Earl matches it with magnificence. The gallery is converting into a museum in the style of a columbarium, according to an idea I proposed to my Lord Northumberland (HWC 38. 429; 27 August 1764).[5]

Throughout the 1760s Walpole was prepared to add incense to the Northumberlands' family pride. He sent to Lady Northumberland an account of heralds in the Percy family: 'I flatter myself that these additional proofs of the greatness of your Ladyship's house will not be unacceptable' (HWC 40. 179; 2 April 1760).[6] And when James Bentham's *History and Antiquities of Ely* (Hazen No. 11) was being compiled, Walpole urged his antiquarian friend, William Cole, to solicit a subscription from the earl and countess for a plate of their ancestor,[7] whose portrait had been discovered painted on an old wall behind Ely Cathedral choir (HWC 1. 160), and whose 'leg and thigh bones, of an enormous size' had been disinterred (HWC 1. 162): '. . . I should think either the Duke or Duchess of Northumberland would rejoice at such an opportunity of buying incense,' he wrote to William Cole 14 June 1769:

> and I will tell you what you shall do. Write to Mr Percy [Thomas (1729–1811), chaplain to the Duke of Northumberland], and vaunt the discovery of Duke Brythnoth's bones, and ask him to move their Graces to contribute a plate. They could not be so unnatural as to refuse – especially if the Duchess knew the size of his thigh-bone (HWC 1. 164–5; 14 June 1769).

'His Royal Highness of Sion' (HWC 33. 109), as Walpole liked to call the duke, and the 'Irish Queen' (HWC 38. 469), as he referred to the duchess after the duke was appointed Lord Lieutenant of Ireland in April 1763, were notorious sycophants to royalty. The duchess was one of Queen Charlotte's bride-maids, and she was appointed Lady of Queen Charlotte's Bedchamber on 2 August 1761 (HWC 38. 96, n. 24). During his Lord Lieutenancy the duke displayed, Walpole writes in the *Memoirs of George III*, a 'profusion and ostentation . . . so great, that it seemed to lay a dangerous precedent for succeeding governors, who must risk unpopularity if more parsimonious; or the ruin of their fortune, should they imitate his example' (G III 1. 332; 38. 235, n. 93). '. . . I do not think it necessary to scatter pearls and diamonds about the streets like their Vice-Majesties of Ireland' (G III 1. 38. 235; 17 November 1763). Before leaving for Ireland, the Northumberlands 'had a levee of Irish . . . and charmed them all', George Montagu wrote Walpole, adding 'they are easily charmed' (HWC 10. 75; 21 May 1763). In her new role, Walpole wrote to Hertford, 'Your Irish Queen [Countess of Northumberland] exceeds the English Queen, and follows her with seven footmen before her chair' (HWC 38. 469; 25 November 1764). A week later Walpole learned from the countess that she 'has added an eighth footman' (HWC 38. 473; 3 December 1764).

Walpole watched the vicissitudes of the duke's political career from the ironic perspective of the son of a fallen prime minister. 'The Opposition have named and firmly believe,' he wrote in May 1767, 'a new administration [will be] composed of Lord Bute's friends, with the Duke of Northumberland at the head' (HWC 22. 521; 24 May 1767). Five years before in March 1762 he had remarked on the duke's appointment as Chamberlain to Queen Charlotte's household, Privy Councillor to the King (HWC 22. 103; 30 November 1762), and Lord Lieutenant of Ireland in 1763 (HWC 11. 3, n. 4). Walpole had observed Northumberland's collisions with John Wilkes during the Middlesex elections at Brentford when Walpole fortified Strawberry Hill, and Lord Northumberland was pelted by the Wilkesite mob rioting in London (HWC 23. 99; 23 March 1769). He viewed sympathetically the humiliation of the Northumberlands when Bute was falling from power: 'Both he [the Earl of Northumberland] and my Lady went on Monday night [20 May 1763] to Bedford House, and were received with every mark of insult. The Duke [John Russell (1710–71), Duke of Bedford] turned his back on the Earl, without speaking to him, and he was kept standing an hour exposed to all their raillery' (HWC 38. 562–3; 20 May 1765). In the Gordon riots, Northumberland was 'forced from his carriage and robbed of his watch on the cry being raised that a gentleman in black who rode with him was a Jesuit confessor' (DNB 15. 864).

Walpole associated the Duke of Northumberland with the folly of political ambition. At the age of sixty-four the duke sought the post of Master of the King's Horse, was appointed, kissed hands 27 November 1778, was sworn 3 December 1778, and retained the position until 1780. Walpole thought it 'a ridiculous promotion: he [Northumberland] was afflicted with the stone, and very lame with the gout' (HWC 33. 93, n. 11).[8] '. . . [I]t would be silly not to know how precarious the tenure is', he told Anne Liddell when ill with the gout, after the Duke of Northumberland at the age of sixty-six resigned the post of Master of the Horse to George Brudenel (1712–90), Duke of Montagu, who was sixty-eight: 'Antiquated dukes may hobble into and out of golden chariots, if they think their corpses look well in them – I should not like to lie in state before I am dead' (HWC 33. 259; 2 January 1781). At the same time, when the household was established for the Prince of Wales, the future George IV, on 27 December 1780, Walpole wrote Horace Mann:

> I do not know all the names, and fewer of the faces that compose it; nor intend. I, who kissed the hand of George the First, have no colt's tooth for the Court of George the Fourth. Nothing is so ridiculous as an antique face in a juvenile drawing room. I believe that they who have spirits enough to be absurd in their decrepitude, are happy, for they certainly are not sensible of their folly – but I, who have never forgotten what I thought in my youth of such superannuated idiots, dread nothing more than misplacing myself in my old age (HWC 25. 109; 31 December 1780).

In 1795 Walpole wrote to Anne Liddell who had urged him to make a speech in the House of Lords:

[A]s I have none of the great abilities and renown of the late Lord Chatham [William Pitt (1708–78), Earl, MP, and prime minister], so I have none of the ambition of aping his death and tumbling down in the House of Lords [where Pitt had a stroke 7 April, d. 11 May 1778], which I fear would scarce obtain for me a sixpenny print in a magazine from Mr Copley.[9]

The best use I have made of my very long life, has been to treasure up beacons to warn me against being ridiculous in my old age. I remember I was in bed with the gout, some years ago, when I was told that the late Duke of Northumberland had been at St James's that morning [3 December 1778] to kiss hands for being appointed Master of the Horse to the King. I said, 'Well, the Duke is three or four years older [two] than I am, he has the gout as I have, and he has the stone, which thank God I have not: now, should anybody come to my bedside, and propose to me to rise and drive about the streets in a gold glass-case, I should conclude they had heard I had lost my senses, though I had not discovered it myself (HWC 34. 210; 11 December 1795).

The vulgar Duchess of Northumberland was equally a beacon to Walpole, warning against vulgarity, ostentation, extravagance, and pride. Unlike the Duchess of Northumberland, Walpole preened himself on not courting royalty:

. . . I am very secure of never being suspected of paying my court for interest, and certainly never seek royal personages, I always pique myself, when I am thrown into their way, upon showing that I know I am nobody, and know the difference between them and me. This I take to be common sense, and do not repent of my behaviour. If I were a grandee, and in place, I would not, like the late Duchess of Northumberland, tag after them [Prince of Wales (1762–1830), and Princess of Wales, Caroline (1768–1821)], calling them, *my Master* and *my Mistress*. I think if I were their servant, I would, as little, like the same Grace, parade before the Queen with more footmen than her Majesty: *that* was impertinent (HWC 34. 23; 11 October 1788).

But Walpole was neither moralistic nor malicious in his censure of Lady Northumberland, whose eccentricities delighted him. Her parties may have been crowded and vulgar (HWC 9. 337; 10. 139; 32. 27), but he rarely missed them. He collected her *bons-mots* assiduously:

. . . [T]here was a vast assembly at Marlborough House [London, March 1765], and a throng in the doorway. My Lady Talbot [Mary de Cardonnel (1719–87)] said, 'Bless me! I think this is like the *Straits* of Thermopylae!' my Lady Northumberland replied, 'I don't know what *Street* that is, but I wish I could get my [arse] through' (HWC 38. 526; 26 March 1765).

He admired her '*bouts-rimés* on a buttered muffin' (HWC 39. 241; Hazen 2420, pp. 10–11). For thirty years he treasured the memory of 'her Vice-Majesty of Ireland' (HWC 10. 108) embarking in her coach from Syon House in 1762 for the races at Newmarket when the Thames was flooding 'with both legs out at the fore-glass' (HWC 10. 108; 12 November 1763). He wrote Anne Liddell from Strawberry Hill in 1794 during

> two new editions of the Deluge, the amplest we ever knew since my grandfather Noah's, except one twenty [thirty-two] years ago, when the late Duchess of Northumberland was overtaken by it [the flood] on the road and was forced to ride with her two legs out of the windows in the front of her post-chaise (HWC 34. 207; 8 December 1794).

CHAPTER 13

Walpole's Portraits in the Letters: Statesmen

Walpole continually forsakes politics in his correspondence while filling his letters with political news. 'I abhor politics' (HWC 31. 105); 'I hate . . . parliament' (HWC 31. 111); 'politics [are] but a farce' (HWC 25. 365). Writing about the last illness of the prime minister, Charles Watson-Wentworth (1730–82), Lord Rockingham, Walpole pretends indifference about Wentworth's successor:

> I am to dine tomorrow [Friday 29 June 1782] with Princess Amelie [Sophia Eleanora (1711–86), daughter of George II] at Gunnersbury, must return on Sunday for the last Drawing-Room at Gloucester House – and on Thursday shall be sovereign of myself again, which is much more important to me than who is to be first lord of the Treasury, if the Marquis [Rockingham] is carried off in his second dictatorship [1782 administration]. Three hours ago I saw just the reverse of what is passing in Lord Rockingham's ante-chamber. It was Lady North, her three daughters and one of her sons taking a solitary promenade on the river [Thames, from their house in Bushey Park], and landing to stroll on the shore, without a single Rosencrans or Guildenstern attending. Forty years ago [1742, when Sir Robert Walpole's ministry fell] I myself was one of the *dramatis personae* in such a scene; and as even then I was perfectly indifferent to the change of decorations [from Downing to Arlington Street], it is not surprising that I should look on them now with much composure – but it was constitution not philosophy: philosophy is only a command of muscles. I never could command mine, when I really cared; and should have made a miserable politician, had I ever felt a sensation of ambition (HWC 33. 337–8; 22 June 1782).

Every scene of falling ministries in the correspondence reminds Walpole of his father's fall from power. But Walpole's disengagement is unconvincing, as in his apology to Anne Liddell for joking about her politics: '. . . [P]olitics must range under one of the four [divisions]: one must admire, lament, laugh at, or be indifferent about, whatever happens. My time of life and the multitude of events I have seen, dispose me to indifference – but to keep up good humour . . .' (HWC 33. 521; 2 August 1786). Richard Bentley's frontispiece for Walpole's *Memoirs of George II* shows Walpole at Strawberry Hill standing under a tree between toga-clad figures of Democritus and Heraclitus, the laughing and weeping philosophers, the words of his family motto – *Fari Quae Sentiat* – subscribed.[1] Of innumerable portraits of politicians in the correspondence, just two – those of Richard Grenville, and John Montagu – are sufficient to show that philosoph-

84.   William Dickinson, after Sir Joshua
Reynolds: *Richard Grenville, Viscount Cobham
and 2d Earl Temple*. RA 1776. Mezzotint
engraving. Photo: Courtesy of the
Huntington Library, Art Collections, and
Botanical Gardens, San Marino, California,
Bute Collection of Mezzotints after
Reynolds. 'He had outlived a fictitious
importance, and was but an historic
Strulbrug' (HWC 30. 272).

ical detachment was not the muse of the Prime Minister of Taste: '[B]eing a speculative, and not a practical politician, my opinion may be biased by outward circumstances. I acknowledge too that I am apt to have strong prejudices both when I like and dislike' (HWC 34. 101; 9 December 1790).

Richard Grenville, Viscount Cobham, 2d Earl Temple (1711–79), 'Historic Strulbrug'. Joshua Reynolds px

Walpole expresses the surprising opinion in identifying Reynolds's portrait of 'Lord Temple' that this *nobleman, half length* is 'the finest portrait he ever painted' (RA 76. 237, p. 21; *marginalia*; plate 84). The comment is surprising because his own portrait in the correspondence of the folly of Temple's political ambition approaches Pope's Sporus in its stringency. Walpole first mentions Temple in 1746 when he and his brother were rising to prominence as Pitt's allies (HWC 30. 107, n. 7; 9 October 1746). In a time of ripening political factions Walpole describes Temple's outrageous conduct to George William 2d Baron Hervey (1721–75) at one of his wife Anne Chambers's assemblies, probably on Wednesday 14 February 1750:

> About ten days ago at the new Lady Cobham's assembly, Lord Hervey was leaning over a chair talking to some women, and holding his hat in his hand – Lord Cobham came up and spit in it – yes, spit in it! – and then with a loud laugh, turned to Nugent

[Robert Nugent (1709–88)], and said, 'Pay me my wager.' In short, he had laid a guinea that he committed this absurd brutality, and that it was not resented. Lord Hervey with great temper and sensibly, asked if he had any further occasion for his hat? – 'Oh! I see you are angry!' – 'Not very well pleased.' Lord Cobham took the fatal hat and wiped it, made a thousand foolish apologies, and wanted to pass it for a joke (HWC 20. 123–4; 25 February 1750).

'Lord Gob-'em' (HWC 20. 124) finally succeeded in making amends with a written apology for what Hervey's mother Mary Lepell called 'the most ridiculous, impertinent, silly piece of boyish play that ever was committed by any gentleman past fifteen' (HWC 26. 30).

Walpole portrays Temple as a treacherous, self-serving, fair-weather friend of William Pitt, who resigned from Pitt's cabinet in a vain attempt to obtain a knighthood which George II refused him. 'To the Garter nobody can have slenderer pretensions', Walpole wrote:

> [H]is family is scarce older than his earldom [1752], which is of the youngest. His person is ridiculously awkward; and if chivalry were in vogue, he has given proofs of having no passion for tilt and tournament. Here ends the story of King George the Second, and Earl Temple the First (HWC 21. 346; 16 November 1759).

After Pitt resigned, Walpole watched Temple continue to court the mob when the old allies, Temple and Pitt, eclipsed George III and Queen Charlotte on Lord Mayor's Day, 9 November 1761:

> . . . [A] young King, and a new Queen were by no means the principal objects of attention. A chariot and pair, containing Mr Pitt and Lord Temple, formed the chief part of the triumph. The reception, acclamation, and distinction paid to Mr Pitt in the streets, and the observance of him in Guildhall, were equal to anything you can imagine (HWC 21. 547; 14 November 1761).

Throughout the convolutions of ministries in the early sixties Cobham exemplifies for Walpole the folly of political ambition after he had himself decided to withdraw from politics: 'To be free from pain and politics is such a relief to me, that I enjoy my little comforts and amusements here [Strawberry Hill] beyond expression', he wrote to George Montagu in 1765:

> No mortal ever entered the gate of ambition with such transport as I took leave of them all at the threshold! Oh! if my Lord Temple knew what pleasures he could create for himself at Stowe, he would not harass a shattered carcass, and sigh to be insolent at St James's! For my part, I say with the bastard in King John [Shakespeare's play, I i 82–3], though with a little more reverence, and only as touching his ambition
>
> > Oh! old Sir Robert, father, on my knee
> > I give heaven thanks I was not like to thee.
> >   (HWC 10. 168; 23 August 1765)

Here Walpole censures his father's political ambition as well as Temple's, but whereas Sir Robert's career served his country well, Walpole thought Temple's character and career ruinous to the nation.

After the Rockingham faction was returned, Walpole wrote: '. . . I dread triumphant friends', meaning, among others, Temple and his brother: 'Lord Temple and George Grenville are very proper to be tied to a conqueror's car and *to drag their slow length along*' (HWC 10. 192; 5 January 1766; adapting Pope, *Essay on Criticism*, line 357). When Temple failed to form an administration six months later and Pitt stayed in power, Walpole celebrated with comical verses, referring to Temple's sister Hester Grenville (1720–1803):

> You may strike up your sackbut, psaltery and dulcimer, for Mr Pitt comes in, and Lord Temple does not. Can I send you [George Montagu] a more welcome affirmative or negative? My sackbut is not very sweet, and there is the ode I have made for it:

> > When Britain heard the woeful news,
> > That Temple was to be minister,
> > To look upon it could she choose
> > But as an omen most sinister?
> > But when she heard he did refuse,
> > In spite of Lady Chat[ham] his sister,
> > What could she do, but laugh, O Muse!
> > – And so she did, till she bepist her.

> If that snake [Temple] had wriggled in, he would have drawn after him the whole herd of vipers, his brother Demogorgon [George Grenville] and all. 'Tis a blessed deliverance! (HWC 10. 223; 21 July 1766).

The tone and imagery of this squib matches exactly the poltical caricatures of the Grenvilles that Walpole was collecting at this time (plate 85).[2] When the Rockingham Whigs' effort to form a ministry finally collapsed, Walpole told George Montagu: 'The fools and the rogues, or if you like proper names, the Rockinghams and the Grenvilles, have bungled their own game, quarrelled and thrown it away' (HWC 10. 244; 31 July 1767).

In spite of such bitter feelings about Temple's political ambition, coloured by memories of his father's career, Walpole continued to have amicable social relations with Lord and Lady Temple. In 1764 he sent them the *The Magpie and her Brood* (40. 366), a verse fable printed at the Strawberry Hill Press. In July 1770 he spent a week at the Temples' country seat, Stowe, Buckinghamshire, at a house-party for Princess Amelia (1711–86). Walpole accepted the invitation apprehensively, but 'took . . . care to avoid politics', and '[t]he party passed off much better than I expected' (HWC 10. 313; 7 July 1770). A small set of only six people including the Temples entertained the princess, and Walpole was at the top of his form: '[A]s I took care to give everything a ludicrous turn as much as I could, the Princess was diverted' (HWC 39. 128). Walpole found the role of courtier demanding and the routine taxing: rising early, dressing for a drawing-room, breakfast at 9:30, tours of 'that province that they call a garden' (HWC 39. 127), dinner at three, cards until ten, supper and bed before midnight.

85.   James Gillray: *Wierd-Sisters; Ministers of Darkness; Minions of the Moon.* 23 December 1791. Coloured aquatint annotated by HW, 9 × 13 in. Courtesy of the Print Collection, Lewis Walpole Library, Yale University. 'If satirical prints could dispatch them [political administrations], they would be dead in their cradle; there are enough to hang a room' (HWC 33. 400–1).

For Walpole, who praised the gardens in his essay on gardening,[3] Stowe was as much 'a Work to wonder at' as it was for Pope (*Epistle to Burlington*, line 70). He sees Temple's seat as simultaneously ludicrous and enchanting, a scene he paints like Watteau, emphasizing the pastoral idyll rather than the political allegory in the garden.

> . . . [M]y meditations on so historic a spot prevented my being tired. Every acre brings to one's mind some instance of parts or pedantry, of the taste or want of taste, of the ambition, or love of fame, or greatness, or miscarriages of those that have inhabited, decorated, planned or visited the place (HWC 10. 313–14; 7 July 1770).

His description of a dramatic entertainment that took place by moonlight in Stowe's Elysian Fields, a satirical passage in the garden that featured temples of Ancient (a Palladian rotunda) and Modern Virtue (a ruin), perfectly illustrates his divided view:

> With a little exaggeration I could make you [George Montagu] believe that nothing ever was so delightful. The idea was really pretty, but as my feelings have lost some-

thing of their romantic sensibility, I did not quite enjoy such an entertainment *al fres-co* so much as I should have done twenty years ago. The evening was more than cool, and the destined spot anything but dry. There were not half lamps enough, and no music but an ancient militia-man who played cruelly on a squeaking tabor and pipe. As our procession descended the vast flight of steps into the garden, in which was assembled a crowd of people from Buckingham and the neighbouring villages to see the Princess and the show, the moon shining very bright, I could not help laughing, as I surveyed our troop, which instead of tripping lightly to such an Arcadian entertainment, were hobbling down, by the balustrades, wrapped up in cloaks and greatcoats for fear of catching cold. . . . we were none of us young enough for a pastoral (HWC 10. 314).

Walpole contributed to 'the chief entertainment of the week' (HWC 10. 315) the following day, Thursday 5 July, when the party assembled for coffee after dinner in the Elysian Fields at an ornamental arch dedicated to Princess Amelia, surrounded by statues of the nine muses and Apollo. Walpole had composed verses for the princess that were placed in the hand of Apollo next to the arch, and Lord Temple helped Lady Mary Coke retrieve them from Apollo's hand 'with some difficulty' (HWC 31. 147). The lines are spoken by Venus, whose temple of Ancient Virtue could be seen from Princess Amelia's arch:

> T'other day with a beautiful frown on her brow
> To the rest of the Gods said the Venus of Stow,
> 'What a fuss is here made of that arch just erected!
> How *our* temples are slighted, our altars neglected!
> Since yon nymph has appear'd, *we* are noticed no more:
> All resort to *her* shrine, all *her* presence adore.
> And what's more provoking, before all our faces
> Temple thither has drawn both the Muses and Graces.'
> 'Keep your temper, dear child,' Phoebus cried with a smile,
> 'Nor this happy, this amiable festival spoil.
> Can your shrine any longer with garlands be drest?
> When a true Goddess reigns, all the false are supprest.'
>   (HWC 10. 315–16)

Thus, Walpole substitutes charming make-believe for politics at Stowe, but he returned with relief to Strawberry Hill: '. . . I should die of the gout or fatigue, if I was to be Polonius to a princess for another week' (HWC 39. 127; 12 July 1770).

Walpole included Lord and Lady Temple among his guests at Strawberry Hill on 11 May 1772, but social intercourse did not change his opinion of Temple's character. He ridicules Temple's reluctance to retire from public life in 1777 with almost Swiftian intensity:

That old ruinous fragment of faction, Lord Temple, has . . . become by his separation from Lord Chatham [William Pitt (1708–78) who married Temple's sister, Hester

Grenville], and by the death of his brother George [Grenville (1712–70)], too insignif-icant and impotent to overturn, awe or even alarm the administration, he has been attempting to wriggle into a little favour by a mongrel mixture of treachery, spying and *informing*, below a gentleman, and even below any Lord, but one [possibly John Montagu, Earl of Sandwich] (HWC 28. 286; 27 February 1777).

A year later, when Temple had reinstated himself with Pitt, Walpole refers to him as 'his [Pitt's] water-gall [secondary rainbow]' (HWC 28. 380; 8 April 1778). When Pitt died Walpole refused to attend the funeral on 9 June 1778: 'I go to no puppet-shows, nor want to see Lord Chatham's water-gall Lord Temple hobble chief mourn-er' (HWC 28. 401; 31 May 1778). After Temple himself died on 11 September 1779, Walpole refers to Swift's living dead in Book III of *Gulliver's Travels* granted eternal life without immortal vigour: 'Lord Temple's death is much more barren [than the dying infant Henry Pelham-Clinton, d. 23 September 1779]. He had outlived a fictitious importance, and was but an historic Strulbrug' (HWC 30. 272; 21 September 1779).

John Montagu (1718–92), 4th Earl of Sandwich: 'The most dissolute and abandoned sad dog in the Kingdom'. Thomas Gainsborough px

At the 1783 Royal Academy exhibition Walpole identified Gainsborough's portrait of 'Lord Sandwich whole length', remarking 'the view of Greenwich [Hospital in the background] – good' (RA 83. 190, p. 10, *marginalia*; plate 86). Walpole's acquaintance with Sandwich dates from his appointment to the Admiralty Board in 1745, when Walpole informed Horace Mann that he would appeal to him to support 'the defence of Tuscany' in the War of the Austrian Succession:

> I shall quite make interest for you: nay, I would speak to our new ally, and your old acquaintance Lord Sandwich, to assist in it; but I could have no hope of getting at his ear, for he has put on such a first-rate tie-wig[4] on his admission to the Admiralty Board, that nothing without the lungs of a boatswain can ever hope to penetrate the thickness of the curls. I think however, it does honour to the dignity of ministers; when he was but a Patriot [a Whig in opposition to Robert Walpole], his wig was not of half its present gravity (HWC 18. 561; 4 January 1745).

Sandwich joined the faction of John Russell (1710–71), 4th Duke of Bedford, and Walpole tells an anecdote about his courtship of his patron:

> He goes once or twice a week to hunt with the Duke [at Woburn Abbey]; and as the lat-ter has taken a turn of gaming, Sandwich, to make his court – and fortune, carries a box and dice in his pocket; and so they throw a main, whenever the hounds are at a fault, *upon every green hill and under every green tree* [*Jeremiah* 2. 20] (HWC 20. 113; 31 January 1750).

Walpole described Sandwich's political tactics during the debate in the House of Lords on Bedford's Turnpike bill (February 1750):

86.   Thomas Gainsborough: *John Montagu, 4th Earl of Sandwich*. RA 1783. Oil on canvas, 92 × 60 in. © National Maritime Museum, London. Photo: Maritime Museum. 'Think to what a government is sunk, when a secretary of state is called in Parliament to his face, *the most profligate sad dog in the kingdom*, and not a man can open his lips in his defence' (HWC 38. 513).

Lord Sandwich, who governs the little Duke [of Bedford] through the Duchess [Gertude Leveson Gower (1715–94)], is the chief object of the Newcastle's hatred. Indeed there never was such a composition! he is as capable of all little knavery, as if he was not practicing all great knavery. During the turnpike contest, in which he laboured night and day against his friend Halifax [George Montagu (1716–71), 2d Earl], he tried the grossest tricks to break agreements, when the opposite side were gone away on the security of a suspension of action (HWC 20. 120–1; 25 February 1750).

Before the 1750s, then, Sandwich registers in Walpole's correspondence as a spectacle in a tie-wig and a knave in politics. By the end of the decade, however, despite Walpole's distaste for Sandwich's politics, a mutual interest in pictures drew them closer together, when Sandwich gave Walpole a coveted portrait of the French courtesan Ninon Lenclos (see Chapter 7). Walpole was so grateful for this portrait 'given . . . me in the prettiest manner in the world', that he wrote to John Chute of the Vyne in Hampshire asking him to bestow political favours on Montagu 'if he should ever meddle in any election in Hampshire' (HWC 35. 100; 26 July 1757). When Walpole visited Sandwich's country seat, Hinchingbrooke, Huntingdonshire, on 31 May 1763 he saw a portrait of Sandwich 'in a Turkish habit, done at Constantinople by Liotard' (*Visits*, p. 49). He admired the house – 'most comfortable, and just what I like; old, spacious, irregular, yet not vast or forlorn', and he thought 'some portraits tolerable, none I think fine'. Referring to a copy of Reynolds's portraits of the Duke of Cumberland after he became alienated from Sandwich, Walpole writes: 'The colours . . . are as much changed as the original to the proprietor' (HWC 10. 79; 30 May 1763).

In November 1763 during the uproar over John Wilkes's *North Briton*, when Walpole voted with the minority 'that general warrants are illegal' (HWC 22. 285) in support of Wilkes's privilege, Sandwich carefully contrived in the House of Lords to smear Wilkes by attributing to him the authorship of a 'blasphemous and bawdy poem' (HWC 22. 187). Walpole informed Horace Mann:

> . . . Lord Sandwich produced to the Lords [Wednesday 16 November 1763], a poem called an *Essay on Woman* written by the same Mr Wilkes, though others say only enlarged by him from a sketch drawn by a late son ['Thomas Potter, son of Dr Potter Archbishop of Canterbury' (HW)] of a late archbishop.[5] It is a parody on Pope's *Essay on Man*. . . . Mr Wilkes complains that he never read it but to two persons, who both approved it highly, Lord Sandwich and Lord Despencer. The style to be sure is at best not unlike that of the last. The wicked even affirm that very lately at a club with Mr Wilkes, held at the top of the playhouse in Drury Lane, Lord Sandwich talked so profanely that he drove two harlequins out of company. You will allow however that the production of this poem so critically was masterly; the secret too was well kept; nor till a vote was passed against it, did even Lord Temple [Richard Grenville (1711–79), Wilkes's political ally] suspect who was the author (HWC 22. 184–5; 17 November 1763).

Walpole summarized the debate in the House of Lords in a letter to Frances Conway:

> Lord Sandwich laid before the House the most blasphemous and indecent poem that ever was composed, called 'An Essay on Woman, with notes by Dr Warburton'. . . . [and] Lord Sandwich moved to vote Wilkes the author; but this Lord Mansfield stopped, advertising the House that it was necessary first to hear what Wilkes could say in his defence (HWC 38. 229–30; 17 November 1763).

Sandwich's parliamentary manoeuvre was voted a breach of privilege by the Lords. Still Walpole admired his political skill in engineering the attack on Wilkes:

> This bomb was certainly well conducted, and the secret, though known to many, well kept. The management is worthy of Lord Sandwich, and like him. It may sound odd from me, with my principles, to admire Lord Sandwich; but besides that he has in several instances been very obliging to me, there is a good humour and an industry about him that are very uncommon. I do not admire politicians; but when they are excellent in their way, one cannot help allowing them their due. Nobody but he could have struck a stroke like this (HWC 38. 231; 17 November 1763).

Sandwich's political manoeuvre turned out to be a Pyrrhic victory. Walpole reported to Francis Conway on 18 November 1763:

Notwithstanding Lord Sandwich's masked battery, the tide runs violently for Wilkes, and I do not find people in general so inclined to excuse his Lordship as I was. One hears nothing but stories of the latter's impiety, and of the concert he was in with Wilkes on that subject. Should this hero die, the Bishop of Gloucester [William Warburton, to whom salacious notes in the *Essay on Woman* were satirically attributed] may doom him whither he pleases, but Wilkes will pass for a saint and a martyr (HWC 38. 232–3).

Among 'stories' circulating in London was a rumour that the convivial Sandwich had been expelled from the Beefsteak Club: 'London never was so entertaining since it had a steeple or a madhouse', Walpole told George Montagu 20 November:

Secretaries of State [Sandwich] turn Methodists on the Tuesday [15 November 1763], and are expelled the playhouse for blasphemy on Friday [18 November 1763]. . . . I know my letter sounds as enigmatic as Merlin's almanac; but *my* events have really happened. . . . [Y]ou know I have long had a partiality for your cousin Sandwich, who has out-Sandwiched himself. He has impeached Wilkes for a blasphemous poem, and has been expelled for blasphemy himself by the Beefstake-club at Covent Garden. Wilkes has been shot by Martin [Samuel Martin (1714–88), in a duel], and instead of being burned at an *auto da fé*, as the Bishop of Gloucester intended, is reverenced as a saint by the mob, and if he dies, I suppose people will squint [alluding to Wilkes's crossed eyes] themselves into convulsions at his tomb, in honour of his memory (10. 110–11).

After the strenuous debate Walpole reiterated the idea that Sandwich was hoist on his own petard:

It has been hard service; and nothing but a Whig point of this magnitude [the issue of Ministers' privilege, or General Warrants] could easily have carried us to the House at all, of which I have so long been sick. Wilkes will live, but is not likely to be in a situation to come forth for some time. The Blasphemous Book [*Essay on Woman*] has fallen ten times heavier on Sandwich's own head than on Wilkes's: it has brought forth such a catalogue of anecdotes as is incredible! (HWC 38. 243; 25 November 1763).

This was one of the rare occasions when Walpole resisted the impulse to collect and retail anecdotes for reasons he explained to his cousin Francis Seymour Conway on 9 December 1763: 'The anecdotes about Lord Sandwich are numerous; but I do not repeat them to you, because I know nothing how true they are, and because he has, in several instances, been very obliging to me; and I have not reason to abuse him' (HWC 38. 260; 9 December 1763).

Writing to Mann, Walpole did repeat one extraordinary anecdote about Sandwich bowdlerized until the Yale edition, à propos of an all-night debate during the Wilkes affair. Isaac Barré (1726–1802) spoke 'with infinite wit and humour' for the motion, ruthlessly attacking Sandwich:

There sat Sandwich under the gallery, while the whole House applied the picture to him! Not a word was offered in his defence. You will ask if he was thunderstruck –

yes, say those who were near him – yet so well he recovered the blow, that at three in the morning he took a coffee-girl who attends in the Speaker's chambers, carried her into one of the rooms, and before he shut the door, laid on the table, while a dissenting minister stood in the passage (HWC 22. 283–4; 11 February 1765).

Walpole was speaking of himself as a member of the silent minority in the House when he wrote to Francis Conway: 'Think to what a government is sunk, when a secretary of state [Sandwich] is called in Parliament to his face, *the most profligate sad dog in the kingdom*, and not a man can open his lips in his defence' (HWC 38. 513; 12 February 1765).

Sandwich's betrayal of his friend and club-mate Wilkes earned him the nickname Jemmy Twitcher after the thief who betrays Macheath in the *Beggar's Opera*. The name, Walpole remarked, 'stuck by the Earl so as almost to occasion the disuse of his title' (HWC 14. 133, n. 10).

Even before the Wilkes commotion had died down, Sandwich, 'the father of lies' as Walpole was calling him (HWC 38. 284), laid 'another egg of animosity'. Sandwich began 'canvassing to succeed Lord Hardwicke [Philip Yorke (1690–1764), 1st Earl], as High Steward of Cambridge [University]' (HWC 38. 248; 2 December 1763), prompting the immediate opposition of the chancellor, Duke of Newcastle, who supported Yorke's son Lord Royston. 'But who can damn the Devil [Sandwich]?' Thomas Gray wrote to Walpole of Sandwich's campaign in January 1764:

He continues his temptations here [Cambridge University] with so much assiduity that I conclude he is not absolutely sure of success yet. . . . Yet he would be chose at present, I have little doubt, though with strong opposition, and in a dishonourable way for him. Yet I have some gleams of hope, for it is in the power of one man [Newcastle, the chancellor] to prevent it, if he will stand the brunt (HWC 14. 131; 27 January 1764).

Lord Hardwicke died on 6 March 1764; the election was scheduled for 30 March. Walpole reported to Francis Conway that Hardwicke's supporters 'are fixed, and the contest at Cambridge will but make them strike deeper root in Opposition' (HWC 38. 341; 11 March 1764).

Gray acknowledged the strength of the opposition, but respected Sandwich's political ingenuity:

The anti-Twicherites [opponents of Sandwich] are numerous and sanguine, and make themselves sure of throwing him out, whatever comes of their own candidate [Philip Yorke (1720–90), Viscount Royston]; but as they are nearly equal, I doubt his Lordship has some trick left to turn the scale (HWC 14. 133; 18 March 1764).

In the end the election on 30 March resulted in a tie: 'Lord Sandwich's contest at Cambridge has taken a strange turn', Walpole informed Horace Mann: 'the numbers for him and Lord Hardwicke [Viscount Royston, 2d Earl] were equal, but both sides pretended to a majority of one. The election broke up in confusion, and *le tout est à recommencer*, with additional heat' (HWC 22. 219; 9 April 1764). Sandwich's 'majority' depended on 'the fraudulent vote of Thomas Pitt' (HWC 14. 133, n. 12), but the vote was reversed on appeal

87A–B.   *HW's transcript and revision of manuscript verses entitled 'The Candidate' (1774) by Thomas Gray (1716–71).* Courtesy of the Lewis Walpole Library, Yale University. 'Methinks I wish you [William Mason] could alter the end of the last line, which is too gross to be read by any females, but such cock bawds as the three dames in the verses. . .' (HWC 28. 170).

when the Court of King's Bench declared Hardwicke elected on 25 April 1765.

Three days before the election Walpole wrote to Francis Conway that 'Lord Sandwich's friends have little hopes. Had I a vote [Walpole, lacking an MA degree, was disqualified], it would not be given for the new Lord Hardwicke' (HWC 38. 355; 27 March 1764). But Walpole was not a strong partisan of Sandwich, and after describing rowdy undergraduate opposition to him – '[T]he juniors burst into the Senate House, elected a fictitious Lord Hardwicke, and chaired him' – he adds:

> The indecent arts and applications which had been used by the *Twitcherites* . . . had provoked this rage. I will give you but one instance: a voter, who was blooded on purpose that morning, was brought out of a madhouse with his keeper. This is the great and wise nation, which the philosopher Helvétius [*De l'esprit* (1758); Hazen, 552] is come to study! When he says of us, *C'est un furieux pays*! he does not know that the literal translation ['violently mad'] is the true description of us (HWC 38. 363; 5 April 1764).

Sometime before the abortive election, when Sandwich was canvassing for votes in

Cambridge, Thomas Gray sent Walpole a satirical squib, later entitled *The Candidate* (plates 87A–B), attacking Sandwich's campaign.[6] Gray's ruthless lampoon reveals an utter contempt for Sandwich, undiluted by Walpole's sympathy or sense of obligation. Gray's lines depict Physic, Law, and Divinity, three old harlots of Cambridge [the faculties of Jurisprudence, Medicine, and Divinity], gossiping about their lecherous suitor, Jemmy Twitcher [Sandwich]. Physic [the faculty of Medicine] will have nothing to do with him, dismissing him for his 'sheep-biting look' (l. 6) 'pickpocket air' (l. 6), syphlitic nose, 'lewd eyes', and awkward gait. Law can tolerate his looks, for Sandwich resembles his great-grandfather, the libertine John Wilmot (1647–80), 2d Earl of Rochester:

> I don't know, says Law, now methinks, for his look,
> 'Tis just like the picture in Rochester's book.[7]
> But his character, Phyzzy, his morals, his life!
> When she died, I can't tell, but he once had a wife.
> They say he's no Christian, loves drinking and whoring,
> And all the town rings of his swearing and roaring,
> His lying, and filching, and Newgate-bird tricks: –
> Not I, – for a coronet, chariot and six.
> (lines 11–18; 28. 169; 16 September 1774)

Walpole supplies a note on Sandwich's wife, Dorothy Fane, whom he had married in 1741: 'Lady Sandwich confined for lunacy, but Lord Sandwich's enemies said she was still shut up after she recovered her senses – at least she never appeared again in the world' (HWC 28. 169, n. 9).

Sandwich's main support during his campaign came from the faculty of Divinity, whose members looked forward to government patronage from Sandwich. Divinity accordingly dismisses her sisters' demurrers, and accepts Jemmy's proposal of marriage:

> What a pother is here about wenching and roaring!
> Why David loved catches, and Solomon whoring.
> Did not Israel filch from th'Egyptians of old
> Their jewels of silver, and jewels of gold?
> The prophet of Bethel, we read, told a lie:
> He drinks; so did Noah: he swears; so do I.
> To refuse him for such peccadillos, were odd;
> Besides, he repents, and he talks about God.
> (lines 23–30)

Then turning to Jemmy Twitcher, the Earl of Sandwich, Divinity adds:

> Never hang down your head, you poor penitent elf;
> Come, buss me, I'll be Mrs Twitcher myself.
> Damn ye both for a couple of Puritan bitches!
> He's Christian enough, that repents, and that stitches [copulates].
> (lines 31–4; 28. 169–70)

Walpole did not share the bitter contempt of 'Jemmy Twitcher's Courtship' (HWC 28. 166), as Mason refers to Gray's attack. Walpole's personal relations with Sandwich inclined him to ignore or extenuate his faults. Walpole tried to persuade Mason to publish Gray's brilliant lines in *Poems* (1775; Hazen 3841) purged of the last word: 'Methinks I wish you could alter the end of the last line, which is too gross to be read by any females, but such cock bawds as the three dames in the verses – and that single word is the only one that could possibly be minded' (HWC 28. 170).

Walpole's character of Sandwich in subsequent correspondence continues this ambivalence: a mixture of shocked amusement at Sandwich's politics, combined with distant but polite social relations. It is noticable that Walpole's portrait of Sandwich in his letters is less critical than that in his *Memoirs*, where Walpole writes scathingly of Sandwich's canvassing of votes in the Cambridge election: 'Ambitious industry was never exerted so indefatigably as by Sandwich on this occasion. There was not a corner of England, nay, not the Isle of Man, unransacked by him for votes. He ferreted out the mad, the lame, the diseased, from their poor retreats, and imported them into the University' (G III 1. 314).[8]

Walpole continued to observe sceptically Sandwich's Machiavellian political career, expressing relief in 1765 '[t]here is no going through another course of patriotism in your [George Montagu's] cousin Sandwich and George Grenville!' (HWC 10. 167; 23 August 1765). He was gratified that Sandwich's protégé, 'his parson [James Scott (1733–1814), a party political writer] Anti-Sejanus [was] hooted off the stage' (HWC 22. 410; 21 March 1766). After the repeal of the Stamp Act he asked George Montagu: 'Are your cousins Cortez and Pisarro [Halifax and Sandwich] heartily mortified that they are not to roast and plunder the Americans?' (HWC 10. 202; 3 March 1766); and he carefully identified Scott, Halifax, Sandwich, and Grenville in a satirical engraving in his collection, 'The Repeal of the Stamp Act' (HWC 22. facing p. 400). When Sandwich was restored to the post of Lord Admiral his administration was so lax and cavalier as to endanger the fleet in the American War of Independence, a situation Walpole described in an anecdote: 'Four days ago [18 July 1778] a person I know sent to the Lord High Admiral's to ask if there was any account of the fleet. The answer, in writing, was, "Lord S. says there is nothing new; catches are going round"' (HWC 33. 30; 22 July 1778).

On several occasions Walpole refers to a more serious matter, Sandwich's court-martial of the admirals Augustus Keppel (1725–86) and Sir Hugh Palliser (1723–96): '. . . the disgraces Lord Sandwich's artifices have brought on the Court by the absurd persecution of Admiral Keppel. It was very near overturning the administration . . .' (HWC 24. 447; 25 February 1779). But Walpole cannot take Sandwich seriously for long in his letters. Reflecting on his 'mortality' at the age of fifty-nine, Walpole jokes about emulating Lord Sandwich in making his exit in the manner of the legendary Countess of Desmond [see Chapter 6]:

> I propose to conclude my career in a manner worthy of an antiquary, as I was in the last century, and when I am satiated with years and honours, and arrived at a comfortable old age, to break my neck out of a cherry tree in robbing an orchard, like the Countess of Desmond at an hundred and forty – but don't mention this last idea, Madam [Anne Liddell], lest that roguish lad the First Lord of the Admiralty should steal the thought from me (HWC 32. 317; 22 August 1776).

88.   Valentine Green, after Nathaniel
Dance: *Martha Ray*. 7 April 1779.
Mezzotint engraving, 19⁷⁄₈ × 16 in.
Courtesy of the Print Collection,
Lewis Walpole Library, Yale
University. 'It is very impertinent in
one Hackman to rival Herod and
shoot Mariamne [Martha Ray]. . . .
and yet it just sets curiosity agog,
because she belongs to Lord
Sandwich at a critical moment'
(HWC 33. 101).

'What trials Lord Sandwich goes through!' (HWC 33. 99; 8 April 1779), Walpole
wrote to Anne Liddell during the court martials of Admirals Keppel and Palliser. Four
months previously, Sandwich's mistress Martha Ray (1745–79; plate 88) had been
murdered on Wednesday 7 April 1779 in Covent Garden:

Last night as Miss Wray [Ray] was getting into her coach in Covent Garden from the
play [Isaac Bickerstaffe's *Love in a Village*], a clergyman shot her through the head –
and then himself. She is dead; but he is alive to be hanged – in the room of Sir Hugh
Palisser (HWC 33. 98; 8 April 1779).

This was much more than a private scandal, and Walpole wildly speculated 'that the
assassin was a dissenter, and instigated by the Americans to give such a blow to the state'
(HWC 33. 98). Walpole quizzed his servants, his cousin Francis Conway, and bought a

copy of the trial of James Hackman (1752–79; Hazen 1609.40.1), who was tried at the Old Bailey on 16 April, and executed at Tyburn on Monday the 19th. Improving on 'the first breath of rumour', Walpole relates to Anne Liddell how Hackman met Martha Ray when she was singing at Lord Sandwich's seat at Hinchingbrooke about 1774:

> The assassin's name is Hackman; he is brother to a reputable tradesman in Cheapside, and is of a very pleasing figure himself, and most engaging behaviour. About five years ago he was an officer in the 68th regiment, and being quartered at Huntingdon, pleased so much, as to be invited to the oratorios at Hinchinbrook, and much caressed there. Struck with Miss Wray's charms, he proposed marriage – but she told him she did not choose to carry a knapsack. He went to Ireland, and there changed the colour of his cloth, and at his return, I think not long ago, renewed his suit, hoping a cassock would be more tempting than a gorget – but in vain (HWC 33. 99–100; 9 April 1779).

Martha Ray went to the play on Wednesday night [7 April 1779] with the singer Catherine Rinni Galli (1724–1804).

> During the play the desperate lover was at the Bedford Coffee-house and behaved with great calmness and drank a glass of *capillaire*. Towards the conclusion he sallied into the piazza [Covent Garden], waiting till he saw his victim handed by Mr Macnamara ['a young Irish Templar']. He came behind her, pulled her by the gown, and on her turning round, clapped the pistol to her forehead and shot her through the head. With another pistol he then attempted to shoot himself, but the ball only grazing his brow, he tried to dash out his own brains with the pistol, and is more wounded by those blows than the ball (HWC 33. 100; 9 April 1779).

Martha Ray, Sandwich's most durable mistress after his wife went insane, had been living with him since 1761 (HWC 33. 98, n. 14) and bore him nine children (HWC 33. 101, n. 11). Walpole gives a poignant description of Sandwich awaiting her return in London the night of her murder:

> Lord Sandwich was at home expecting her to supper at half-an-hour after ten. On her not returning an hour later he said something must have happened – however, being tired, he went to bed at half-an-hour after eleven, and was scarce in bed before one of his servants came in, and said Miss Wray was shot. He stared, and could not comprehend what the fellow meant – nay, lay still, which is full as odd a part of the story as any – at twelve came a letter from the surgeon to confirm the account – and then he was extremely afflicted (HWC 33. 100–1; 9 April 1779).

'[C]an one believe such a tale?' (HWC 33. 98), Walpole asked the day after the murder. The next day he was equally confounded:

> Now upon the whole, Madam [Anne Liddell], is not the story full as strange as ever it was? Miss Wray has six [nine] children, the eldest son is fifteen [Robert Montagu (1763–1830)], and she was at least three times as much [she was thirty-four]. To bear

a hopeless passion for five years, and then murder one's mistress – I don't understand it (HWC 33. 101; 9 April 1779).

Walpole can't dismiss it as mere newspaper sensation, a crime of passion, because he shares Sandwich's affliction as if he had been admitted to his room the night of the murder:

> I do not love tragic events *en pure perte* [for nothing]. If they do happen, I would have them historic. This is only of kin to history, and tends to nothing. It is very impertinent in one Hackman to rival Herod, and shoot Mariamne[9] – and *that* Mariamne, a kept mistress! and yet it just sets curiosity agog, because she belongs to Lord Sandwich at a critical moment – and yet he might as well have killed any other inhabitant of Covent Garden (HWC 33. 101; 9 April 1779).

'Sandwich at a critical moment' (HWC 33. 101) may refer to the campaign of Charles Fox to remove Sandwich as First Lord of the Admiralty, a parliamentary motion defeated on Monday 19 April 1779, the same day that '[t]he poor assassin was executed' (HWC 24. 460; 20 April 1779). The crime tending to nothing engaged Walpole's deepest emotions, not only because it was:

> a shocking murder, committed on the person of a poor woman connected with a material personage on the great stage [Lord Sandwich]. . . . She was allowed to be most engaging, and so was the wretched lover, who had fixed his hopes of happiness on marrying her, and had been refused, after some encouragement, I know not how much. On his trial yesterday [Friday 16 April 1779] he behaved very unlike a madman, and wishes not to live – he is to suffer on Monday [19 April], and I shall rejoice when it is over, for it is shocking to reflect that there is a human being at this moment in so deplorable a situation (HWC 24. 459–60; 17 April 1779).

A week earlier Walpole had written Cole '[t]he poor criminal in question I am persuaded is mad' (HWC 2. 156; 12 April 1779).

Walpole's intensely vivid account of Martha Ray's murder further illustrates how the portraits in Walpole's letters differ from the *Memoirs*. In the letters Walpole writes to correspondents who depend on him for accounts more vivid than the newspapers; he breathes the first warm breath of rumour from servants, reads the account of the trial as soon as it is printed, collects reports straight from the mouths of ministers at the Admiralty, and records details from the bedroom of Lord Sandwich the night of the murder. We can see him speculating, making up his mind, changing his mind, re-creating the scene of the murder like an eye witness, covering the story with leaf-gold, above all deepening and enriching the portrait of Sandwich who appears as a caricature even in verse satires as brilliant as Gray's, and who disappears completely in the wooly personifications of Churchill.[10] After reading Walpole's description of Sandwich waiting for Martha Ray in his London house, we can never dismiss him as the whore-monger of the caricatures.

We get only a few glimpses of Sandwich, in public and private, in Walpole's correspondence of the 1780s: 'near massacred' (HWC 33. 184; 7 June 1780) on his way from the Admiralty to the House of Lords during the Gordon riots; his narrow escape from a motion censuring his mismanagement of the Admiralty (HWC 25. 243, n. 19; 8 February 1782), a result Walpole referred to as 'one culprit . . . whitewashed' (HWC 33. 326; 9 February 1782). Summing up Sandwich's administration later in 1782 Walpole hands down a severe verdict: '. . . [T]hough certainly a man of abilities, [Sandwich] was grown obstinate, peevish, intractable, and was not born for great actions. He loved subtlety and tricks and indirect paths, qualities repugnant to genius' (HWC 25. 276; 5 May 1782). But Walpole maintained a civil relationship, if not a friendship, with Sandwich. In 1785, he loaned him a book on Cromwell (HWC 42. 127; Hazen 2913), that led to the first of several meetings in Berkeley Square that Sandwich described to the author of the book, Mark Noble: 'I have this morning had a long interview with Mr Walpole, he is everything you could wish with regard to your business [a second edition of the book], but an absolute cripple with the gout, and confined to his chair' (HWC 42. 134, n. 2). Walpole concludes his correspondence with the extraordinary Lord Sandwich: 'Forgive me for concluding abruptly, for I have not breath to say more; and am, with great respect and gratitude/Your Lordship's most obedient humble servant' (HWC 42. 128; 1 January 1785).

CHAPTER 14

Walpole's Portraits in the Letters: 'Out-pensioners of Bedlam'

Chevalier D'Éon: 'A Complication of Abominations'

At the 1765 Society of Artists exhibition Walpole identifies two portraits of French diplomats who figured in a scandal that entertained London from 1763 to 1765. The first, a portrait of *An officer, half length*, is by François-Xavier Vispré (1730–90), a French painter and engraver working in London after 1760. Walpole identifies the sitter as 'Monsieur Deon', adding 'there is a print of it' (SA 65. 146, p. 14; plate 89). The second, by Chevalier Vanloo (Carlo, 1705–65), *Portrait of a gentleman, three quarters* (SA 65. 144, p. 14), Walpole identifies as 'Comte de Guerchy', 'well-coloured', also noting a print.

In May 1763 Walpole had entertained a party of French visitors, including the Chevalier D'Éon (Charles-Geneviève-Louis-Auguste-André-Timothée de Beaumont, 1728–1810) at a 'très jolie fête au château de Straberri' (HWC 10. 69; 17 May 1763) just as D'Éon was beginning to practice his confidence tricks on British and French ministers. 'We break-fasted in the great parlour, and I had filled the hall and large cloister by turns, with French horns and clarinets' (HWC 10. 71). D'Éon had arrived in London in September 1762 as secretary to the French ambassador, Louis-Jules-Barbon Mancini-Mazarini (1716–98), the Duc of Nivernois, who had been sent on a special mission to negotiate a peace treaty to end the Seven Years War.[1] When the duke returned to Paris after the treaty was ratified, Louis XV sent D'Éon back to London to serve as chargé d'affaires, and secret agent until Nivernois's successor as ambassador, Claude-Louis-François de Regnier (1715–67), Comte de Guerchy (1715–67) arrived. Elevation to the rank of minister plenipotentiary turned D'Éon's head, and gave him delusions of grandeur. He refused to resign his post when de Guerchy arrived, or to give up the emolument and secret documents entrusted to him. In November 1763 Walpole's correspondent, the English ambassador to France, Francis Seymour Conway (1718–94) wrote from Paris that '[h]e [D'Éon] is generally treated here as a madman' (38. 238; 19 November 1763). Walpole gives similar reports of his desperate expedients to maintain his position in London.

D'Éon produced a forged letter from Louis XV dated 4 October 1763 'ordering him to disregard the recall, to disguise himself as a woman, and to remain in England incognito' (38. 238, n. 14). By November the paranoid D'Éon was imagining that the new French ambassador de Guerchy had hired an assassin to murder him, and was quarreling with him in public. Walpole describes to Horace Mann 'the fatal night at Lord Halifax's' when swords were drawn (38. 244):

89.   François-Xavier Vispré: *Charles de Beaumont, Chevalier D'Éon*. Mezzotint engraving, 13 × 7½ in. HW's extra-illustration (Hazen 2374). Courtesy of the Lewis Walpole Library, Yale University. 'D'Éon, even by his own account, is as culpable as possible, mad with pride, insolent, abusive, ungrateful, and dishonest, in short, a complication of abominations' (HWC 38. 356).

90.   L. J. Cathelin, after J. Ducreux: *Charles de Beaumont, Chevalier D'Éon as a Woman. c.* 1787. Line engraving, 12½ × 9¾ in., HW's extra-illustration (Hazen 2374). Courtesy of the Lewis Walpole Library, Yale University. 'I have found her [la Chevalière d'Éon] altered again! . . . . I now found her loud, noisy and vulgar' (HWC 33. 510).

You have seen some mention in the papers of Monsieur Deon, who from secretary to Monsieur de Nivernois became plenipotentiary, an honour that has turned his brain. His madness first broke out upon one Vergy [Pierre-Henri Treyssac de (d. 1774)] an adventurer, whose soul he threatened to put into the chamber-pot and make him drink it. This rage was carried so far one night at Lord Halifax's [George Montagu, 2d E. of Halifax (1716–71)], that he was put under arrest. Being told his behaviour was a breach of the peace, he thought it meant the *peace* he had signed, and grew ten times madder. This idea he has thrust into a wild book that he has published [Hazen 1609.54.26]; the titlepage of which would divert you; he states all his own names, titles and offices, Noble Claude, Geneviève, Louis, Auguste, Caesar, Alexandre, Hercule, and I don't know what, Docteur en Droit – the *chute* from Caesar to Master Doctor is admirable. The conclusion of the story is, that the poor creature has all the papers of the negotiation in his hands, and threescore thousand livres belonging to the Comte de Guerchy, and will deliver neither one nor t'other. He is recalled from home, and forbidden the Court here, but enjoys the papers and lives on the money, and they don't know how to recover either. Monsieur de Guerchy has behaved with the utmost tenderness and humanity to him. This minister is an agreeable man and pleases much (HWC 22. 190–1; 12 December 1763).

The following March D'Éon published 'a most scandalous quarto, abusing Monsieur de Guerchy outrageously' – *Lettres, mémoires et négociations particulières du Chevalier d'Éon* (London, 1764) – which Walpole described as 'a complication of abominations' (HWC 38. 356; 27 March 1764; Hazen 2374). Walpole dated, annotated, and extra-illustrated with eight prints one of two editions of the scandalous and 'wonderful book' (22. 216). D'Éon's *Lettres* were filled with libels on Nivernois, César-Gabriel de Choiseul, Duc de Praslin (1712–85), Secretary of State, and other French officials:

> Resentment, pride, and frenzy, precipitated him into a literary war with them. . . . he has not only published the Duc de Praslin's letters, and abused de Guerchy intolerably, but has sacrificed Nivernois's letters too, and the private correspondence between the latter and Praslin. . . . Deon's book is full of wit and parts – and what makes it more provoking, our ministers know not what to do, nor how to procure any satisfaction to Guerchy (22. 217–18; 9 April 1764).

Finally, on Thursday 19 April the king ordered the attorney-general to file a writ of indictment against D'Éon. Walpole reported 'that poor lunatic was at the opera on Saturday, looking like Bedlam. He goes armed, and threatens, what I dare say he would perform, to kill or be killed, if any attempt is made to seize him' (38. 378; 20 April 1764). On 9 July D'Éon's case was tried by Lord Mansfield at the King's Bench Bar, Westminster, where D'Éon pleaded *nolo contendere*, and was found guilty (22. 247–8; 27 July 1764). But he absconded before he could be sentenced, after hiding out in a house of ill repute (22. 263; 25 November 1764). According to Walpole's *Memoirs*, D'Éon had been nursing the paranoid fantasy that Guerchy had hired an assassin, Pierre-Henri Treyssac de Vergy to assassinate him (38. 467, n. 14). Before absconding D'Éon persuaded his putative assassin to swear an affadavit dated 11 October 1764 before Sir John Eardley Wilmot (1709–92), Puisne-Judge of the Court of King's Bench: 'Vergy, his antagonist, is become his convert. . . . has made an affadavit. . . . that Monsieur de Guerchy had hired him to stab or poison D'Éon. . . . the story is as clumsy as it is abominable' (38. 467; 25 November 1764).

In November 1764 Vergy published two letters (Hazen 1609. 56. 2–3) to Étienne-François de Choiseul-Stainville (1719–85), Duc de Choiseul, which Walpole interpreted as a French version of John Wilkes's *North Briton*:

> Wilkes and Churchill, you know, were the father and mother of Deon. This madman has begotten another, or rather has transmuted his old enemy de Vergy into an ally. The latter having been ten months in prison for debt, has been redeemed by Deon, and in gratitude or in concert, has printed (and sent about) a French *North Briton*, in which he pretends to confess that he was brought over by Monsieur de Guerchy to cut Deon's throat. This legend is so ill put together, that on the face of it, it confutes itself. However he has tacked an affadavit or oath to it; and I hear within these days he has deposed the same oath before Judge Wilmot. . . . [T]he whole embroil is vexatious enough to poor Guerchy, who is in a country where to have any scandal

believed, it is not necessary to swear to it. His very being a foreigner would induce half this good town to supply the affadavit, without knowing anything of the matter (22. 262–3; 15 November 1764).

So it turned out, because five months later, on 1 March, 'a bill of indictment was found by the grand jury of Middlesex . . . against a foreigner, for a conspiracy against the life of the Chevalier d'Éon' (*London Chronicle*, 2–5 March; 38. 522, n. 2).'I told him,' Walpole wrote to Francis Conway about his conversation with de Guerchy, 'I had absolute proof of his innocence, for I was sure, that if he had offered money for assassination, the men who swear against him would have taken it' (38. 523; 26 March 1765).

On a trip to Paris in October 1765 Walpole met some of the French ministers involved in the D'Éon affair, and compared them to their portraits in the pamphlet wars.

I dined at the Duc of Praslin's with five-and-twenty tomes of the *corps diplomatique*; and after dinner was presented, by Monsieur de Guerchy, to the Duc de Choiseul. The Duc de Praslin is as like his own letters in D'Éon's book [Hazen 2374] as he can stare; that is, I believe, a very silly fellow. His wisdom is of the grave kind. His cousin, the first minister [Choiseul], is a little volatile being, whose countenance and manner had nothing to frighten me for my country. I saw him but for three seconds, which is as much as he allows to any one body or thing. Monsieur de Guerchy, whose goodness to me is inexpressible, took the trouble of walking everywhere with me, and carried me particularly to see the new office for state papers [Dépôt des Archives des Affaires Étrangères at Versailles, opened 1763] (39. 14–15; 2 October 1765).

Walpole sounds disappointed when the D'Éon 'interlude . . . [was] almost concluded' (22. 263; 25 November 1764): '[W]ell! what trumperies, I tell you!' he exclaimed to Francis Seymour Conway:

Wilkes is outlawed, D'Éon run away, and Churchill dead [the poet Charles Churchill (d. 4 November 1764)] – till some new genius arises, you must take up with operas, and pensions, and seven footmen [the Northumberlands' retinue]. – But patience! your country is seldom sterile long (38. 469; 25 November 1764).

It was a long wait before D'Éon returned to the stage of Walpole's correspondence, when in his second prolonged sojourn in England 1785–90 he was appearing in London society dressed as a woman (plate 90). This caused an even greater sensation than the first 'vexatious embroil' (22. 262). D'Éon's biographers have retrospectively coloured his life from childhood with the stain of transvestism: doubts about gender as a child when he was supposedly dressed as a girl, appearing as a woman before Catherine the Great in St Petersburg in the role of diplomatic courier, and Louis XV's supposititious orders to conduct his secret mission in London disguised as a woman.

Early in January 1786, Walpole discovered that he had dined at the miniature-painter Maria Cosway's Schomberg House in Pall Mall in company with D'Éon without recognizing him/her:

I received a little Italian note from Mrs Cosway [Maria Hadfield (1759–1838)] this morning, to tell me that as I had last week met at her house an old acquaintance without knowing her, I might meet her again this evening [Friday, 27 January 1786] *en connaissance de cause* as Mlle la Chevalière d'Éon, who, as Mrs Cosway told me, had taken it ill that I had not reconnoitred her, and said she must be strangely altered – the devil is in it if she is not! – but alack! I have found her altered again! adieu to the abbatial dignity that I had fancied I discovered – I now found her loud, noisy and vulgar – in truth I believe she had dined a little *en dragon* [D'Éon had been promoted to captain of dragoons in the French army in 1757]. The night was hot, she had no muff or gloves, and her hands and arms seem not to have participated of the change of sexes, but are fitter to carry a chair than a fan (33. 510; 27 January 1786).

D'Éon makes her final appearance in Walpole's correspondence when couplets from Harrington's translation of Ariosto, quoted in Thomas Warton's *Observations on the Fairy Queen* (Hazen 1840; 1762), reminded him how she appeared in uniform during his first sojourn in London:

. . . I lighted upon two lines that at first sight reminded me of Mlle D'Éon,

> Now when Marfisa had put off her beaver,
> To be a woman everyone perceive her –

but I do not think that is so perceptible in the Chevalière. She looked more feminine as I remember her in regimentals, than she does now. She is at best a hen-dragoon, or an herculean hostess [i.e., an inn-keeper]. I wonder she does not make a campaign in her own country, and offer her sword to the almost-dethroned monarch [Louis XVI (1754–93)], as a second Joan of Arc (11. 68; 4 September 1789).

Few pictures illustrate more clearly than D'Éon's the dynamics of Walpole's passion for portraits and the curiosities of human nature. A compound of press reports, extra-illustrated pamphlets, letters, memoirs, eye-witness observations, notes in exhibition catalogues – all melt together to add another portrait to Walpole's imaginary museum.

George Townshend (1753–1811), 4th Baron Ferrers (1770), Earl of Leicester (1784), 2d Marquis Townshend (1807): 'Mad About Pedigree'. Joshua Reynolds px

Walpole identifies Reynolds's portrait of George Townshend 4th Baron Ferrers, as 'son of Lord Townshend' (RA 75. 231, p. 22; *marginalia*; plate 91), 4th Viscount (1724–1807). Ferrers first appears in the correspondence in January 1779 when he decided to consult Walpole about improvements to the family seat in Staffordshire. Walpole wrote to his antiquarian correspondent, William Cole on 3 January 1779:

Lord de Ferrers, who deserves his ancient honours, is going to repair the Castle of Tamworth, and has flattered me that he will consult me. He has a violent passion for

91.   Sir Joshua Reynolds: *George Townshend, 4th Baron Ferrers, Earl of Leicester, 2d Marquess Townshend*. RA 1775. Oil on canvas, 94 × 56½ in. Private Collection. Photo: © Christie's Images Ltd. 2000. 'He has a violent passion for ancestry' (HWC 2. 135).

ancestry – and consequently I trust will not stake the patrimony of the Ferrarii, Townshends and Comptons, at the hazard table. A little pride would not hurt our nobility, cock or hen (2. 135–6; 3 January 1779).

In this remark Walpole expresses that mixture of amusement and admiration characteristic of his attitude to Ferrers throughout their relationship.

Walpole saluted Ferrers as 'a great herald arising', adding that 'I hope to make him a Gothic architect' (2. 146; 18 February 1779). Within a few months Cole found in his collection an illuminated-manuscript pedigree of the Ferrers family 'five yards in length' (2. 153, n. 14), which he offered to loan to Walpole until 'you and Lord Ferrers have satisfied your curiosity' (2. 154; 7 April 1779). In early June Walpole was preparing for Lord Ferrers's visit to Strawberry Hill on Saturday 5 June 1779, 'and I have got to treat him an account of ancient paintings in the hall of Tamworth Castle' (2. 165; 2 June 1779). A year later Lord Ferrers returned the favour by identifying arms on painted altar doors from St Edmundsbury, which Walpole had bought at auction (2. 219–21; 30 May 1780). On 23 April 1784 Ferrers was elected president of the Society of Antiquaries, but Walpole was clearly sceptical of his zeal for titles.

After Ferrers was created Earl of Leicester in a splendid ceremony at St James's Palace on Thursday 6 May 1784 (39. 410, n. 13), Walpole wrote that Ferrers was 'mad about pedigree, and called himself heir to the title, because as an hundred others were, he was descended from a female Sidney' (34. 28, n. 11). Following a visit to Penshurst in 1788, the Sidneys' estate in Kent, Ferrers 'fell in love with, and wants to purchase it', Walpole informed Anne Liddell:

> In the mansion he found a helmet, and put it on – but unfortunately it had been made for some paladin, whose head was not of the exact standard that a genuine Earl of Leicester's should be, and in doffing it, he almost tore one of his ears off. I am persuaded he tried it with intention of wearing it at the next coronation, for when he was but two-and-twenty [1775], he called on me one morning and told me he proposed to claim the championry of England, being descended from the eldest daughter of Ralph de Basset [1335–90; 3rd Lord Basset of Drayton], who was champion before the Flood or before the Conquest, I forget which; whereas the Dymocks [Lewis (1763–1820) and John (d. 1784)] come only from the second; and he added, 'I did put in my claim [in the Herald's office] at the coronation of Queen Elizabeth.' A gentleman who was with me, and who did not understand the heraldic tongue, hearing such a declaration from a very young man, stared and thought he was gone raving mad – and I, who did understand him, am still not clear that the gentleman was in the wrong (34. 28; 19 October 1788).

Walpole thought that John Dymoke had 'admirably' performed the ceremonial office of Champion of England at George III's coronation Tuesday 22 September 1761 (9. 388): '[H]e [Dymoke] rode into Westminster Hall armed *cap-a-pie* and challenged anyone who disputed the King's rights' (9. 388, n. 25).

A year before he died Walpole reminisced with George Farington about Lord Leicester's 'passion for ancestry', repeating the story '[w]hen he was only twenty-two years old, he applied to Lord Orford [HW] for his opinion, whether he should not take the title of Lord Bassett, being descended from Margery, eldest daughter of a peer of that title' (15. 330; 24 July 1796). Walpole adds an anecdote about Leicester's attempt to buy a title from his father in 1787:

> Lord Leicester, when his father [George Townshend (1724–1807), 4th Vct. of Raynham, cr. Earl of Leicester 1784], was to be created a Marquess, offered to join in a settlement of £12,000 if he would make Leicester the title and not Townshend. Which his father refused to do, and added, his son might choose any second title but Townshend (15. 330).

And two months before Walpole died on 10 January 1797 he 'mentioned [again] Lord Leicester's passion for heraldry and ancestry, and ridiculed Lord Leicester's going to brokers' shops to hunt for pictures of ancestors. "The late Lord Chesterfield," said he, "humorously spoke of ancestry, by saying he was descended from Adam de Stanhope and Eve de Stanhope"' (15. 334; 10 January 1797).

Edward Wortley Montagu (1713–76): 'Our Greatest Miracle'.
Matthew William Peters px

Reynolds's portraits of aristocrats do not exclusively preoccupy Walpole. He always had an eye for portraits of eccentrics. At the 1776 Royal Academy exhibition, he admired a portrait by Matthew William Peters identified in the catalogue as *Mr. Wortley Montague in his dress as an Arabian prince* (No. 222; plate 92). Walpole's annotation reads: 'very good, in Rembrandt's manner' (RA 76. 222, p. 20, *marginalia*).

Montagu was the son of Lady Mary Wortley-Montagu (Mary Pierrepont, [1689–1762]) whom Walpole had encountered on the Grand Tour, and disliked with an intensity bordering on misogyny. Walpole expressed an incestuous disgust for her on the Grand Tour, identifying himself with her alienated son Edward in a letter to the rake Henry Fiennes Clinton (1720–94), 9th Earl of Lincoln:

> I did not doubt but Lady Mary would be glad of having you flesh of her flesh, but did not imagine she would try to bring it about by making you of her blood; of her poxed, foul, malicious, black blood! I have gone in a coach alone with her too, and felt as little inclination to her as if I had been *her son*. She is a better specific against lust than all the bawdy prohibitions of the Fathers. She comes up to one of Almanzor's rants in a play of Dryden – /The thought of me shall make you impotent! (30. 10; 31 January 1741).[2]

Walpole watched the career of Montagu, child of a brilliant, licentious mother, and an avaricious father, with a mixture of curiosity and compassion. After Montagu was elected to Parliament as MP for Huntingdon County, on 18 July 1747, Walpole wrote to ask Mann about Lady Mary who was then living in Italy: 'Do you know anything of Lady Mary? Her adventurer son is come into Parliament, but has not opened' (19. 450; 24 November 1747).

Four years later Montagu had been making a splash in Paris and London as an extravagant dandy:

> Our greatest miracle is Lady Mary Wortley's son, whose adventures have made so much noise: his parts are not proportionate, but his expense is incredible. His father [Edward Wortley-Montagu (1678–1761)] scarce allows him anything: yet he plays, dresses, diamonds himself, even to distinct shoe buckles for a frock, and has more snuff-boxes than would suffice a Chinese idol with an hundred noses. But the most curious part of his dress, which he has brought from Paris, is an iron wig; you literally would not know it from hair – I believe it is on this account that the Royal Society have chosen him of their body [elected 31 May 1750] (HWC 20. 226; 9 February 1751).

His annual allowance was 'granted on condition that he never be in the same city with his father' (20. 226, n. 41).

Later in 1751 Walpole closely followed one of Montagu's adventures in Paris, well documented in the press. Montagu and an Irish MP, Theobald Taaffe (1708–80; 19. 450, n. 13), were arrested, imprisoned, and tried for cheating and robbing a broker, Abraham

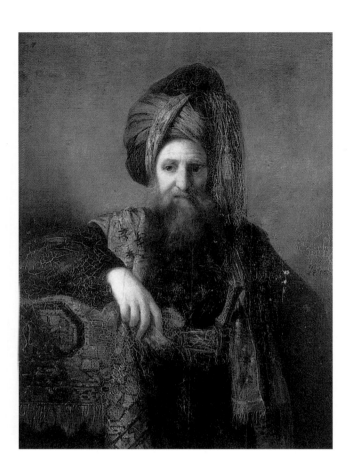

92. Matthew William Peters: *Edward Wortley Montagu*. RA 1776. Oil on canvas, 46 × 34 in. In a Private Scottish Collection. Photo: Scottish National Portrait Gallery. 'Our greatest miracle is Lady Mary Wortley's son, whose adventures have made so much noise' (HWC 20. 226).

Payba, alias James Roberts, out of 870 louis d'ors at hazard with loaded dice on 24 September 1751. But it turned out Payba owed them both money. They were acquitted at the trial in January 1752 in the criminal chamber of the Châtelet, where Montagu had been incarcerated.

Montagu and Taaffe were in prison awaiting trial when Walpole gave Horace Mann a summary of the pending case, which he was piecing together from newspaper reports in the *Daily Advertiser*:

All the letters from Paris have been very cautious of relating the circumstances. The outlines are, that these two *gentlemen* who were pharoah bankers to Madame de Merepoix [Anne de Beauvau (1707–91)], had travelled to France to exercise the same profession, where it is supposed they cheated a Jew, who would afterwards have cheated them of the money he owed, and that to secure payment, they broke open his lodgings and bureau, and seized jewels and other effects; that he accused them; that they were taken out of their beds at two o'clock in the morning, kept in different prisons [the Châtelet and Fort L'Évêque] without fire or candle for six and thirty hours; have since been released on excessive bail; are still to be tried [20–5 January 1752], may be sent to the galleys, or dismissed home, where they will be reduced to keep the best company, for I suppose nobody else will converse with them. . . . Wortley you know has been a perfect Gil Blas [Le Sage's picaresque rogue (1715); Hazen No. 1571], and for one of his last adventures is thought to have added the famous Miss Elizabeth Ashe to the number of his wives (20. 287–9; 22 November 1751).

Walpole disapproved of Montagu's recklessness, but he thought worse of the parents than the son. When Montagu's father died in 1761 leaving his son a legacy of £1000 per annum from an estate 'worth half a million' Walpole remarked: 'The son you perceive is not so well treated by his own father, as his companion Taaffe is by the French Court, where he lives and is received on the best foot' (21. 473; 27 January 1761). When Lady Mary died on 21 August 1762 her bequest of one guinea to her son Edward Montagu was a calculated insult (22. 72, n. 19). 'I told you of Lady Mary Wortley's death and will,' Walpole wrote sarcastically to Horace Mann, 'but I did not then know that with her usual maternal tenderness, and usual generosity, she has left her son one guinea' (22. 81; 26 September 1762).

The last glimpses we get of Montagu in the correspondence are Mann's references to his preparation for a 'journey to Aetheopia. They say he has put a daughter into a convent at Rome. He wears his whiskers, I am told, and at home the dress of that country sometimes to accustom himself to it' (22. 113; 25 December 1762). This is the figure of the adventurer we see in Peters's portrait fourteen years later. And it is as an adventurer rather than as an author that Walpole remembers him in a note to the Mann correspondence: his 'adventures deserve better to be known than his own writings' (21. 472, n. 10). Walpole is referring to Montagu's books in his library: *Reflections on the Rise and Fall of the Antient Republicks* (1759; Hazen 2727), and *Observations on a Supposed Antique Bust at Turin* (1763; Hazen 1609. 56. 1).

CHAPTER 15

Walpole's Portraits in the Letters: 'Modern Literati'

The Daily Advertiser (26 April 1770) lists Walpole among the guests who attended the Royal Academy dinner and private viewing on Sunday 23 April 1770 at 125 Pall Mall (HWC 23. 211, n. 12). Walpole dated his catalogue 'April 23d', writing his verdict on the title-page: 'In this exhibition were some very fine things, and fewer bad than any of the preceding.'

Samuel Johnson (1709–84), 'Saucy Caliban'. Joshua Reynolds px

Walpole identified 'busts in profile' painted by Reynolds of 'Dr Goldsmith' (No. 151) and 'Dr Johnson' (No. 152; plate 93) exhibited at the Royal Academy's second exhibition (1770). The artist Joseph Farington (1747–1821) records Walpole's reminiscences about Reynolds's abortive attempt to introduce him to Johnson at the 1770 exhibition (see Chapter 8):

> Lord Orford [HW] said yesterday [Sunday 24 July 1796, referring to Boswell's account in the *Life*] that he felt great compassion for the wretched state of Johnson's mind in his last illness. The relation one can scarcely read without horror.[1] Lord Orford never was acquainted with Johnson; Sir Joshua Reynolds offered to bring them together, but Lord Orford had so strong a prejudice against Johnson's reputed manners, that he would not agree to it (HWC 15. 332–3; 25 July 1796).

Walpole had been moved to compassion by Boswell's account of Johnson's last illness, but throughout his life he inveighed against the 'tasteless pedant' (29. 111) with a vehemence that prompted Farington to remark: 'I observed . . . that age had not weakened the prejudices of Lord Orford. . . . His resentments are strong; and on the other side his approbation, when he does approve, unbounded' (15. 333).

Walpole's portrait of Johnson in the correspondence falls little short of caricature. Soon after the publication of Johnson's *Dictionary* (15 April 1755), Walpole used it to make a witty joke about a royal god-child – Augusta, Princess of Wales's campaign against George III's intention of marrying her eldest son to Sofie Karoline (1737–1817) of Brunswick-Wolfenbüttel: 'Her Ladyship's eldest boy declares violently against being *bewolfenbuttled* – a word which I don't pretend to understand, as it is not in Mr Johnson's new dictionary' (35. 255; 19 October 1755; Hazen 5). Playful witticism is soon supplanted in Walpole's correspondence with the censorious William Mason, by more astringent remarks, as when he pretends to forswear writing because of the popularity of Johnson's work:

93.   James Watson, after Sir Joshua Reynolds: *Samuel Johnson*. Mezzotint engraving. Photo: Courtesy of the Huntington Library, Art Collections, and Botanical Gardens, San Marino, California, Bute Collection of Mezzotints after Reynolds. 'He [Johnson] has other motives than lucre, – prejudice. . . and pedantry are the hags that brew his ink' (HWC 29. 180).

My last volume of the *Anecdotes of Painting* has long been finished [vol. 4, 1772, published 1780] . . . but there I take my leave of Messieurs the readers. Let Dr Johnson please this age with the fustian of his style and the meanness of his spirit! both are good and great enough for the taste and practice predominant. I think this country sinking fast into ruin (HWC 28. 166; 23 August 1774).

The fustian and meanness probably refer to Johnson's conversation, copiously reported in the newspapers before Boswell's *Tour* (1786), and to criticism of Johnson's *Shakespeare* (1765). Commenting on Garrick's omission of the graveyard scene in *Hamlet*, Walpole writes:

Dr Johnson has dared to say that when Shakespeare arrived at being sublime, he was bombast; that is, Johnson had no idea of sublimity but in the pomp of diction, and he himself in his common conversation is always hyperbolic and pedantic. He talks like Ancient Pistol, and is the very thing he condemns (HWC 29. 370).[2]

Walpole compliments Mason's *Life of Gray* (1775) by derogating Johnson: 'As you have . . . [not] imitated the teeth-breaking diction of Johnson . . . you cannot expect to please the *reigning* taste' (HWC 28. 185; 3 April 1775). He adds tautology to his bill of complaint, comparing Johnson to Garrick as 'woeful' overrated authors:

> Posterity would believe me . . . who will see those [writings] of another modern idol, far less deservedly enshrined, Dr Johnson. I have been saying this morning, that . . . [Johnson] deals so much in triple tautology, or the fault of repeating the same sense in three different phrases, that I believe it would be possible, taking the ground-work for all three, to make one of his Ramblers into three different papers, that should all have exactly the same purport and meaning, but in different phrases. It would be a good trick for somebody to produce one and read it – A second should say, 'Bless me, I have this very paper in my pocket, but in quite other diction'; and so a third (HWC 33. 88–9; 1 February 1779).

Johnson's *Lives of the Poets* (1779–81), and particularly the drubbing Johnson gave Gray, provoked Walpole's most bitter attacks on Johnson. He wrote to William Mason, Gray's biographer:

> Apropos to Gray, Johnson's life, or rather criticism on his odes, is come out; a most wretched, dull, tasteless, *verbal* criticism, yet timid too. But he makes amends, he admires Thompson and Akenside, and Sir Richard Blackmore, and has reprinted Dennis's criticism on *Cato*, to save time and swell his pay. In short as usual, he has proved that he has no more ear than taste. Mrs Montague [Elizabeth Robinson (1720–1800), author of *An Essay on the Writings and Genius of Shakespear* (1769)] and all her Maenades intend to tear him limb from limb for despising their moppet Lord Lyttelton [Sir George (1709–73)] (HWC 29. 97; 27 January 1781).

One of the 'six times' (11. 276) Walpole was in a room with Johnson occurred on Sunday 4 February 1781 at a meeting of the Maenad-Bluestockings at Margaret Smith, Lady Lucan's in Charles Street, Berkeley Square:

> I think I shall soon compass a transcript of Gray's life by Demogorgon [Samuel Johnson] for you. I saw him last night at Lady Lucan's, who had assembled a *blue-stocking* meeting in imitation of Mrs Vesey's Babels. It was so blue, it was quite mazarine-blue. Mrs Montague kept aloof from Johnson, like the West from the East (HWC 29. 104; 5 February 1781).

Johnson had referred to 'poor Lyttelton' making craven acknowledgments to favorable reviewers of his *Dialogues of the Dead* [Hazen 131; Lives 10 (1781): 11–12]:

> Apropos, *poor Lyttelton* were the words of offence. Mrs Vesey [Elizabeth (1715–91)] sounded the trumpet. It has not I believe produced any altercation, but at a bluestocking meeting held by Lady Lucan, Mrs Montagu and Dr Johnson kept at different ends of the chamber and set up altar against altar there. There she told me as a

mark of her high displeasure that she would never ask him [Johnson] to dinner again. I took her side and fomented the quarrel, and wished I could have made Dagon [God of the Philistines] and Ashtaroth [Goddess of the Zidonians] scold in Coptic (29. 115–16; 3 March 1781).

Walpole's scenario invites a satirical engraving by Gillray. After Mason received from Walpole a transcript of Johnson's *Life of Gray*, 'blubber' of 'saucy Caliban' (HWC 29. 106), Mason replied:

. . . now let me thank you for your transcript of Johnson, which is certainly the meanest business that ever disgraced literature. . . . I have a great mind to weave it into a mock epic could I get the least hint of a squabble between Queen Astaroth and Dagon. If that matter goes further, pray give me early intelligence (HWC 29. 121).

Johnson's *Lives of the Poets*, especially his treatment of Gray, prompted Walpole to cast Johnson as the hero of a new *Dunciad* in a Ciceronian tirade:

I dipped into them [*Lives of the Poets*, 1779], and found that the tasteless pedant admires that wretched buffoon Dr King [William (1663–1712)], who is but a Tom Brown in rhyme; and says that *The Dispensary* [by Samuel Garth (1661–1719)], that *chef-d'oeuvre*, can scarce make itself read. This is prejudice on both sides. . . . But Dr Johnson has indubitably neither taste nor ear, criterion of judgment, but his old woman's prejudices. . . . I am glad that the measure of our dullness is full. I would have this era stigmatize itself in every respect, and be a proverb to the nations around, and to future ages. We want but popery to sanctify every act of blindness. Hume should burn the works of Locke, and Johnson of Milton, and the atheist and the bigot join in the same religious rites, as they both were pensioned by the same piety. Oh! let us not have a ray of sense or throb of sensation left to distinguish us from the brutes! let total stupefaction palliate our fall, and let us resemble the Jews, who when they were to elect a God, preferred a calf! (HWC 29. 110–11; 19 February 1781).

Walpole condemned Johnson's *Life of Gray* for its verbal criticism, but 'sense . . . [overwhelmed] by words' (28. 143) is the basis for his attack on the *Life of Pope*: 'Sir Joshua Reynolds has lent me Dr Johnson's life of Pope, which Sir Joshua holds to be a *chef-d'oeuvre*. It is a most trumpery performance and stuffed with all his crabbed phrases and vulgarisms, and much trash as anecdotes' (HWC 29. 130; 14 April 1781). He then quotes a 'farrago of Demogorgon jargon', as Mason acknowledged (29. 132):

The machinery in *The Rape of the Lock* he calls *combinations of skilful genius with happy casualty*, in English I guess a *lucky thought*. . . . Pope's not transcribing the whole *Iliad* as soon as he thought he should . . . concludes with this piece of bombast nonsense, *he that runs against time has an antagonist not subject to casualties*. . . . Was poor good sense ever so unmercifully overlaid by a babbling old woman! How was it possible to marshal words so ridiculously? He seems to have read the ancients with no view but of pilfering polysyllables, utterly insensible to the graces of their simplicity. . . .

Hurlothrumbo talked plain English in comparison of this wight on stilts (HWC 29. 130–1; 14 April 1781).

Walpole's is referring to the mock opera *Hurlothrumbo* (Hazen 2403, 1729) in which the eponymous hero talks nonsense and the author, Samuel Johnson of Cheshire (1691–1773), walks upon stilts.

The small-minded Mason asks in reply: 'How can poor Sir Joshua be such an oaf to admire such a writer, when his own style is so free of those blemishes?' (HWC 29. 132; 21 April 1781). Neither Walpole nor Mason could transcend contemporary prejudice against Johnson's sesquipedalian diction; understanding of its metaphorical power had to await William Wimsatt's classic study, *Philosophical Words* (1948). Mason, who was then hoping to persuade Reynolds to annotate his translation of du Fresnoy (1783; Hazen 3890), reveals his usual prejudice: 'I shrewdly suspect he [Reynolds] will show Johnson my translation and that, as he will certainly abuse it, Sir Joshua will lay aside the thought of annotations' (HWC 29. 132).

Mason's fears of Johnson's criticism, like Walpole's, proved groundless. Johnson wrote to Reynolds 19 February 1783 of Mason's translation: 'I find him better than exact, he has his author's [du Fresnoy's] distinctness and clearness without his dryness and sterility' (HWC 29. 132, n. 9). Walpole characterized their mutual fear of Johnson's criticism when he reported to Mason Edward Gibbon's anecdote about 'somebody [who] asked Johnson if he was not afraid that *you* [Mason] would resent the freedoms he has taken with Gray, – *No, no Sir, Mr Mason does not like rough handling'*. To which Walpole vaingloriously adds: 'I hope in the Muses [a satire in progress?] that you will let him see who had most reason to fear rough handling. The saucy Caliban!' (HWC 29. 106; 9 February 1781). Responding to the false report that he had tried to prevent Johnson from reading his tragedy, *The Mysterious Mother*, in manuscript, Walpole later admitted to Anne Liddell that his fear of Johnson's censure had been unwarranted: '[Y]ou know, Madam, I never reverenced him, yet had no reason to be in terrible fear of his criticisms, for he really, as far as I have heard, always spoke civilly of my publications' (HWC 33. 579; 4 October 1787). Boswell confirms this hypothesis: 'Talking to me of Horry Walpole . . . Johnson allowed that he got together a great many curious little things, and told them in an elegant manner' (HWC 33. 579, n. 7). This is high praise from Johnson, and Boswell elsewhere quotes his reference to 'Horace Walpole, who is read with pleasure.'[3]

Another important dimension of Walpole's prejudice against Johnson concerns Johnson's status as a professional writer. He treasured anecdotes that his Twickenham neighbour, Sir John Hawkins, who was preparing his *Life of Johnson* (1787), told him on Sunday 3 February 1782: 'When Dr Johnson was at work on his Shakspeare, Sir John said to him, "Well! Doctor, now you have finished your dictionary [1755], I suppose you will labour your present work [editing Shakespeare] *con amore* for your reputation." "No Sir," said Johnson, "nothing excites a man to write but necessity"' (HWC 29. 179, 7 February 1782).[4] Hawkins added the story of a clergyman for whom Johnson refused to write a sermon:

'No Sir,' said the mercenary, 'I cannot write but for money; since I have dealt with the heathens (the booksellers) I have no other inspiration. I knew they could not do without me, and I made them pay five guineas a sheet for my *Rasselas*; you must pay me, if I write for you'. . . . I do not know why he called the booksellers *heathens*, unless for their worshipping such an uncouth idol as he is; yet he has other motives than lucre, – prejudice, and bigotry, and pride, and presumption, and arrogance, and pedantry are the hags that brew his ink, though wages alone supply him with paper (HWC 29. 179–80; 7 February 1782).

The gentleman amateur author with a private press at Strawberry Hill, supported by sinecures, simply cannot understand a writer who writes to earn a living. Once again Walpole supplies a hint for a satirical engraving: Johnson's Muses as 'the hags that brew his ink'.[5]

After Johnson's death in 1784, Walpole delighted in the rivalry of Johnson's biographers, composed satirical epigrams, and annotated Boswell's *Tour to the Hebrides* (1785) and *Life of Johnson* (1791; Hazen 3294). His epigram 'On Dr Johnson's Biographers' satirizes Boswell, Mrs Piozzi, and a dozen others who rushed memoirs into print:

> In Johnson's fate Acteon's re-occurs,
> Each piecemeal torn by his own pack of curs.
> (12. 258)

Walpole's copy of the *Tour* contains several satirical engravings (plate 94), and another epigram summing up his reaction to the *Tour*:

> When boozy Bozzy belch'd out Johnson's sayings,
> And half the volume fill'd with his own brayings,
> Scotland beheld again before her pass
> A brutal bulldog coupled with an ass.
> (33. 509, n. 15; Hazen 3069)

Walpole admired Boswell's *Life* (1791) for its 'gossiping [and] . . . numbers of proper names' (HWC 11. 275), but he censured Boswell for practicing what Dr Charles Blagdon (1748–1820) had called:

a new kind of libel, by which you may abuse anybody, by saying, some dead person said so and so of somebody alive – Often indeed Johnson made the most brutal speeches to living persons, for though he was good-natured at bottom, he was very ill-natured at top. He loved to dispute to show his superiority. If his opponents were weak, he told them they were fools; if they vanquished him, he was scurrilous (HWC 11. 275; 26 May 1791).

Walpole was pleasantly surprised to find he had escaped whipping: 'I expected amongst the excommunicated to find myself, but am very gently treated' (11. 275–6). Walpole decries Boswell's speculation that his prejudice against Johnson resulted from resentment of Johnson's parliamentary reporting of his father's speeches in the *Gentleman's Magazine*: '. . . I did not read then, or ever knew Johnson wrote till Johnson died, nor

94. *Scotch Worship of an English Idol*
[Johnson]*; and his High Priest*
[Boswell]. *c.* 1786. Anonymous etching,
10½ × 13 in. The Pierpont Morgan
Library, New York. Photo: Morgan
Library. 'When boozy Bozzy belch'd
out Johnson's sayings,/And half the
volume fill'd with his own
brayings,/Scotland beheld again before
her pass/A brutal bulldog coupled
with an ass' (HWC 33. 509, n. 15).

have looked at since. Johnson's blind Toryism and known brutality left me aloof, nor did I ever exchange a syllable with him' (11. 276). On several occasions Walpole 'sewed up . . . [his] mouth' when in the presence of Boswell (33. 466; 20 June 1785). When Boswell solicited anecdotes for Johnson's *Life of Gray*, Walpole refused:

> I said very coldly, I had given what I knew to Mr Mason. B. [Boswell] hummed and hawed and then dropped, 'I suppose you know Dr J. [Johnson] does not admire Mr Gray' – Putting as much contempt as I could into my look and tone, I said, 'Dr Johnson don't! – humph!' – and with that monosyllable ended our interview (HWC 11. 276; 26 May 1791).

In summary, Walpole's portrait of Johnson in the correspondence is a caricature: Demogorgon, the modern idol of booksellers and misguided readers, is the hero of Walpole's new *Dunciad*. His view derives from a gentleman writer's profound distrust of a professional writer, a 'mercenary' with strong intellectual convictions who takes literature seriously. Walpole cannot understand Johnson's outrage at the desecration of Elgin and Aberdeen Cathedrals expressed in Johnson's *Journey to the Western Islands* (1775; Hazen 3108). Walpole rejoices that the lead removed from the roofs – 'this cargo of sacrilege' – was lost at sea: 'I confess I have not quite so heinous an idea of sacrilege as Dr Johnson. . . . I doubt that uncharitable anathema is more in the spirit of the Old Testament than of the New' (HWC 15. 149–50; 1 January 1781). Then too, Walpole's pleasure in drawing caricatures must be added to his portrait of Johnson. He gives a more balanced and less entertaining view of Johnson in his retrospective 'General Criticism on Dr Johnson's Writings', where he complains once again about

95.   Sir Joshua Reynolds: *Edward Gibbon*. RA 1780.
Oil on canvas, 29 × 24½ in. By permission of the Earl
of Rosebery. Photo: Antonia Reeve Photography for
the Scottish National Portrait Gallery. 'I well knew
his vanity, even about his ridiculous face and person,
but thought he had too much sense to avow it so palpably' (HWC 29. 98).

the 'vicious', 'encumbered' style, but concedes that '[t]here is meaning in almost every
thing Johnson says. . . . he is often profound, and a just reasoner . . . when prejudice,
bigotry, and arrogance do not cloud or debase his logic' (*Works* 4. 361).

Edward Gibbon (1737–94): 'Vanity is not Vice'. Joshua Reynolds px

'Mr Gibbon . . . good and like' Walpole wrote in his catalogue annotating Reynolds's
Portrait of a Gentleman (RA 80. 18, p. 4, *marginalia*; plate 95), identifying an intellectual
friend who both intimidated and delighted him. Their acquaintance dates from 1761
when Gibbon presented Walpole with his first book, *Essai sur l'étude de la littérature*
(Hazen 1786, London 1761), inscribed by Gibbon 'From the author', and annotated by
Walpole with this succinct biographical vignette of the historian: 'Son of Alderman
Gibbon, seduced in France to turn Papist, but recovered by his father to the religion of
his country. Afterwards author of the celebrated Roman history' [Hazen 1786]. In return
for this book Walpole sent Gibbon the first two volumes of his *Anecdotes of Painting*
(1762).

   An exchange of books began this uneasy friendship. Gibbon continued the exchange
by presenting Walpole with the first volume of the *Decline and Fall*, published on
Saturday 17 February 1776 (28. 243, n. 15; Hazen 3188). Walpole, suffering from the gout
when he received his copy on Monday 12 February, had his secretary send a message of
thanks the same day, expressing the 'greatest admiration of the style, manner, method,
clearness, and intelligence' of the first chapter (41. 333; 12 February 1776). Two days later,
when he had read a 'great part' of the first volume, Walpole singled out for praise Gibbon's

amiable modesty. . . . [betraying] no dictatorial arrogance of decision. . . . The strongest [impression on me] is the thirst of being better acquainted with you – but I reflect that I have been a trifling author, and am in no light profound enough to deserve your intimacy, except by confessing your superiority so frankly, that I assure you honestly I already feel no envy, though I did for a moment (41. 335; 14 February 1776).

Walpole urges Gibbon to finish his *magnum opus*. Taking a 'liberty as an older man' [HW's fifty-eight to Gibbon's thirty-eight], he warns Gibbon 'never to let your charming modesty be corrupted by the acclamations your talents will receive', admitting to one 'sensation of vanity. . . . that your sentiments on government agree with my own' (HWC 41. 335; Wednesday 14 February 1776).

In a letter to William Mason written the following Sunday Walpole explains why Gibbon's book had intimidated him:

Lo, there is just appeared a truly classic work: a history, not majestic like Livy, nor compressed like Tacitus; not stamped with character like Clarendon; perhaps not so deep as Robertson's *Scotland* [Hazen 321 (1759)], but a thousand degrees above his *Charles* [*Charles V*, Hazen 2943 (1769)]; not pointed like Voltaire, but as accurate as he is inexact; modest as he is *tranchant* and sly as Montesquieu [Hazen 1163] without being so *recherché*. The style is as smooth as a Flemish picture, and the muscles are concealed and only for natural uses, not exaggerated like Michael Angelo's to show the painter's skill in anatomy; nor composed of the limbs of clowns of different nations, like Dr Johnson's heterogeneous monsters. This book is Mr Gibbon's *History of the Decline and Fall of the Roman Empire*. . . . I know him a little, never suspected the extent of his talents, for he is perfectly modest, or I want penetration, which I know too, but I intend to know him a great deal more (HWC 28. 243–4; 18 February 1776).

Walpole did get to know Gibbon better, but no mortal could live up to such a dazzling first impression of perfect modesty. Two years later on a Saturday morning 17 June 1778, Gibbon visited Walpole at Arlington Street in London with the witty George Selwyn, and held his own in conversation:

. . . [Gibbon] told me a very good thing of Hare [James Hare (1747–1804), MP]. The Duke of Northumberland [Sir Hugh Smithson (1715–86)] had lost a great cast at Almack's [the gambling club] t'other night, and was paying his money round the table. Hare looked at him and said to himself – but aloud, 'An ox roasted whole for the benefit of the paupers of Westminster!' (HWC 33. 6, n. 12).

Nevertheless, when Gibbon lent Walpole a proof-copy of volume two of the *Decline and Fall* in November 1780 before publication on 1 March 1781, the book occasioned a quarrel and Gibbon turned into the butt of Walpole's anecdotes. An acerbic letter written by Walpole to the cynical Reverend William Mason recounts the argument:

You will be diverted to hear that Mr Gibbon has quarreled with me. He lent me his second volume in the middle of November. I returned it with a most civil panegyric [missing]. He came for more incense, I gave it, but alas! with too much sincerity, I added, 'Mr Gibbon, I am sorry *you* should have pitched on so disgusting a subject as the Constantinopolitan history. There is so much of the Arians and Eunomians, and semi-Pelagians; and there is such a strange contrast between Roman and Gothic manners, and so little harmony between a Consul Sabinus and a Ricimer, Duke of the palace, that though you have written the story as well as it could be written, I fear few will have patience to read it.' He coloured; all his round features squeezed themselves into sharp angles; he screwed up his button-mouth and rapping his snuff-box, said, 'It had never been put together before' – *so well* he meant to add – but gulped it. He meant *so well* certainly, for Tillemont [Louis le Nain de, 1637–98], whom he quotes in every page, has done the very thing. Well from that hour to this [mid-November 1780 to 27 January 1781] I have never seen him, though he used to call once or twice a week; nor has sent me the third volume [published 1 March 1781], as he promised. I well knew his vanity, even about his ridiculous face and person, but thought he had too much sense to avow it so palpably.

Concluding with complaints about 'the style . . . far less sedulously enamelled than the first volume', and a specious charge about 'flattery to the Scots', Walpole finishes his portrait by transforming the modest author of the first volume into a Witwould – 'so much for literature and its fops!' (HWC 29. 97–9; 27 January 1781). As frequently happened, William Mason brings out a malicious streak in Walpole. The insecure and vulnerable author of the *Anecdotes of Painting* delights in belittling his intellectual superior.

How he would have cringed had he known that Gibbon had written a devastating review of Walpole's own feeble and wrong-headed work of history, *Historic Doubts on the Life and Reign of Richard the Third* [1 February 1768].[6] Walpole wrote a reply to Gibbon's anonymous review, and to the notes of David Hume that accompanied it, a piece of special pleading revealing more vanity than Walpole attributes to Gibbon: 'Mr Hume had shown me the notes last year [1768] in MS, but this conduct appeared so paltry, added to Mr Hume's total silence, that I immediately wrote an answer', Walpole writes in *Short Notes*, 'not only to these notes [Hume's] but to other things that had been written against my *Doubts*' (HWC 13. 44–5; 1769). 'However, as I treated Mr Hume with the severity he deserved', he adds vaingloriously, 'I resolved not to print this answer, only to show it to him in MS and to leave it behind as an appendix to and confirmation of my *Historic Doubts*' (13. 45).

It is possible that Walpole made up all or part of the dialogue in the snuff-box anecdote to amuse Mason. He quotes one name that figures in Gibbon's unpublished third volume (HWC 29. 98, n. 18; 27 January 1781). Walpole apparently suffered some feelings of guilt for ridiculing Gibbon when he wrote sanctimoniously to Mason a week later: 'The lost sheep is found; but I have more joy in one just person than in ninety and nine sinners that do not repent [*Luke* 15. 4]; in short, the renegade Gibbon is returned to me, after ten or eleven weeks, and pleads having been five of them at Bath' (29. 106; 9 February 1781). The penitent sinner Gibbon had given Walpole volume three, published 1 March 1781, by the time he wrote to Mason to say he found it as tedious and confusing as the second: 'He has made me a present of these volumes and I am sure I shall have fully paid for them when I have finished them' (29. 115; 3 March 1781). The enamelled style of volume one

96.   Attributed to Raphael Lamar West: *Some Body & No Body*. 15 February 1787. Coloured line engraving, 14 × 9½ in. Courtesy of the Print Collection, Lewis Walpole Library, Yale University. 'I [HW] am glad no caricaturist is present; he would certainly draw Mr G[ibbon] and me like the old print for children of Somebody and Nobody' (HWC 34. 194).

had been replaced, Walpole thought, by 'rhetoric diction': 'the style which is translating bad Latin into English, that may be turned into classic Latin' (29. 115).

When the final volumes of the *Decline and Fall* were published on 27 April 1788, Walpole redeemed himself for some of these judgments and his humiliation of the author. He wrote to Anne Liddell:

> I am a little surprised, I confess, at your Ladyship's finding it laborious to finish Mr Gibbon [vols. 4–6], especially the last volume, which I own too, delighted me the most – perhaps because I was best acquainted with the subjects of it. In the other volumes I was a little confounded by his leaping backwards and forwards, and I could not recollect all those *fainéant* [idle] emperors of Constantinople, who come again and again, like the same ships in a moving picture [the Eidophusikon]. How he could traverse such acres of ill-written histories, even to collect such a great work, astonishes me (HWC 34. 39–40; 10 February 1789).

By the time Walpole finished reading the *Decline and Fall* he confirmed his first favorable impression, and abandoned the idea of the 'fop of literature' he had invented to amuse his cynical friend William Mason. Comparing Gibbon to William Robertson (1721–93), the Scottish historian, Walpole sums up the superiority of Gibbon's history painting: '. . . as he [Robertson] has not the genius, penetration, sagacity and art of Mr Gibbon, he cannot melt his materials together, and make them elucidate and even improve and produce new discoveries – in short, he cannot like Mr Gibbon make an *original* picture with some bits of mosaic' (HWC 34. 131–32; 23 November 1791).

On Saturday 30 November 1793 Walpole and Gibbon both attended Margaret Smith, (d. 1814) Lady Lucan's stylish salon where they had met before for cards (33. 313; 1781). Walpole 'said to the person next me, "I am glad no caricaturist is present; he would certainly draw Mr G[ibbon] and me like the old print for children of Somebody and Nobody"' (HWC 34. 194; 9 December 1793). The print (plate 96) contrasts the plumpness of 'Somebody' (Gibbon) and the skeletal leaness of 'Nobody' (Walpole). But Walpole's witticism refers to more than physical appearances. He is comically characterizing here his painful realization of the difference between himself and a writer he recognized, to his credit, as one of the greatest of his time. A year before he died, Walpole was even able to forgive Gibbon his vanity: '"The Diary of Gibbon [Hazen 3189],"' Farington records Walpole saying during his last illness (Sunday 24 July 1796),[7] '"gave me a better opinion of his [Gibbon's] heart . . . than I had before. It exhibits some weaknesses, but vanity is not vice"' (HWC 15. 331).

CHAPTER 16

Walpole's Portraits in the Letters: Group Portraits

Reynolds's Bedford Children

Considering his fascination with portraits of individual characters it is paradoxical that Walpole's most extended commentary on pictures in the correspondence concerns two group portraits or conversation pieces. The first, Reynolds's portrait of the Bedford children acting the story of St George and the Dragon, inspired in Walpole a whimsical fantasy, and a flight of self-dramatization. The second, Zoffany's picture of the *Tribuna* (RA 80. 68, p. 6), the Grand Duke's Gallery at Florence filled with Grand Tourists looking at masterpieces of classical statuary and Italian painting, caused him to question his own preference for portraiture. Reynolds's *Bedford Children* illustrates, then, the power of a conversation piece to liberate Walpole's imagination. Zoffany's *Tribuna* illustrates the collision between Walpole's taste for portraits and the Grand Tour taste, dramatizing a battle of pictures corresponding to Swift's *Battle of the Books*, the perennial struggle between classic and romantic taste in art.

The year before Reynolds exhibited his *Portrait of a nobleman with his brothers, and a young lady* (RA 77. 286, p. 22), Walpole saw the picture at least once in Reynolds's studio in Leicester Fields, but he didn't think much of it: 'I have seen the picture of St George,' he told Anne Liddell in December 1776, 'and approve the Duke of Bedford's [Francis Russell (1765–1802)] head, and the exact likeness of Miss Vernon [Caroline Vernon (1751–1829)], but the attitude is mean and foolish, and expresses silly wonderment' (HWC 32. 337; 17 December 1776). In a manuscript note to the catalogue Walpole elaborated these objections to the attitudes of the children:

Duke of Bedford as St George killing the dragon and his brothers, Miss Caroline Vernon as Sabrina [Sabra]. There are fine parts in this picture, but all the limbs flat and not round, and her figure too long. This picture is at Mr Rigby's [Richard Rigby (1722–88), MP] at Mistley in Essex, a print of it (RA 77. 286, p. 22; plate 97).[1]

But it is clear from an earlier reference to the *Bedford Children* in August 1776, possibly after a previous visit to Reynolds's studio, that Walpole attached a more personal value to the picture. Reynolds's painting figures in Walpole's fanciful ruminations in a letter to Anne Liddell about growing old, and the younger generation's readiness to 'declare us veterans Strulbrugs [Swift's immortals] a little before our time':

97.   Valentine Green, after Sir Joshua Reynolds: *Francis Russell, 5th Duke of Bedford, his brothers, and Miss Vernon acting 'St George and the Dragon'*. RA 1777. Mezzotint engraving. Private Collection, destroyed 1949. Photo: Courtesy of the Huntington Library, Art Collections, and Botanical Gardens, San Marino, California, Bute Collection of Mezzotints after Reynolds. '. . . I will prevent all clamour, by adopting St George's motto, "Honi soit qui mal y pense" ' (HWC 32. 317).

. . . [W]e silly folks in the country despair of recovering the province of wisdom, that is keeping young people forever in leading strings while we enjoy the world and dispose of all its blessings over our bottles. The picture of St George has opened my eyes. I will launch into the world again, and propose to be prime minister to King George V [HW's imaginary son of George IV (1762–1830), Prince of Wales], and lay a plan for governing longer than Cardinal Fleury [Louis XV's prime minister 1726–43], by surfeiting all the young nobility at Eton and Westminster schools with sugar-plums. In the meantime if I grow deaf like the late or present governor [Robert Darcy (1718–78), and George Brudenell (1712–90) to the Prince of Wales], I will have Master George V taught to talk to me upon his fingers, which will teach both him and me to spell, for it would not be proper to have him bawling secrets of state to me through a speaking-trumpet – and when I came to be minister [like the drunkard Granville Leveson Gower],[2] I will secure the attachment of all the young senators by getting drunk with them every night till six in the morning; and if I should never be sober enough to give away places, which is the only real business of a minister, I will marry a Scotch wife [like Gower's Lady Susanna Stewart (1731–1805)], who shall think of nothing else. I will do still more, and what no minister yet could ever compass, I will prevent all clamour, by adopting St George's motto, 'Honi soit qui mal y pense' [motto of the English Crown and the Order of the Garter: 'Shamed be he who thinks evil of it'], which if inscribed on the picture now in agitation, will certainly hinder anybody's smiling at it.

As one cannot entirely divest oneself of one's character,/ – But finds the ruling passion strong in death [Pope, *Epistle to Cobham*, lines 262–3], I propose to conclude my career in a manner worthy of an antiquary, as I was in the last century, and when I am satiated with years and honours, and arrived at a comfortable old age, to break my neck out of a cherry tree in robbing an orchard, like the Countess of Desmond [Catherine Fitzgerald (d. 1604); see Chapter 6] at an hundred and forty (HWC 32. 316–17; 22 August 1776).

Walpole dismissed the story as 'the foolish legend of St George' (2. 164; 1779), but silly as the picture seemed to Walpole, it inspired him to draw this ludicrous self-portrait in an exuberant return to childhood. He imagines himself a modern Saint George, prime minister and councillor to an unborn monarch, George V, who will serve longer than Louis XV's minister, outdo the deaf, drunken, and doddering governors of the Prince of Wales, the future George IV, and die, like the Countess of Desmond, by falling out of a cherry tree.

Zoffany's Tribuna, Equivocating About Portraits

Johann Zoffany's picture of *A Room in the Gallery of Florence, called the Tribuna, in which the principal part is calculated to shew the different styles of the several masters* (RA 80. 68, p. 6; plate 98), Walpole described in his catalogue as a 'most curious picture with much merit' (*marginalia*). He devoted so much commentary to this picture perhaps because it brought to the surface a latent contradiction between the taste for old masters he had repudiated after the Grand Tour, and the preference for portraits he had adopted as Prime Minister of Taste. In any event, Zoffany's picture inspires equivocations from Walpole that are not easy to explain.

George III and Queen Charlotte had commissioned from Johann Zoffany (1733–1810) a picture of the *Tribuna*, a room in the Grand Duke's Gallery (the Uffizi) in Florence designed in 1588 to house the rarest treasures of the Medici collection.[3] Horace Mann wrote to Walpole in August 1772 that 'he [Zoffany] has been sent here [Florence] to make a perspective view of the *Tribuna* with small figures (portraits) as spectators. This, it seems, is his style, and it is said he is excellent in it' (HWC 23. 430; 25 August 1772). Walpole responded sceptically to Horace Mann's news:

> Zoffanii is delightful in his real way, and introduces the furniture of a room with great propriety; but his talent is neither for rooms simply or portraits. He makes wretched pictures when he is serious. His talent is to draw scenes in comedy, and there he beats the Flemish painters in their own way of detail. Butler [Samuel Butler (1612–80)], the author of *Hudibrass* [Hazen 1822], might as well be employed to describe a solemn funeral, in which there was nothing ridiculous – This [the Tribuna commission], however, is better than his going to draw naked savages and be scalped, with that wild man Banks [Sir Joseph (1744–1820)], who is poaching in every ocean for the fry of little islands that escaped the drag-net of Spain (23. 435–6; 20 September 1772).

Walpole facetiously makes it seem as if the naturalist Banks had withdrawn from Captain Cook's second expedition so that Zoffany, whom he had recruited to draw

98.   Johann Zoffany: *The Tribuna of the Grand Duke's [Ufizzi] Gallery, Florence*. RA 1781. Oil on canvas, 48⅝ × 61 in. The Royal Collection © 2000 Her Majesty Queen Elizabeth II. Photo: Royal Collection Enterprises, Ltd. 'The idea I always thought an absurd one. It is rendered more so by being crowded with a flock of travelling boys, and one does not know or care whom' (HWC 24. 527).

Patagonian penguins in the south seas, was enabled to copy Raphaels and Titians in the finest art gallery in Europe.

Walpole's decided opinions of Zoffany's 'real way', and talent for comedy, derive from his notes on pictures Zoffany had exhibited for a decade at the Society of Artists exhibitions and at the Royal Academy from 1770 to 1772. Walpole had praised ('good', 'excellent') a half-dozen of Zoffany's theatrical conversation pieces of David Garrick in character parts, in particular as Abel Drugger in Ben Jonson's *Alchemist*: 'This most excellent picture . . . one of the best pictures ever done by this genius' (RA 70. 212, p. 20; HW's MS note).[4] Walpole disagreed with Mann about Zoffany's aptitude for portraits: he criticized Zoffany's half-length portrait of George III as 'very like, but most disagreeable and unmeaning figure' (RA 71. 230, p. 22, *marginalia*). When Zoffany sent a religious history painting, *The repose, in the flight into Egypt*, to the Academy's 1775 exhibition, Walpole labelled it 'very poor' (RA 75. 352, p. 31), proof of wretchedness 'when he is serious' (23. 435).[5] But significantly Walpole had admired

99.   Johann Zoffany: *The Academicians of the Royal Academy*. RA 1772. Oil on canvas, 39¾ × 58 in. The Royal Collection ©
2000 Her Majesty Queen Elizabeth II. Photo: Royal Collection Enterprises, Ltd. 'This excellent picture was done by candle
light. He [Zoffany] made no design for it, but clapped in the artists as they came to him' (RA 72. 290, p. 25; HW's MS note).

Zoffany's *Portraits of the Academicians of the Royal Academy* (plate 99), a serious picture
that anticipates his *Tribuna*: 'This excellent picture was done by candle light. He made
no design for it, but clapped in the artists as they came to him; and yet all the attitudes are easy and natural, most of the likenesses strong. There is a print from it' (RA
72. 290, p. 25; MS note).

Zoffany 'clapped in' the portraits of the spectators in the *Tribuna* too, but strangely
enough neither Walpole nor Mann approved of them: 'You will laugh,' Mann wrote to
Walpole on 28 September 1775, 'when I tell you that Mr Zoffany is now waiting for me
in the next room to put my portrait into the picture which the King sent him hither to
make of the *Tribuna* of the Gallery. It is a most curious and laborious undertaking' (23.
519; 28 September 1773). When Zoffany was about half-way through, Mann wrote to
Walpole that '[t]he one-eyed German, Zoffany . . . has succeeded amazingly in many
parts. . . . but [the Tribuna picture] is too much crowded with (for the most part) unin-
teresting portraits of English travellers then here' (24. 33–4; 23 August 1774).

Zoffany continued to introduce portraits of spectators into the *Tribuna* until he returned to England in 1779, when Walpole went to visit Zoffany's studio in London on Friday 12 November 1779:

> I went this morning to Zoffanii's, to see his picture or portrait of the Tribune at Florence. . . . The first thing I looked for, was *you* [Horace Mann] − and I could not find you. At last I said, 'Pray, who is *that* Knight of the Bath? [standing to the right, with a sword] − 'Sir Horace Mann' − 'Impossible!' said I − My dear Sir, how you have left me in the lurch! − you are grown fat, jolly, young − while I am become the skeleton of Methusalem! (24. 527; 12 November 1779).

After teasing Mann about his *avoir du poids*, Walpole goes on to reiterate Mann's complaint about the crowd of spectators:

> The idea ['a perspective view of the *Tribuna*, with small figures (portraits) as spectators' (23. 430)] I always thought an absurd one. It is rendered more so by being crowded with a flock of travelling boys, and one does not know or care whom. You and Sir John Dick, as Envoy and Consul, are very proper. The grand ducal family [Peter Leopold II (1747−92), Grand Duke of Tuscany 1765−90][6] would have been so too. Most of the rest are as impertinent as the names of churchwardens stuck up in parishes, whenever a country church is repaired and whitewashed (24. 526−7; 12 November 1779).

Walpole's complaint about the crowd of 'travelling boys . . . one does not know' is odd because he had admired a similar crowd of figures in Zoffany's *Royal Academicians*, and more than half a dozen of twenty-two spectators in Zoffany's *Tribuna* were people Walpole knew intimately. The charming figure of Richard Edgecumbe (1764−1839), standing to the left, hands on knees looking over the shoulder of Charles Loraine Smith (1751−1835; plate 100) who is sketching the statue of Cupid and Psyche, is the only 'travelling boy' in the picture. Edgecumbe was the son of one of Walpole's oldest friends, George, 1st Earl of Mount Edgecumbe (1720−95), a boy Walpole introduced to Mann when planning Edgecumbe's Grand Tour in 1784 (25. 518; 9 August 1784). Walpole's old friend and correspondent, Sir Horace Mann, standing to the right wearing the red ribband of the Order of the Bath, escaped censure because he was the envoy at Florence who had made arrangements for Zoffany to paint the Tribuna. Sir John Dick (1720−1804), consul at Leghorn from 1754 to 1776, was known to Walpole for 'the zeal he showed about your [Mann's] ribband' (23. 367; 21 January 1772).

Another person in Zoffany's *Tribuna* Walpole knew well was Mann's protégé, the artist Thomas Patch (1725−82), standing in the group admiring Titian's *Venus*. Mann had introduced Patch to Walpole, who collected his landscape paintings and engravings: 'I am transported with them!' Walpole said of Patch's engraved copies of Massacio sent to him by Mann: 'Tell me more of this Patch, and if you have a mind to please me quite, send me a drawing by him of yourself, of your whole person, exactly as you are' (23. 266−7; 20 January 1771). Patch's conversation pieces of English Grand Tourists were exactly in the humourous, Hogarthian style Walpole believed was Zoffany's forte: 'Patch was excellent in

100.   Johann Zoffany: *The Tribuna* (detail). The Royal Collection © 2000 Her Majesty Queen Elizabeth II.
Photo: Royal Collection Enterprises, Ltd. Left middleground: Richard Edgcumbe looks over the shoulder of
Charles Loraine Smith, while Zoffany holds a Raphael Madonna in front of George Nassau Clavering, Earl
Cowper.

caricatura,' Walpole wrote in his *Book of Materials* (1771, p. 11), 'and was in much favour with the young English nobility who visited Florence; many of whom allowed him to represent them and their governors ludicrously' (HWC 26. 45).

Three other people in Zoffany's *Tribuna* who Walpole was not intimate with but certainly knew include first of all, Felton Hervey (1712–73) who is seated in a chair conversing with Horace Mann. Walpole had described Hervey as a vainglorious hero when he was preparing for the Siege of Prague in 1742: 'Felton Hervey's warhorse, besides having richer caparisons than any of the expedition, had a gold net to keep off the flies – in winter' (18. 69–70; 8 October 1742). Second, George Finch, Earl of Winchilsea (1752–1826), who is staring in a daze at the statue of *Venus de Medici*, was one of Walpole's heroes who had volunteered for the American War in 1776 (32. 308, n. 17). Third, Walpole had drawn his own caricature in a letter to William Mason of another portrait in the picture, James Bruce (1730–94), the African traveller who was in Florence in January 1774 en route to Abyssinia:

> Would you believe that the great Abyssinian, Mr Bruce, whom Dr B[urney] made me laugh by seriously calling the *intrepid traveller* [*General History of Music* 1. 214; Hazen 3163], has had the intrepidity to write a letter to the Doctor [Charles Burney], which the latter has printed in the book, and in which he intrepidly tells lies . . . (28. 248; 29 February 1776).

When Bruce published his *Travels* in 1790 (Hazen 4018) Walpole thought it 'the most absurd, obscure, and tiresome book I know' (39. 475; 7 July 1790).

In the same letter which criticizes the crowd of portraits in the *Tribuna* Walpole admits in a postscript another exception, a character he drew at full length in his correspondence:

> I do allow Earl Cowper a place in the Tribune: an English Earl, who has never seen his earldom, and takes root and bears fruit at Florence, and is proud of a pinchbeck principality in a third country, is as great a curiosity as any in the Tuscan collection (24. 529; 12 November 1779).

George Nassau Clavering Cowper (1738–89), Viscount Fordwich, created 3rd Earl Cowper in 1764, was an English peer and MP who visited Florence in 1759 on the Grand Tour and decided to settle there, becoming a friend of the Grand Duke, a patron of artists, and a lavish entertainer. In the correspondence Walpole drew his own satirical portrait of Earl Cowper, whom he censured for emigrating to Italy, and for neglecting his peerage, his friends, and his responsibilities as MP. 'To tell you [Horace Mann] the truth, the Earl I conclude is a madman – therefore I wonder he does *not* come home' (24. 187; 22 March 1776).

Cowper had a passion for titles – the Order of St Hubert, the Green Ribbon of the Thistle, two orders of English Knighthood, the Bath and the Garter. He also had the ambition to become a 'principied Earl' (25. 646) by assuming the title of Prince of the Holy Roman Empire. Walpole understood the irony: 'It would be a sort of poetic justice,' Walpole wrote Mann, 'if he [Cowper] should send his son to England, and the boy should refuse to return to him. I am sorry other climates cannot repair the eccentricities our own climate occasions' (24. 242; 20 September 1776). This is a passage Walpole explained in a note to the Mann correspondence: 'Lord Cowper from the moment he went to travel would not return to England, but settled at Florence, and though entreated in the most earnest manner, would not visit his father before the latter's death' (24. 242, n. 9; 20 September 1776).

Horace Mann described Cowper's protracted, expensive, and futile quest for a foreign title, and received Walpole's verdict: 'Your new Prince of Nassau is perfectly ridiculous – a real peer of England to tumble down to a tinsel titularity! Indeed an English coronet will not be quite so weighty as it was!' (24. 302; 14 May 1777), another passage in Cowper's epistolary portrait explained in Walpole's notes: 'Earl Cowper had obtained a titular principality from the Emperor; imagining that he should take place of English Dukes, but finding his mistake and that it would give him no precedence at all here [England], he dropped the title of Prince' (24. 302, n. 13).

Cowper was very popular in Florence, and Mann maintained good relations with his family. Mann 'prepared a sumptuous dinner' and represented George III in gala liveries at the christening of Cowper's son on Thursday 22 August 1776 (24. 238, n. 6). Mann told Walpole he had encouraged Zoffany to include Lord Cowper in the picture 'if he thought the variety more picturesque' (24. 539; 10 December 1779).

Zoffany's portrait of Cowper standing to the extreme left pointing with his left hand at the statue of the Satyr with the Cymbals, participates in an anecdotal drama that Walpole would have enjoyed if he was aware of it. Three figures to the right of Lord Cowper, Zoffany put himself in the picture holding a painting by Raphael of a Madonna and Child. Sometime in the mid-seventies Zoffany had sold Raphael's Niccolini *Madonna* to Lord Cowper. Zoffany had asked 5000 guineas, but eventually accepted '500 guineas *plus* an annual pension of £100 for life which Zoffany received for forty years'. Oliver Millar speculates that when Zoffany introduced his own figure into the picture commissioned by the king and queen holding up Cowper's Raphael, the pantomime may have been calculated to get Cowper another title. Cowper wrote to George III 23 April 1780 to offer him the Madonna and a self-portrait by Raphael for £2500 pounds. 'The king did not, unfortunately, accept this offer and the Earl never got the Garter.'[7]

It is clear, then, that Walpole knew several of the *dramatis personae* of Zoffany's picture well. So the question remains, why should Walpole find a picture of his favourite gallery filled with portraits of people he knew an 'absurd' idea (24. 527)? Walpole's quibbling letter describing the *Tribuna* in Zoffany's studio does little to answer the question. Like most commentators on Zoffany's picture Walpole admired the scrupulously exact finishing of details: 'The execution is good,' Walpole remarks: 'most of the styles of painters happily imitated; the labour and finishing infinite, and no confusion, though such a multiplicity of objects and colours' (24. 527; 12 November 1779). This said, Walpole starts to find fault, almost as if he thinks he must live up to Mann's expectations of his connoisseurship. '. . . [F]inishing infinite', he concedes, but he finds:

> Titian's Venus . . . the principal object, is the worst finished. . . . but the greatest fault is in the statues. To distinguish them, he has made them all of a colour, not imitating

the different hues of their marbles – and thus they all look alike, like casts in plaster of Paris – however it is a great and curious work – though Zoffanii might have been better employed (24. 527).

In this comment on the colour of the statuary Walpole is surely straining at gnats. His concession about 'a great and curious work' exposes his specious criticism. Walpole then starts to ride another hobby-horse, his pre-conceived idea of Zoffany's 'real way' (23. 435): 'He is the Hogarth of Dutch painting, but, no more than Hogarth, can shine out of his own way. He might have drawn the Holy Family well, if he had seen them *in statu quo*' (24. 92–3; 17 April 1775). 'His talent is representing natural humour: I look upon him as a Dutch painter polished or civilized' (24. 527; 12 November 1779).

Horace Mann's long reply to Walpole's letter does not explain the absurdity of Zoffany's *Tribuna*, but it expresses prejudices that made the picture controversial, and eventually unacceptable to the king and queen. 'Your opinion of his laborious performance in all the parts you mention,' Mann writes obsequiously, 'agrees with that of our best judges here, but they found great fault in the perspective, which they say is all wrong' (24. 539; 10 December 1779). Mann refers to Zoffany as the 'one-eyed German' (24. 33). He was interested in rumors circulating in Italy that Zoffany was a bigamist: 'So then it is not true that he was hanged for bigamy?' (24. 539). We have no evidence that Walpole shared these prejudices about Zoffany's nationality or marital arrangements. Nor is there evidence that Walpole shared Mann's concern about the indecency of Titian's nude Venus: 'I should think,' Mann wrote, 'the naked Venus which is the principal figure will not please her Majesty so much as it did the young men to whom it was showed' (24. 540).

Portraits were undoubtedly Walpole and Mann's mutual concern. Mann writes of conversations with Zoffany in Italy:

> I told him often of the impropriety of sticking so many figures in it, and pointed out to him the Great Duke and Duchess, one or two of their children . . . and Lord Cowper. He told me that the King had expressly ordered mine [Horace Mann's portrait] to be there, which I did not believe, but did not object to it, but he made the same merit with all the young travellers then at Florence, some of whom he afterwards rubbed out . . . and filled up their places elsewhere (24. 539–40).

Mann is here referring to rumours that Zoffany was selling places in the royal picture, charging Grand Tourists 20 guineas for a sitting, removing them after they departed from Florence, and substituting others on the same terms. '. . . [T]he impropriety of crowding in so many unknown figures was still greater' (24. 540), Mann believed, because it was a lucrative royal commission. Mann concludes his report with an apology for his own portrait:

> As to the question you make me of my own personage, I can only say that everybody thought it like me, but I suppose he took pains to lessen my pot-belly and the clumsiness of my figure, and to make me stand in a posture which I never kept to but then. I remember, for it was several years ago, that I was sadly tired when I was tortured by him to appear before their Majesties in my best shape and looks (24. 540).

101.   Samuel Scott: *Walpole's View of Pope's Villa, Twickenham, c.* 1759. Oil on canvas, 18½ × 36 in. Courtesy of the Lewis Walpole Library, Yale University. 'Some monuments of our predecessors ought to be sacred. . . . Refined taste went to work [on Pope's garden]' (HWC 25. 177).

In August 1781, a year after the *Tribuna* was exhibited at the Royal Academy, Walpole recognized a different value in Zoffany's puzzling picture when he learned that Leopold II (1747–92), Grand Duke of Tuscany, was making alterations to the gallery. First, '[t]he Great Duke had removed many of the curiosities and practiced another door in it, so that it was become a passage room' (25. 177; HW's note). Second, '[t]he Great Duke had fetched from Rome the group of Niobe and her children, and placed them round a chamber, by which means they remained in strange unmeaning attitudes and no longer expressed their story' (25. 177; HW's note). During the campaign for Gibraltar, Walpole wrote to Horace Mann:

> . . . [E]verything is a theme for moralizing, from Gibraltar to the Tribune at Florence. If that inestimable chamber is not inviolate, what mortal structure is! Zoffanii's picture, however, will rise in value, as a portrait of what that room *was* – yet its becoming more precious will not, I doubt, expedite the sale of it. It is a pity that they who love to display taste, will not be content with showing their genius without making alterations; and then we would have more samples of the styles of different ages. Some monuments of our predecessors ought to be sacred (HWC 25. 177; 23 August 1781).

At last Walpole recognized the painting for what it was, the portrait of a room Galileo had called 'una guardaroba, una tribuna . . . di tutta eccelenza' (Millar p. 12). Walpole finishes moralizing on the fate of the *Tribuna* by comparing its desecration to the alterations the Earl of Stanhope had made to Pope's villa and gardens at Twickenham (*Works* 2. 428; plate 101) in the early 1760s:

Refined taste went to work; the vocal groves were thinned, modish shrubs replaced them – and light and three lanes broke in; and if the muses wanted to tie up their garters, there is not a nook to do it without being seen. Poor Niobe's children, who now stand in a row as if saying their catechism, will know how to pity them! (25. 177–8; 23 August 1781).

Portraits were certainly the most interesting part of Zoffany's picture to Walpole, but when talking to Horace Mann who was supplying English aristocrats like Northumberland and Carlisle with copies of old masters, Walpole steps out of character for a moment when confronted with Zoffany's hybrid picture, and speaks in the voice of Hogarth's connoisseur, an English gentleman who patronizes Italian art. Comparing conversation-piece portraits in the same room with Raphael, Titian, and the Venus de Milo, the Prime Minister of Taste defers to Grand Tour taste. Nevertheless, Walpole remained a portraitist, as we shall see when we look at his own group portrait in the correspondence, the saga of the Gunning sisters.

CHAPTER 17

Walpole's Portraits in the Letters: The Gunninghiad

'Et in Arcadia Ego': The Ghost of Maria Gunning; Joshua Reynolds px

In the correspondence Walpole painted his own group portrait depicting two generations of the Irish Gunning family, starting with the sensational début of the beautiful
sisters Maria (1732–60) and Elizabeth Gunning (1733–90) in the London social world
of the early 1750s, ending in the 1790s with a scandal surrounding Elizabeth Gunning
the younger (1769–1823), a story as long and complicated as Galsworthy's *Forsyte Saga*.
For a frontispiece to his Gunninghiad Walpole used *Portraits of two ladies, half lengths, Et
in Arcadi[a] ego* (RA 69. 91, p. 11; plate 102), a double portrait Reynolds exhibited at
the first Royal Academy exhibition which occasioned Walpole's remarkable identification of Maria Gunning's ghost in Reynolds's picture: 'Mrs Crewe [Frances Anne
Greville (d. 1818)] and Mrs Bouverie [Henrietta Fawkener (1751–1825)] moralising on
the tomb of Lady Coventry [Maria Gunning (1732–60)]' (RA 69. 91, p. 11; *marginalia*).
Walpole was acquainted with both of Reynolds's living sitters, the ladies Bouverie and
Crewe, both 'standard' (21. 451) beauties in London society. In May 1764 he was help-
ing to spread the false report circulating in newspapers that the future Lady Bouverie,
the fourteen-year-old Henrietta Fawkener, was engaged to be married to John Crewe
(1742–1829), MP and a member of Walpole's card-playing society: 'Lady Falkener's
daughter is to be married to a young rich Mr Crewe, a Maccarone [fop], and of our
loo' (HWC 38. 394; 27 May 1764). The rumor was unfounded. On 30 June 1764 by
special license Henrietta Fawkener married Edward Bouverie (1738–1810), MP. Two
years later, on 4 April 1766, Henrietta Fawkener's intimate friend Frances Anne
Greville married the maccarone, John Crewe (38. 394, n. 19). Sometime in June of that
year the Ladies Bouverie and Crewe were hoping to breakfast with Walpole at
Strawberry Hill, 'very desirous of seeing the place' (39. 75), and until the end of his life
Walpole kept up social relations with both ladies who eventually became part of the
'agreeable society at Richmond' (11. 148).[1]

This is enough to establish that Walpole was acquainted with the Ladies Crewe and
Bouverie from the time of their marriages in the 1760s until the end of his life, but
how can we account for Walpole's identification of Maria Gunning's ghost in the
tomb? We have no evidence that the Ladies Crewe and Bouverie were acquainted with
Lady Coventry. Moreover, it seems unlikely that Reynolds's imitation of *Et in Arcadia
ego* 'I [Death] too live in Arcadia', a sublime theme in Renaissance painting borrowed
from Poussin and others, had a contemporary monument in mind. On the other hand,

102.   Sir Joshua Reynolds: *Portraits of two ladies . . . Et in Arcadia Ego*. RA 1769. Oil on canvas, 39¾ × 50 in. Private Collection. Photo: Courtesy of the Huntington Library, Art Collections, and Botanical Gardens, San Marino, California, Bute Collection of Mezzotints after Reynolds. 'Mrs Crewe and Mrs Bouverie moralising on the tomb of Lady Coventry' (HW's interlineated MS note, RA 69. 91, p. 11).

Maria Gunning, Lady Coventry, is a frequent subject in Walpole's correspondence, where he draws a vivid character portrait of her. In fact, Walpole had been 'moralising' about Maria Gunning in his letters for nearly two decades before Reynolds exhibited the portrait. Thus it seems likely that the idea of the Ladies Bouverie and Crewe moralising on the tomb of Lady Coventry in the picture is Walpole's own invention, his own reading of Reynolds's famous double portrait. If so, Walpole's social iconography is perfectly characteristic of the Prime Minister of Taste interpreting a picture that had baffled Samuel Johnson. Leslie and Taylor record a conversation in Reynolds's studio when Johnson admitted his ignorance about the title of the picture, *Et in Arcadia Ego*:

> 'What can this mean?' said Dr. Johnson. 'It seems very nonsensical – I am in Arcadia.' 'Well, what of that? The King could have told you,' replied Sir Joshua. 'He saw it yesterday, and said at once: 'Oh, there is a tombstone in the background. Ay, ay, Death is even in Arcadia.'[2]

In a classic study Erwin Panofsky demonstrates that King George III translated the Latin inscription correctly, interpreting the inscription as a *memento mori* spoken by Death – 'I too reside in Arcadia' – as opposed to the nostalgic, elegiac meditation on mortality expressed by Poussin's picture in the Louvre.[3] Disgusted with allegory, Walpole substitutes social for art-historical iconography, imagining Reynolds's fashionable sitters reflecting on the hard 'fate of young women of quality' (HWC 25. 75).

In a letter about ministerial changes Walpole writes in June 1751 that the arrival in London of the Gunning sisters had eclipsed the fame of the Pelham brothers, Thomas and Henry, and George Grenville (1712–70), 1st Lord of the Treasury:

103. Francis Cotes: *Maria Gunning, Countess of Coventry*. 1751. Pastel on paper, 23½ × 17½ in. In a Private Scottish Collection. Photo: Antonia Reeve Photography for the Scottish National Portrait Gallery. 'These [Maria and Elizabeth Gunning] are two Irish girls of no fortune, who are declared the handsomest women alive' (HWC 20. 260).

104. Francis Cotes: *Elizabeth Gunning, Duchess of Hamilton and Argyll*. 1751. Pastel on paper, 23¼ × 17¼ in. By courtesy of the National Portrait Gallery, London. Photo: NPG Picture Library.

The two Miss Gunnings, and a late extravagant dinner at White's [club] are twenty times more the subject of conversation than the two brothers, and Lord Granville. These are two Irish girls of no fortune,[4] who are declared the handsomest women alive. I think their being two [plates 103 and 104], so handsome and both such perfect figures, is their chief excellence, for singly I have seen much handsomer women than either: however, they can't walk in the park, or go to Vauxhall, but such mobs follow them that they are generally driven away (20. 260; 18 June 1751).

Even before their marriages the Gunning sisters were bywords for beauty. Walpole tells Mann an anecdote about Mrs Mary Taylor, the housekeeper at Hampton Court Palace, who once showed visitors the Gunning sisters as the 'Beauties of Hampton Court', instead of Kneller's twelve paintings of ladies of the court of William and Mary (HWC 20. 272; 31 August 1751). Early the next year, in a parody of the *St James's Evening Post*, Walpole introduces a ribald advertisement after the entry 'To be sold, the whole nation': 'To be covered by any Earl going one-and-twenty, the two Miss Gunnings' (9. 129; 9 January 1752).

On 5 March 1752 Maria Gunning married George William, 6th Earl Coventry, 'a

105.   Sir Joshua Reynolds: *Emilia Mary Lennox, Countess and Marchioness of Kildare, and Duchess of Leinster*. 1753. Oil on canvas, 50 × 39 in. Private Collection. Photo: Photographic Survey, Courtauld Institute of Art.

106.   Francis Cotes: *Penelope Atkins, Mrs. George Pitt, Lady Rivers*. 1752. Pastel on paper, 25 × 20 in. By courtesy of the National Portrait Gallery, London. Photo: NPG Picture Library.

grave young Lord, of the remains of the patriot breed . . . [who] has long dangled after the eldest [Gunning sister]' (20. 302; 27 February 1752). Shortly thereafter, Walpole conducted one of the beauty contests he delighted in at an assembly in London, an anecdote he introduces into his *Memoirs* that 'may at least be as amusing as the more serious follies committed by and about [John] Wilkes':

> Soon after Lady Coventry was married, I was at an assembly at Bedford House, and drew together, her [Maria Gunning], the charming Lady Emily Lenox [(1731–1814); plate 105], then [not until 1761] Marchioness of Kildare, and since [1766] Duchess of Leinster, and Mrs Penelope Pitt [Penelope Atkins (1725–95); plate 106], since [1776] Lady Rivers (the two last celebrated in my poem of *The Beauties*); I said I wanted to decide which was the handsomest. They said I should declare. I replied that was hard, but since they insisted, I would – and 'I give it,' added I, 'to Lady Kildare, because she does what you both try to do – blush' (G III, 3. 131 n. 1).

'Ten queens of beauty sure I see!/Yet sure the true is Emily', Walpole had written in *The Beauties* (1746; HWC 30. 326; lines 62–3) of Emilia Lennox, already a celebrated beauty at fifteen. He later praised her as one of the 'capital beauties' at George III's coronation (38. 122), 'as handsome as the Graces' (38. 126). Penelope Atkins, who married the brutal George Pitt in 1746, had impressed Walpole at a masquerade celebrating the Peace of Aix-la-Chapelle at the King's Theatre in the Haymarket, where she appeared 'in vast beauty . . . [wearing] a red veil, which made her look gloriously handsome' (20. 49; 3 May 1749). A year later he heralded her as one of the 'court beauties' about to visit Italy: 'I think you [Horace Mann] will find her one of the most glorious beauties you ever saw' (20. 58; 17 May 1749).

Although Walpole did not give the golden apple to Maria Gunning at Bedford House, he eagerly anticipated her contention with rival beauties in Paris on her honeymoon. 'Our beauties are travelling Paris-ward', he informed Horace Mann:

> Lady Caroline Petersham [née Fitzroy (1722–84)] and Lady Coventry are just gone thither. It will scarcely be possible for the latter to make as much noise there as she and her sister have in England. It is literally true that a shoemaker at Worcester got two guineas and an half by showing a shoe that he was making for the Countess, at a penny apiece. I can't say that her genius is equal to her beauty: she every day says some new *sproposito* ['howler']. She has taken a turn of vast fondness for her Lord: Lord Downe [Henry Pleydell Dawnay (1727–60), 3rd Viscount] met them at Calais, and offered her a tent bed, for fear of bugs in the inns. 'Oh!' said she, 'I had rather be bit to death, than lie one night from my dear Cov!' – her dear Cov proposed to carry the chambermaid in the same vehicle with them, by placing a stool for her in the fore part – 'No, my Lord,' said the Countess in broad Irish, 'then you will put your legs between her thighs as you used to do between mine.' – I can conceive my Lady Caroline making a good deal of noise even at Paris; her beauty is set off by a genius for the extraordinary, and for strokes that will make a figure in any country (20. 324; 27 July 1752).

In October Walpole reported that:

> Our beauties are returned [from Paris], and have done no execution. The French would not conceive that Lady Caroline Petersham ever had been handsome,[5] nor that my Lady Coventry has much pretence to be so now. . . . Poor Lady Coventry was under piteous disadvantages, for besides being very silly, ignorant of the world, breeding, speaking no French, and suffered to wear neither red nor powder, she had that perpetual drawback upon her beauty, her Lord [George William Coventry (1722–1809), 6th Earl], who is sillier in a wise way, as ignorant, ill-bred, and speaking very little French himself; just enough to show how ill-bred he is. The Duke de Luxemburg [Charles Montmorency-Luxembourg (d. 1764)] told him he had called up my Lady Coventry's coach; my Lord replied, *Vous avez fort bien fait* ['you have done very well']. He is jealous, prude, and scrupulous; at a dinner at Sir John Bland's [1722–55; gambler, MP, and suicide], before sixteen people, he coursed his wife round the table, on suspecting she had stolen on a little red, seized her, scrubbed it off by force with a napkin, and then told her, that since she had deceived him and broke her promise, he would carry her back directly to England. They were pressed to stay for the great fête at St Cloud [given by Louis-Philippe de Bourbon (1725–85), Duc d'Orléans, 24 September at his palace], he excused himself, 'because it would make him miss a music meeting at Worcester' [the three choirs festival inaugurated in 1720].

And she excused herself from the fireworks at Madame Pompadour's [20 September at Bellevue, featuring a luminous figure of the Dauphin attacked by monsters vomiting flames], 'because it was her dancing-master's hour.' I will tell you [Horace Mann] but one more anecdote, and I think you can not be imperfect in your ideas of them. The Maréchale de Lowendahl [Freiherre Ulrik Lovendal (1700–55)] was pleased with an English fan Lady Coventry had, who very civilly gave it her: my Lord made her write for it next morning, 'because he had given it her before marriage, and her parting with it would make an irreparable breach' and send an old one in the room of it! She complains to everybody she meets, 'how odd it is that my Lord should use her so ill, when she knows he has so great a regard that he would die for her, and when he was so good as to marry her without a shilling!'. . . . I don't know whether you will not think all these very trifling histories; but for myself, I love anything that marks a character strongly (20. 337–9; 28 October 1752).

Back in London Lady Coventry was humiliated by her husband with the collusion of Walpole at a private ball at Jermyn Street in London given by George Pitt (1721–1803), whose portrait by Thomas Gainsborough was also exhibited at the Royal Academy in 1769 (RA 69. 36, p. 6; plate 107).[6] '. . . I shall tell you an historiette of our beauty, my Lady Coventry', Walpole wrote to Horace Mann.

I was lately at a private ball with her at George Pitt's. We supped in the library, and sitting near the books, Mr Churchill [Walpole's brother-in-law, Charles Churchill (1720–1812)] took down a Bible, and said, 'Who can tell me which is first, Solomon's song or his wisdom?' You will not think there was much brimstone in this speech: however, the fair Countess put herself (I say *put herself*, for you never saw anything more done on purpose) into an outrageous passion, said it was blasphemous and impious, and she wished the house would fall upon his head. This set us all into violent laughing: she called out, 'My Lord Coventry, if you laugh any more, I *will* cry!' She then would have risen from table; nobody would stir. At last we went into the ballroom; my Lord stood with his back to the chimney-glass; she stood before him, scolding immoderately, and at the same time setting herself in the glass over his shoulder.
   Lord Holderness [Robert Darcy (1718–78), 4th Earl] came up to her, and said, 'Well! Madam, as you have quarelled with my Lord, I hope you will let me be your paramour tonight!' 'Yes,' said she, 'with all my heart, and I will be your *Thisbis* [Thisbe].' – I was so entertained with all this folly, to call it nothing else, that I was determined it should not end so, but begged all the women, to take my Lord [Coventry] out and make him dance so continually, that the quarrel might not be made up when they went home. The idea took like wildfire: the women were so delighted with the thought of depriving the Countess of that night's perquisites of her beauty, that they made the Earl dance, till he and themselves were ready to faint, and till I believe my Lady wished that she had interested herself a little less about Solomon's understanding, which was not the point on which she really wished her wise Lord should resemble him (20. 367; 27 March 1753).

Like a cruel and unfeeling character in *Evelina*, Walpole would not have escaped Frances Burney's satire. Few of us would share Horace Mann's obsequious response to this

107.   Thomas Gainsborough: *George Pitt, Baron 1st Lord Rivers*. RA 1769. Oil on canvas, $91\frac{1}{2} \times 60$ in. © 2000 The Cleveland Museum of Art, Gift of the John Huntington Art and Polytechnic Trust. Photo: Cleveland Museum. 'She [Penelope Atkins Pitt] is the most amiable of beings, and the most to be pitied – her brutal half mad husband. . . has heaped upon her every possible cruelty' (HWC 23. 451).

episode: 'I thank you for the historiette of the handsome Countess. . . . There never was anything so clever as the method you took to punish her' (20. 375–6; 4 May 1753).

A year later Walpole describes Lady Coventry's dancing with George II and flirting with the rake and gambler, Frederick St John, 2d Viscount Bolingbroke (1734–87):

> T'other night [Monday 25 February 1754] they danced minuets for the entertainment of the King at the masquerade; and then he sent for Lady Coventry to dance: it was quite like Herodias – and I believe if he had offered her a boon, she would have chosen the head of *St John* – I believe I told you [Richard Bentley] of her passion for the young Lord B[olingbroke] (35. 162–3; 2 March 1754).

Vignettes of this affair and others with the Duke of Cumberland continue in the correspondence until the year Maria Gunning died. In April 1756 Walpole reports her appearance on the Causeway, a circular drive between Grosvenor Gate and the Serpentine in Hyde Park, and his teasing her at supper at Francis Seymour Conway's in Grosvenor Street:

. . . [I]t [the Causeway] is the new office, where all lovers now are entered. How happy she must be with Billy [William Augustus (1721–65), Duke of Cumberland] and Bully [Lord Bolingbroke]! I hope she will not mistake, and call the former by the nickname of the latter! At a great supper t'other night at Lord Hertford's, if she was not the best humoured creature in the world, I should have made her angry; she said in a very vulgar accent, if she drank any more, she should be *muckibus* [intoxicated] – 'Lord,' said Lady Mary Coke, 'what is that?' – 'Oh! it is Irish for *sentimental*!' (9. 185; 20 April 1756).

Walpole tells another 'gossiping story' of Maria Gunning's toast at Woburn House, seat of John Russell (1710–71), 4th Duke of Bedford: '[A]fter dinner, the Duchess, my Lady Gower [Louisa Egerton (1723–61)] and six-and-twenty people at table, the Duke asked my Lady Coventry for her toast – she gave, *The Best*. Rigby [Richard (1722–88), MP] said, who says we can't drink my Lady Coventry's health before her face?' (37. 430; 22 January 1756).

Lady Coventry's silliness, ignorance, and vanity are recurring themes in Walpole's portrait. He describes how his beautiful niece Maria Walpole (1736–1807), about to be presented at court, 'distracted' Lady Coventry, 'who t'other day told Lady Anne Conolly [Anne Wentworth] how she dreaded Lady Louisa's [Louisa Lennox's] arrival – "But," said she, "now I have seen her, I am easy"' (9. 235; 16 May 1759). Lady Coventry displayed her clothes for King George II's birthday on Saturday 10 November to George Selwyn (1717–91): '. . . [T]hey are blue with spots of silver the size of a shilling and a silver trimming and cost my Lord [Coventry] will know what – she asked George how he liked them – he replied, "Why, you will be change for a guinea"' (9. 253–4; 8 November 1759).

In the spring of 1759 Walpole entertained both of the Gunning sisters at Strawberry Hill where he conducted another of his paragones: On Wednesday 30 May Maria's younger sister Elizabeth Gunning (1733–90) sat in the shell bench on his terrace with two other beauties. On Friday 1 June Walpole gave the golden apple to Maria Gunning, who was by this time suffering from tuberculosis.

Strawberry Hill is grown a perfect Paphos [temple of Aphrodite in Cyprus], it is the land of beauties. . . . Yesterday [Friday 1 June 1759] the t'other, more famous Gunning [Maria, Lady Coventry] dined there [on the terrace at Strawberry Hill] – she has made a friendship with my charming niece [Maria Walpole], to disguise her jealousy of the new Countess's beauty. There were they two, their lords, Lord Buckingham and Charlotte [Maria's younger sister] (9. 237; 2 June 1759).

In a note to his *Memoirs*, Walpole describes the outcome of this contest:

I had dined with her [Lady Coventry] in the foregoing June with my niece, the beautiful Lady Waldegrave, then just married [Tuesday 15 May 1759], since [1766] Duchess of Gloucester. They stood in the window [at Strawberry Hill] in the full sun, and though Lady Coventry was wasted and faded, and Lady Walpole in all her glow of beauty, in spite of my partiality to my niece, I could not but own to myself that Lady Coventry was still superior. It was a less triumph, as Lord Pembroke [Henry Herbert (1734–94), 10th Earl] was so fickle, that Lady Coventry gave great uneasiness to his lovely wife, Lady Elizabeth Spencer [(1737–1831)], who, in the Madonna style, was divinely beautiful (G III, 3. 131 n.).

By the end of 1759 it was clear that Lady Coventry was ill – dying of tuberculosis and, according to rumour, 'white lead' (10. 237), the toxic chemical in eighteenth-century cosmetics. Walpole's correspondence traces her dying with more compassion than he showed at Pitt's party. 'The kingdom of beauty is in as great disorder as the kingdom of Ireland. My Lady Pembroke [Lady Elizabeth Spencer] looks like a ghost – poor Lady Coventry is going to be one' (9. 264; 23 December 1759). A month later, January 1760, Walpole writes:

[t]here has been cruel havoc among the ladies; my Lady Granby [Frances Seymour (1728–60)] is dead, and the famous Polly [in *The Beggar's Opera*], Duchess of Bolton [Lavinia Beswick (1708–60)], and my Lady Besborough [Caroline Cavendish (1719–60)]. . . . Poor Lady Coventry is near completing this black list (9. 271–2; 28 January 1760).

Lady Coventry had a reprieve. In April she was flirting with Lord Bolingbroke near Walpole in Westminster Hall at the murder trial of Laurence Shirley (1720–60), 4th Earl Ferrers. Walpole wrote to George Montagu:

The seats of the peeresses were not near full, and most of the beauties absent; the Duchess of Hamilton [Elizabeth Gunning] and my niece Waldegrave [Maria Walpole], you know, lie in – but to the amazement of everybody, Lady Coventry [Maria Gunning] was there – and what surprised me much more, looked as well as ever. I sat next but one to her, and should not have asked if she had been ill – yet they are positive she has few weeks to live. She and Lord Bolinbroke seemed to have very different thoughts, and were acting over all the old comedy of eyes (9. 280; 19 April 1760).

By the end of May, newspapers had printed a false report of Lady Coventry's death, when Walpole wrote to William Wentworth (1722–91), 2d Earl of Strafford, on 7 June 1760: 'The pretty Countess is still alive, was thought actually dying on Tuesday night [3 June 1760], and I think will go off very soon' (35. 302; 7 June 1760). In August Walpole was still keeping a death watch on the 'poor Countess' (38. 69), 'the beautiful Maria Gunning' (21. 429, HW's note, 1 August 1760). 'My Lady Coventry is still alive, sometimes at the point of death, sometimes recovering. They fixed the spring; now the autumn is to be critical for her' (21. 429). At last she succumbed on 30 September 1760, and Walpole learned that her sister Elizabeth had caught the disease. After her first husband James Hamilton had died, Elizabeth Gunning had married in 1759 John Campbell (1723–1806), Marquis of Lorn, later 5th Duke of Argyll:

The charming Countess is dead at last; and as if the whole history of both sisters was to be extraordinary, the Duchess of Hamilton [Elizabeth Gunning (1733–90), remarried to John Campbell; (plate 108)] is in a consumption too and going abroad directly. Perhaps you [Horace Mann in Florence] may see the remains of these prodigies, you will see but little remains; her features were never so beautiful as Lady

108.   François-Hubert Drouais: *Elizabeth Gunning,
Duchess of Hamilton and Argyll.* 1763. Oil on canvas,
29 × 23¼ in. In a Private Scottish Collection.
Photo: Antonia Reeve Photography for the Scottish
National Portrait Gallery.

Coventry's, and she has long been changed, though not yet I think above six and
twenty. The other [Lady Coventry] was but twenty-seven (21. 438; 5 October 1760).

The Campbells set out for Italy in the last week of October, when Walpole reiterated his warning to Horace Mann about Elizabeth Gunning's decay, and described her
sister Maria's deathbed[7]:

> I think the Duchess [Elizabeth Gunning, Duchess of Hamilton] will not answer your
> expectation. She never was so handsome as Lady Coventry, and now is a skeleton. It
> is hard upon a standard beauty, when she travels in a deep consumption. Poor Lady
> Coventry concluded her short race with the same attention to her looks. She lay con-
> stantly on a couch with a pocket glass in her hand, and when that told her how great
> the change was, she took to her bed the last fortnight, had no light in her room but
> the lamp of a tea-kettle, and at last took things in through the curtains of her bed,
> without suffering them to be undrawn. The mob who never quitted curiosity about
> her, went, to the number of ten thousand, only to see her coffin. If she had lived to
> ninety like Helen, I believe they would have thought that her wrinkles deserved an
> epic poem. Poor thing! how far from ninety! She was not eight and twenty! (21.
> 450–1; 1 November 1760).

Lady Coventry died at Croome Court, Worcestershire, the Coventrys' seat, was buried
at Pirton, and later returned to Croome. That presumably is where Walpole imagines the
scene of Reynolds's double portrait, *Et in Arcadia Ego* (RA 69. 91).
It seems reasonable to conclude that the moralising Walpole implicitly attributes to the

Ladies Bouverie and Crewe consists of his own meditation on the fate of a standard beauty like Lady Coventry in his own society. The London début, the notoriety, the marriage to a titled fool, the rival belles in Paris and London, the masquerades, balls, dinners, flirtations, and Walpole's own egregious cruelty constitute the world of Hogarth's *Marriage à la Mode*, and Pope's *Epistle to a Lady*. Walpole's portrait of Lady Coventry in his correspondence is worthy to stand in the company of Hogarth and Pope.

Elizabeth Gunning (1733–90), Duchess of Hamilton and Argyll. Joshua Reynolds px

At the first Society of Artists exhibition, Walpole identified Reynolds's portrait of *A Lady*, *whole length* as 'Elizabeth Hamilton Duchess of Hamilton' (SA 60. 47, p. 7; *marginalia* and MS note; plate 109). Reynolds's portrait was a deliberate bid to make a sensation at the first art exhibition, and to out-do his rivals, Allan Ramsay (1713–84) and Francis Cotes (1725–70). A wonderful synthesis of neo-classical motifs borrowed from Tintoretto, Kneller, Ramsay, and a Westminster Abbey monument by Laurent Delvaux, Reynolds's portrait identifies Elizabeth Gunning with Venus by the attribute of the doves, and by '[t]he relief on the side of the plinth [showing] the shepherd Paris, who . . . chose Venus as the most beautiful of the three goddesses'.[8]

Like Paris in the Greek myth, Walpole compared the beauty of Elizabeth Gunning to her rivals, including her sister Maria whom he thought more beautiful:

> The Duchess was more delicate than her sister [Maria Gunning, Lady Coventry], with the most beautiful hands and arms in the world; but Lady Coventry was still handsomer, had infinite life and vivacity, the finest eyes in the world, nose, and mouth, excepting that both had bad teeth. Lady Coventry danced like a nymph, and was too kind a one. The Duchess always preserved her character (G III, 3. 131, n. 1).

In the correspondence Walpole compares Elizabeth Gunning's first marriage to the dissolute James, 6th Duke of Hamilton (1724–58) with her sister's marriage to George William Coventry (1722–1809):

> About six weeks ago Duke Hamilton, the very reverse of the Earl [Lord Coventry], hot, debauched, extravagant, and equally damaged in his fortune and person, fell in love with the youngest [Gunning] at the masquerade [King's Theatre, Haymarket; 16 January 1752] and determined to marry her in the spring. About a fortnight since at an immense assembly at my Lord Chesterfield's,[9] made to show the house which is really most magnificent, Duke Hamilton made violent love at one end of the room, while he was playing at pharaoh at the other end; that is, he saw neither the bank nor his own cards, which were of three hundred pounds each. He soon lost a thousand.
>
> I own I was so little a professor in love, that I thought all this parade looked ill for the poor girl; and could not conceive, if he was so much engaged with his mistress as to disregard such sums, why he played at all. However, two nights afterwards, being left alone with her while his mother and sister were at Bedford House, he found himself so

impatient, that he sent for a parson. The Doctor refused to perform the ceremony without license or ring: the Duke swore he would send for the Archbishop – at last they were married with a ring of the bed-curtain at half an hour after twelve at night at Mayfair Chapel.[10] The Scotch are enraged [because the bride was Irish]; the women mad that so much beauty has had its effect; and what is most silly, my Lord Coventry declares now he will marry the other (20. 302–3; 27 February 1752].

The newly married sisters were the cynosure of fashionable society, Walpole wrote on 23 March 1752:

The world is still mad about the Gunnings: the Duchess of Hamilton was presented [at court, St James's Palace] on Friday [20 March]; the crowd was so great, that even the noble mob in the Drawing-Room clambered upon chairs and tables to look at her. There are mobs at their doors to see them get into their chairs; and people go early to get places at the theatres when it is known they will be there. Dr Sacheverel [Henry (1674–1724), incendiary Tory preacher] never made more noise than these two beauties (HWC 20. 311–12).

After Elizabeth Gunning's first husband, James, 6th Duke of Hamilton died from a cold caught while hunting, aged only thirty-four, Walpole gives a facetious account of her second marriage (3 February 1759) to John Campbell (1723–1806), Marquess of Lorn, later (1770) 5th Duke of Argyll. Again Walpole compares Elizabeth to her sister Maria:

What an extraordinary fate is attached to those two women! Who could have believed that a Gunning would unite the two great houses of Campbell and Hamilton [bitter rivals for generations]? For my part, I expect to see my Lady Coventry Queen of Prussia. I would not venture to marry either of them these thirty years, for fear of being shuffled out of the world *prematurely* to make room for the rest of their adventures. The first time Jack [Campbell] carries the Duchess into the Highlands, I am persuaded that some of his second-sighted subjects will see him in a winding-sheet, with a train of kings behind him as long as those in Macbeth (38. 7; 28 January 1759).

Walpole kept watch on the Gunning sisters throughout the decade, as a connoisseur of what he calls 'standard' beauties (21. 451). We have already observed the beauty contest Walpole staged at Strawberry Hill for Maria Gunning. On Wednesday 30 May 1759 he staged another for Elizabeth Gunning. The Duchesses of Hamilton (Elizabeth Gunning, plate 110), Richmond [Lady Mary Bruce (1740–96); plate 111], and Lady Ailesbury [Caroline Campbell (1721–1803)] dined on the terrace at Strawberry Hill: 'There never

---

109.   Sir Joshua Reynolds: *Elizabeth Gunning, Duchess of Hamilton*. SA 1760. Oil on canvas, 93 × 57 in. Board of Trustees of the National Museums and Galleries on Merseyside (Lady Lever Art Gallery, Port Sunlight). Photo: Lever Art Gallery. 'The Duchess [Elizabeth Gunning] was more delicate than her sister [Maria Gunning], with the most beautiful hands and arms in the world; but Lady Coventry [Maria Gunning] was still handsomer' (G III 3. 131–2 n.).

110.   Katherine Read: *Elizabeth Gunning, Duchess of Argyll, c.* 1769. Pastel on paper, 23 × 18¼. In a Private
Scottish Collection. Photo: Antonia Reeve Photography for the Scottish National Portrait Gallery.

111.   Sir Joshua Reynolds: *Lady Mary Bruce, Duchess of Richmond.* 1758–60. Oil on canvas, 29½ × 24½ in. The
Trustees of the Goodwood Collection. Photo: Paul Mellon Centre for Studies in British Art.

was so pretty a sight as to see them all three sitting in the shell' (HWC 9. 237; 2 June 1759).
Walpole imagines himself talking in old age about these legendary beauties:

> . . . [A] thousand years hence, when I begin to grow old, if that can ever be, I shall
> talk of that event and tell young people how much handsomer the women of my
> time were than they will be then; I shall say, 'Women alter now. I remember Lady
> Ailesbury looking handsomer than her daughter the pretty Duchess of Richmond, as
> they were sitting on the shell on my terrace with the Duchess of Hamilton, one of
> the famous Gunnings' (9. 237; 2 June 1759).

John Campbell (1723–1806), 5th Duke of Argyll, and 'The Gunninghiad': *'A Tissue of Effrontery, Folly, and Imposture'. Thomas Gainsborough px*

Gainsborough's three-quarter-length portrait of *A nobleman*, identified by Walpole as the
'Duke of Argyll' (John Campbell [1723–1806], 5th Duke; plate 112), introduces a scandal
that requires revision of the biblical adage to read: 'the sins of the mothers shall be visited
on the daughters'. Campbell's portrait serves as the occasion for Walpole's Gunninghiad, a

112.   Thomas Gainsborough: *John Campbell, Marquess of Lorn, and 5th Duke of Argyll*. RA 1779. Oil on canvas, 30 × 25 in. In a Private Scottish Collection. Photo: Antonia Reeve Photography for the Scottish National Portrait Gallery '. . . . The Duchess of Hamilton [Elizabeth Gunning] is going to marry Col. [John] Campbell. . . . It is match that would not disgrace Arcadia' (HWC 21. 267).

113.   Richard Cosway: *George Spencer, Marquess of Blandford. c.* 1747. Oil on panel, 29³⁄₄ × 24 in. By kind permission of His Grace the Duke of Marlborough. Photo: Blenheim Palace.

story he tells in the correspondence about Major-General Campbell's niece Elizabeth that observes most of the conventions of the eighteenth-century English novel. Walpole was in Campbell's company at least once when Campbell was Marquess of Lorn (1761–70) at a ball in Burlington Street given by her 'mad Grace' (20. 226), the eccentric Lady Catherine Hyde (1701–77), Duchess of Queensberry, in March 1764.

> I do not know whether what I am going to tell you [Francis Seymour Conway] did not border a little upon Moorfields [Bedlam]. The gallery where they danced was very cold. Lord Lorn, George Selwyn, and I, retired into a little room, and sat comfortably by the fire. The Duchess looked in, said nothing, and sent a smith to take the hinges of the door off. We understood the hint, and left the room, and so did the smith the door. This was pretty legible (38. 343; 11 March 1764).

Shortly after returning from Italy by way of revolutionary France in August 1790 where he 'had his chaise pelted, and the coronet over his arms rubbed out' (11. 107; 2 August 1790), John Campbell came home to discover a hornet's nest of gossip about a great match in his wife's family. His wife's namesake and niece, Elizabeth Gunning the younger (1769–1823), only daughter of his wife's brother, General John Gunning

(1741–97) and the novelist Susannah Minifie (1740–1800), was rumoured to be engaged to marry the eldest son of the Duke of Marlborough, George Spencer, Marquess of Blandford (1766–1840; plate 113).

Walpole's cousin, Henry Seymour Conway, told him 'peremptorily' (39. 479) that the engagement was certain, but Walpole remained sceptical:

> Though I cannot yet believe it will be, there is certainly much more probability than I thought of another Gunning becoming a duchess. General Conway wrote to me [letter missing] that it is all settled, and that she [Elizabeth Gunning the younger] is to have the same jointure as the Duchess of Marlborough [Lady Caroline Russell (1743–1811)] – but *Lady Clackmannan* [probably John Campbell's sister, a gossip] who has questioned (you may be sure) both the Duke [John Campbell, Duke of Argyll, the bride-to-be's uncle] and Lord Lorne [Argyll's son, George William Campbell (1768–1839)], says, the former answered cooly, 'They tell me it is to be,' but the other told her he knew nothing of the matter, and that he had even not seen Lord Blandford. The Duchess of Gloucester [Maria Walpole] says that Mrs [Caroline] Howe, who is apt to be well informed, does not believe it. My incredulity is still better founded, and hangs on the Duchess of Marlborough's wavering weathercock-hood, which always rests at forbidding the banns (11. 108; 2 August 1790).

In a matrimonial intrigue more complicated than a novel by Richardson, the next crucial event in the plot – announcement of the engagement – seems to have taken place at Little Strawberry Hill, the house Walpole was leasing to his correspondents in this affair, Mary and Agnes Berry. On Sunday 10 October, the day before the Berrys departed on a continental tour, then and there the younger Elizabeth Gunning, whose family was living in Twickenham, 'announced that she was to be married to Lord Blandford' (11. 123, n. 12) on 20 October 1790. Walpole was present and thought that he detected disbelief in the Duke of Argyll's eldest daughter, Lady Augusta Clavering, on this occasion: 'You know on the famous night at your house,' Walpole wrote to Mary Berry, 'when Gunnilda [HW's nickname for Elizabeth Gunning the younger] pretended that her father [General John Gunning] had received Lord Blandford's appointment of the wedding day, we suspected, when they were gone, that we had seen doubts in Lady Augusta's face . . . but she protests she had then no suspicion' (11. 229; 27 March 1791).

The marriage had not taken place by 20 October, and Walpole was even more sceptical about the '*Marchioness to be or not to be*' (11. 123) when he wrote to the Berrys on 22 October:

> to send you the progress of a history that at the eve of your departure revived so strangely, without having had a beginning. In its present stage [Sunday 24 October 1790 'after dinner'] it is a war of duchesses. The bride's aunt [Elizabeth Gunning (1733–90), 5th Duchess of Argyll] firmly asserts it is to be; the bridegroom's grandmother [Gertrude Leveson Gower (1715–94), 4th Duchess of Bedford] positively denies it – and she ought to know as first inventress. In the meantime no *sposo* [bridegroom] appears, nor his parents [George Spencer and Caroline Russell, Duke and

Duchess of Marlborough], Marlborough House wanting repainting – in short, everybody but the ducal aunt [Elizabeth Gunning] suspects *the* letter was fictitious somewhence or other (11. 123–4; 22 October 1790).

Elizabeth Gunning, Duchess of Argyll, died on 20 December 1790, dismissing the duke with a wave of her hand just before she expired (39. 480; 23 December 1790). Throughout her last illness the matrimonial conspiracy of her niece and her matrimonially ambitious mother seemed to be in doubt. '. . . [I]n no *Gazette* . . . do I find that Miss Gunning is a marchioness', Walpole writes on 31 October 1790 (11. 128): 'The Marquisate is just where it was – to be and not to be – Duchess Argyll is said to be worse' (11. 136; 8 November 1790); 'The Gunning match remains, I believe, *in statu quo non*' (11. 153; 26 November 1790). Supping with the actress Elizabeth Farren in Green Street, Grosvenor Square, on Friday 12 November 1790,[11] Walpole did collect an important morsel of gossip about the Marquess of Blandford who was then visiting at Horton, Dorset: '[Gossip] . . . says he [Blandford] has heard of his pretended letter, laughs at it, and protests it is not his, nor is there the least foundation for it' (11. 142; 13 November 1790). On December 17, three days before the Duchess of Argyll died, Walpole reports the Marquess of Blandford's wedding appointment letter to be a forgery:

The famous letter and another to the same purport, of which we were told the night before you [the Berry sisters] set out, is discovered to be a forgery, but the writer not found out, yet supposed to be the very person [Gunnilda] who repeated it to us (11. 163; 17 December 1790).

General John Gunning (1741–97) promoted the match until he began to suspect that the Marquess of Blandford's love-letters were being forged by his wife and daughter: 'The Gunninghiad draws to a conclusion', Walpole wrote prematurely to Mary Berry on 29 January 1791:

The General a few weeks ago, to prove the equality of his daughter to any match, literally put into the newspapers [unlocated] that he himself is the thirty-second descendant in a line from Charlemagne – *oui, vraiment* – yet he had better have, like Prior's Madam,

To cut things short, gone up to Adam – [*Alma*, 2. line 374].

However, this Carlovingian hero does now allow that *the letters* are forgeries, and rather suspects the novelist his lady [Susannah Minifie] for the authoress – and if she is, probably Miss Charlemagne [Gunnilda] is not quite innocent of the plot, though she still maintains that her mother-in-law elect [Caroline Russell, Duchess of Marlborough] did give her much encouragement; which, considering her Grace's conduct about her children, is not the most incredible part of this strange story (11. 185–6; 29 January 1791).

In a long letter to Agnes Berry dated 13 February 1791 Walpole described the dénouement of the Gunninghiad, which was dragging its slow length along. After more suspicious love-letters had been received, General Gunning:

> sent *all* the letters down to the Marquis [George Spencer at Blenheim], desiring to be certified of their authenticity, or the contrary. . . . The Marquis immediately distinguished the two kinds, owned the few letters that disclaimed all inclination for Miss Charlemagne [Gunnilda]; disavowed the rest. Thence fell the General's wrath on his consort (11. 196).[12]

Enter Major-General John Campbell, 5th Duke of Argyll, who seems to have been a bewildered bystander to his sister-in-law's matchmaking designs. Gunnilda's uncle and father

> thought it expedient that Miss Charly's character should be cleared as far as possible. . . . She was ordered to draw up a narrative [untraced], which should be laid before the Duke of Marlborough and if allowed by him, to be shown for her vindication. She obeyed, and her former assertions did not suffer by the new statement – but one singular circumstance was added – she confessed – ingenuous maid! – that though she had not been able to resist so dazzling an offer [George Spencer, Marquess of Blandford's proposal forged by her mother and herself], her heart was still her cousin's, the other Marquis (11. 197; 13 February 1791).

The 'other Marquis' in this *opera buffa*, was none other than the Duke of Argyll's son, Gunnilda's first cousin George William Campbell (1768–1839), Marquess Lorn, 'Miss Charly's' true love while she was participating in her mother's plot to entrap the future Duke of Marlborough.

Walpole summarises an affadavit published in the *St James's Chronicle*, 19 April 1791: '. . . Miss [Gunnilda] pretended her mama had an aversion to Lord Lorn . . . and that she did not dare to acquaint so tender a parent with her lasting passion for him' (11. 252; 23 April 1791). Or, as she puts in a letter: 'she [Susannah Minifie, her mother] detests the person dearest to me on earth' (11. 252, n. 12).

This exculpatory narrative by a blameless witness was approved by 'a confidential junto' (11. 197) at Argyll House in London,[13] and sent to Blenheim on the morning of 3 February by General Gunning. Within twenty-four hours Argyll's stable-groom, whom Walpole calls Carloman [man of Charlemagne], returned with a 'wonderful acquittal of the damsel', a letter purporting to be from George Spencer, 4th Duke of Marlborough, himself:

> declaring how delighted he and his princess had been at their son's having made choice of so *beautiful* and *amiable* a virgin for his bride; how greatly they had encouraged the match, and how chagrined they were, that from the lightness and inconstancy of his [George Spencer, Marquess of Blandford's] temper the proposed alliance was quite at an end (11. 197–8; 13 February 1791).

'You may still suspect,' Walpole continues his letter to Agnes Berry, 'and so did some of the Council, that every tittle of this report and of the letter, were not gospel' (11. 198). Walpole goes on to recount clues that led to suspicion that the duke's letter was another forgery: the 'Duke' mis-spelled his eldest son's name, the sealing wax was black, 'and nobody could discover for whom such illustrious personages were in mourning' (11. 198).

On Tuesday 8 February the general tested his doubts by consulting Henry John Spencer (1770–95), the duke's second son on leave from the embassy at the Hague: '. . . [T]he letter was shown to him; he laughed and said it had not the least resemblance to his father's hand' (11. 198). After this 'negative detection' (11. 198) took place, Walpole disclosed 'the most positive and wonderful unravelling'. On 9 February Essex Bowen, an army captain on half-pay wrote to General Gunning that his wife, Margaret Lyster, a friend of Gunnilda's:

> had lately [1 February 1791] received from her [Gunnilda] a copy of a most satisfactory testimonial from the Duke of Marlborough in her favour (though, note, the narrative was not then gone to Blenheim) and begging the gentlewoman's husband [Captain Bowen] would transcribe it and send it to her, as she wished to send a copy to a friend in the country. The husband had done so, but had had the precaution to write at top *copy*, and before the signature had written *signed* M., both which words Miss [Gunnilda] had erased, and then delivered the gentleman's identic transcript to the groom [William Pearce] to be brought back as from Blenheim – which the *steady* groom on being examined anew, confessed, and that being bribed by Miss Gunning he had gone but one post [to General Gunning's house at Twickenham], and invented the rest (11. 198–9; 13 February 1791).

In a postcript Walpole corrects himself, placing blame for the forgery on Gunnilda's mother, Susannah Minifie, and her sister Margaret, another novelist: 'The whole *Minifry* are involved in the suspicions, as they defend the damsel, who still confesses nothing; and it is her mother, not she, who is supposed to have tampered with the groom, and is discarded too by her husband [General John Gunning]' (11. 200). The same day (9 February 1791) General Gunning evicted his wife from his house in Twickenham, she took refuge with her daughter in Pall Mall with Gertrude Leveson-Gower (1715–94), the Dowager Duchess of Bedford, whom Walpole suspected of having hatched the whole plot ('first inventress', 11. 123). 'In fact, there never was a more extraordinary tissue of effrontery, folly, and imposture' (11. 199; 13 February 1791), Walpole concluded, signing what he hoped would be the last chapter of a saga named after one of Mrs Manley's [Mary de la Rivière (1663–1724)] romances: 'Eginhart, Secretary to Charlemagne [General Gunning] and the Princess Gunnilda [Elizabeth Gunning] his daughter' (11. 200, and n. 33; 13 February 1791).

But within five days Walpole was writing to Mary Berry 'a shocking (not a fatal) codicil to Gunnilda's story' (11. 201). At 4 A.M. on 10 February, 'after the explosion, the Signora Madre [Susannah Minifie] took a post chaise and four and drove to Blenheim'. The Marquess was not at Blenheim, so she pursued him to Kirtlington Park, Oxfordshire: '. . . [F]inding him there, she began about her poor daughter – but he interrupted her, said there was an end put to all that, and desired to lead her to her chaise, which he insisted on doing, and did' (11. 201; 18 February 1791). In *A Letter to the Duke of Argyll* (1791), Susannah Minifie describes her frantic 'journey of a hun-

114.   After a drawing by Francesco Bartolozzi: *Elizabeth Gunning the younger.* From Madame de Barneveldt, *Memoirs*, 2d ed., 2 vols. (London: Vernor & Hood, 1796), vol. 1, frontispiece. By permission of the British Library. 'There is a medallion of Gunnilda supported by two – cupids not marquises, her name and four verses beneath' (HWC 11.218).

115.   James Gillray: *The Siege of Blenheim – Or – The New System of Gunning Discoverd.* 5 March 1791. Coloured line engraving, 9¾ × 13¾ in. © Copyright The British Museum. 'There is published a Grub print not devoid of humour . . . . Miss astride a cannon is firing a volley of forged letters at the Castle of Blenheim' (HWC 11.220).

dred and forty miles, without taking off my clothes for two nights, or any refreshment whatever, but one glass of water and one of wine' (11.201, n. 4). Walpole concludes: 'I think this is another symptom of the Minifry being accomplices to the daughter's enterprises' (11.201). The stable-groom's confession to taking a bribe, and Captain Bowen's testimony about the Gunnings' forgeries of the letter to the duke:

she [Susannah Minifie] resolutely disowned . . . [and] desired the Duke of Argyll to let her take an oath on the Bible of her perfect innocence of every circumstance of the whole transaction, which you may be sure he did not permit – *n'importe* – the next day . . . she went before a justice of peace [William Hyde], swore to her innocence and ignorance throughout, even of the note to Mrs Bowen, and then said to the magistrate, 'Sir, from my youth you may imagine I do not know the solemnity of an oath; but to convince you I do, I know my salvation depends on what I have now sworn' – solve all this if you can! is it madness? – does even romance extend its inventions so far? or its dispensations? – it is but a burlesque part of this wonderful tale, that old crazy Bedford [Gertrude Leveson-Gower] exhibits Miss every morning in the Causeway in Hide Park, and declares her protégée some time ago refused the hand of your acquaintance Mr Trevilyan [John (1761–1846)] – Except of the contending opera houses [Pantheon, and King's Theatre, Haymarket], one can hear nothing but Miss Gunning – but it is now grown so disgusting a story, that I shall be glad to hear and report to you no more about it (11.201–2; 18 February 1791).

At this point the Gunninghiad takes another literary turn, as Susannah Minifie advertises in the *Gazetteer* (23 February 1791) that she was preparing to tell all in *A Letter from Mrs Gunning, Addressed to His Grace the Duke of Argyll* (11. 197, n. 7). Susannah Minifie's threat prompted the duke 'to collect counter-affadavits' (11. 204), 'a cartload' delivered to mother and daughter at a house in St James's Street 'in order to prevent the publication of their libel – but it only enraged the . . . [mother], who vows she will print all she knows – that is, anything she has heard by their entire intimacy in the family, or, no doubt, what she can invent or misrepresent – what a Medusa!' (11. 205–6; 26 February 1791). Susannah Gunning's pamphlet, *A Letter*, did not get into print until Monday 21 March at noon; it sold out by four o'clock in the afternoon (11. 225, n. 17). In the meanwhile the 'mad' Minifry, 'outpensioners of Bedlam' (11. 217), as Walpole calls the scribbling sisters, 'sent a new narrative to the Duke of Marlborough, wherein the infanta [Gunnilda] maintains to his Grace's face, that she passed three *days* with him and the Duchess this summer [August 1790] at

Sion though it was but three *hours*', (11. 217). The duke was amazed by the claim to intimacy that Walpole calls 'a new style of romancing . . . I can scarce believe while I repeat it' (11. 217; 11 March 1791). At the same time Susannah Minifie was puffing her forthcoming libel in *The Saint James's Chronicle*, proof of a frontispiece (untraced) was sent to the Duke of Argyll: 'There is a medallion of Gunnilda supported by two – Cupids not marquises, her name, and four verses beneath' (11. 218; 11 March 1791; plate 114).[14]

This portrait medallion was apparently not used to illustrate Susannah Minifie's pamphlet. Walpole mentions instead James Gillray's engraved satire, *The Siege of Blenheim – or – The New System of Gunning Discover'd*[15]:

> There is published a Grub print not void of humour, called 'The New Art of Gunning'; Miss [Elizabeth Gunning] astride a cannon is firing a volley of forged letters at the Castle of Blenheim, and old Gertrude [Leveson-Gower], emaciated and withered, and very like, lifting up her hoop to shelter injured innocence, as she calls her (11. 220; 11 March 1791; plate 115).

The Dowager Duchess of Bedford is saying to mother and daughter: 'Come under my protection, deary's. I'll hide you in Bedfordshire; and find one of my little Granny-boys to play with Missy' (11. 220, n. 30).

After all this build-up, Susannah Minifie's pamphlet, once published, was a let-down. '. . . [I]t disappoints everybody', Walpole commented. 'It is neither romantic, nor entertaining, nor abusive, but on the General [John Gunning] and Mr and Mrs Bowen [Captain Essex Bowen, and his wife Margaret Kirwan Lyster (1747–1832), who exposed the forged letter in *A Statement of Facts*], and the General's groom [William Pearce]' (11. 225; 19 March 1791). Although the pamphlet was addressed to the Duke of Argyll, Susannah Gunning's furious conspiracy theory did not even mention him:

> Of the House of Argyll she says not a word. In short, it is a most dull incoherent rhapsody, that gives no account at all of the story that gave origin to her book, and at which no mortal could guess from it; and the 246 pages [HW's mistake for 147] contain nothing but invectives on her four supposed enemies, and endless tiresome encomiums on the virtues of her *glorious darling*, and the unspottable innocence of that harmless lambkin[16] – I would not even send it to you if I had an opportunity – you would not have patience to go through it – and there I suppose the absurd legend will end – I am heartily tired of it (11. 226; 19 March 1791).

But Walpole adds '[o]ne word more of the Gunnings' (11. 228; 27 March 1791) that turned into a torrent of gossip: first, Captain Bowen's announcement 'by the channel of the papers that he shall prosecute her [Susannah Minifie] for the libel' (11. 228; 27 March 1791); second, 'her congratulations on their intended course of law' (*Gazetteer* 24 March; 11. 228, n. 14); third, the general's reaction to newspaper publicity of his 'claimed descent from Charlemagne. . . . "It is true, I am well born, but I know no such family in Ireland as the Charlemagnes"' (11. 229; 27 March 1791); fourth, Gunnilda's letter of apology to the Marquess of Blandford 'in her own name and *hand*, begging his pardon (for promising herself marriage in his name) but imputing the first thought to his grandmother [Gertrude Leveson-Gower], whom she probably inspired to think of it' (11. 229); fifth, the Duchess of Marlborough's showing the Duchess of Bedford the letter in a futile attempt 'to open her eyes on her protégée' (11. 229); sixth, the mother and daughter's flight to France, 'terrified by Capt. Bowen's prosecution – and there I hope will terminate that strange story, for in France there is not a marquis left to marry her' (11. 229; 27 March 1791).

Captain Bowen never went to law, but on 19 April Walpole reports that Bowen:

> published a little pamphlet of affadavits [*A Statement of Facts, in Answer to Mrs Gunning's Letter* (1791), which prove that Gunnilda attempted to bribe her father's groom to perjure himself, but he begged to be excused. Nothing more appears against the mother. . . . Still I am persuaded that both the mother [Susannah Minifie] and the aunt [Margaret Minifie] were in the plot, whatever it was (11. 252; 23 April 1791).

In July 1791 Walpole wrote that the Gunnings had lost 'their place in the town-talk' (11. 307; 4 July 1791), but he cannot leave off in his letters 'the stale story of the Gunning' (11. 253). With 'scarce a penful of news' for the Berrys he says his last word on the subject:

> – *en attendant, voici* [in the meanwhile, here are] the Gunnings again. The old gouty General [John Gunning, Gunnilda's father] has carried off his tailor's wife [Rebecca Howard (1767–1805)] – or rather, she him – whither, I know not – probably not far, for the next day the General was arrested for £3,000 and carried to a sponging house, whence he sent Cupid with a link to a friend to beg help, and a crutch. This amazing folly is generally believed,[17] perhaps because the folly of that race is amazing – so is their whole story. The two beautiful sisters [Maria and Elizabeth Gunning the elder] were going on the stage, when they are at once exalted almost as high as they could be, were Countessed and double-Duchessed – and now the rest of the family have dragged themselves through all the kennels of the newspapers! – it is but a trifling codicil, that t'other day poor old Bedford [Gertrude Leveson-Gower] made Miss Gunning read her daughter Marlborough's [Caroline Russell's] letter on Lord Blandford's [George Spencer's] marriage to a lady that came to visit her [Susan Stewart (1767–1841), daughter of a Scot [John, 7th Earl of Galloway] (11. 365–6; 9 October 1791).

'[T]he Marquis of Blandford', Walpole wrote to the Berry sisters on 16 September 1791, '[is] literally married, *malgré* [in spite of] the Duchess' (11. 352).

At last Walpole could honestly write that 'the Gunninghiad is completed . . . by a marriage, like other novels of the Minifies' (11. 196; 13 February 1791). It was 'the termination of a legend' (11. 196), an 'absurd legend' Walpole had pretended to be 'heartily tired of' (11. 226). But even with marriage the story for Walpole had not entirely come to an end. In June 1791 he transcribed for the Berry sisters one of several versions of a parody of the Gunninghiad illustrated by a print (plate 116), and verses to be sung 'To the tune of *The Cow with the* Crumpledy *Horn*, etc' ('The House that Jack Built')[18]:

116.   Isaac Cruikshank: *This is the House that Jack Built.* 2 June 1792. Coloured line engraving, 16 × 13¼ in. ©
Copyright The British Museum. Walpole transcribes a parody of verses set to the tune of *The Cow with the
Crumpeldy Horn,* for the grand finale of his Gunninghiad (HWC 11. 279).

This is the note that nobody wrote;

This is the groom that carried the note that nobody wrote;

This is Ma'am Gunning who was so very cunning to examine the groom that carried the note that nobody wrote.

This is Ma'am Bowen to whom it was owing, that Miss Minify Gunning was so very cunning to examine the groom that carried the note that nobody wrote.

These are the Marquises shy of the horn, who caused the maiden all-for-*Lorn*, to become on a sudden so tatter'd and torn, that Miss Minify Gunning was so very cunning to examine the groom etc.

These are the two Dukes whose sharp rebukes made the two Marquises shy of the horn, and caused the maiden all-for-Lorn etc.

This is the General somewhat too bold, whose head was so hot, though his heart was so cold, who proclaim'd himself single before it was meet, and his wife and his daughter turn'd into the street, to please the two Dukes, whose sharp rebukes etc. etc. etc.

(HWC 11. 279; 2 June 1791).

PART IV

Conclusion: Walpole's Self-Portrait, the Prime Minister of Taste

CHAPTER 18

Walpole's Self-Portrait,
The Prime Minister of Taste

A Masquerade of Self-Portraits

'Having drawn you this picture of myself, Madam, a subject I have to say so much upon' (31. 17), Walpole begins a paragraph in a letter to Mary Lepell. Like Reynolds and many other artists, Walpole's favourite subject for portraiture was himself. Walpole's passion for self-dramatisation in the correspondence amounts to a masquerade of self-portraits. Madame du Deffand was one of the first to recognize the protean variety of Walpole's self-portraits, referring to him as 'l'hiéroglyphe Walpole' (3. 31), and 'un logogriphe sans mot', 'a charade without a word' (4. 31). He compares himself to Alceste tormented by a bore in Molière's *Misanthrope* (3. 44); he turns himself into '*Horace the Magnificent*' on the Grand Tour (17. 505). He signs himself the 'Duchess of Ruffham' [Rougham, a village south of Houghton House] (18. 238, n. 14); 'The Abbot of Strawberry' (40. 125); the author of scandalous chronicles, 'Abbé de Brantôme' (32. 53); 'Dunce Scotus' (32. 297); 'Horace Trismegistus' (32. 59); 'Jack the Giant-Killer' (32. 175); 'Noah' (35. 228); 'The Governor of Barataria or Sancho Panza' (32. 211); and 'YO EL REY' (33. 378).

Wearing a waistcoat embroidered by Anne Liddell, he sees himself as Don Quixote reflected in a window at No. 5 Arlington Street, London:

I rose; the first object was to examine more attentively the inspired vest in the full sun against which it shone gorgeously – but, alas! as I crept to the window, in the glass I beheld – What do you think, Madam? – such an emaciated, wan, wrinkled, poor skeleton, that – O! adieu, visions, goddesses, odes, vests of roses, and immortal Strawberry – I thought I saw a thinner Don Quixote attired by the duchess for sport [*Don Quixote*, Part II, ch. 31] – Shocked, sunk from my altitudes, and shrinking into myself, I bade Philip Pança [Philip Colomb, HW's servant] fold up the vest, and vowed never to dress up my ghost like Adonis, but to consecrate the dear work of dear fingers to the single word (I *will* believe in the charming ode, Friendship [Anne Liddell's verses had compared Walpole to Horace] – and may the memory of that word, the vest and the ode, exist, when Strawberry Hill, its tinsel glories, and its master are remembered nowhere else! (32. 220; 1 January 1775).

In this typical virtuoso performance of self-dramatisation, he compares himself to Horace and Aeneas in the same letter.

117.   John Carter: *Three Sketches of Horace Walpole*. 1788. Watercolour vignettes, 5¾ × 9 in. Courtesy of the Lewis Walpole Library, Yale University. 'Having drawn you [Mary Lepell] this picture of myself, Madam, a subject I have to say so much upon, will not your good nature apply it as it deserves?' (HWC 31. 17).

The word 'skeleton' (32. 220) introduces another of Walpole's favourite masks – old age (44. 15–16; plate 117). A review of such references includes a dozen impersonations of Methusalah: 'I am Methuselam on most things and a boy on others, and one don't love to tell people that one's passions are too superannuated or too juvenile' (22. 341). In the same comedy of the *senex amans* wooing the Berry sisters he plays the 'old fool' (32. 320), the 'antediluvian' (12. 5), 'an old patriarch' (32. 382), one of the 'elderly Arcadians' (32. 114), and, most famously, 'a wrinkled Adonis' (32. 13). 'I roll about in a chariot decorated with Cupids, and look like the grandfather of Adonis' (10. 176).

Walpole is equally fond of identifying himself with Swift's Strulbrugs from the third book of *Gulliver's Travels*. Attempting to beg off a visit, he writes a Gothic excuse:

> If it is possible that Madam d'Andelot [Comtesse d'Andlau] should know that there is such an antediluvian as I remaining, why would not your Ladyship be so good as to say that Strulbrugs are dispensed with from making visits? – if I must, I must – so the first dark night, I will order my coffin and pair, and *appear* to her (33. 461; March 1785).

Apologizing for a letter threadbare of news, he plays the parts of 'Strulbrug' and 'old sailor':

> This is all my journal contains, Madam – but what better can you expect from a Strulbrug? and one so insipid as to be content with being so? – nay, it is not an unpleasant state. Having outlived all one's passions and pursuits, and not having acquired avarice in lieu, one sits down tranquilly like an old sailor that has been in many storms, and sees the crowd bustling and jostling or playing the fool, and feels the comfort of idleness and indifference, and the holiday luxury of having nothing to do. . . . I can but smile with thinking how you will be disappointed on receiving, instead of a letter, the reflections of a Strulbrug on his own inanity. When Swift drew the character, he did not know it – poor man! the turbulence of his own temper, and the apprehensions of his own decay, made him conceive it as a miserable condition – on the contrary it is almost a gay one, when one can be sensible of it and of all its enjoyments (33. 463–4; 7 June 1785).

Walpole never tires of the theatrical game of witty impersonation to entertain his correspondents: 'The town, who like the devil when one has once sold oneself to him, never permits one to have done playing the fool' (9. 416). In a letter to Mason Walpole casts himself in the role of 'vieux fou', 'old fool' in Voltaire's comedy (1725; Hazen 3057): 'I am tempted to sign my name in French, for the pleasure of quoting the following lines from Voltaire's *Indiscret*, the ridiculous parts of which suit me exactly. . . .

> Horace est un vieux fou, plutôt qu'un vieux seigneur
> Tout chamarré d'orgueil, pétri d'un faux honneur,
> Assez bas à la cour, important à la ville
> Et non moins ignorant qu'il veut paraître habile
> (28. 366–7; Scene iii, lines 15–18).

Responding to William Mason's complimentary 'Ode to Walpole', Walpole identifies himself with privileged visitors to Richmond Park and members of Parliament in a complicated piece of self-deprecation, defending himself against charges about Chatterton:

. . . [M]y *native eloquence*[1] which your partiality honours [line 30], proves what I have long suspected it was, only easy verbiage. In the early part of my life I wished to have it known that I was not a fool – doctors differ on the method and on the success: now, when I was grown much more indifferent to fame, you have bestowed on me more than I should ever have presumed to ask. I am now like people that have a ticket to Richmond Park which they lend to others when they can go in without, by being known to be in favour with the proprietor [the king], or like country squires returned for two places, who make their option for the county, and resign their family borough, on which perhaps there is not a tenement left standing. I choose my niche in your verses (28. 432–3; 25 August 1778).

The metaphors of admission and election suggest Walpole's ineradicable sense of marginality, especially poignant because he is assuming his inferiority to an irretrievably second-rate poet. But the insecurity that Mason awakened in Walpole, who had an absurdly inflated opinion of Mason's poetry – 'I allow your full superiority' (29. 144) – is uncharacteristic. More often Walpole plays comic roles, as when he identifies himself mock-heroically with Rousseau's Julie in describing a mishap to his parakeet at Strawberry Hill:

I have been in still more danger by water: my perroquet was on my shoulder as I was feeding my gold-fish, and flew into the middle of the pond: I was very near being the Nouvelle Éloise [Hazen 819], and tumbling in after him; but with much ado I ferried him out with my hat (35. 308; 5 July 1761).

Equally playful is Walpole's comparison of himself to the inhabitant of a weather-house, a toy hygroscope: 'My letters depend on events, and I am like the man in the weather-house that only comes forth on a storm' (23. 297; 26 April 1771). Thus Walpole insists 'on making a comedy of myself' (5. 398). '. . . I laugh at all serious characters . . . and at myself' (19. 4).

The Self-Portrait of the Trifler

These constantly varied impersonations in Walpole's masquerade of self-dramatisation are mere vignettes, blending into his self-portrait of the trifler drawn at full length in the correspondence. Derived from the code of self-deprecation necessary to the courtesy-book gentleman, the pose of the trifler was often motivated by Walpole's distaste for compliments. Here is a typical disclaimer, written in response to William Cole's compliments on Walpole's *Anecdotes of Painting*, the book that began their correspondence:

> But now, my good Sir, how could you suffer your prejudiced partiality to me to run away with you so extravagantly, as to call me one of the greatest characters of the age?. . . . But if you are blind towards me, I am not so to myself. I know not how others feel on such occasions, but if anyone happens to praise me, all my faults gush into my face, and make me turn my eyes inward and outward with horror. What am I but a poor old skeleton, tottering towards the grave, and conscious of ten thousand weaknesses, follies, and worse! And for talents, what are mine, but trifling and superficial; and, compared with those of men of real genius, most diminutive! Mine a great character! Mercy on me! I am a composition of Anthony Wood [(1632–95), antiquarian and biographer] and Madame Danois [Marie Berneville, Comtesse d'Aulnoy, writer of fairy tales; Hazen 1776], and I know not what trumpery writers. This is the least I can say to refute your panegyric, which I shall burn presently. . . . We have been friends above forty years . . . does it become us, at past threescore each, to be saying fine things to one another? Consider how soon we shall both be nothing! (2. 269; 4 May 1781).

Early in life Walpole articulated his gospel of trifles while at Cambridge, when writing to George Montagu about the pleasures of remembering schooldays at Eton:

> I think at our age 'tis excess of joy, to think, while we are running over past happinesses, that 'tis still in our power to enjoy as great. Narrations of the greatest actions of other people, are tedious in comparison of the serious trifles, that every man can call to mind of himself, while he was learning those histories: youthful passages of life, are the chippings of Pit's diamond, set into little heart-rings with mottoes: the stone itself more worth, the filings more genteel, and agreeable. Alexander at the head of the world never tasted the true pleasure, that boys of his own age have enjoyed at the head of a school (9. 2–3; 6 May 1736).

Sir Thomas Pitt (1653–1726; plate 118), Governor of Madras and grandfather of William Pitt, Earl of Chatham, bought the diamond Walpole refers to for £20,000, and in 1717 sold it to Louis XV for £125,000 (9. 2, n. 2). The 'chippings of Pit's diamond' are Walpole's metaphor for 'serious trifles'.

In Walpole's mind the jewel of dynastic and political power is of less value than sentimental trifles of private life. Walpole's metaphor suggests that he was already preparing himself at the age of nineteen for 'a life of letter-writing' (10. 15; 22 February 1762) instead of politics. Discouraged by Montagu's neglect of their friendship, Walpole

118. Sir Godfrey Kneller: *Thomas 'Diamond' Pitt*. Private Collection. Photo: By courtesy of the National Portrait Gallery, London '. . . [S]erious trifles . . . are the chippings of Pit's diamond, set into little heart-rings with mottoes' (HWC 9. 2-3).

returned to the theme thirty years later in another letter to his classmate just before visiting Paris after his disillusionment with politics in the 1760s.

> If I did not hate the world I know, I should not seek another. My greatest amusement will be in reviving old ideas. The memory of what made impressions on one's youth is ten times dearer than new pleasures can be. . . . My mind is such a compound from the vast variety that I have seen, acted, pursued, that it would cause me too much pains to be intelligible to young persons. . . . The trifles that amuse my mind, are the only points I value now. I have seen the vanity of everything serious, and the false-hood of everything, that pretended to be serious. I go to see French plays and buy French china, not to know their ministers, to look into their government, or think of the interests of nations (10. 171; 31 August 1765).

Walpole's unpublished autobiographical notes on his life (13. 3–51), essentially a chronology of his publications, unmistakeably reveal the importance he attached to his career as a writer. But the gentleman-author invariably dismisses his own writings as trifles: '. . . I write more trifling letters than any man living' (38. 94; 14 July 1761). His letters to Horace Mann are 'errant trifles' (17. 1). 'My books, my virtu, and my other follies and amusements take up too much of my time', he says to George Montagu (9.

32; 17 June 1746). And he declares to Thomas Gray '. . . [my writings] are the most hasty trifles in the world' (14. 167; 18 February 1768). Walpole refers to his forged letter to Rousseau that caused a sensation as 'a trifle that I wrote lately' (35. 117; 15 January 1766). He replies to George Nicol's proposal to publish an edition of his works with characteristic self-deprecation: 'I would no more hear of a splendid and ornamented edition of my trifling writings, than I would dress my old, emaciated, infirm person in rich and gaudy clothes' (42. 371; 30 August 1790). Describing a portfolio of nobleman's etchings he was compiling, Walpole writes to Mason:

> I who, simpleton as I was, loved to be an author, am so ashamed of my own stuff, and so convinced that nobody but you and Gray could write, have taken shame to myself, and forsworn the press; yet as I cannot be idle, it is impossible. I have invented a new and very harmless way of *making books* which diverts me as well,[2] and brings me to no disgrace (28. 195; 7 May 1775).

Here is a typical reproof valiant to Thomas Warton's compliment upon his *Anecdotes of Painting*: '. . . how can you, Sir, approve such hasty, superficial writings as mine, you, who in the same pursuits are so much more correct, and have gone so much deeper?' (40. 254; 21 August 1762). He refuses to accept the title of a learned author that William Cole gives him: '. . . [T]he reviewers and such *literati* have called me *a learned and ingenious gentleman*. I am sorry they ever heard my name, but don't let them know how irreverently I speak of the erudite . . .' (1. 368–9; 25 April 1775). He answers Cole's request for 'prints of me' with his usual self-abasement: 'The owner sets very little value on them, since he sets very little indeed on himself; as a man, a very faulty one, and as an author, a very middling one; which whoever thinks a comfortable rank is not at all of my opinion' (1. 337; 21 July 1774). He refuses John Nichols' offer to 'change any passages that criticize my own work' in Nichols' second edition (1782) of his *Biographical Anecdotes of Hogarth* (Hazen 2435):

> . . . I should blush to myself if I even wished for that complaisance. Good God! Sir, what am I, that I should be offended at or above criticism or correction? I do not know who ought to be – I am sure, no author. I am a private man, of no consequence, and at best an author of very moderate abilities (41. 448; 31 October 1781).

Walpole was 'ashamed' of the compliments in the advertisement to a Dublin edition of *The Mysterious Mother* (1791): 'To any *eminence in literature* I am sure I have no pretensions; an *amiable character* I wish I deserved; and of *high rank* I certainly am not, nor ever aspired above being a private commoner, and have proved a very insignificant one' (42. 324; 4 April 1791).

Walpole refuses to accept Robert Jephson's compliment on the epilogue he provided for Jephson's tragedy *Braganza* (17 February 1775 at Drury Lane): '. . . I could not refuse Mr Tighe's request of writing an epilogue, though I never was a poet, and have done writing. . . . I am ashamed of it' (41. 287; 24 February 1775). He refuses to contribute to John Berkenhout's *Biographical History of Literature* (Hazen 3291 [1777]):

> My life has been too insignificant to afford materials interesting to the public. In gen-

eral, the lives of mere authors are dry and unentertaining; nor, though I have been one occasionally, are my writings of a class or merit to entitle me to any distinction. . . . My own works . . . are dead and buried; but as I am not impatient to be interred with them, I hope you [Berkenhout] will leave that office to the parson of the parish (41. 255–6; 6 July 1773).

Receiving 'great encomiums on my taste and knowledge' with a presentation copy of a mathematical treatise, Walpole ridicules the compliment as usual:

. . . I am warranted to insert this certificate among the *testimonia authorum*, before my next edition of the *Painters* [*Anecdotes of Painting*]. No, I assure you, I am much more just – I have sent the gentleman word what a perfect ignoramus I am, and did not treat my vanity with a moment's respite (38. 359; 27 March 1764).

Responding to Anne Liddell's encouragment of Strawberry Hill editions, Walpole replies:

. . . I have several reasons for lamenting daily that I ever was either author or editor. . . . No, Madam, I have lived to attain a little more sense; and were I to recommence my life, and thought as I do now, I do not believe that any consideration could induce me to be an author. I wish to be forgotten. . . . In short . . . I have great contempt for middling writers. We have not only betrayed want of genius, but want of judgment – how can one of my grovelling class open a page of a standard author, and not blush at his own stuff? I took up the first part of *Henry IV* t'other day, and was ready to set fire to my own printing-house (33. 574; 15 September 1787).

When Anne Liddell gave Walpole's character to Jean Huber, a Swiss engraver, Walpole replied:

I hate to have anybody think better of me than I deserve; and I must say your Ladyship's partiality to me, at least your favour, is apt to rate me above the common run of men, which I know I am not. I never had anything like a solid understanding on one side, or wit on the other (32. 327; 13 October 1776).

Reflecting on attacks on his writings 'which like water-balloons hop, hiss, hop up again once or twice at intervals, stink and perish forever', Walpole continues:

I have done with the world – and were it to begin again, the last vocation I would embrace, should be that of author. My veneration for true genius is profound; my indifference to a mediocrity of fame, which at most can fall to my lot, total; my contempt for the fry of Grub Street, supreme (29. 295; 5 May 1783).

In this passage Walpole may be referring to the publication of his second book, *Royal and Noble Authors* (1759), when he remarks to Montagu: 'Nothing tempts me to launch out again; every day teaches me how much I was mistaken in my own parts, and I am in no danger now but of thinking I am grown too wise; for every period of life has its mistake' (9. 411; 23 December 1761). When Henry Fox circulated some of Walpole's manuscript verse, he replied:

> You frighten me out of my wits . . . a fair step towards making me in earnest a poet, a title I should dread. . . . I never thought poetry excusable, but in the manner I sent you mine, just to divert anybody one loves for half an hour. . . . But to make anything one writes, especially poetry, public, is giving everybody leave under one's own hand to call one fool. You think me modest, but all my modesty is pride – while I am unknown, I am as great as my own imagination pleases to make me – the instant I get into that dreadful Court of Requests [the stone-paved lobby connecting the Houses of Lords and Commons, HWC 20. 123, n. 30] you talk of, I am as silly a fellow as Thompson [James Thomson (1700–48)] or Glover [Richard (1712–85)] (30. 104–5; 24 July 1746).

When William Gilpin dedicated his *Essay on Prints* (Hazen 338; 1781) to Walpole with a compliment to his *Anecdotes* 'and the valuable researches he [Walpole] has made to improve them [the polite arts]', Walpole commented: '. . . [H]e [Gilpin] talks of my researches, which makes me smile; I know as Gray would have said, how little I have *researched*, and what slender pretensions are mine to so pompous a term' (29. 97; 27 January 1781).

In a letter egregiously flattering William Mason's writings, Walpole says he wishes he had confined himself to marginalia:

> There is nothing pleases me so much as humbling myself to the level of my talents. Writing notes in my books, as it requires only truth and memory, and no parts, suits me exactly; and had I always known myself as well as I do now, I should never have soared out of my sphere, and my works would have been highly valued, as I should have never had above one reader to each, the person who buys my books at my auction (28. 292; 13 March 1777).

In another letter Walpole invidiously compares his verses to Mason's: '. . . Mine at best were factitious rills that, like the artificial cascatelle of Hagley [Lord Lyttelton's gardens in Worcestershire], played for moments to entertain visitors, and were not the natural bounty of the soil . . . [compared to] your torrent' (28. 242; 18 February 1776). After the publication of his third book, *Anecdotes of Painting*, Walpole writes to Dalrymple: 'I am . . . forced to confess to you, that I have met with so many discouragements in virtù and literature. . . . Whatever is the cause, I am almost as sick of the profession of editor, as of author' (15. 99; 23 February 1764). 'I have always tried', he writes to Cole, 'to divest myself of the self-love of an author' (2. 143; 4 February 1779). And when embroiled in the Chatterton controversy he remarks: 'I have taken a thorough dislike to being an author' (2. 85; 3 June 1778).

Walpole's pose of the trifler, it is clear from these belittling remarks, afforded the amateur author a convenient defense against the professionals: 'I never publish a sheet, but buzz! out fly a swarm of hornets, insects that never settle upon you, if you don't strike at them; and whose venom is diverted to the next object that presents itself' (38. 362; 5 April 1764). But Walpole's self-deprecation has deeper roots than a mere rhetorical tactic, and although we do not intend to put Walpole on the couch, we should at least enquire whether the pose of the trifler has psychological or philosophical underpinnings. Consider this telling remark in a letter to George Montagu after the publication of *Royal and Noble Authors* (April 1758):

> . . . [A]s to writing, I am absolutely winding up my bottom [skein of thread], for twenty reasons. The first and perhaps the best, I have writ enough – the next; by what I have writ, the world thinks I am not a fool. . . . My last reason is, I find my little stock of reputation very troublesome . . . it has dipped me in *erudite* correspondences – I receive letters every week that compliment my learning – now as there is nothing I hold so cheap as a learned man, except an unlearned one, this title is insupportable to me (9. 227; 24 October 1758).

Walpole's sense of himself as the son of a hero, Sir Robert Walpole, whom he never tired of celebrating throughout his life, probably accounts for the almost obsessive strain of self-deprecation in his self-portrait: 'a rag of quality' at the funeral of George II (9. 321); 'a mere younger brother' (13. 108); 'a most indifferent figure' (28. 114); a 'tinsel' wit (31. 16); a person who understands 'nothing useful' (31. 331); 'a reprobate' (32. 190); always 'kicking down the pail of my fortune' (32. 260); one to whom trade is 'Coptic' (33. 545); 'a blockhead' at Eton (37. 161); 'a perfect goose about details of business' (38. 528); 'a credulous old simpleton' (33. 577); and a scribbler of 'gossiping babble' (33. 577). 'I never did anything that signified' (29. 88). Walpole further declares: 'Genius I absolutely have not. . . . I have so much littleness in my mind. . . . an idol of mud . . . [would] blush . . . seeing itself crowned with laurel!' (29. 82–3); 'I know nothing' (21. 368); 'I think meanly of myself' (15. 146); 'I always confess my own faults' (38. 39).

Walpole's view of compliments as anathema derives from this conviction of his own insignificance, a conviction that is more than merely rhetorical: 'You say you love and *adore* me', he writes to Horace Mann in disbelief:

> Jesus! my dear Sir! what an object of adoration! You put me in mind of what I have read in some traveller, who viewing some Indian temple, that blazed with gold and jewels, was at last introduced into the *sanctum sanctorum*, where behind the veil sat the object of worship – an old baboon! – and perhaps poor Pug's inside, as well as out, was fairer than mine! (24. 433; 5 January 1779).

This may be as much playfully grotesque self-caricature as self-disgust, but it carries self-deprecation to extremes.

Taken out of context, some of Walpole's remarks seem shocking, as does this startling one in a letter to Anne Liddell, a letter occasioned by his not understanding 'a syllable' of George Colman's comedy, *The Man of Business* (Hazen 1810. 21. 9): 'No, I shall never be fit for anything as long as I live. A miscarriage I was born and shall die, without any merit but that of being/Your Ladyship's most attached H.W.' (32. 191–2; 19 February 1774). Anne Liddell had suffered a recent miscarriage, and one suspects Walpole was not baring his soul, but ending a letter with a *coup de théâtre*.

The same thing may be true of a series of virtually nihilistic remarks, prompted less by philosophy than a love of extremes. Commiserating with Horace Mann about a set-back in his consular career, Walpole offers facile consolation: 'What are rank and fortune, if they do not secure content? I was born at the top of the world; I have long been nobody, and am charmed to be so. . . . when one is emperor of one's self, all is harmony and sunshine' (23. 367; 21 January 1772). Reflecting on the completion of his designs for Strawberry Hill, Walpole writes complacently, again to Horace Mann:

> I have all my life been blessed with knowing my own mind. I never wished to be *anybody*, that is, anything; and when the moments have arrived, in which I might have been what I pleased, I resisted them, and persisted in my nothinghood. I hated Parliament, resolved to quit it, and did: was told I should repent, but never have – There ends my panegyric on myself (24. 100–1; 7 May 1775).

An attitude of indifference and *nil admirari* appears to be more characteristic than pretensions to nihilism in Walpole's self-portrait as trifler. Lonely after the Berry sisters went abroad in 1790, he consoles himself as philosopher manqué: '. . . [N]o wonder then that I am unhappy. . . . I pique myself on no philosophy, but what a long use and knowledge of the world had given me, the philosophy of indifference to most persons and events' (11. 112; 10 October 1790). On at least three occasions he identifies himself with a type of indifference, 'the country squire who was hunting as the battle of Edgehill was going to be fought . . . an instance of philosophic indifference in the height of a civil war, unparalleled till the present age' (29. 147; 14 June 1781). But writing to William Cole in 1778 about the 'impending war with France', Walpole's pose of philosophical indifference falters: '. . . [T]hough I am only a spectator, I cannot be as indifferent to the melancholy aspect of the times, as the country gentleman was, who was going out with his hounds, as the two armies at Edgehill were going to engage!' (2. 75; 23 April 1778).

He adopts the same pose of indifference to parry a compliment from Anne Liddell:

> I have no more vanity than hypocrisy – and if you would only substitute *indifference*, in the place of all the attributes you have so graciously bestowed on me, you would find it the sole key to almost every action of my life for some time past, and I believe for all to come (33. 1; 1778).

Writing from Bath after William Pitt asked Walpole to move the address at the opening of Parliament on 11 November 1766, Walpole again carries the pose of indifference to histrionic extremes:

> This coming into the world again, when I am so weary of it, is as bad and ridiculous as moving an address would be. I have no affectation, for affectation is a monster at nine-and-forty; but if I cannot live quietly, privately, and comfortably, I am perfectly indifferent about living at all. I would not kill myself, for that is a philosopher's affectation . . . but I shall always drive very near, before I submit to do anything I do not like. In short, I must be as foolish as I please, as long as I can keep without the limits of absurdity (39. 79; 18 October 1766).

The Herald of Fame

The story of Walpole's edition of the *Life* (1764) of Edward Lord Herbert of Cherbury (1583–1648) provides us in conclusion with a revealing portrait of the Prime Minister of Taste. We see Walpole collecting ancestors, managing family stories, preparing his audience to share his enthusiasm for one of his eccentric heroes, becoming a broker of reputations, and balancing his own views against public opinion. We are concerned here not with the discussion of another of Walpole's portraits in the correspondence but with the politics of portraiture, Walpole's role as portraitist, and his motives as a portrait collector.

Six years after opening the Strawberry Hill Press Walpole wrote excitedly to Bishop Charles Lyttelton on 10 July 1762 about the manuscript of Lord Herbert's autobiography:

> I have got a most delectable work to print, which I had great difficulty to obtain, and which I must use while I can have it. It is the life of the famous Lord Herbert of Cherbury, written by himself – one of the most curious pieces my eyes ever beheld (40. 287; 10 July 1763).

Walpole had just discovered the manuscript on a visit to Ragley, Warwickshire, as he explains in a letter to George Montagu:

> It is nothing less than the most curious book that ever yet set its foot in the world – I expect to hear you scream hither. . . . I found it a year ago at Lady Hertford's [Isabella Fitzroy, Countess of Hertford] to whom Lady Powis [Barbara Herbert (1735–86)] had lent it. I took it up, and soon threw it down again, as the dullest thing I ever saw. She [Lady Hertford] persuaded me to take it home. My Lady Waldegrave [Maria Walpole] was here [Strawberry Hill] in all her grief – [the poet, Thomas] Gray and I read it to amuse her – we could not go on for laughing and screaming (10. 129–30; 16 July 1764).

The swashbuckling career of the young courtier of James I, filled with duels, gallantry, and vanity surpassing Boswell's seemed screamingly comic to Walpole and his friends, but he was soon determined to print it at the Strawberry Hill Press.

'I begged to have it to print', Walpole continues the story.

> Lord Powis [Henry Arthur Herbert (1703–72), Earl of Powis], sensible of the extravagance [Cherbury's reckless career] refused. I insisted – he persisted. I told my Lady Hertford, it was no matter, I would print it, I was determined. I sat down and wrote a flattering dedication to Lord Powis, which I knew he would swallow. He did, and gave up his ancestor (10. 130).

Walpole's dedication praised Lord Powis for transmitting to posterity 'this record of his [Lord Herbert's] glory (10. 130, n. 11). However, the screams of laughter that had greeted the reading of Cherbury's chivalric exploits in the field and the boudoir prompted editorial caution:

> But this [dedication] was not enough. I was resolved the world should not think I admired it [Lord Herbert's autobiography] seriously (though there are really fine pas-

sages in it and good sense too) – I drew up an equivocal preface, in which you [George Montagu] will discover my opinion; and sent it with the dedication (10. 130).

Walpole's dissemblance about Lord Cherbury can easily be taken for unequivocal panegyric. Walpole praises the autobiographer unreservedly for his honesty: 'Foibles, passions, perhaps some vanity, surely some wrongheadedness; these he scorned to conceal, for he sought truth, wrote on truth [*De Veritate* (Hazen 167; 3rd ed. 1656)], was truth' (*Works* 1. 231). Walpole goes on to quote the Powises:

> . . . [T]here must have been a wonderful fund of internal virtue, of strong resolution and manly philosophy, which in an age of such mistaken and barbarous gallantry, of such absurd usages and false glory, could enable lord Herbert to seek fame better founded, and could make him reflect that there might be a more desirable kind of glory than that of a romantic duellist (*Works* 1. 231).

Walpole resolves contradictions between the street fighter and philosopher with a characteristic *bon mot*: 'I will anticipate the reader's surprise, though it shall be but in a word: to his astonishment he will find, that the history of don Quixote was the life of Plato' (*Works* 1. 231). But Walpole's quixotic philosopher, Lord Herbert, also commands his admiration: Herbert's biography of Henry VIII (1683; Hazen 19) is called 'a masterpiece of historic biography' (*Works* 1. 230); as a soldier Herbert's 'chivalry was drawn from the purest founts of the Fairy Queen' (*Works* 1. 232). 'As a public minister, he [Herbert] supported the dignity of his country, even when its prince [James I] disgraced it' (*Works* 1. 232). In Walpole's mind Herbert's life was exemplary: 'Valour and military activity in youth; business of state in the middle age; contemplation and labours for the information of posterity in the calmer scenes of closing life: this was lord Herbert: the deduction he will give himself' (*Works* 1. 232).

In *Royal and Noble Authors* (1758) Walpole had drawn a portrait of Lord Herbert equally equivocal. He describes Herbert's autobiography as 'perhaps the most extraordinary account that ever was given seriously by a wise man of himself' (*Works* 1. 363). Walpole again dwells on contradictions in the character of the quixotic philosopher, illustrated by an anecdote about 'his lordship putting up a solemn prayer for a sign to direct him whether he should publish his treatise *De Veritate* or not . . . [interpreting] a sudden noise as an imprimatur' (*Works* 1. 361 n.). 'There is no stronger characteristic of human nature', he observes, 'than its being open to the grossest contradictions' (*Works* 1. 361–2, n.).

Walpole's self-conscious equivocations in presenting his portrait of Cherbury may have resulted from attacks on Walpole's 'freedom with great names' in *Royal and Noble Authors*, in particular his controversial portrait of Sir Philip Sidney (plate 119). There Walpole portrayed Sidney as the archetype of undeserved and exaggerated fame. He describes how '[a] thousand accidents of birth, court-favour or popularity, concur sometimes to gild a slender proportion of merit. . . . No man seems to me so astonishing an object of temporary admiration as . . . the famous sir Philip Sidney' (*Works* 1. 342). Sidney's valor from Walpole's view was nothing extraordinary in 'an age of heroes' (*Works* 1. 342), and his writing was overrated: 'This was all my criticism pretended to

119. George Vertue: *Sir Philip Sidney. c.*
1745. Line engraving, $14\frac{1}{2} \times 19\frac{1}{4}$ in.
Courtesy of the Print Collection, Lewis
Walpole Library, Yale University. 'This
was all my criticism pretended to say, that
I could not conceive how [Sidney]. . .
had obtained such immense reputation'
(*Works* 1. 342, n.).

say, that I could not conceive how a man who in some respects had written dully and
weakly, and who at most was far inferior to our best authors, had obtained such
immense reputation' (*Works* 1. 342 n.).

Walpole's heretical judgment on Sidney conforms to his family motto – *Fari quae sentiat* (say what you think) – and to the high-minded ideal of historiography he asserts in
the introduction to *Royal and Noble Authors*:

No authority, under divine, is too great to be called in question; and however venerable monarchy may be in a state, no man ever wished to see the government of letters
under any form but that of a republic. As a citizen of that commonwealth, I propose
my sentiments for the revision of any decree, of any honorary sentence, as I think fit:
my fellow-citizens, equally free, will vote according to their opinions (*Works* 1. 249).

Thus Walpole, Prime Minister of Taste, promulgates his fearless, iconoclastic doctrine as
herald of the Temple of Fame.

But Walpole's letter to George Montagu about the reception of his edition of Cherbury's life shows that the doctrine was easier to pronounce than to put into practice:

The thing most in fashion is my edition of Lord Herbert's *Life*; people are mad after it – I believe, because only two hundred [copies] were printed – and by the numbers that admire it, I am convinced that if I had kept his Lordship's council [Lord Powis urged Walpole to tone down Herbert's extravagance], very few would have found out the absurdity of it. The caution with which I hinted at its extravagance has passed with several for approbation, and drawn on theirs. This is nothing new to me; it is when one laughs out at their idols, that one angers people. I do not wonder now that Sir Philip Sidney was the darling hero, when Lord Herbert, who followed him so close and trod in his steps, is at this time of day within an ace of rivalling him. I wish I had let him; it was contradicting one of my own maxims, which I hold to be very just; that it is idle to cure the world of any folly, unless one could cure it of being foolish (10. 139–40; 16 December 1764).

Walpole took great pains to control the distribution, and influence the reception of Cherbury's *Life*. Powis and Walpole shared equally the 200 copies of the Strawberry Hill edition, and Walpole distributed presentation copies with caveats, the usual disclaimers about triviality, and expressions of his own enthusiasm for the book: [To Lord Harcourt:] '. . . the most singular book that ever was written' (35. 452; 21 August 1764); [To Lord Lincoln:] 'I think it will amuse you for an hour, as it is one of the most extraordinary books ever published' (30. 175; 6 August 1764); [To William Mason:] '. . . by far the most curious and entertaining book that my press has produced . . . you will think it the most delightful book you ever read, and yet out of 150 pages [171] you had better skip the fifty first' (28. 3; 29 December 1763); [To Thomas Warton:] 'a most singular book . . . not . . . unworthy of keeping company with those paladins . . . in your notes on Spenser [*Observations on the Fairy Queen* (1762; Hazen 1840)]' (40. 368; 30 October 1764). William Cole reacted to the philosophical Quixote just as Walpole had prepared him to respond: 'The book delighted me excessively as well as surprised me: who could have believed that the philosophic author of *De Veritate* [Paris 1624] could have lived and acted the part of Don Quixote in reality?' (HWC 1. 70; 2 August 1764). David Dalrymple's acknowledgment of the copy Walpole sent him shows that he perfectly understood Walpole's intentions as an editor:

[I]t is indeed a curiosity that is perhaps unequalled. They who despise anecdotes will I hope acknowledge now that things may be instructive and valuable, though not generally known. It were to be wished that other men of quality would imitate the example of Lord Powis and trust their ancestors in your hands (15. 102; 26 September 1764).

Despite such acknowledgments, one of the presentation copies, Gilly Williams's, occasioned what may be the most influential and most mistaken judgment of Walpole's character. 'Horry [HW] has published Lord Herbert's *Life*', George James ('Gilly') Williams (1719–1805) wrote to George Selwyn 29 September 1764, 'with a very extraordinary dedication to Lord Powis. I have not read it, reserving it for the post-chaise, but I am told nothing is more odd and entertaining' (HWC 30. 176). A month later (19 October 1764) Williams wrote again to Selwyn:

> As to your question about Don Quixote, Horry says Lord Herbert was a Don Quixote with the austere philosophy of Plato: he does not tell you Plato was a Quixote. I wish most heartily he [Walpole] had the managing of other old family stories. . . . I can figure no being happier than Horry. *Monstrari digito praetereuntium* 'to be pointed out by the finger of passers by' has been his whole aim. For this he has wrote, printed, and built. To this we owe Lord Herbert, and I hope in future shall owe much more diversion (30. 176).

Williams is alluding to Horace's *Odes* (IV iii, 21–3), a passage where the poet acknowledges that he owes his fame to his muse – 'This is all thy gift, that I am pointed out by the finger of those passing by as the minstrel of the Roman lyre'.[3] The allusion, however, does not apply very well to Walpole's character. The author of *Royal and Noble Authors* and the *Anecdotes of Painting*, the architect of Strawberry Hill with its antiquarian collection of portraits, the equivocal editor of Edward Herbert's *Life*, did not rejoice in fame like his namesake, the classical poet. The fear of ridicule was Walpole's ruling passion. Williams's comment would have been more apt if the infinitive *monstrari* were changed from passive to active voice: 'to point' rather than 'to be pointed at' was Walpole's heart's desire as herald of fame.

But it is not easy to say what Walpole is pointing at in his portrait of Lord Cherbury. When Thomas Nugent's translation of the life of Benvenuto Cellini (1500–71) appeared in 1771 (Hazen 3181), Walpole compared it ironically to Herbert's in a letter to William Wentworth:

> I am angry with him [Cellini] for being more distracted and wrong-headed than my Lord Herbert. Till the revival of these two, I thought the present age had borne the palm of absurdity from all its predecessors. But I find our cotemporaries are quiet good folks, that only game till they hang themselves, and do not kill everybody they meet in the street. Who would have thought we were so reasonable? (35. 342, 20 June 1771).

This is certainly an opinion Walpole did not disclose to Lord Powis about his ancestor. Distracted, wrong-headed, extravagent, absurd, a reckless bully prepared to kill everyone he meets in the street – these are aspects of Herbert's character Walpole hopes 'the world should not think I admired' (10. 130).

One of Walpole's motives as an editor was to conceal his own enthusiasm for Herbert's unconventional character lest he be thought ridiculous. How thoroughly Walpole identified with Lord Herbert is suggested by his account of a visit in 1765 to Chantilly, the Château of Henri, Duc de Montmorency (1534–1614), that Herbert had frequently visited before and after he became ambassador to France: 'I gave my Lord Herbert's compliments to the statue of his friend the Constable [Montmorency was appointed Constable of France by Henri IV in 1593]', Walpole wrote to Mary Lepell (31. 46; 15 September 1765), referring to the equestrian statue standing before the Château.

It is significant that Walpole never mentions the portrait frontispiece (plate 120) to Lord Herbert's *Life*, one of the most attractive features of his edition, except to com-

120.   Anthony Walker after Isaac Oliver: *Portrait of Edward Herbert, Lord Herbert of Cherbury* (1583–1648). *The Life of Edward Lord Herbert of Cherbury, Written by Himself*, ed. HW (Strawberry Hill, 1764), front. By courtesy of the National Portrait Gallery, London. Photo: NPG Picture Library. 'I paid twenty guineas for the portrait of Lord Herbert before his Life. . . . it vexed me exceedingly' (HWC 15. 112).

120 A.   Isaac Oliver (d. 1617): *Edward Baron Herbert of Cherbury. 1610–13*. Oil on vellum, 7⅛ × 9 in. Powis Castle, Welshpool, Montgomery, Wales. Photo: National Trust Photographic Library/Powis Estate Trustees/Courtauld Institute.

plain about the price. 'Our engravers are so extravagant, though so indifferent, that I have almost given over the pleasure of having engravings', he wrote to Dalrymple. 'I paid twenty guineas for the portrait of Lord Herbert before his Life. . . . It vexed me exceedingly' (15. 112; 8 November 1767). The miniature portrait by Isaac Oliver (d. 1617) dated 1610 (plate 120A), engraved by Anthony Walker (1726–65), depicts Herbert armour-clad lying next to a stream in a wooded landscape. Readers of Walpole's edition found the frontispiece 'as romantic as the *Life* itself' (1. 72; 2 August 1764). George Montagu wrote to say '. . . I am in love with the charming couchant hero. I never saw so charming a figure so well graved, so sweet a romantic landscape – all Tasso, all Spencer, all truth, all honesty, all spirit' (10. 133–4; 30 August 1764). William Cole requested a separate impression of the print: 'I wish you had given us some little history of that print' (HWC 1. 71–2; 2 August 1764). That history was provided fifteen years later by John Bowle (1725–88), editor of *Don Quixote* (1781), who found a specific quotation from Cervantes in Oliver's picture.[4]

The Enemy of Artists

It comes as no surprise to discover that the Prime Minister of Taste, playing the herald of fame, should turn out to be the enemy of artists. The *locus classicus* for this attitude can be found in Walpole's account of a conversation with William Hogarth (1697–1764) while he was writing his *Anecdotes of Painting*. Although Walpole collected Hogarth's engravings and admired his work, particularly the portrait of Thomas Bambridge Hogarth gave to him (plate 121),[5] this conversation reveals how profoundly the patron was intimidated by the artist.

Walpole visited Hogarth's studio in the spring of 1761 'to see a portrait he is painting of Mr Fox [Charles James (1749–1806)]' (9. 365; 5 May 1761). He wrote to George Montagu:

Hogarth told me he had promised, if Mr Fox would sit as he liked, to make as good a picture as Vandyke or Rubens could. I was silent – 'Why now,' said he, 'You think

this very vain, but why should not one speak truth?' This *truth* was uttered in the face of his own Sigismonda [SA 61. 43, p. 6], which is exactly a maudlin whore tearing off the trinkets that her keeper had given her, to fling at his head. She has her father's picture in a bracelet on her arm, and her fingers are bloody with the heart, as if she had just bought a sheep's pluck in St James's market. As I was going, Hogarth put on a very grave face, and said, 'Mr Walpole, I want to speak to you'; I sat down, and said, I was ready to receive his commands. For shortness, I will mark this wonderful dialogue by initial letters (9. 365).

Although Walpole says 'this conversation is literal' (9. 366), it reads like a satirical redaction rather than a transcript:

H[ogarth]. I am told you are going to entertain the town with something in our way [*Anecdotes of Painting* (1762)]. W[alpole]. Not very soon, Mr Hogarth. H. I wish you would let me have it, to correct; I should be sorry to have you expose yourself to censure. We painters must know more of those things than other people. W. Do you think nobody understands painting but painters? H. Oh! So far from it, there's Reynolds, who certainly has genius; why, but t'other day he offered £100 for a pic-

ture that I would not hang in my cellar; and indeed, to say truth, I have generally found that persons who had studied painting least, were the best judges of it – but what I particularly wanted to say to you was about Sir James Thornhill [(1675–1734), Hogarth's father-in-law] . . . I would not have you say anything against him; there was a book published some time ago, abusing him, and it gave great offence – he was the first that attempted history in England, and I assure you some Germans have said he was a very great painter. W. My work will go no lower than the year 1700, and I really have not considered whether Sir J. Thornhill will come within my plan or not; if he does, I fear you and I shall not agree upon his merits. H. I wish you would let me correct it – besides, I am writing something of the same kind myself, I should be sorry we should clash. W. I believe it is not much known what my work is; very few persons have seen it. H. Why, it is a critical history of painting, is not it? W. No, it is an antiquarian history of it in England; I bought Mr Vertue's MSS, and I believe the work will not give much offence. Besides, if it does, I cannot help it: when I publish anything, I give it to the world to think of as they please. H. Oh! if it is an antiquarian work, we shall not clash. Mine is a critical work; I don't know whether I shall ever publish it – it is rather an apology for painters – I think it owing to the good sense of the English, that they have not painted better. W. My dear Mr Hogarth, I must take my leave of you, you now grow too wild – and I left him – if I had stayed, there remained nothing but for him to bite me. I give you my honour this conversation is literal, and perhaps, as long as you have known Englishmen and painters, you never met with anything so distracted. I had consecrated a line to his genius (I mean for wit) in my preface; I shall not erase it, but I hope nobody will ask me if he was not mad (9. 365–6; 5 May 1761).

Walpole's transcription of this astonishing conversation, almost too good to be true, is saturated with irony. He bristles with the patron's suspicion and hostility to artists, irritated by Hogarth's boast of outdoing Van Dyck and Rubens, annoyed by Hogarth's objection to amateurs' poaching on artist's territory ('our way'), and by the professional's assumption that 'nobody understands painting but painters'. He cannot have appreciated Hogarth's unwarranted assumption that Walpole's essay might criticize a gentleman architect, Sir James Thornhill, and that publication would expose him to censure. Walpole bridles at Hogarth's impertinent offer to correct his essay, and Hogarth's indecent haste in conceding that Walpole's 'antiquarian history' would not clash with his own 'critical' apology for painters. Finally, Walpole must have been insulted by Hogarth's ironic parting shot, which appears to be a dig at English patrons' neglect of English artists: 'I think it owing to the good sense of the English [patrons], that they [English artists] have not painted better.' This pointed remark prompts Walpole's hasty exit. Walpole's extreme characterization of Hogarth as an animal wild enough to bite, mad and distracted, clearly reveals Walpole's deep-seated alienation from artists.[6]

The Prime Minister of Taste, Homo Ludens

Although the herald of fame and the enemy of artists describe Walpole's activity and attitude as a collector of portraits, these roles do not characterise the element of play and parody that is the soul of his attitude to the arts. I would like to conclude, therefore, with the speculation that Walpole's career as Prime Minister of Taste amounted to a more or less deliberate parody of his father's political career as England's first prime minster.

'If I should prove a mere younger brother,' Walpole wrote to his Eton classmate, Richard West, 'and not turn to any profession, would you receive me?' (13. 108; 17 August 1736). Financed by sinecures, brought up to believe all professions ignoble, Walpole was asking a question that proved to be the most perplexing of his life. How could Walpole 'receive' himself without a profession? While disclaiming pretensions to authorship, Walpole became a writer for reasons he makes clear in a letter to George Montagu: '. . . [B]y what I have writ, the world thinks I am not a fool . . . having always lived in terror of that oracular saying . . . "The sons of heroes are loobies [louts]"' (9. 227; 24 October 1758). This statement is important because it reveals that his father, Robert Walpole, was a definite source of Walpole's uneasiness about his career, and his unceasing self-belittlement. The continuing dilemma of Walpole's life remained the struggle to find a vocation and to reconcile any vocation with his status as a gentleman.[7]

How could the son of the first pre-eminently successful British prime minister pretend to a career in politics? Inheriting a seat in Parliament through his father's influence, Walpole made no attempt at a parliamentary career: he spoke rarely in Parliament and then only to defend his father's reputation, and was otherwise content to remain an inconspicuous backbencher. 'Oh! how unlike him I am!' Walpole exclaims in a letter to Mann: 'How incapable of copying him even in a diminutive sphere!' (23. 522). 'My father is ever before my eyes – not to attempt to imitate him, for I have none of his matchless wisdom, or unsullied virtues, or heroic firmness' (24. 507). Remembering his father's prime ministership Walpole compares himself to Hamlet: '. . . [L]ike Hamlet on the sight of Yorick's skull, I recollected the prosperity of Denmark when my father ruled, and compared it with the present moment!' (25. 7; 13 January 1780). But Walpole can also say 'with the bastard in King John [I. i. 82–3]', quoting Shakespeare in reference to his father's political ambition: 'Oh! old Sir Robert, father, on my knee/I give heaven thanks I was not like to thee' (10. 168). Writing from King's Lynn while electioneering in March 1761, Walpole clearly indicates that he thinks his 'new vocation' (9. 350) of politics absurd. He formally repudiated politics after his cousin Conway's betrayal, and meant what he said when he told John Stuart, Prime Minister, third Earl of Bute: 'I know myself too well to think I can ever be of any use but as a virtuoso and anti-quarian' (40. 188).

The story of a son whose genius was stifled by a dominating father, living in his father's shadow, has the makings of tragedy, but Walpole believed that 'Life is a farce' (33. 432) and cast himself in a comic role. Yet we must not make Macaulay's mistake of tak-ing Walpole's rhetoric of self-deprecation at face value. Voltaire, as impatient with Walpole as with Congreve for belittling his career as a writer, penetrated the disguise of the gentleman-author when he remarked in a letter: 'Your father was a great minister and a good orator, but I suspect he would not have been able to write like you' (41. 152; 15 July 1768). Samuel Johnson shrewdly recognised in *Idler* (45) that self-deprecation is a form of self-aggrandizement,[8] and we can justifiably interpret Walpole's self-portrait of the trifler as ironic.

The constant theme of his rhetoric in the correspondence disguises a courtesy-book gentleman who used the mask of the trifler to emulate his father's political career in the world of art. Walpole was joking when he said he planned to 'launch into the world again, and propose to be prime minister to King George V' (32. 316). But Walpole's 'vocation to virtu', as George Robins called it,[9] was no joke, but a lifetime devoted to building in his mind an imaginary museum of portraits of the English aristocracy. '. . . [V]os estampes, vos antiques, peuvent-ils vous suffire pour toute occupation?', ('Your antiquities, are they enough to occupy you entirely?') (7. 65), Madame du Deffand asked incredulously. The arts did suffice, perfectly, because Walpole became a 'pretty universal virtuoso' (38. 357), ceaselessly collecting English portraits, and drawing his own match-less portraits of himself and his contemporaries in his letters.

Virtuosoship permitted Walpole to imitate his father's career in the arena of taste where he could not be outdone, humiliated, or ridiculed. Sinecures enabled Walpole to live the life of an aristocrat. He pursued a career in the politics of taste that amounts to a fascinating imitation of his father's political career. Instead of the politics of power, Walpole embarked on the politics of powerlessness and play. Instead of a Palladian power-house[10] – Houghton, Norfolk – Walpole built a Gothic play-house, at Strawberry Hill, Middlesex. Instead of a collection of capital pictures by old masters, Walpole collected portraits. Instead of a foreign policy, Walpole undertook a Grand Tour. Instead of buying and selling places at elections, Walpole bought pictures at auc-tions. Instead of manipulating a king, a court, and a Parliament, Walpole ranged portraits of royalty and peers in grangerized books. Instead of a cabinet of ministers, Walpole con-vened a Committee of Taste. Instead of parliamentary oratory at the dispatch box, Walpole whispered private gossip in witty letters.

The career of the Prime Minster of Taste, motivated by rivalry with his father, chal-lenges the assumption of Ketton-Cremer and Wilmarth Lewis that Walpole was a moth-er's boy.[11] The younger son takes up the portfolio of taste for the aristocracy, represents his constituency of aristocrats in Houses of Lords where he rummages for their portraits, catalogues their pictures, identifies and attributes their portraits, collects their *bons-mots*, and covers the banalities of their existence with the leaf-gold of his letters. Walpole's own distaste for parliamentary politics may have been the result of witnessing his father's fall

122.   Jean-Antoine Watteau: *l'Embarquement pour Cythère* (Embarcation for Cythera). 1718. Oil on canvas, 51⅛ × 75⅝ in. © Photo: RMN-Gerard Blot. Musée du Louvre, Paris.

from power after two decades of libellous and bloody opposition politics that pitted his father against his favourite poet, Alexander Pope.[12] The politics of taste offered a sanctuary, a character, and a career to a younger son intimidated by power politics.

The mask of the aristocratic trifler served Walpole well, transforming an insignificant younger son into a Prime Minister of Taste whose fame eclipsed his father's. Throughout his life he witnessed the decline and fall of Houghton House. At the same time Strawberry Hill was becoming a mecca for tourists, receiving its apotheosis during the Strawberry Hill sale of 1842. Walpole's idea of taste as 'extemposed judgment'[13] – intuitive rather than intellectual discrimination – helped to rescue it from the connoisseurs; and his example encouraged greater freedom of individual taste.[14] His career as portraitist vigorously defended the genre connoisseurs slighted, and helped to establish the reputation of English portrait painting and engraving in the teeth of connoisseurs' snobbery.

Walpole's aristocratic gospel of trifles seems anachronistic in modern democratic culture, but his wit, irony, parody, and persiflage, playing on the arts of life, offer us a valuable legacy. We have been too ready to accuse Walpole of malicious and satirical mockery, branding him the 'representative scoffer' (HWC 2. 225, n. 9) when he was merely playful.[15] Johan Huizinga's estimate of Walpole as the exemplary eighteenth-century man of play, *homo ludens*, is a better likeness than Macaulay's biased portrait of the trifler:

> If ever a style and a *Zeitgeist* were born in play it was in the middle of the 18th century. . . . The Classicism of Adam, Wedgwood and Flaxman was born of the 18th century's light and playful touch. . . . We can actually observe Romanticism being born in play, as a literary and historical fact. Its birth-certificate is provided by the letters of Horace Walpole. Perusing them, one becomes increasingly aware that this remarkable man, the father of Romanticism if ever it had one, still remained extremely classicist in his views and convictions.[16]

Ideas of 'zeitgeist' and classic-to-romantic teleology have been discredited, and few would now describe Walpole as the 'father of romanticism', but *homo ludens* Walpole certainly was, and Huizinga's book makes it perfectly clear that the playful man in the Aristotelian sense is more than a trifler.

Walpole drew the portrait of himself as Prime Minister of Taste at a cost. I do not think it romantic to see in his self-portrait one of Watteau's pictures of Harlequin. In his youth Walpole painted watercolour copies of Watteau's pictures (13. 91),[17] and repeatedly compared himself to Harlequin, the comic character in the Italian *commedia dell'arte* who wears a mask and parti-coloured costume, constantly committing blunders and absurdities: 'Harlequin, my dear favourite Harlequin, my passion, makes me more melancholy than cheerful' (10. 176), Walpole writes of himself to George Montagu. But Walpole never removed himself completely from his father's shadow, and his self-deprecation occasionally leads him close to nihilism. 'Je fais un plaisir de négatifs', (I take pleasure in negatives) (6. 82); 'I am perfectly indifferent about living' (39. 79). As far as we can tell, except for his mother (HWC 37. xiii), Walpole never experienced intimacy in human relationships: 'Je n'aime que moi', (I love only myself) (5. 262). Surrounded by society, he preferred to live a life of self-sufficiency and almost monastic isolation. He forfeited a chance to achieve excellence in a profession because he could not bring himself to take his career as a writer seriously, although it is clear from his autobiographical notes (13. 1–51) that he thought of himself as a writer. Compared to Pope who sacrificed everything to his art, Walpole wasted his literary talent in trifles. And yet he was able to paint in his inimitable letters an unforgettable picture of the Indian summer of the English aristocracy. This picture, like his own self-portrait, is filled with unfailingly playful wit, but we are looking at a Watteau painting (plate 122) of the embarkation of the English aristocracy for the island of oblivion.

Short Titles and Abbreviations

Aedes: Horace Walpole, *Aedes Walpolianae: or, A Description of the Collection of Pictures at Houghton Hall in Norfolk, The Seat of Sir Robert Walpole, Works* (1798), vol. 2.

Anecdotes: Horace Walpole, *Anecdotes of Painting in England*, ed. Ralph N. Wornum, 3 vols, 1876.

BM Satires: British Museum, Department of Prints and Drawings, *Catalogue of Prints and Drawings . . . Political and Personal Satires*, 10 vols., 1870– 1952.

Constable, *Canaletto*: W. G. Constable, *Canaletto: Giovanni Antonio Canal 1697–1768*, 2d ed., rev. by J. G. Links. Oxford, 1989.

Crown, 'Sketches': Patricia Crown, 'An Album of Sketches from the Royal Academy Exhibitions of 1780–1784,' *Huntington Library Quarterly* 44. 1 (Winter 1980) 61–6.

DNB: *Dictionary of National Biography*, eds. Leslie Stephen and Sidney Lee, reissue, 22 vols, (1908– 9).

G III: Horace Walpole, *Memoirs of the Reign of King George the Third*, ed. G. F. Russell Barker, 4 vols, 1894.

GVN: *The Notebooks of George Vertue*, Walpole Society vols 18, 20, 22, 24, 26, 29. Oxford, 1930–47. Cited in text by volume and page, spelling and syntax normalized.

Hayes, *Landscape*: John Hayes. *The Landscape Paintings of Thomas Gainsborough.* 2 vols. London, 1982.

Hazen: *A Catalogue of Horace Walpole's Library*, 3 vols. New Haven and London, 1969. Cited in text by book number.

Hearn, *Dynasties*: Karen Hearn, ed. *Dynasties: Paintings in Tudor and Jacobean England 1530–1630*. London, 1995.

HW: Horace Walpole (1717–1797).

HWC: W. S. Lewis, ed. *The Yale Edition of Horace Walpole's Correspondence.* 48 vols. New Haven, 1937–83. Cited in text by volume and page; translations from French letters (HWC 3–8) by the author.

HW Portraits: 'The Portraits of Horace Walpole', by C. Kingsley Adams and W. S. Lewis. Walpole Society, 1968–70, vol. 42, pp. 1–34.

Johnson, *Cotes*: Edward Mead Johnson. *Francis Cotes*. London, 1976.

Kerslake: John Kerslake. *Early Georgian Portraits*. 2 vols. London, 1977.

Larsen: Erik Larsen. *The Paintings of Anthony Van Dyck.* 2 vols. Düsseldorf, 1988.

Lloyd, *Cosway*: Stephen Lloyd. *Richard & Maria Cosway: Regency Artists of Taste and Fashion.* Edinburgh: Scottish National Portrait Gallery, 1995.

LWL: Lewis Walpole Library, Farmington, CT.

Mannings, *Reynolds*: David Mannings, *Sir Joshua Reynolds: Catalogue raisonné*. New Haven and London, 2000.

Millar, *Early Georgian*:
Oliver Millar. *The Tudor, Stuart and Early Georgian Pictures in the Collection of Her Majesty the Queen*. London, 1963.

Millar, *Later Georgian*:
Oliver Millar. *The Later Georgian Pictures in the Collection of Her Majesty the Queen*. 2 vols. London, 1969.

Millar, *Zoffany's Tribuna*:
Oliver Millar. *Zoffany and his Tribuna*. London, 1966.

Piper, 1963: David Piper. *Catalogue of Seventeeth-Century Portraits in the National Portrait Gallery 1625–1714*. Cambridge, 1963.

Piper, *English Face*: David Piper. *The English Face*. 2d ed. Malcolm Rogers. London, 1992.

Pressly, *Life*: William L. Pressly. *The Life and Art of James Barry*. New Haven and London, 1981.

RA: Academy of Arts, London. Collection of Cat-alogues anno-tated by HW (1769–96; Hazen 3885). Countess Rosebery, Dalmeny House, South Queens-ferry, West Lothian, Scotland. Cited in text by year of exhibition, cata-logue number of exhibit, and page. E.G., RA 69. 91, p. 11 = The First Exhibition of the Royal Academy, 1769; exhibit No. 91, Reynolds's *Et in Arcadia Ego*; page 11.

RA Index: Index to Royal Academy Exhi-bitions 1769– 1795, unpublished typescript of exhibited pictures, illustrated with photocopies, at the Courtauld Institute of Art, London.

Roux, *Graveurs*. Marcel Roux. *Graveurs du XVIII Siècle*. vol. 4. Paris: Bibliothèque Nationale, 1940.

SA: Society of Arts, Artists, and Free Society. Collection of Catalogues Annotated by HW (Hazen 3885). Lewis Walpole Library, Farm-ington, CT. Cited in text by year of exhibition, catalogue number of exhibit, and page. E.g., SA 61. 43, p. 6 = Society of Artists Catalogue 1761; exhibit No. 43, Hogarth's *Sigis-munda*; page 6.

Scharf: George Scharf. *A Descriptive and Historical Catalogue of the Coll-ection of Pictures at Woburn Abbey*. London, 1890.

Seznec, *Salons*: Jean Seznec, ed. *Diderot Salons*. 4 vols. Oxford, 1967.

Strong, *Icon*: Roy Strong, *The British Icon: Elizabethan & Jacobean Portraiture*. New Haven and London, 1969.

Strong, *Tudor*: Roy Strong, *Tudor & Jacobean Portraits*. 2 vols. London, 1969.

Van Erffa and Staley: Helmut von Erffa, and Allen Staley. *The Paintings of Benjamin West*. New Haven and London, 1986.

Visits: 'Horace Walpole's Journal of Visits to Country Seats', ed. Paget Toynbee, Walpole Society, vol. 16 (1927–8) 9–80.

Wheelock: Arthur K. Wheelock, Jr., Susan J. Barnes, and Julian S. Held. *Anthony van Dyck*. New York, 1990.

White, *Dutch Pictures*:
Christopher White, *The Dutch Collection of Pictures in the Collection of Her Majesty the Queen*. Cam-bridge, 1982.

Works: *The Works of Horatio Walpole, Earl of Orford*, 5 vols. 1798.`

YCBA: Yale Center for British Art, New Haven, CT.

Notes

Chapter 1   Introduction, The Trifler Restored

1   See Kenneth Clark, 'Ruins and Rococo: Strawberry Hill', *The Gothic Revival*, 3d ed. (London: J. Murray, 1962) 50–75. See also Michael McCarthy, *The Origins of the Gothic Revival* (New Haven and London, 1987), and Clive Wainwright, *The Romantic Interior* (New Haven and London, 1989).

2   See Thomas Babington Macaulay, review of *Letters of Horace Walpole, Earl of Orford, to Sir Thomas Mann, Edinburgh Review* 58 (October 1833), 227–58. For a typical example of Macaulay's conflation of Walpole's character with his collection, see p. 2: 'Serious business was a trifle to him, and trifles were his serious business . . . he unbent his mind in the House of Commons. And, having indulged in the recreation of making laws and voting millions, he returned to more important pursuits, to researches after Queen Mary's comb, Wolsey's red hat, the pipe which Von Tromp smoked during his last sea-fight, and the spur which King William stuck into the flank of Sorrel.'

3   See R. W. Ketton-Cremer, *Horace Walpole: A Biography*, 3d ed. (1940; London, 1964).

4   See *The History of Tom Jones, A Foundling*, ed. Martin C. Battestin, 2 vols., The Wesleyan Edition of the Works of Henry Fielding (Oxford, 1975), Book XV, chap. 1, 2: 783.

5   See Hazen 309, *An Account* (1722), and Hazen 310: *Two Discourses*. I. *An Essay on the Art of Criticism as It Relates to Painting. . . .* II. *An Argument in Behalf of the Science of a Connoiseur* (London, 1719). See also 'The Complicated Richardson' (c. 1734), *Hogarth's Graphic Works*, comp. Ronald Paulson (New Haven and London, 1965) 1: 314–15, plate 337.

6   For a clear account of Richardson's criticism, see Lawrence Lipking, *The Ordering of the Arts in Eighteenth-Century England* (Princeton, 1970), chap. 5.

7   See Samuel Johnson, *Rasselas*, ed. Gwin J. Kolb, The Yale Edition of the Works of Samuel Johnson, vol. 17, chap. 11, 46.

8   See Rensselaer W. Lee, '*Ut Pictura Poesis*: The Humanist Theory of Painting', *Art Bulletin* 12 (1940), 197–209.

9   See Jonathan Richardson the younger's MS interlineated note in the annotated French translation of *Works* (Amsterdam, 1728) now in the London Library: *Description de divers fameux tableaux . . . en Italie*, vol. 3, 103. Hereafter cited Richardson, *Annotated Works* (1728).

10   See Walter Alison Phillips, *Encyclopedia Britannica*, 11th ed., 11. 604, s.v. 'gentleman'.

11   See Reginald C. Haggar, *A Dictionary of Art Terms* (New York, 1962), 318.

12   See *OED* 16. 344, quoting E. H. Gombrich, *Art and Illusion*, III vi. 193.

13   See Sir Thomas Hoby, trans., *The Book of the Courtier, by Baldasare Castiglione* (London, 1928), 1. 41, hereafter cited in the text by part and page.

14   See HW's compliment to his friend and correspondent, George Simon, 2d Earl Harcourt (1736–1809), whom he calls 'quite Count Castiglione the perfect courtier' (HWC 33. 463).

15   My quotations, hereafter cited in the text are taken from Walpole's annotated copy of the first edition, 2 vols. (London, Dodsley, 1774; Hazen 436).

16   The year Chesterfield died (1773) Walpole told Anne Liddell about Chesterfield's buying a landscape 'which somebody was so good as to paint a few months ago for Claud Lorrain [1600–82]' (23. 466): 'My Lord Chesterfield bought a Claud t'other day for four hundred guineas and a Madame de la Valière [a mistress of Louis XIV] for four. He said, "Well! if I am laughed at for giving so much for a landscape, at least it must be allowed that I have my women cheap." Is not it charming to be so agreeable quite to the door of one's coffin?' (HWC 32. 102–3; 11 March 1773).

17   See HW Portraits, A 13, plates 13 and 17a.

18   HW, *Memoirs of King George II*, ed. John Brooke, 3 vols. (New Haven, 1985) 3. 43.

Chapter 2   No Connoisseur: Collecting on the Grand Tour

1   For the hang of the Downing Street pictures in Sir Robert Walpole's collection, see 'Drawings of the two principal apartments of the Treasury-House in Downing street, as it was altered and fitted up by Sr. Robert Walpole', in the extra-illustrated *Aedes Walpolianae* (Hazen 3546; Metropolitan Museum of Art, New York; acc. no. 25. 62), leaves 67–70.

2   See Joseph Addison, *Remarks on Several Parts of Italy* (1726; Hazen 1844), 225.

3   For a summary of HW's acquisition of the eagle and present location, see HWC 3. 405, n. 4: 'In 1936 Walpole's eagle was in the possession of Earl Weymiss, Gosford House, Longniddry, East Lothian'.

4   According to Mary Berry, 'Mr Walpole in these letters calls the Strawberry committee those of his friends [principally John Chute and Richard Bentley] who had assisted in the plans and Gothic ornaments of Strawberry Hill' (HWC 35. 177, n. 7 a). See W. S. Lewis, 'The Genesis of Strawberry Hill', *Metropolitan Museum Studies* 5. 63.

5   See *Epistles to Several Persons*, ed. F.W. Bateson, *The Twickenham Edition of the Poems of Alexander Pope* [hereafter TE] (London, 1951) 3. 2, 130.

6   See Lord Byron, 'Preface' to *Marino Faliero* (1820), *The Complete Poetical Works*, ed. Jerome J. McGann, 4 vols. (Oxford, 1980–6) 4. 305.

7   Walpole also thought the eagle a convenient place on which to hang his verses. Mary Berry notes that he was planning in 1792 to hang round the eagle's neck 'some lines . . . [he] had written extolling the Duke of York's [Frederick (1763–1827)] military fame, and conquests in Holland, which the unfortunate issue of the campaign obliged him to suppress'. See HWC 12. 11, n. 8.

8   See Adolf Michaelis, *Ancient Marbles in Great Britain* (Cambridge, 1882), 68–9, 300.

9   See Lesley Lewis, *Connoisseurs and Secret Agents in Eighteenth Century Rome* (London, 1961).

10   See R. A. G. Carson, *Principal Coins of the Romans*, vol. 2 *The Principate* 31 BC-AD 296 (London, 1980), 86, No. 745.

11   See Johann Joachim Winckelmann, *Description des pierres gravées du feu Baron de Stosch* (Florence 1760; Hazen 3767).

12   See E. H. Toelken, *Erklärendes Verzichniss der antiken vertuft geschnittenen Steine der Königlich Preussischen Gemmensammlung* (Berlin, 1835), 324.

13   See Winckelmann (1760) for references to Stosch's Galla Placidia.

14   See the manuscript in HW's library, *A Collection of the Spintrian Medals of Tiberius* (Hazen 2599).

15   Including Francis I (1708–65), Holy Roman Emperor and Grand Duke of Tuscany (HWC 21. 149), Madame de Pompadour (21. 201), Frederick the Great (21. 186), and George III (21. 478).

16   See illustration, HWC 18, opp. 45. See also *Medallic Illustrations of the History of Great Britain and Ireland* (Lon-don, 1907–11), Part III, plate clx, no. 1 (HWC 18, vii).

17   Elsewhere in notes to his transcription of the Mann correspondence, Walpole refers to 'Baron Stosch, a great virtuoso and antiquary, settled at Florence' (20. 475, n. 11).

18   *Connoisseurs and Secret Agents* (1961), 50, and 54.

19   See references to medals from Stosch's collection in Walpole's SH Description, *Works* 2. 451, Nos. 8 and 21. See also HW's MS note in SH Description (1774; Hazen 2523. 95) on 'Germanicus [plate 7], very fine intaglia on cornelian . . . from the collection of the marquis Riccordi at Florence. In Baron Stosch's collection of pierres gravées [Hazen 3762] which have the names of their artists, there is another Germanicus with the name of the same workman Epitynchanes. It is larger than Mr Walpole's and represents that prince younger, but it is imperfect, the lower part being broken off directly from the chin.'

20   My translation of a letter in French quoted by Lewis, *Connoisseurs and Secret Agents*, 72.

21   My translation of a letter in French quoted by Lewis, *Connoisseurs and Secret Agents*, 58.

22   See, for example, the Andrea dell Sarto 'not in good keeping' that Horace Mann bought for HW 'by accident at Paulin Dolce's sale' (18. 214; 30 April 1743), 'a dirty picture vastly spoilt and ill-used' attributed to Guido Reni (17. 138), and a copy of Guido, 'a wretched raw daub' HW commissioned from Donato Creti (18. 292; 14 August 1743).

23   The first was Correggio's *La Notte*. See Richardson, *Tableaux en Italie, Annotated Works* (1728) 3. 676–7: 'La fameuse Notte du Corrége. . . . . éffectivement, c'est peut-être la première Pièce du Monde, pour le Clair-obscur' (It is perhaps the first picture in the world for chiaroscuro).

24   See Richardson's description of Correggio's *St Jerome and the Virgin* in the church of Saint Anthony Abbate at Parma, *Tableaux en Italie, Annotated Works* (1728), 662–3: 'Il est exquis & parfaitement bien conservé, fort beau & fort éclatant' (It is exquisite and perfectly well preserved, very beautiful and very striking).

25   Dr Robert Bragge (d. 1777), a dealer of unsavoury reputation Walpole and his father had dealings with. See Iain Pears, *The Discovery of Painting* (New Haven and London, 1988),192–6.

26   For Walpole's attribution to Domenichino, see *Aedes Walpolianae, Works* 2. 278. For the attribution to Giovanni Battista Salvi, called Sassoferrato

(1609–85), see *Hermitage Catalogue of European Painting* (Leningrad, 1976), 133, Inventory 1506. For the definitive identification of the picture as a copy by Salvi of an engraving after Pierre Mignard (1612–95), see Jean-Claude Boyer, and François Macé de Lépinay, 'The Mignardes, Sassoferrato and Roman Classicism During the 1650s,' *Burlington Magazine* 123 (February 1981), 69–75.

27 See Richard E. Spear, *Domenichino*, 2 vols. (New York and London, 1982) No. 85 (1623–5), pl. 264, and colour plate 6.

28 See, for example, Domenichino's *Cumaean Sibyl*, Spear No. 51 (1616–17), pls. 171–2.

29 See HW, *Book of Materials* (Hazen 2615), 1 (1759), p. 105.

30 See Richardson, *Annotated Works* (1728), 'Historical and Chronological List of Painters', 1. 217–20.

31 Francis Haskell, *Patrons and Painters* (New Haven and London, 1980), 130–1.

32 See Hazen 2483 (1st ed. 1747); Hazen No. 3931 (2d ed. 1752); Hazen 3932 (3d ed. 1767); and *Works* (1798).

33 See Hazen No. 3546, now in the possession of the Metropolitan Museum of Art, leaf 59 verso. For the print, François de Poilly after Pierre Mignard's drawing of Salvi's picture, see José Lothe 'L'Oeuvre gravé de François et Nicolas de Poilly d'Abbeville' (Paris: Commission des travaux historiques de la ville de Paris, 1994), No. 308. See also Boyer and Lépinay, 'The "Mignardes" ', *Burlington Magazine* (February 1981), 68–76.

34 See Lada Nikolenko, *The Grove Dictionary of Art*, ed. Jane Turner (London, 1996) 21. 497–9.

35 See Boyer and Lépinay, 'The "Mignardes" ', 69.

36 Cited by Boyer and Lépinay, p. 70, n. 6: Abbé de Monville, *La Vie de Pierre Mignard, Premier Peintre du roy* (Paris 1730). lvi–lvii. For Walpole's Amsterdam edition of the following year, see Hazen 998: Simon Philippe, Mazière de Monville, *La Vie de Pierre Mignard* (Amsterdam, 1731).

37 Quotations from Richardson's *Annotated Works* (1728), *Un Discours sur la science d'un connoisseur*, 2. 194 and 198; and *Un Essai sur l'art de critiquer, en fait de Peinture*, 2. 84.

38 For Burlington's *Madonna della Rosa* (c. 1630), see Spear No. 107, 1. 284–5, pl. 351; for his father's *The Rebuke of Adam and Eve* (1628–30), see Spear No. 104, 1. 279–81, pl. 344.

Chapter 3   Keeper of the Prime Minister's Pictures

1 See MS 'Drawings of the two principal apartments of the Treasury-House in Downing-street as it was altered and fitted up by Sir Robert Walpole', extra-illustrated *Aedes Walpolianae*, Metropolitan Museum of Art (Hazen 3546). For

the best recent study of Robert Walpole's collection, see Andrew Moore, *Houghton Hall: The Prime Minister, The Empress and the Heritage* (London, 1996).

2 *Sir Robert Walpole* [vol. 2]: *The King's Minister* (London, 1960) 2. 87. See also *Sir Robert Walpole*: [vol. 1] *The Making of a Statesman* (London, 1956). Hereafter cited in text.

3 'Howard, the framemaker, acted for him at the Duke of Portland's sale in 1711.' See Denys Sutton, 'Aspects of British Collecting, Part I, iv. The Age of Sir Robert Walpole,' *Apollo* 114 (November 1981), 334.

4 See Richardson's annotated *Works* (1728) 3. 567, marginalia by Jonathan Richardson, Jr.

5 For Maratti's *History of Rebecca*, see H. Avray Tipping, 'Houghton Hall, Norfolk,' *English Homes*, Period V–vol. I, *Early Georgian, 1714–1760* (London, 1921), 97.

6 See James Lees-Milne, *Earls of Creation* (London, 1962).

7 Andrew Moore, *Dutch and Flemish Painting in Norfolk* (London, 1988), 11.

8 See the Dyce copy at the Victoria & Albert Museum (Hazen 2483), 73.

9 See Oliver Goldsmith, *The Vicar of Wakefield*, *Collected Works*, Arthur Friedman (ed.), 5 vols. (Oxford, 1966), vol. 4, ch. 16. 83.

10 Iain Pears, *The Discovery of Painting*, New Haven and London, 1988, 77.

11 Ibid., 84, and n. 126 (245–6), plate 25, and p 81.

12 *Richardsoniana* (London, 1776) vol. 1. 336, quoted by Pears, 196–7.

13 For John Ellis, see GVN 3. 38; Denys Sutton, *Aspects of British Collecting*, Part I, iv, 'The Age of Sir Robert Walpole', *Apollo* 114 (November 1981), 334; and Edward Croft-Murray, *Decorative Painting in England 1537–1837*, vol. 2 (London, 1970), 204–5. For the price of Van Dyck's *Holy Family*, see Gerald Reitlinger, *The Economics of Taste* (New York, 1961), 474.

14 Throughout this paragraph I rely on Walpole's annotations in the Dyce copy of *Aedes Walpolianae* (Hazen 2483).

15 Quoted by Denys Sutton, *Aspects of British Collecting*, Part I, iii, 'Augustan Virtuosi,' *Apollo* (November 1981), 313.

16 For typology of contemporary collectors, see Frank Hermann, *The English as Collectors* (London, 1972), and Denys Sutton, *Aspects of British Collecting*, Part II, v, 'New Trends,' *Apollo* 116 (December 1982). 358–72.

17 See Hieronymus Tetius [Girolamo Teti], *Aedes Barberinae ad Quirinalem . . . descriptae* (Rome, 1642; Hazen 3725). See Francis Haskell, *Patrons and Painters* (1980). 54–6, and plate 9.

18 Francis Henry Taylor, *The Taste of Angels: A History of Art Collecting from Ramses to Napoleon*

19   See the manuscript list of presentation copies in the annotated Dyce copy at the Victoria & Albert Museum (Hazen 2483), including Richard Bentley, John Chute, Thomas Gray, Frederick Louis (1707–51; Prince of Wales), Horace Mann, George Montagu, Arthur Pond, Mr Reynolds, Sir Luke Schaub, Joseph Spence, and James West.

20   See the Dyce copy of the first edition in the Victoria & Albert Museum (Hazen 2483); a copy of the second edition (1752) in the Morgan Library (Hazen 3931); a copy of the third edition (1767) in the Louis Walpole Library (Hazen 3932); and the copy in Walpole's posthumous *Works* (vol. 2, 1798). See also the extra-illustrated fair copy, possibly Thomas Kirgate's hand, in the Metropolitan Museum of Art (Hazen 3546).

21   R. W. Ketton-Cremer, *Horace Walpole, A Biography* (New York, 1940), 98.

22   Pears, op. cit., 203.

23   Walpole commissioned a portrait from John Wootton (1682–1764), to whom Patapan sat 6 May 1743: 'Patapan sits to Wootton tomorrow for his picture. He is to have a triumphal arch at a distance, to signify his Roman birth, and his having barked at thousands of Frenchmen in the very heart of Paris' (HWC 18. 220–1).

24   See George Vertue, *Catalogue of the Curious Collection of Pictures of George Villiers, Duke of Buckingham* (1758; Hazen 2479.3), with an introduction by HW.

25   See George Vertue (ed.), *Catalogue and Description of King Charles the First's Capital Collection of Pictures, by Abraham van der Dort* (London, 1757; Hazen 2478).

26   See *Epistles to Several Persons*, F. W. Bateson (ed.), TE 3.2 (London, 1951), 151, line 204.

27   See Oliver Millar, 'Philip, Lord Wharton, and his Collection of Portraits,' *Burlington Magazine* 136 (August 1994), 517–30.

28   See *Aedes Walpolianae passim*, and Hazen 3546, leaf 58 for *Moses in the Bullrushes*. See also Walpole's portfolios of engravings after such artists as Raphael, and Guido Reni (Hazen 3609 and 3610).

29   See, for example, Walpole's discussion of 'an anachronism which may be pardoned in a painter' in Le Mer's *Consulting the Sibylline Oracles* (*Works* 2. 256).

30   See Lawrence Stone's epigraph from Psalm 49 for *The Crisis of the Aristocracy 1558–1641* (Oxford, 1967): 'Their inward thought is that their houses shall continue for ever and their dwelling places to all generations; they call their lands after their own names. Nevertheless man being in honour abideth not; he is like the beasts that perish.'

31   John Butt (ed.), *Imitations of Horace*, TE 4 (New York and Oxford, 1942), *Epistle* II ii (1737), 183, lines 246–51.

32   Quoted by Pears, op. cit., 248, n. 155. A unique, priced copy of the catalogue in the Bodleian library lists 125 lots 'of which 60 were sold for a total of £851. 11s. 6d. Other sales of the Walpole collection took place in 1748/49 and 1751.'

33   See Butt, op. cit., TE 4 (New York and Oxford, 1942), *Satires* II ii (1734), 69, lines 175–8.

34   See *A Set of Prints engraved after the most capital paintings in the collection of . . . the Empress of Russia, lately in the possession of the Earl of Orford at Houghton in Norfolk. With plans, and descriptions of the paintings from* Aedes Walpolianae, 2 vols. (London: Boydell, 1788; Hazen 3572). See also Gregory M. Rubenstein, 'Richard Earlom (1743–1822) and Boydell's *Houghton Gallery*,' *Print Quarterly* 8, 1 (March 1991), 1. 27.

35   See Denys Sutton, 'Aspects of British Collecting – Part II, Cross-Currents in Taste,' *Apollo* 116 (December 1982), 388; and Frank Hermann, *The English as Collectors*, 82.

36   Edward Croft-Murray lists three of Cipriani's easel pictures in storage at Houghton Hall, Norfolk, not including *Theodore and Honoria*. See *Decorative Painting in England*, 2 (1970), 186, No. 8.

37   Maynard Mack (ed.), TE 3.1 (London, 1950), Epistle II, 89, line 288.

Chapter 4   *George Vertue: Walpole's Privy Councillor for Portraits*

1   See *HW Portraits*, A. 10.1: 13, plate 9.

2   See 'Some Account of George Vertue', GVN 1. 1–21, and 'The Life of Mr. George Vertue', *Works* 4. 119–29.

3   GVN 1. facing p. 1, plate II, 'W. Humphrey fec't.'

4   See GVN 1, frontispiece, plate I, and notes GVN 1. 162.

5   See Roy Strong, *The English Icon: Elizabethan & Jacobean Portraiture* (London, 1969), No. 30, colour plate. The sitters have recently been renamed Lady Mary Neville and her son, Gregory Fiennes, 10th Baron Dacre, and the picture dated 1559. See Susan Foister, 'Nobility Reclaimed', *Antique Collector* (April 1986), 58–60.

6   HW's friend, the antiquary Michael Lort, welcomed his *Anecdotes* 'as one of the desiderata in literature, materials collected with zeal, industry and fidelity by one man [Vertue], disposed, digested and embellished by the parts and genius of another [HW]' (16. 142; 14 March 1762).

7   See Strong, *op. cit.*, 10 and 91, No. 30.

8   For *The Battle of the Spurs*, see Oliver Millar, *The Tudor, Stuart, and Early Georgian Pictures in the Collection of Her Majesty the Queen* (London, 1963), No. 23. 54, plate 9.

9   See Louise Lippincott, *Selling Art in Georgian*

London: The Rise of Arthur Pond (New Haven and London, 1983).

10   Vertue devotes almost half of his autobiography to an account of the generosity of his patrons. See GVN 1. 8–14.

11   See 'List of Persons to whom I have given the *Aedes Walpolianae*,' (Hazen 2483; Dyce copy, Victoria & Albert Museum), back endpaper *verso*.

12   See, for example, Vertue's copy of a portrait of Mary, Queen of Scots in Walpole's collection (HWC 40. 365); Walpole's large portfolios of Vertue's prints and drawings (Hazen 3664–5); and Walpole's 'List of Vertue's Works,' appendix to his *Life of Vertue* (*Works* 4. 130–54).

13   Walpole owned another miniature he called Lady Anne Clifford, and attributed to Nicholas Dixon. See typescript catalogue of pictures at the Lewis Walpole Library, p. 192.

14   See *Works* 4. 85; and HWC 1. 355, n. 10.

15   See Sir Wallace Notestein, *Four Worthies* (1957), 158–60; G. F. Russell Barker, DNB 4. 512; and GEC 3. 295–7. For Anne Clifford's iconography, see George C. Williamson, *Lady Anne Clifford* (Kendal, 1922), ch. 20.

16   For the portrait of the dancing Countess, Lucy Harrington (1581–1627) by Marcus Gheeraerts, see George Scharf, *Catalogue of Pictures at Woburn Abbey* (1890), No. 75. 53–4; Cornelius Johnson's portrait is Scharf, No. 74. 53.

17   For the portrait of Edward Courtenay (1526–56), 11th Earl of Devonshire, see Scharf, No. 10.

18   See HWC 15. 112–15; and 42. 320–2.

19   See Lawrence Lipking, *Ordering of the Arts* (Princeton, NJ, 1970). 136.

20   See, for example, compliments from Lord Beauchamp (HWC 38. 151); Michael Lort (16. 142), and Henry Zouch (16. 46).

21   J. Douglas Stewart challenges Walpole's idea of 'a dichotomy in Kneller's oeuvre'. See *Sir Godfrey Kneller and the English Baroque Portrait* (Oxford, 1983), 80 and 83.

22   See here and throughout this paragraph S. R. Gardiner, DNB 20. 1179–94.

Chapter 5   Portraits at Strawberry Hill – I

1   See HWC 32, p. 140, n. 13, and illustration facing page. See also Walter Strickland, 'Hugh Douglas Hamilton,' Walpole Society 2 (1912–13), 99–110.

2   See also the silhouette portrait of Anne Liddell by Jean Huber (1721–86) that consoled Walpole for her absence from the Coronation of George III: HWC 32. 1, pl. facing page.

3   See HWC 9. 279–80 for Walpole's description of the trial. Ferrers was found guilty of murdering his steward John Johnson, and executed at

Tyburn. Walpole owned a transcript of the trial (Hazen 1112), and a pen and wash drawing by Samuel Wale (pl. 32; LWL 765/O/76).

4   Quotations with normalized spelling taken from Walpole's MS *Book of Materials* 1 (1759; Hazen 2615), 63–4, and 'Walpoliana: A Dream of Horace Walpole,' *Blackwood's Magazine* 221 (April 1927), 454–6.

5   Granville Leveson, 2d Earl Gower (1721–1803), Walpole's friend and London neighbour in Arlington Street, who had been appointed George II's Master of the Horse on 2 July 1757.

6   See George Vertue (ed.), *Catalogue and Description of King Charles the First's Capital Collection*, by Abraham van der Dort (d. 1640), introduction by HW (London, 1757; Hazen 2478).

7   Selwyn 'erected a good marble bust [by Roubiliac] of the Martyr in a little gallery' at his seat, Matson, Gloucestershire. See HWC 1. 341.

8   See Richard Bentley, *Drawings and Designs* (Hazen 3585): 'Sketch of the Gallery at Strawberry Hill', pencil, ink, and wash drawing

9   To place Walpole's dream in a psychological context, see Terry Castle, 'The Spectralization of the Other in *The Mysteries of Udolfo*', *The New Eighteenth Century* (New York and London, 1987), Ch. 11. 231–53, n. 307–10.

10   See John Gough Nichols, 'The Pictures Once at Strawberry Hill Attributed to English History,' *Notes and Queries*, Ser. III, vol. 10 (28 July 1866), 61.

11   See C. W. C. Oman, *Coinage of England* (Oxford, 1931), 242, pl. XXV (7).

12   The label text for *Virgin and Child with Saints* (c. 1472), now in the Metropolitan Museum on loan to the Department of European Paintings (L.1999.45), ascribes the triptych to Hugo van der Goes. See Claus Grimm, 'A Rediscovered Work by Hugo van der Goes', *Journal of the Walters Art Gallery* 46 (1988), 77–91. See also the exhibition catalogue, *From Van Eyck to Bruegel: Early Netherlandish Painting in the Metropolitan Museum of Art*, ed. Maryan W. Ainsworth and Keith Christiansen (New York, 1998), 208, 210 (figs. 79a and 79b).

Chapter 6   Portraits at Strawberry Hill – II

1   Notes on Edmund Waller's *Works* (1729; Hazen 472).

2   See Walpole's 'Notes to the Pictures at Woburn Abbey' (1791), *Annual Register* 43 (1801), No. 24. 489–90.

3   See Edward Hyde, Earl of Clarendon, *The History of the Rebellion and Civil Wars in England*, 3 vols. (Oxford, 1702–17; Hazen 41) 1. 57.

4   *Annual Register* 43, No. 26, p. 488.

5   See George Scharf, *Catalogue of Pictures at*

Woburn Abbey (1890), No. 118. 80–1.

6 See Sir Anthony Weldon's *The Court and Character of King James I* (1650; Hazen 1767); David Lloyd's *State Worthies* (1670; Hazen 1752); Arthur Wilson's *Life and Reign of King James* (1653; Hazen 910); collections of trials (Hazen 870, and 1724); and Edmund Sawyer (ed.), *Memorials of Affairs of State . . . Compiled from the Papers of Sir Ralph Winwood* (1725; Hazen 1100).

7 Quoted by Jill Finsten, *Isaac Oliver: Art at the Courts of Elizabeth I and James I*, 2 vols. (New York and London, 1981), vii.

8 Quoted by Graham Reynolds, 'A Masterpiece by Isaac Oliver', *Victoria & Albert Museum Yearbook* (1974), 9.

9 See Graham Reynolds, *English Portrait Miniatures*, rev. ed. (Cambridge, 1988), 28, fig. 15; and Roy Strong, *The English Renaissance Miniature* (London, 1983), 166.

10 See *Isaac Oliver* (1981) op.cit., 77–8.

11 Alexander Pope, 'Epistle to a Lady,' *Epistles to Several Persons* (ed.), F. W. Bateson, TE 3. 2. 48, lines 15–16.

12 See Rensselaer W. Lee, ' "*Ut Pictura Poesis*": The Humanist Theory of Painting," ' *Art Bulletin* 12 (1940), 197–209. Quotations from Richardson's discussion of Van Dyck's portrait of the Countess of Exeter are taken from *Two Discourses, I: An Essay on the Whole Art of Criticism as it Relates to Painting, Works* (London, 1773).

13 The phrase is Lawrence Lipking's, *The Ordering of the Arts* (1970), 114–15.

14 On the trial, see Augustus Jessopp, DNB 3. 1313–14, s.v. Thomas Cecil, 1st Earl of Exeter; Samuel R. Gardiner, 'The Fall of the Howards', *History of England* (New York: AMS P, 1965), 3, ch. 27. 189–94; Charles Wallace, *James I* (1934; rpt. Freeman, New York, 1969); and David Matthew, *James I* (London, 1967), ch. 19, 'The Howards' Fall', 269–71.

15 See *Catalogue of Pictures and Drawings in the Holbein-Chamber at Strawberry-Hill* (Hazen 2619. 4). For Walpole's drawing of the 'Chimney side' of the Holbein Chamber showing Müntz's copy hanging at top left, see Walpole's extra-illustrated *Description of Strawberry Hill* (1774; Hazen 2523).

16 See George Edward Cokayne, *The Complete Peerage*, rev. by Vicary Gibbs *et al.* (London, 1810–), 4. 249– 50.

17 Walpole revived this exploded hypothesis in *Historic Doubts* (1768): 'The old countess of Desmond, who had danced with Richard, declared he was the handsomest man in the room except his brother Edward, and was very well made' (*Works* 2. 166). Vicary Gibbs refers to the legend of the Countess of Desmond dancing with Richard III as 'the most ornamental' of 'various imaginary embellishments given by Horace Walpole'. See GEC 4 (1916), 250, n.

18 Vicary Gibbs asserts that '[h]er death took place in 1604 . . . but *not*, upon any good evidence, by *falling down from a cherry tree*, as was sung by Tom Moore in his Fudge Letters where he relates/ 'That she lived to much more than a hundred and ten/And was killed by a fall from a cherry tree then./What a frisky old girl!' See GEC 4 (1916), 250, n.

Chapter 7 Portraits at Strawberry Hill – III

1 See Louis Dimier, 'French Portrait-Drawings at Knowsley [Hall, Lancashire],' *Burlington Magazine* 18 (December 1910), 162–8.

2 Quoted by Allen Hazen, *Horace Walpole's Library*, No. 3655, 'Portfolio containing 180 engravings of illustrious persons in France'.

3 See Oliver Millar, *The Tudor, Stuart, and Early Georgian Pictures in the Collection of Her Majesty the Queen*, 2 vols. (London, 1959), No. 260, 1. 125, pl. 108.

4 Two lines of Millamant HW attributes to Lady Wishfort from William Congreve's *Way of the World*, IV. vi, 1, and V. xiii, 36.

5 See oval portraits on copper of Mme de Sévigné, 'when a young widow', and a similar picture of her daughter and chief correspondent, Madame de Grignan, in the Tribune at Strawberry Hill 'on the side opposite to the altar' (*Works* 2. 491).

6 In 1781 HW subscribed to three sets of a five-volume history of the Medici family by Jacopo Raguccio Galluzi (Hazen, Nos. 32, and 3097). When the books arrived at Berkeley Square, he told Horace Mann: 'as you may guess . . . [I] turned to the story of Bianca Capello. It is a little palliated, yet I think was clearly an empoisonment'. See HWC 25. 193; 18 October 1781.

7 See the fictitious collection by Louis D'amours, *Lettres de Ninon de Lenclos au Marquis de Sévigné* (Amsterdam, 1750; Hazen 1185). See also HWC 39. 242, n. 33.

8 See Edgar H. Cohen, *Mademoiselle Libertine: A Portrait of Ninon de Lanclos* (Boston, 1970), 262–5. See also Émile Magne, *Ninon de Lanclos*, trans. Gertrude Scott Stevenson (London, 1926), 208–11: 'Probably no woman has ever had so much romantic nonsense written about her as has Ninon de Lanclos' (287–8).

9 See Antoine Bret's *Mémoires* (1751; rpt. 3 vols. 1775; not in Hazen). The passage from Madame du Deffand's letter (HWC 6. 136) is my translation.

10 The verses allude (line 3) to Jean de la Fontaine (1621–93), 'L'Écrevisse et sa fille' (*Fables* XII. x; Hazen 941), and (line 6) to *Matthew* VII, 3–5, and *Luke* VI, 412.

11 See H. C. Barnard, *Madame de Maintenon and*

Saint-Cyr (1934; rpt. London, 1971).

12 See Émile Magne, *Ninon* (1926), 290.

13 For the picture, now in the National Portrait Gallery (No. 1030), *see* Oliver Millar, *The Later Georgian Pictures in the Collection of her Majesty the Queen* (London, 1965), No. 975. 88, pl. 135. For Walpole's frame and inscription, see *The Autobiography and Correspondence of Mary Granville, Mrs. Delany*, Lady Llanover (ed.), Second Series, 3 vols. (London, 1862) 3. 497–8, and facsimile of HW's inscription, facing 3. 498. See also Jacob Simon, *The Art of the Picture Frame* (London, 1996), 113–14 (figs. 121–2), and 165 (Cat. 54).

14 Marcia Pointon, *Hanging the Head: Portraiture and Social Formation in Eighteenth-Century England* (New Haven and London, 1993), 34–5.

Chapter 8 Identifying Portraits: Walpole's Catalogues and Letters

1 I am defining Walpole's portraits in the correspondence in accordance with Ralph Rader's idea of literary portraiture in Boswell's *Life of Samuel Johnson* (1791). See Ralph Rader, 'Literary Form in Factual Narrative: The Example of Boswell's Johnson', *Essays in Eighteenth-Century Biography*, Philip B. Daglian (ed.), (Bloomington and London, 1968), 26–9.

2 For Walpole's annotated exhibition catalogues, see Hazen 3885. Catalogues of the Society of Arts, Society of Artists, and Free Society dating from the 1760s, are in the Lewis Walpole Library, Farmington, CT (Hazen 3885, nos. 1–14). Bound photocopies of the LWL catalogues are at the Paul Mellon Centre, Bedford Square, London. Walpole's annotated Royal Academy catalogues, twenty-eight numbers (1769–1797), including interleaved pamphlet reviews, are at Dalmeny Castle, West Lothian, Scotland. These were photocopied when disbound by the Courtauld Institute of Art, University of London, Somerset House for the uncompleted Royal Academy Index.

3 See *Notes by Horace Walpole . . . on the Exhibition of the Society of Artists*, Hugh Gatty (ed.), Walpole Society, vol. 27 (1938–59), 60. See also Algernon Graves, *The Society of Artists of Great Britain 1760–1791: A Complete Dictionary of Contributors* (London, 1907).

4 See 'The Papers of the Society of Artists of Great Britain', Walpole Society, vol. 6 (Oxford, 1918), 116–20.

5 See also Walpole's extended comment on this picture quoted by Nicholas Penny (ed.), *Reynolds* (London, 1986), No. 42. 205–7.

6 A conversation piece, portraits of Richard Edgcumbe, George Williams, and Richard Selwyn, semi-annual visitors to Strawberry Hill

Walpole called 'my out of town [party]' (HWC 9. 417, n. 12). See also *Works* 2. 401.

7 See Morris R. Brownell, 'Good Offices for Artists', *Samuel Johnson's Attitude to the Arts* (Oxford, 1989), 49.

8 In his 1763 Society of Arts catalogue Walpole recorded an anecdote about a precursor-exhibit of Madame Tussaud's gallery, a plaster of paris statue of an old man by Benjamin Rackstrow (d. 1772) that 'every body mistook . . . for real' (S. Arts 63, p. 16; HW's MS note). Walpole was taken in too, as he told his cousin Henry Seymour Conway: 'Do you know that, though apprised of what I was going to see, it deceived me, and made such impression on my mind, that, thinking on it as I came home in my chariot, and seeing a woman steadfastly at work in a window in Pall Mall, it made me start to see her move' (HWC 38. 199; 1 May 1763).

9 For HW's presentation copies, see Hazen, vol. 3. 246 (No. 3885), sold at Christie's 12 February 1982 (lot 157).

10 British Museum, Burney Papers. This and subsequent press references are taken from photocopies documenting the unpublished Royal Academy Index at the Courtauld, and files of newspaper notices compiled by Clare Lloyd-Jacob at the Paul Mellon Centre, London.

11 See 'The Royal Academy Exhibition in 1771', a watercolour drawing by one of the exhibitors (No. 12. 4), Michel Vincent, called Charles Brandoin (1733–1807) of Chelsea, signed and dated 1771 (Huntington Art Gallery; acc. no. 63. 52; plate i, front endpaper).

12 Many of the guests listed figure in Walpole's correspondence as correspondents, acquaintances, or visitors to Strawberry Hill: for example, Richard Owen Cambridge (1717–1802); George Grenville (1753–1813), 3rd Earl Temple; William Ponsonby (1704–93), 2d Earl Bessborough; Henry Temple (1739–1802), 2d Viscount Palmerston.

13 *Public Advertiser*, Saturday 17 April 1771. 3. Walpole noted three other purchases in the catalogue: (1) Jeremiah Meyer's miniature portrait enamel (No. 131. 14): 'The King bought it'. (2) Benjamin West's *Death of General Wolfe* (No. 210. 20): 'Ld Grosvenor [Sir Richard Grosvenor (1731–1802)] gave £400 for this'.(3) George Mullins's landscape: 'purchased by Mr Walpole' (No. 267. 24).

14 For the date of this conversation, see HWC 43, 148, *corrigenda* HWC 11. 276, n. 30).

15 The portrait cannot be traced, but the engraving annotated by HW is in the British Museum, Department of Prints and Drawings, Anderdon 61. See also the Royal Academy Index, Courtauld Institute, neg. 629/23 (14).

16 See Martyn Anglesea, 'David Garrick and the Visual Arts', diss., University of Edinburgh, 1971.

17 See App. 1: 'The Nicoll Affair', HWC 14. 193–233.

18 See Martin Postle, 'Patriarchs, Prophets and Paviours: Reynolds's Images of Old Age', *Burlington Magazine* 130 (October 1988), 735–44.

19 On Samuel Dyer's portrait, see Algernon Graves and William Vine Cronin, *A History of the Works of Sir Joshua Reynolds*, 4 vols. (London, 1899–1901) 1. 271–2. For Walpole's pamphlet attributed to Richard Baker, see *Observations on the Pictures Now in Exhibition at the Royal Academy, Spring Gardens, and Mr. Christie's* (London, 1771).

20 See William Congreve, *Love for Love*, Emmett L. Avery (ed.), Regents Restoration Drama Series (Lincoln Nebr., 1966), 72–4. See also *The London Stage 1660–1800*, ed. G. W. Stone (1962), pt. 4 vol. 3, 1444.

21 See James Watson, sc., *The Artist's son, Horace, as David*, mezzotint, RA Index, Courtauld re-photo.

22 See Edgar Wind, 'The Revival of History Painting', *Journal of the Warburg and Courtauld Institute* 2 (1938–9), 116–19; and Charles Mitchell, 'Benjamin West's *The Death of General Wolfe* and the Popular History Piece', *Journal of the Warburg and Courtauld Institute* 7 (1944), 20–33.

23 See James Barry, *Works* (1869) 1. 174.

24 See quotations from the *Gazetteer* (8 May 1771), *Lady's Magazine*, and clipping from an unidentified newspaper dated 25 April 1771 (Victoria & Albert Museum cuttings) in the Royal Academy Index at the Courtauld.

25 See Rudolf and Margot Wittkower, *Born Under Saturn, The Character and Conduct of Artists* (New York, 1963).

26 Cf. Walpole's comment on Gainsborough's painting 'In the style of Rubens, and by far the finest landscape ever painted in England, and equal to the great masters' (RA 77. 136. 12). See also HW's remark on RA 81. 94. 6; pl. 58: 'Gainsborough has two pieces with land and sea, so free and natural that one steps back for fear of being splashed' (HWC 29. 138; 6 May 1781). See John Hayes, *The Landscape Paintings of Thomas Gainsborough: A Critical Text and Catalogue Raisonné*, 2 vols. (London, 1982) 1. 138, pl. 169.

27 Sandby started a drawing, finished by Edward Edwards, of Walpole's Gallery at Strawberry Hill, now LWL. See Hazen 3582, and HWC 41. 189, n. 3.

28 See John C. Riely, 'Horace Walpole and "The Second Hogarth,"' *Eighteenth-Century Studies* 9 (Fall 1975), 28–44. See also BM Satires Nos. 4763, and 4918, and Courtauld Institute photo 814/4 (26).

29 See William T. Whitley, 'Notes on the Catalogues of Eighteenth-Century Exhibitions', *Artists and Their Friends in England 1700–1799*, 2 vols. (London and Boston, 1928) 2. 366: '. . . even our chief authority [for identification of eighteenth-century English portraits], Horace Walpole, is not infallible'.

30 Quoted by Matthew Hodgart (ed.), *Horace Walpole: Memoirs and Portraits* (New York, 1963), 47. Hereafter cited in the text from *Memoirs of the Reign of King George the Third*, G. F. Russell Barker (ed.), 4 vols. (London and New York, 1894).

31 See Romney Sedgwick (ed.), *Some Materials Towards Memoirs of the Reign of King George II, by John Lord Hervey*, 3 vols. (London, 1931) 1. lviii. Sedgwick writes that '[t]he existence of *Memoirs* by the celebrated Lord Hervey . . . was first announced by Horace Walpole in his *Catalogue of Royal and Noble Authors*' (1. xi). See also 'Memoirs from his [Hervey's] first coming to court to the death of the queen [a manuscript]' (Walpole, *Works* 1. 453). For Hodgart's evaluation of Walpole's *Memoirs of George III*, see *Memoirs and Portraits* (1963), xiii.

32 For 'The Death of Lord Hervey, or A Morning at Court, A Drama' (1736), see *Memoirs*, Sedgwick (ed.), 2. 574–5, 585–96.

Chapter 9 Walpole's Portraits in the Letters: Maria Walpole

1 For Dorothy Clement's children, see HWC 9. 13, n. 3; and 43. 111.

2 Walpole admired Maria Walpole's *lèse-majesté*, and compared her to Mary Magdalaine Lombard (1695–1783), a French stay-maker's daughter married to Horatio Walpole, Ambassador to France (1723–30), who answered the French Queen's [Marie-Catherine Leszczyńska (1703–68)] question – 'What family do you belong to? – "D'*aucune* [none], Madame"' – answered my aunt. Don't you think that *aucune* sounded greater than Montmorency would have done? One must have a great soul to be of *Aucune* or *Maria* families, which is not necessary, to be a Howard' (HWC 23. 435; 20 September 1772).

3 See HW Portraits, A 6, pl. 5, p. 9 for Rosalba's portrait of Walpole dated 1741 in 'a grey coat with gold lace, [and] ermine-lined mantle embroidered with blue, white and red flowers and green leaves'.

4 The colour of the Duke of Gloucester's servants as well as the Prince of Wales's.

5 For HW's irony, see Penny, *Reynolds* (1986), No. 122, 292–3. For pictures Walpole may be parodying, see *Lady Elizabeth Keppel, Adorning a Statue of Hymen* (SA 62. 87. 6); *Lady Sarah Bunbury Sacrificing to the Graces* (SA 65. 104. 12); and *Three Ladies [the Montgomery sisters] Adorning a Term of Hymen* (RA 74. 216. 22).

6 Frederick Lord North (1732–92) resigned the following year on 20 March 1782. See HWC 29. 201; 21 March 1782.

7 See *The Compleat Country Dancing Master* (Hazen 1784, 1718–19). For the music, see *The Autobiography and Correspondence of Mary Granville, Mrs. Delany*, Lady Llanover (ed.), 4 (1862), 169.

Chapter 10   Walpole's Portraits in the Letters: Marriage à la Mode

1 See Ellis K. Waterhouse, *Reynolds* (London, 1973), 11, and pl. 94.

2 Frances's father was Henry Pelham (1695–1754), MP and prime minister; her mother Lady Catherine Manners (1701–80).

3 The balding John Manners (1721–70), Marquis of Granby, MP and army officer, whose father gave him twenty-four thousand pounds not to wear a wig. See HWC 38. 481.

4 See Niccolo Francescò Haym, *Del Tesoro Brittanico parte prima*, 2 vols. (London, 1719–20; Hazen 269) 2. 35, 124–5, and plate facing 2. 124.

5 See Claude Prosper Jolyot de Crébillon, *Les Égarements du coeur et de l'esprit, ou memoires de M. de Meilcoeur* (The Hague, 1736; Hazen 1026).

6 See Pierre Carlet Chamblain de Marivaux, *La Vie de Mariane, ou les avantures de Madame la Comtesse de★★★* (Paris, 1742; Hazen 997); and Marivaux's *Le Paysan parvenu* (Frankfurt, 1737; Hazen 1228), and the English translation (Hazen 1902; 1735).

7 See Lady Louisa Stuart, *Notes . . . on George Selwyn*, W. S. Lewis (ed.), (New York, 1928), 25.

8 See Elizabeth, Duchess of Northumberland, *Diaries of a Duchess*, James Greig (ed.), (1926), 44.

9 First printed in *Works* (1798) 4. 393.

10 See Walpole's praise of William Kent's garden design at Esher in 'On Modern Gardening,' *Works* 2. 539. See also Morris R. Brownell, *Alexander Pope & the Arts of Georgian England* (Oxford, 1978), 178, and pl. 37.

11 'Spitalfields, a district and parish in the east of London, between Bishopsgate and Bethnal Green, inhabited by weavers of silk and other poor people'. See Henry B. Wheatley, *London Past and Present* (London, 1891) 3, 291.

12 Walpole's parody of Colley Cibber's remark on Mrs Oldfield in the 'Preface' to *The Provoked Husband*, 'an expression . . . much ridiculed at the time' (HW). See HWC 23. 132, n. 8 (19 July 1769).

13 See BM Satires, 3. 744–6, Nos. 3030–3.

14 Walpole's description of the 'droll print' is quoted in relation to *Gisbal's Preferment* (May 1762), 'an etched satire on the relationship of Lord Bute and the Princess of Wales' (BM Satires 4. 60–3, No. 3849), but Rosemary Baker and Joan Sussler inform me that the print is not in the collections of the British Museum or the Lewis Walpole Library.

15 Walpole describes six of these triumphs, some-times ironically. For example: '[No.] 4. Princess Augusta [Princess Dowager of Wales (1719–72)], a bird of paradise, *Non habet parem* [she has no equal] – unluckily this was translated, *I have no peer*. People laughed out [Princess Augusta was rumored to be having an affair with Lord Bute], considering where this was exhibited [in the house of the mistress of the Duke of Kingston]' (HWC 38. 204, n. 13).

16 For the funeral procession of Eleanor of Castile (d. 28 November, 1290), wife of Edward I, see HWC 32. 146, n. 10. For Mousseline la Sérieuse, see 'Princesse d' Astracan' in *Les Quatre Facardins* (1730) in the fairytale by Anthony Hamilton, *Works* (1749; Hazen 982). See HWC 32. 146, n. 13.

17 Walpole wrote satiric verses 'On the Duchess of Kingston's Going to Rome . . . addressed to the Pope'. See HWC 24. 14, n. 17).

18 See *The Trial of Elizabeth Duchess Dowager of Kingston for Bigamy, Before the Right Honourable the House of Peers, in Westminster-Hall, in Full Parliament* (London, 1776). Walpole's copy has not been traced, but Hazen lists two other records of the trial in Walpole's library: *The Kingston Cause Impartially Stated* (1776; Hazen 1609. 37. 1), and *A Brief for her Grace the Duchess of Kingston* (1776; Hazen 1609. 58. 21).

19 See William K. Wimsatt, Jr., 'James Boswell: The Man and the Journal,' *Yale Review* 49 (September 1959), 80–92.

20 *The London Chronicle* locates her in an apartment of Henry Fiennes Clinton (1720–94), 2d Duke of Newcastle's, adjoining Westminster Hall. See HWC 28. 262, n. 9.

21 A character Walpole believed she had inherited from her mother, Harriet Chudleigh (d. 1756): '. . . [w]hat a heroine her mother was – at least I have not forgotten this story. . . . She was coming home late at night, with two of the old [Chelsea] pensioners as patrol, walking behind the coach. She was asleep, and was awakened by three footpads, one of whom held a pistol at her breast. She coolly put her head out of the other window, and said, "Fire!" The patrol fired, and shot the robber. The daughter [Elizabeth Chudleigh] does not degenerate' (HWC 24. 198; 24 April 1776).

Chapter 11   Walpole's Portraits in the Letters: Scandal

1 For Donald Greene's denial that Johnson made this remark, see 'Boswell's *Life* as "Literary Biography" ', John Vance (ed.), *Boswell's Life of Johnson: New Questions, New Answers* (Athens, GA, 1985), 165–6.

2 See Nicholas Penny, *Reynolds* (1986), No. 48. 214–16.

3 See ibid., No. 203. 389, and Dorothy George, BM Satires 5 (1935), No 6112.

Chapter 12   Walpole's Portraits in the Letters: Aristocrats

1   See Arthur T. Bolton, 'Syon House, Middlesex – III, A Seat of the Duke of Northumberland', *Country Life* 46 (20 December 1919), 838, fig. 1. For Batoni's *The Wedding of Cupid and Psyche* (1753–5), see Anthony M. Clark, *Pompeo Batoni: A Complete Catalogue* (Oxford, 1983) No. 186, 262–4.

2   See Walpole's invitation dated Monday 8 June ?1759, a card designed by Richard Bentley, HWC 40, facing 153.

3   Theresa Cornelys (1723–97) was proprietor of Carlisle House, Assembly Rooms in Soho opened in 1760. William Almack (d. 1781) opened Assembly Rooms in King Street, St James, on 20 February 1765. See DNB.

4   See *Epistles to Several Persons*, F. W. Bateson (ed.), TE 3.2. 148, lines 155–6.

5   For alterations to Northumberland House, *see* Arthur T. Bolton, *The Architecture of Robert and James Adam (1758–1794)* 1. 246–73.

6   See Thomas Hearne, *A Collection of Curious Discourses Written by Eminent Antiquaries* (Oxford, 1720; Hazen 657).

7   See James Bentham, *The History and Antiquities of the Conventual and Cathedral Church of Ely*, 2d ed., 2 vols. (Norwich, 1812; Hazen 11) 1. 83–6, 285.

8   See *The Last Journals of Horace Walpole During the Reign of George III from 1771–1783*, Francis Steuart (ed.) (1910) 2. 212.

9   For *The Death of Chatham*, see Jules David Prown, *John Singleton Copley in England 1774–1815*, vol. 2 (Cambridge, MA, 1966), ch. 12, 'The Death of Chatham 1779–1781', 2. 275–91.

Chapter 13   Walpole's Portraits in the Letters: Statesmen

1   See Wilmarth S. Lewis, *Horace Walpole* (New York, 1960), xxi, 85, and pl. 28.

2   See, for example, *The Repeal of the Stamp Act*, HWC 22, facing 400. BM Satires 4. 368–73, No. 4140. HW's annotated print is in the New York Public Library.

3   See HW's 'On Modern Gardening', *Works* 2. 517–45. See also Morris R. Brownell, *Alexander Pope & the Arts of Georgian England* (Oxford, 1978), 195–207.

4   See Valentine Green's engraving dated 1774 after Zoffany's portrait of Lord Sandwich 'probably painted at the time of Sandwich's appointment as First Lord of the Admiralty': Mary Webster, *Johan Zoffany (1733–1810)* (London, 1976), No. 17. 29.

5   For *The Essay on Woman*, *see* HWC 22, p. 184, n. 14, and *An Essay on Woman* (London, 1871). See also E. R. Watson, 'John Wilkes and the Essay on Woman', *Notes and Queries*, 11th ser. 9 (1914), 121+.

6   See HWC 28. 169–70, n. 7; and HWC 29. 377, App. 7. See also 'The Candidate', *The Poems of Thomas Gray, William Collins, Oliver Goldsmith* (ed.), Roger Lonsdale, Longmans' Annotated English Poets (London, 1969), 243–52.

7   See Rochester's *Works* (London, 1718; Hazen 176), front. HW noted on his MS copy of Gray's *Candidate* that 'Lord Sandwich was great-grandson of Lord Rochester and resembled his portraits'. See HWC 28. 169, n. 8. Walpole saw Lord Sandwich's portrait of 'Lord Rochester, father of Lady Sandwich [his mother]', on a visit to his seat, Hinchingbrooke, Huntingdonshire 30 May 1763. See HW *Visits*, 49.

8   See *The Poetical Works of Charles Churchill* (ed.), Douglas Grant (Oxford, 1956), 546, quoting HW, G III 1. 314.

9   Herod's first wife, murdered by him in a fit of jealousy. See *The Oxford Companion to French Literature* (1959), 453.

10   See Charles Churchill's lifeless poem, *The Candidate*, *Works* (1956), 349–72.

Chapter 14   Walpole's Portraits in the Letters: 'Out-pensioners of Bedlam'

1   See John Knox Laughton, DNB 5. 831–55. Walpole remarked that 'Nivernois has about as much life as a sick favourite child' (HWC 38. 203).

2   See *The Works of John Dryden*, vol. 11 (Berkeley CA 1978), *The Conquest of Granada*, Pt. I, vi, 297.

Chapter 15   Walpole's Portraits in the Letters: 'Modern Literati'

1   See *Boswell's Life of Johnson*, George Birkbeck Hill (ed.), and L. F. Powell, 6 vols. (Oxford, 1934–50) 4. 394–419.

2   See 'Walpole on Garrick's Alterations of Hamlet' (1773; HWC 29. 370).

3   See *The Private Papers of James Boswell*, Frederick A. Pottle (ed.), 18 vols. (New York, 1928–34) 9. 272.

4   Cf. James Boswell, *Life* 3. 19: 'No man but a blockhead ever wrote, except for money'.

5   See Morris R. Brownell, *Samuel Johnson's Attitude to the Arts* (Oxford, 1989), ch. 8, 'Johnson Caricatured and Illustrated', and Appendix, 'Subject Pictures of Johnson', 185–6. See also HW's copy of Boswell's *Journal of a Tour to the Hebrides with Samuel Johnson* (London, 1785; Hazen 3069), extra-illustrated with caricatures of Johnson and Boswell.

6   For Gibbon's review of Walpole's *Doubts*, see Edward Gibbon, *Miscellaneous Works*, John Baker Holroyd, Earl of Sheffield (ed.), 3 vols. (London, 1796–1815) 3. 156–7.

7   See J. E. Norton, *Bibliography of Gibbon* (Oxford, 1940), 190.

Chapter 16   Walpole's Portraits in the Letters:
Group Portraits

1 The painting was destroyed by fire. For the mezzotint by Valentine Green, see Chaloner Smith 8/53.

2 Walpole is referring to the Lord President of the Council, nominee for prime minister, and 'notorious drunkard', Granville Leveson, 2d Earl Gower (1721–1803), his neighbour in Arlington Street. See HWC 32. 317, n. 5.

3 For HW's commission for 'drawings of the gallery' (Hazen 3570) from a 'little man' on the Grand Tour, see HWC 17. 58 (1741), and 18. 292 (14 August 1743).

4 See also SA 62. 138. 9; SA 63. 137. 10; SA 65. 167. 15; and SA 66. 198–9. 14.

5 Cf. HWC 24. 92, 17 April 1775: 'Zofanii has sent over a wretched Holy Family'.

6 For Zoffany's portrait of Leopold II, see Oliver Millar, *Zoffany and his Tribuna* (London, 1966), 25, pl. 26.

7 See ibid., 28, and n. 2.

Chapter 17   Walpole's Portraits in the Letters:
The Gunninghiad

1 For Walpole's visits to the House of Bouverie, see HWC 11. 341–2.

2 See Charles Robert Leslie, and Tom Taylor, *Life and Times of Sir Joshua Reynolds*, 2 vols. (London, 1865) 1. 325. See also Morris R. Brownell, *Samuel Johnson's Attitude to the Arts* (1989), 56–7.

3 See Erwin Panofsky, ' "Et in Arcadia Ego": On the Conception of Transience in Poussin and Watteau,' *Philosophy & History: Essays Presented to Ernst Cassirer*, Raymond Klibanski (ed.), and H. F. Paton (Oxford, 1936), 223–54.

4 Cf. HW, G III, 1. 130 n.: 'It is very remarkable that this great lady and her sister, Lady Coventry, had been originally so poor, that they had thoughts of being actresses; and when they were first presented to the Earl of Harrington, the Lord-Lieutenant, at the Castle of Dublin, Mrs. Woffington, the actress, lent clothes to them. They no sooner appeared in England than their beauty drew crowds after them wherever they went'.

5 Caroline Fitzroy (1722–89), Lady Petersham, and Countess of Harrington looked 'as handsome as crimson could make [her]' (HWC 9. 106) on a visit to Vauxhall with Walpole in June 1750. Walpole praised her 'ebon tresses' in *The Beauties* (HWC 30. 325). At the coronation she was 'noble at a distance, and so covered with diamonds, that you would have thought she had bid *somebody* or other, like Falstaff, *rob me the Exchequer*' (38. 126–7. 1761), alluding to her affair with Lord Barrington, Chancellor of the Exchequer.

6 Twenty years later Walpole wrote this report on Pitt's cruelty to his wife, Penelope Atkins (1725–95), Lady Rivers: 'She is the most amiable of beings, and the most to be pitied – her brutal half mad husband, with whom she is still not out of love, and who has heaped on her every possible cruelty and provoking outrage, will not suffer her to see, or even hear from one of her children. . . . Then all her beauties and good nature are poisoned by deafness and danger of blindness' (23. 451; 22 December 1772).

7 Cf. HW, G III, 3. 131 n.

8 See Nicholas Penny (ed.), *Reynolds* (1986), No. 36. 197–9.

9 For Chesterfield House in South Audley Street, see Wheatley, *London Past and Present* 1. 388–9. and *Country Life* 51 (1922), 235–42; 308–14.

10 St George's Chapel, Hyde Park Corner, frequented for clandestine marriages. See Horace Bleackley, *Story of a Beautiful Duchess* (1908), 43–4.

11 The following April 1791 Walpole supped again at Elizabeth Farren's, where amateur actors like Lady Dorothy Hobart (d. 1798) 'treated the players [professionals] with acting as many characters as ever they did, particularly Gunnilda and Lady Clackmannan [probably Lady Greenwich]'. See HWC 11. 237; 3 April 1791).

12 That is, Susannah Minifie's eviction from John Gunning's Twickenham house. See 11. 196, n. 7; 13 February 1791.

13 The members of the junto were: General John Gunning (1741–97); John Campbell (1723–1806), 5th Duke of Argyll; his brother, Lord Frederick Campbell (1729–1816); Walpole's first cousin and confidant throughout the Gunninghiad, Henry Seymour Conway (1719–95); and Andrew Stuart (1725–1801), a lawyer portrayed by Reynolds in this exhibition (RA 79. 254. 20; HW *marginalia*).

14 See *Mémoires of Madame de Barneveldt . . . with . . . portrait of the translator* [Elizabeth Gunning the younger] *by Bartolozzi*, 2d ed., 2 vols. (London, 1786), front. See DNB 8. 792–3.

15 See BM Satires, 6. 848–9, No. 7980.

16 See *The Naked Truth, or the Sweet Little Angel Turned Out for Lorn* (25 March 1791), BM Satires, 6. 849–50, No. 7981.

17 See *The Remarkable Trial of General Gunning for Adultery* (1792), and *An Apology for the Life of Major General Gunning* (1792). See HWC 11. 366, nn. 23–4.

18 'This is the House that Jack Built' (2 January 1792), BM Satires, 6. 955–6, No. 8163.

Chapter 18   Walpole's Self-Portrait,
The Prime Minister of Taste

1 Mason's compliment ('Epistle to Horace Walpole', line 30; HWC 28. 431), referring to Walpole's pam-

phlet in the Chatterton controversy, *A Letter to the Editor of the Miscel-lanies of Thomas Chatterton* (1778; Hazen 1609. 39. 13).

2 See Walpole's compilation, *A Collection of Prints Engraved by Various Persons of Quality* (Hazen 3588).

3 See Horace: *The Odes and Epodes*, trans. C. E. Bennett (London, 1918), 293.

4 'He [Cherbury] is habited in his hose and doublet, and his recumbent posture is that of the Cavallero de las Espeyos [the knight of the Mirrors in Don Quixote, Part II, Chap. 12].' See HWC 42. 43; 28 December 1782.

5 For Walpole's eloquent praise of the portrait of Bambridge in the Gaols Committee sketch (1729), see John Nichols, *Biographical Anecdotes of William Hogarth* (London, 1781), 14–15: 'The scene,' he [Walpole] says, 'is the committee; on the table are the instruments of torture. A prisoner in rags, half-starved, appears before them; the poor man has a good countenance, that adds to the interest. On the other hand is the inhuman gaoler. It is the very figure that Salvator Rosa would have drawn for Iago in the moment of detection. Villainy, fear, and conscience are mixed in yellow and livid on his countenance, his lips are contracted by tremor, his face advances as eager to lie, his legs step back as thinking to make his escape; one hand is thrust precipitately into his bosom, the fingers of the other are catching uncertainly at his button-holes. If this was a portrait, it is the most striking that ever was drawn; if it was not, it is still finer'. See John Kerslake, *Early Georgian Portraits*, 1. 330–8, pl. 943 (Fitzwilliam Museum), and Ronald Paulson, *Hogarth: His Life, Art and Times*, 2 vols. (New Haven and London, 1971) 1. 196–202.

6 See Rudolf and Margot Wittkower, *Born Under Saturn* (London, 1963).

7 The conflict between the gentleman and the writer is the thesis of Paul Yvon's biography, *La vie d'un dilettante: Horace Walpole (1717–1797), essai de biographie psychologique et littéraire* (Paris, 1924).

8 See Samuel Johnson, *The Idler and Adventurer*, W.

J. Bate (ed.), *et al.*, The Yale Edition of the Works of Samuel Johnson, vol. 2 (New Haven and London, 1968. *Idler* 45, 2. 139).

9 See George Robins and Samuel Woodburne, *A Catalogue of the Classic Contents of Strawberry Hill Collected by Horace Walpole* (London, 1842), xxi.

10 See Mark Girouard, *Life in the English Country House* (New Haven and London, 1978), chap. 1.

11 See R. W. Ketton-Cremer, *Horace Walpole: A Biography*, 3rd ed. (London, 1964) 28; and HWC 40. xviii.

12 See Maynard Mack, *The Garden and the City: Retirement and Politics in the Later Poetry of Pope 1731–1743* (Toronto, 1969).

13 See HW, *Book of Materials*, vol. 1 (1759; Hazen 2615), 105.

14 See Joseph Burke, *English Art 1714–1800*, The Oxford History of English Art, vol. 9 (Oxford, 1976), 140: 'In opposing the Liberty of Taste to the Rule of Taste he [Walpole] drew attention to one of the greatest achievements of the eighteenth century, the creation of a playground of the imagination.'

15 Joseph Banks's biographer so labels Walpole's remark deriding colonial voyages that 'carried our abominable passions amongst them [natives]' (HWC 2. 225). See Edward Smith, *The Life of Sir Joseph Banks* (London and New York, 1911), 173–5.

16 Johan Huizinga, *Homo Ludens: A Study of the Play-Element in Culture* (New York, 1950), 189.

17 See HWC 13. 91, n. 8, for HW's watercolour copies (now LWL) of Jean-Antoine Watteau (1684–1721), *A Rural Ball*, *A Music Lesson*, and *A Conversation*, signed and dated 1736 and 1738. See also *Le Rêve de l'artiste*, Watteau's painting in Sir Robert Walpole's collection: *A Catalogue of the Right Honourable Sir Robert Walpole's Collection of Pictures*, HW's MS inventory dated 1736, Pierpont Morgan Library, New York; and Martin Eidelberg, 'Watteau Paintings in England in the Early Eighteenth Century', *Burlington Magazine* 117 (September 1975), 579.

Notes to the Illustrations

99   Zoffany px. *The Academicians*. See Millar, *Later Georgian*, 152–4, No. 1210.

100   Zoffany px. *The Tribuna* (detail). See Millar, *Zoffany's Tribuna*, front.

102   After Reynolds. *Et in Arcadia Ego*. See Mannings, *Reynolds*, No. 445.

103   Cotes px. *Maria Gunning*. See Johnson, *Cotes*, 53, No. 19.

104   Cotes px. *Elizabeth Gunning*. See Johnson, *Cotes*, 52, No. 16.

105   Reynolds px. *Emilia Lennox*. See Mannings, *Reynolds*, No. 620.

106   Cotes px. *Penelope Atkins*. See Johnson, *Cotes*, 61, No. 78.

109   Reynolds px. *Elizabeth Gunning*. See Mannings, *Reynolds*, No. 810.

111   Reynolds px. *Mary Bruce*. See Mannings, *Reynolds*, No. 1119.

113   Cosway px. *George Spencer*. See Lloyd, *Cosway*, 122, No. 94.

115   Gillray del. *Siege of Blenheim*. See BM Satires 6: 848–9, No. 7980.

116   Cruikshank del. *The House that Jack Built*. See BM Satires 6: 955–6, No. 8163.

117   Carter del. *Three Sketches*. See *HW* Portraits, A 16, 1: 20.

120A Oliver px. *Herbert of Cherbury*. See Piper, *English Face*, 66–7.

121   Hogarth px. *The Gaols Committee*. See Kerslake 1: 330–8.

Index

NOTE: Page numbers in italic refer to a Plate. Where information in a note has been indexed, the note number is given after the page number. Works of art are entered under the artist's name, unless anonymous, in which case the index entry is under the title of the work. HW=Horace Walpole. This index was prepared by Jane A. Horton.

'monumenting' portraits 109-11, 131, 142, 143
Moore, Andrew 41-2
More, Sir Antonio 85
Morgan, Thomas 113
Moysey, Mary 193, 194
Mullins, G. 161
Müntz, Johann Heinrich 117, 125, 150-1
Muzell, Heinrich Wilhelm ('Stoschino') 22

Nanteuil, Robert: *Marie de Rabutin-Chantal 128*
Nash, Treadway Russell 108
National Gallery proposal 66
Neapolitan school: HW on 48
Newnham Paddox, Warwickshire 106
Nichols, John 308, 336n.5
Nichols, John Gough 101
Nicol, George 308
nil admirari code 2, 9-10, 11, 312
Ninon *see* L'Enclos
Noble, Mark 242
Nollekens, Joseph 154
Norris, Sir John 77
North, Frederick, 8th Lord North 176-7
North, Lady Anne 176-7
North, Lady Catherine 176-7
Northampton *see* Howard, Henry
Northumberland *see* Seymour; Smithson
Northumberland House, London 218, 219-20, *219*
Nugent, Thomas 317

O'Brien, William 202-4, *202*, 205
O'Hara, Charles 117-18, *119*
Oliver, Isaac
    Edward Baron Herbert of Cherbury 317-18, *318*, *319*
    Lady Called Frances of Somerset 113-14, *113*
Oliver, Peter 88
Olonne, Madame de (Catherine-Henriette
    d'Angennes) 129, 144-5, *144*
Opie, John: *Mary Granville, Mrs Delany* 141-2, *143*
Orford *see* Walpole
Orford House, Chelsea 38, 40, 45
Orlandi, Pellegrino 32
Ossory *see* Fitzpatrick; Liddell
Oxenden, Sir George 82-3
Oxford *see* Cavendish, Henrietta; Harley, Edward

Palliser, Sir Hugh 238, 239
Palma family 48
Palmer, Theophilia ('Offy') 154-5, *154*
Pannini, Giovanni 25
Panofsky, Erwin 278
Paoli, General Pasquale 164
Parker, Mark 25
Parr, Catherine
    discovery of body 106-8, *108*
    portraits of 106
Parr, Thomas (Old Parr) 121
Pass, William 88

Patapan (HW's dog) 49, *50*, 329n.23
Patch, Thomas *268*, 270, 272
    Gathering at the Casa Manetti 13
Peacham, Henry 4
Pears, Iain 43, 47, 60
Pelham, Frances 182-9, *183*
Pelham, Henry, MP 185, 188
Pelham, Thomas 182, 183
Pembroke *see* Herbert, Henry
Pennant, Thomas 121-2
Penny, Edward 29-30, 31
Peters, Matthew William 154
    Edward Wortley Montagu 250, *251*, 252
Petersham *see* Fitzroy, Caroline
Petitot, Jean 125, 147
    Madame la Comtesse d'Olonne 144-5, *144*
Philibert, Comte de Grammont (anon.) 126-7, *127*
Picart, Bernard 24
Pierrepont, Evelyn, 2d Duke of Kingston-upon-Hull
    191, 192-3, 194
Pierrepont, Mary, Lady Wortley-Montagu 166, 250, 252
Pinkerton, John 159, 178
Pitt, Anne 187, 188
Pitt, George, Baron 1st Lord Rivers 282, *283*, 335n.6
Pitt, Penelope (*née* Atkins), Lady Rivers 280-1, *280*,
    335n.6
Pitt, Penelope, Viscountess Ligonier 153, *208*, 209-10
Pitt, Sir Thomas: Pitt's diamond 306, *307*
Pitt, William, 1st Earl of Chatham 227, 228, 230, 231
Pius VI, Pope 194, 195, 198
Pleneuf, Agnès Berthelot de *see* Prie
Plumb, J.H. 38, 42-3
Poilly, François de: *Madonna and Child* 34, *34*, 35
Pointon, Marcia 142, 143
Poisson, Abel-François, Marquis de Marigny 126-7
politics 7, 222, 307
    HW's political career 161-2, 223, 321-2
    HW's portraits of statesmen 225-42
Pomfret *see* Fermor, Thomas
Pompadour, Jeanne-Antoinette Poisson, Marquise de
    129, 139, 144
Pond, Arthur *24*, 77
Ponsonby, William, Lord Duncannon 21, 22
Poor Bill dinner 220
Pope, Alexander 323
    Epistle on Taste 41
    Epistle to Burlington 12, 51, 221, 229
    Epistle to a Lady 176, 186, 189, 287
    Essay on Man consoles HW 68
    estate poetry 59-60
    HW resembles *Dunciad* Grand Tourist 11
    Johnson's *Life* of 256-7
    Twickenham villa 275-6, *275*
Pordenone (Giovanni Antonio Licino)
    HW on 48, 51
    Prodigal Son 49, 51
Portland *see* Harley, Margaret
portraiture

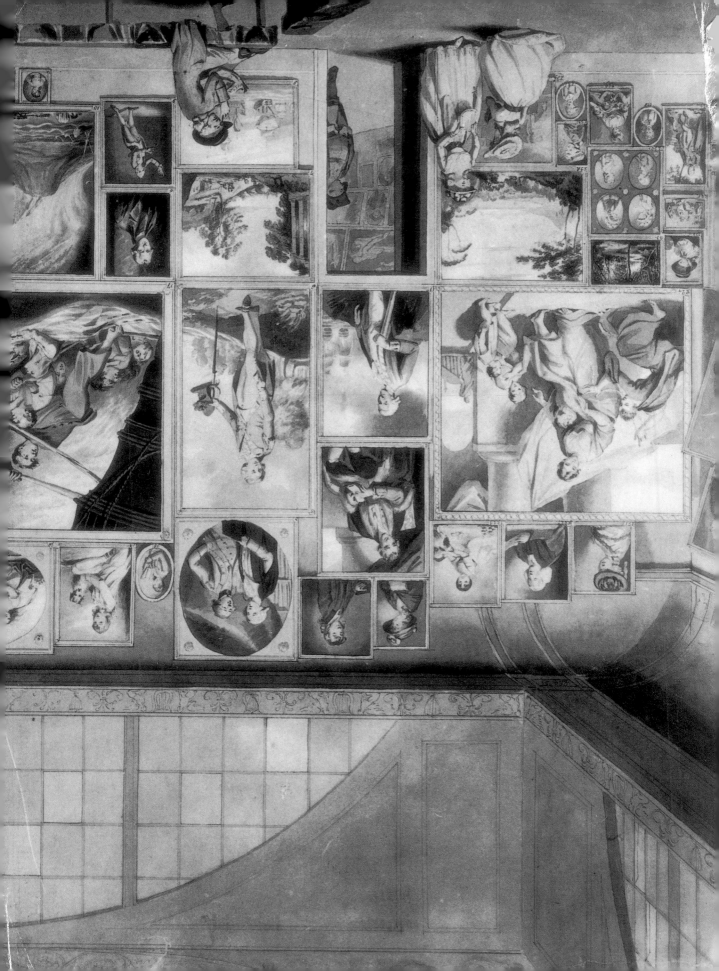